Data Warehouse Design

Modern Principles and Methodologies

About the Authors

Matteo Golfarelli is an associate professor of Computer Science and Technology at the University of Bologna, Italy, where he teaches courses in information systems, databases, and data mining. Before devoting himself full time to data warehousing, he was a researcher in the fields of robotics and pattern recognition. He completed his education at Brown University in Providence, Rhode Island. He has co-authored more than 60 articles published in international journals and conference papers, and authored a book on information system engineering. He has taken part in several research projects and research contracts on data warehousing. Thanks to his experience in the field of business intelligence, he served as an external auditor during many PhD examinations. Since 2008, he has served as program co-chair of the Business Intelligence Systems Conference. He is also member of the Editorial Board of the *International Journal of Data Mining, Modelling and Management*. He can be contacted at matteo.golfarelli@unibo.it.

Stefano Rizzi is a full professor of Computer Science and Technology at the University of Bologna, Italy, where he teaches courses in advanced information systems and software engineering. He has published approximately 100 articles about information systems, mobile robotic systems, and pattern recognition in international journals and conference papers. He has joined several research projects mostly focused on data warehousing and has taken part in research contracts between his university and other enterprises. From 2002 to 2004, he served as scientific supervisor of the University Data Warehouse project managed by the University of Bologna. In 2003, he was appointed program chair of the Sixth ACM International Workshop on Data Warehousing and OLAP (DOLAP) in New Orleans. He is now a member of the DOLAP steering committee. In September 2003 he delivered a keynote address entitled "Open Problems in Data Warehousing: Eight Years Later" at the International Workshop on Data Warehouse Design and Management (DMDW 2003, Berlin, Germany). He served as an area editor for data warehousing in the *Encyclopedia of Database Systems*, edited by Tamer Özsu and Ling Liu (Springer). He can be contacted at stefano.rizzi@unibo.it.

Both authors have been working with data warehousing since 1997. They are well-known within the international community of researchers in this field mainly due to their publications on conceptual design. They have led courses and lectures on data warehousing for several companies, institutions, and universities in Italy and abroad. Both authors were invited to present keynote addresses and to participate in panels on research topics related to data warehousing in international workshops. In 1998 and 2002, they organized two workshops on data warehouse design at the University of Bologna. Both workshops addressed business analysts and designers. In 2001, they led a tutorial on data warehousing at the 17th International Conference on Database Engineering in Heidelberg, Germany. In 2004, they were invited to the Perspective Seminar "Data Warehousing at the Crossroads" in Dagstuhl, Germany. The goal of this seminar was to define new guidelines for data warehouse research in the years to come.

Data Warehouse Design

Modern Principles and Methodologies

Matteo Golfarelli
Stefano Rizzi

Translated by Claudio Pagliarani

New York Chicago San Francisco
Lisbon London Madrid Mexico City
Milan New Delhi San Juan
Seoul Singapore Sydney Toronto

The McGraw·Hill Companies

Library of Congress Cataloging-in-Publication Data

Golfarelli, Matteo.
[Data warehouse. English]
Data warehouse design : modern principles and methodologies / Matteo Golfarelli,
Stefano Rizzi ; translated by Claudio Pagliarani.
    p. cm.
Includes bibliographical references and index.
ISBN 978-0-07-161039-1 (alk. paper)
1. Data warehousing. 2. Database design. I. Rizzi, Stefano. II. Title.
QA76.9.D37G56813 2009
005.74'5—dc22

2009014666

McGraw-Hill books are available at special quantity discounts to use as premiums and sales
promotions, or for use in corporate training programs. To contact a special sales representative,
please visit the Contact Us page at www.mhprofessional.com.

Data Warehouse Design: Modern Principles and Methodologies

The translation of this work has been funded by SEPS

SEGRETARIATO EUROPEO PER LE PUBBLICAZIONI SCIENTIFICHE

S·E·P·S
SEGRETARIATO EUROPEO PER LE PUBBLICAZIONI SCIENTIFICHE

Via Val d'Aposa 7 - 40123 Bologna - Italy
seps@seps.it - www.seps.it

 234567890 QFR/QFR 154321

ISBN   978-0-07-161039-1
MHID   0-07-161039-1

Sponsoring Editor Wendy Rinaldi	**Copy Editor** Lisa Theobald	**Composition** International Typesetting and Composition
Editorial Supervisor Jody McKenzie	**Proofreader** Bev Weiler	**Illustration** International Typesetting and Composition
Project Manager Madhu Bhardwaj, International Typesetting and Composition	**Indexer** Jack Lewis	**Art Director, Cover** Jeff Weeks
Acquisitions Coordinator Joya Anthony	**Production Supervisor** Jim Kussow	**Cover Designer** Kelly Par

Contents at a Glance

Contents

Acknowledgments

We are very glad to thank all those people who directly and indirectly helped us to write this book. First of all, we would like to warmly thank Dario Maio, who embarked on our research in data warehousing in 1997. Thanks also to Boris Vrdoljak for collaborating with us to develop the algorithm for conceptual design from XML sources; to Paolo Giorgini and Maddalena Garzetti for their collaboration for the paragraphs on Tropos methodology; and to Iuris Cella for sharing with us his enterprise viewpoint on business intelligence. We are also in debt to Gruppo Sistema s.r.l., especially Daniele Frisoni and Erika Prati, for their case study. Acknowledgment is also made to many final-year university students who wrote their dissertations on data warehousing in collaboration with enterprises. Their work introduced specific design issues that can be found in different fields of application. All the enterprises with which we have been collaborating so far have also made very positive contributions. They drew our attention to real problems of which university researchers would hardly be aware. Special thanks to our relatives and friends for patiently tolerating our absences while writing this book over the last few months.

Foreword

Data Warehousing is an important topic. It lies at the heart of business information, and information lies at the heart of the modern organization, whether the organization is a business, a non-profit organization, or a governmental agency. Organizations use information like any living organism uses information—to regulate internal operations and to react to external stimuli. Human organizations use information about their internal operations to manage costs and to allocate resources properly. They use information about the external world to manage their customers, manage suppliers, and react to competition and markets. Organizations that use information well tend to thrive compared to their peers. Organizations that do not, tend to struggle compared to their peers.

Information is more important today than ever before. What is different today is the vastness of the information that is being generated and stored. The analog world we live in is becoming digital, and in a digitized world every event can be recorded, categorized, and stored for later analysis. Every business transaction, every web site visit, every image viewed, every call made, and every dollar spent is being digitized and recorded. In the past, a purchase would occur as an "analog transaction" between a store clerk and a customer. Today, that same transaction occurs over the Internet or through a store point-of-sale system where it is instantly recorded.

Unlike older analog events, today's digital events are multidimensional. In the former analog world, a purchase event would be recorded as, "Product X was purchased for Y dollars." In today's digital world, that same purchase event might include ten additional attributes or dimensions including things like the following: time of day, day of week, purchaser name, discount level, product packaging, product promotion, color, style, stock location, salesperson name, and a listing of all other products in the purchaser's market basket. Every digital event has the ability to be recorded with dozens of other attributes or dimensions that can shed additional light on the event itself.

Unlike older analog events, today's digital events are not just being recorded and recalled as isolated events. Instead they are being correlated with one another. Business intelligence systems can tie together interrelated events so that decision-makers can see a series of events assembled in a time-flow or a process-flow, as cause-and-effect relationships, or even as a predictive calculation. Using the purchase example above, in an analog world all purchase events would be summed together to determine the total sales of each product in a day. In a digital world, companies want to track each customer's purchase patterns and product preferences along with the effects of promotions and product placement so that they can sell more to every customer and can predict future inventory requirements and demand levels.

Unfortunately, a digital world does not automatically organize all of the data it produces. In fact, the explosion of digitization has caused a situation in which every system captures data, organizes it, and tags it in its own way without regard to how any other systems might capture, organize, and tag related data. The data warehouse becomes the location where this disparity is homogenized according to an overarching model of the business encoded in the data models of the warehouse.

The biggest implication of a digitized world is that organizations will capture more events, they will associate more dimensions to every event, and they will correlate those events with one another in ever sophisticated, inventive, and unpredictable ways. This means much more data, more interrelationships between data items, and more sophisticated data extractions. It has become quite common today to see data warehouses containing 50TB of data, spanning dozens of dimensions, and containing hundreds of primary metrics. All of these characteristics add up to the paramount requirement for data warehouses to deliver very high performance (at high volumes) and to be very flexible in its usage and evolution. These are the true challenges of modern data warehouse design—high performance combined with high flexibility/functionality.

Data warehousing is an engineering discipline. As with all engineering disciplines, high performance is almost always a tradeoff with high flexibility/functionality. It is often an order of magnitude easier to achieve a high performing system as long as you are willing to forego future flexibility. Similarly, an engineer can create a highly flexible/functional system but always at the expense of high performance. Engineering is the magic that creates a workable balance between high performance and high flexibility/functionality. And this remains the biggest challenge for the data warehouse engineer. Multidimensional databases (i.e., cube databases) can deliver high performance, but are restricted to just those calculations and views that are created as part of the cube model. By contrast, object oriented databases were intended to provide almost infinite data retrieval flexibility and smooth data model evolution, but could never achieve high performance or high scalability. Modern relational databases offer the best promise of high performance at high scale, as well as high flexibility in data extraction when they are paired with a powerful Business Intelligence (BI) technology that can create arbitrarily complex SQL.

Data warehousing is an engineering discipline. Many people wish it were not. Many people wish that data models were not complex. They wish that aggregation strategies and indexing schemes were straightforward. They wish that all data interrelationships need not be defined explicitly. They wish all BI tools could logically model any data structure. They wish that all data structures were equally high performing. But none of these things are true. It takes hard work to design, populate, and evolve a data warehouse that is flexible and high performing.

This book provides the engineering framework, the techniques, and the tools that data warehouse engineers need to deliver predictably successful data warehouses. It is an important book for the next generation of data warehouse engineers who will begin to harness the full power of the new digital world.

Mark Stephen LaRow
Vice President of Products
MicroStrategy

Preface

A data warehouse is a repository for historical, integrated, and consistent data. It is equipped with tools that offer company management the opportunity to extract reliable information to be used as a support for a decision-making process. Data warehousing involves processes that extract relevant data from an enterprise information system, transform the data, integrate it, remove any flaws and inconsistencies, store it into a data warehouse, and provide end users with access to the data so that they can carry out complex data analysis and prediction queries.

Data warehouse systems are currently well established within several medium to large organizations, and it is widely acknowledged that they play a strategic role when it comes to providing end users with easy access to key information that would otherwise be hardly available. The data warehousing phenomenon was born in the corporate world as an answer to users' increasing demands. The academic world first ignored this phenomenon and mainly considered it a mere technological issue until it realized the complexity of data warehousing and the challenges involved. For all intents and purposes, the topic of data warehousing became a major part of international scientific conferences in the field of databases. Since then, many meetings and workshops have been devoted exclusively to data warehousing.

After more than a decade spent in teaching database design, we started our research in the field of data warehousing. Our goal was to discover whether the design techniques developed and tested for relational systems should be thrown away or partially applied to data warehouse design as well. It immediately became clear that the fundamental issues related to conceptual modeling of user requirements had been completely neglected on the one hand. On the other hand, outstanding researchers had already written tons of pages on how to optimize data warehouse performance, which definitely plays a basic role in this field.

We both fervently believe in the importance of adopting a methodological approach based on solid software engineering principles when creating any software system. In particular, we support the need for accurate conceptual modeling when developing databases. Common data warehouse design practices show a surprising lack of sound methodological approaches and conceptual models. To fill this gap, we have endeavored to work out a comprehensive, well-founded design methodology that can safely guide designers through the different phases of a data warehouse project. Our methodology is centered on the use of a conceptual model that can show the specific features of data warehouse applications, while being based on an easy-to-use and simple formalism that designers can use to design and create better projects. The effectiveness of the methodology and conceptual model we propose is substantiated by its adoption for a large number of projects by several Italian software houses and consultants.

This book aims at meeting two different needs. The most urgent need is to create a wide-ranging collection of design techniques and make them part of a systematic and comprehensive methodological framework, acting as a reference for designers. The other urgent need is to counterbalance the lack of books that are suitable for students, even though several universities are currently offering courses in data warehousing. This book collects and systematizes the latest important data warehouse design research results, and sums up what we have learned as many different companies have experimented with our design techniques.

Our academic backgrounds and professional experiences have not only contributed to reaching a compromise between a pragmatic approach and a formal one to data warehousing, but it has also raised awareness on enterprise-specific applications and on cutting-edge research results. We wanted this book to provide a lot of examples. We have also included a real case study to maximize the educational impact of this information.

The increasing diffusion of our methodology in the corporate world compelled us to provide a Computer-Aided Software Engineering (CASE) tool to support the core data warehouse design phases and the related project documentation. Readers interested in such a tool can access it at www.qbx-tool.com

Intended Audience

This book was written for database designers, companies, and institutions that are interested in approaching the domain of decision support systems, and for students attending advanced courses in information systems and databases. Readers should already be familiar with the basics of relational and Entity-Relationship models, as well as information systems and information system design to take maximum advantage of the concepts presented throughout this book.

Organization

Chapter 1 introduces the basic definitions used in the field. It reviews a large number of functional architectures that can be adopted and closely studies a few critical points to help the reader understand the entire process: feeding data warehouses from source data, the multidimensional model that is fundamental for building data warehouses, and the main user options for accessing data warehouse information. Both main approaches to data warehouse implementation are briefly described: the approach based on the relational model and the approach using proprietary multidimensional solutions. In the chapters that follow, we focus on the first approach because it is far more popular than the second.

Chapter 2 reports a lifecycle of data warehouse systems and suggests a methodological approach for designing them. The chapter provides the reference point for the chapters that follow. Seven phases of the lifecycle are presented, and each of the chapters that follows is devoted to a particular phase. Chapter 2 suggests that data warehouse design should consist of three main phases—conceptual, logical, and physical—that have led to successful development of traditional information systems. Chapter 2 also outlines three different design scenarios: a data-driven scenario, a requirement-driven scenario, and a mixed scenario. These scenarios are presented to support the profound differences in real-life companies and aim to make our methodological approach more flexible.

Chapter 3 depicts the phase of data source analysis and reconciliation that feeds a data warehouse. This phase is vital to making sure that the information retrieved meets top quality standards requirements. The activities devoted to the integration of multiple heterogeneous data sources are studied in depth.

Chapter 4 deals with the requirement analysis phase that needs to be carefully carried out to ensure that the system under construction never falls short of end users' needs and expectations. We introduce two different approaches: an informal approach based on simple glossaries and a formal approach used for requirement-driven design or mixed design.

Chapter 5 suggests the conceptual model—the Dimensional Fact Model (DFM)—on which the methodological approach hinges. We gradually introduce the structures for this model to help readers deepen their knowledge from modeling basics to the subtlest shades of representation required in real-life applications.

Chapter 6 is devoted to conceptual design and shows the reader how to use the documentation on data sources and user requirements to create a conceptual schema for a data warehouse.

Chapter 7 describes the phase leading to the expression of workloads in conceptual schemata. This topic is vital for the following logical and physical design phases, that show designers how to optimize performance. This chapter also tackles the main topics related to data volume definition.

Chapter 8 introduces the most popular logical modeling approaches for relational data warehouses. In this chapter, we pay particular attention to the description of the well-known star schema and to redundant views to improve data warehouse performance.

Chapter 9 is about logical design on the basis of conceptual schemata and discusses logical optimization strategies and techniques for designers—the foremost techniques are materialized views. This chapter provides possible implementations based on relational schemata for each DFM construct.

Chapter 10 describes how to feed data warehouses. In this phase, data is extracted from sources, transformed, cleansed, and then used to populate data warehouses.

Chapter 11 lists and analyzes the main index categories that can be used in data warehouse systems and the main join algorithms.

Chapter 12 describes physical design. It first tackles the selection of the most suitable indexes, but also deals with other topics related to physical design, such as sizing up and allocation.

Chapter 13 shows the reader how to create useful and comprehensive project documentation to be used for reference and to help with future system maintenance.

Chapter 14 reviews a case study based on real-world experience and demonstrates how to solve problems following the basic methodological steps described in the preceding chapters.

Chapter 15 introduces readers to business intelligence, a wider domain that has its roots in data warehouse systems and benefits from advanced solutions and architectures used to meet the needs of business actors.

Reading Suggestions

We suggest three different ways to take advantage of our book so as to meet the expectations of three main groups of readers and make our book enjoyable to the largest number of readers.

For Beginners

Our book provides beginners with a comprehensive overview of the main design issues, specified by the following sections:

Chapter 1: All

Chapter 2: Sections 2.1, 2.2, 2.3, 2.4

Chapter 3: Introduction

Chapter 4: Introduction

Chapter 5: Sections 5.1, 5.2.1, 5.2.3, 5.2.4, 5.2.6, 5.2.9

Chapter 6: Introduction, 6.5

Chapter 7: Sections 7.1.1, 7.1.5

Chapter 8: Sections 8.1, 8.2, 8.3

Chapter 9: Introduction

Chapter 10: Introduction

Chapter 12: Section 12.2

Chapter 13: All

Chapter 15: All

For Designers

Decision support system designers can use this book as a methodological handbook for data warehouse design and as a reference for detailed solutions to specific problems.

Chapter 1: All

Chapter 2: All

Chapter 3: All

Chapter 4: All

Chapter 5: Sections 5.1, 5.2, 5.3, 5.4, 5.5

Chapter 6: Sections 6.1, 6.2, 6.4, 6.5

Chapter 7: All

Chapter 8: All

Chapter 9: Sections 9.1, 9.2.1, 9.3.2

Chapter 10: All

Chapter 11: Sections 11.1, 11.2.1, 11.4, 11.6

Chapter 12: All

Chapter 13: All

Chapter 14: All

For Students

This book also provides students attending courses in advanced information systems with a comprehensive report on both theoretical and application issues. It also meets the needs for practice-oriented university courses.

Chapter 1: All

Chapter 2: Sections 2.2, 2.3, 2.4

Chapter 3: All

Chapter 4: Section 4.2

Chapter 5: All

Chapter 6: All

Chapter 7: All

Chapter 8: All

Chapter 9: All

Chapter 10: Introduction

Chapter 11: All

Chapter 12: Sections 12.1, 12.2

Chapter 14: All

Chapter 15: All

Introduction to Data Warehousing

Information assets are immensely valuable to any enterprise, and because of this, these assets must be properly stored and readily accessible when they are needed. However, the availability of too much data makes the extraction of the most important information difficult, if not impossible. View results from any Google search, and you'll see that the *data = information* equation is not always correct—that is, too much data is simply too much.

Data warehousing is a phenomenon that grew from the huge amount of electronic data stored in recent years and from the urgent need to use that data to accomplish goals that go beyond the routine tasks linked to daily processing. In a typical scenario, a large corporation has many branches, and senior managers need to quantify and evaluate how each branch contributes to the global business performance. The corporate database stores detailed data on the tasks performed by branches. To meet the managers' needs, tailor-made queries can be issued to retrieve the required data. In order for this process to work, database administrators must first formulate the desired query (typically an aggregate SQL query) after closely studying database catalogs. Then the query is processed. This can take a few hours because of the huge amount of data, the query complexity, and the concurrent effects of other regular workload queries on data. Finally, a report is generated and passed to senior managers in the form of a spreadsheet.

Many years ago, database designers realized that such an approach is hardly feasible, because it is very demanding in terms of time and resources, and it does not always achieve the desired results. Moreover, a mix of analytical queries with transactional routine queries inevitably slows down the system, and this does not meet the needs of users of either type of query. Today's advanced data warehousing processes separate *online analytical processing (OLAP)* from *online transactional processing (OLTP)* by creating a new information repository that integrates basic data from various sources, properly arranges data formats, and then makes data available for analysis and evaluation aimed at planning and decision-making processes (Lechtenbörger, 2001).

Let's review some fields of application for which data warehouse technologies are successfully used:

- **Trade**   Sales and claims analyses, shipment and inventory control, customer care and public relations
- **Craftsmanship**   Production cost control, supplier and order support
- **Financial services**   Risk analysis and credit cards, fraud detection
- **Transport industry**   Vehicle management
- **Telecommunication services**   Call flow analysis and customer profile analysis
- **Health care service**   Patient admission and discharge analysis and bookkeeping in accounts departments

The field of application of data warehouse systems is not only restricted to enterprises, but it also ranges from epidemiology to demography, from natural science to education. A property that is common to all fields is the need for storage and query tools to retrieve information summaries easily and quickly from the huge amount of data stored in databases or made available by the Internet. This kind of information allows us to study business phenomena, learn about meaningful correlations, and gain useful knowledge to support decision-making processes.

1.1 Decision Support Systems

Until the mid-1980s, enterprise databases stored only *operational data*—data created by business operations involved in daily management processes, such as purchase management, sales management, and invoicing. However, every enterprise must have quick, comprehensive access to the information required by decision-making processes. This strategic information is extracted mainly from the huge amount of operational data stored in enterprise databases by means of a progressive selection and aggregation process shown in Figure 1-1.

FIGURE 1-1
Information value
as a function of
quantity

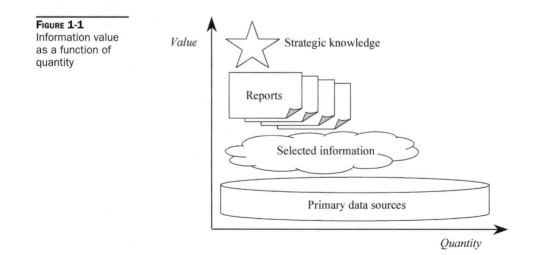

An exponential increase in operational data has made computers the only tools suitable for providing data for decision-making performed by business managers. This fact has dramatically affected the role of enterprise databases and fostered the introduction of *decision support systems*. The concept of decision support systems mainly evolved from two research fields: theoretical studies on decision-making processes for organizations and technical research on interactive IT systems. However, the decision support system concept is based on several disciplines, such as databases, artificial intelligence, man-machine interaction, and simulation. Decision support systems became a research field in the mid-'70s and became more popular in the '80s.

Decision Support System

A *decision support system (DSS)* is a set of expandable, interactive IT techniques and tools designed for processing and analyzing data and for supporting managers in decision making. To do this, the system matches individual resources of managers with computer resources to improve the quality of the decisions made.

In practice, a DSS is an IT system that helps managers make decisions or choose among different alternatives. The system provides value estimates for each alternative, allowing the manager to critically review the results. Table 1-1 shows a possible classification of DSSs on the basis of their functions (Power, 2002).

From the architectural viewpoint, a DSS typically includes a model-based management system connected to a knowledge engine and, of course, an interactive graphical user interface (Sprague and Carlson, 1982). Data warehouse systems have been managing the data back-ends of DSSs since the 1990s. They must retrieve useful information from a huge amount of data stored on heterogeneous platforms. In this way, decision-makers can formulate their queries and conduct complex analyses on relevant information without slowing down operational systems.

System	Description
Passive DSS	Supports decision-making processes, but it does not offer explicit suggestions on decisions or solutions.
Active DSS	Offers suggestions and solutions.
Collaborative DSS	Operates interactively and allows decision-makers to modify, integrate, or refine suggestions given by the system. Suggestions are sent back to the system for validation.
Model-driven DSS	Enhances management of statistical, financial, optimization, and simulation models.
Communication-driven DSS	Supports a group of people working on a common task.
Data-driven DSS	Enhances the access and management of time series of corporate and external data.
Document-driven DSS	Manages and processes nonstructured data in many formats.
Knowledge-driven DSS	Provides problem-solving features in the form of facts, rules, and procedures.

TABLE 1-1   Classification of Decision Support Systems

1.2 Data Warehousing

Data warehouse systems are probably the systems to which academic communities and industrial bodies have been paying the greatest attention among all the DSSs. Data warehousing can be informally defined as follows:

> **Data Warehousing**
>
> *Data warehousing* is a collection of methods, techniques, and tools used to support *knowledge workers*—senior managers, directors, managers, and analysts—to conduct data analyses that help with performing decision-making processes and improving information resources.

The definition of data warehousing presented here is intentionally generic; it gives you an idea of the process but does not include specific features of the process. To understand the role and the useful properties of data warehousing completely, you must first understand the needs that brought it into being. In 1996, R. Kimball efficiently summed up a few claims frequently submitted by end users of classic information systems:

- *"We have heaps of data, but we cannot access it!"* This shows the frustration of those who are responsible for the future of their enterprises but have no technical tools to help them extract the required information in a proper format.

- *"How can people playing the same role achieve substantially different results?"* In midsize to large enterprises, many databases are usually available, each devoted to a specific business area. They are often stored on different logical and physical media that are not conceptually integrated. For this reason, the results achieved in every business area are likely to be inconsistent.

- *"We want to select, group, and manipulate data in every possible way!"* Decision-making processes cannot always be planned before the decisions are made. End users need a tool that is user-friendly and flexible enough to conduct ad hoc analyses. They want to choose which new correlations they need to search for in real time as they analyze the information retrieved.

- *"Show me just what matters!"* Examining data at the maximum level of detail is not only useless for decision-making processes, but is also self-defeating, because it does not allow users to focus their attention on meaningful information.

- *"Everyone knows that some data is wrong!"* This is another sore point. An appreciable percentage of transactional data is not correct—or it is unavailable. It is clear that you cannot achieve good results if you base your analyses on incorrect or incomplete data.

We can use the previous list of problems and difficulties to extract a list of key words that become distinguishing marks and essential requirements for a *data warehouse process*, a set of tasks that allow us to turn operational data into decision-making support information:

- *accessibility* to users not very familiar with IT and data structures;
- *integration* of data on the basis of a standard enterprise model;
- *query flexibility* to maximize the advantages obtained from the existing information;

- *information conciseness* allowing for target-oriented and effective analyses;
- *multidimensional representation* giving users an intuitive and manageable view of information;
- *correctness and completeness* of integrated data.

Data warehouses are placed right in the middle of this process and act as repositories for data. They make sure that the requirements set can be fulfilled.

Data Warehouse

A *data warehouse* is a collection of data that supports decision-making processes. It provides the following features (Inmon, 2005):

- It is subject-oriented.
- It is integrated and consistent.
- It shows its evolution over time and it is not volatile.

Data warehouses are subject-oriented because they hinge on enterprise-specific concepts, such as customers, products, sales, and orders. On the contrary, operational databases hinge on many different enterprise-specific applications.

We put emphasis on integration and consistency because data warehouses take advantage of multiple data sources, such as data extracted from production and then stored to enterprise databases, or even data from a third party's information systems. A data warehouse should provide a unified view of all the data. Generally speaking, we can state that creating a data warehouse system does not require that new information be added; rather, existing information needs rearranging. This implicitly means that an information system should be previously available.

Operational data usually covers a short period of time, because most transactions involve the latest data. A data warehouse should enable analyses that instead cover a few years. For this reason, data warehouses are regularly updated from operational data and keep on growing. If data were visually represented, it might progress like so: A photograph of operational data would be made at regular intervals. The sequence of photographs would be stored to a data warehouse, and results would be shown in a movie that reveals the status of an enterprise from its foundation until present.

Fundamentally, data is never deleted from data warehouses and updates are normally carried out when data warehouses are offline. This means that data warehouses can be essentially viewed as read-only databases. This satisfies the users' need for a short analysis query response time and has other important effects. First, it affects data warehouse–specific database management system (DBMS) technologies, because there is no need for advanced transaction management techniques required by operational applications. Second, data warehouses operate in read-only mode, so data warehouse–specific logical design solutions are completely different from those used for operational databases. For instance, the most obvious feature of data warehouse relational implementations is that table normalization can be given up to partially denormalize tables and improve performance.

Other differences between operational databases and data warehouses are connected with query types. Operational queries execute transactions that generally read/write a small number of tuples from/to many tables connected by simple relations. For example, this applies if you search for the data of a customer in order to insert a new customer order. This kind of query is an OLTP query. On the contrary, the type of query required in data warehouses is OLAP. It features dynamic, multidimensional analyses that need to scan a huge amount of records to process a set of numeric data summing up the performance of an enterprise. It is important to note that OLTP systems have an essential workload core "frozen" in application programs, and ad hoc data queries are occasionally run for data maintenance. Conversely, data warehouse interactivity is an essential property for analysis sessions, so the actual workload constantly changes as time goes by.

The distinctive features of OLAP queries suggest adoption of a *multidimensional* representation for data warehouse data. Basically, data is viewed as points in space, whose dimensions correspond to many possible analysis dimensions. Each point represents an event that occurs in an enterprise and is described by a set of measures relevant to decision-making processes. Section 1.5 gives a detailed description of the multidimensional model you absolutely need to be familiar with to understand how to model conceptual and logical levels of a data warehouse and how to query data warehouses.

Table 1-2 summarizes the main differences between operational databases and data warehouses.

NOTE *For further details on the different issues related to the data warehouse process, refer to Chaudhuri and Dayal, 1997; Inmon, 2005; Jarke et al., 2000; Kelly, 1997; Kimball, 1996; Mattison, 2006; and Wrembel and Koncilia, 2007.*

Feature	Operational Databases	Data Warehouses
Users	Thousands	Hundreds
Workload	Preset transactions	Specific analysis queries
Access	To hundreds of records, write and read mode	To millions of records, mainly read-only mode
Goal	Depends on applications	Decision-making support
Data	Detailed, both numeric and alphanumeric	Summed up, mainly numeric
Data integration	Application-based	Subject-based
Quality	In terms of integrity	In terms of consistency
Time coverage	Current data only	Current and historical data
Updates	Continuous	Periodical
Model	Normalized	Denormalized, multidimensional
Optimization	For OLTP access to a database part	For OLAP access to most of the database

TABLE 1-2 Differences Between Operational Databases and Data Warehouses (Kelly, 1997)

1.3 Data Warehouse Architectures

The following architecture properties are essential for a data warehouse system (Kelly, 1997):

- **Separation**   Analytical and transactional processing should be kept apart as much as possible.

- **Scalability**   Hardware and software architectures should be easy to upgrade as the data volume, which has to be managed and processed, and the number of users' requirements, which have to be met, progressively increase.

- **Extensibility**   The architecture should be able to host new applications and technologies without redesigning the whole system.

- **Security**   Monitoring accesses is essential because of the strategic data stored in data warehouses.

- **Administerability**   Data warehouse management should not be overly difficult.

Two different classifications are commonly adopted for data warehouse architectures. The first classification, described in sections 1.3.1, 1.3.2, and 1.3.3, is a structure-oriented one that depends on the number of layers used by the architecture. The second classification, described in section 1.3.4, depends on how the different layers are employed to create enterprise-oriented or department-oriented views of data warehouses.

1.3.1   Single-Layer Architecture

A single-layer architecture is not frequently used in practice. Its goal is to minimize the amount of data stored; to reach this goal, it removes data redundancies. Figure 1-2 shows the only layer physically available: the source layer. In this case, data warehouses are *virtual*.

FIGURE 1-2
Single-layer
architecture for
a data warehouse
system

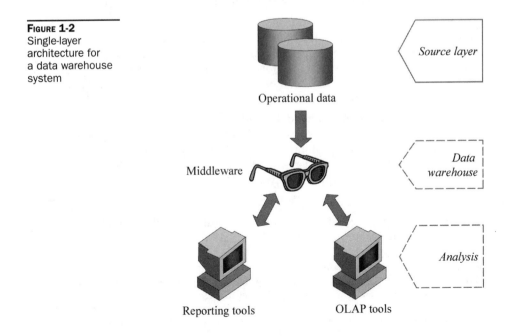

Operational data

Source layer

Middleware

Data warehouse

Reporting tools   OLAP tools

Analysis

This means that a data warehouse is implemented as a multidimensional view of operational data created by specific *middleware*, or an intermediate processing layer (Devlin, 1997).

The weakness of this architecture lies in its failure to meet the requirement for separation between analytical and transactional processing. Analysis queries are submitted to operational data after the middleware interprets them. It this way, the queries affect regular transactional workloads. In addition, although this architecture can meet the requirement for integration and correctness of data, it cannot log more data than sources do. For these reasons, a virtual approach to data warehouses can be successful only if analysis needs are particularly restricted and the data volume to analyze is huge.

1.3.2   Two-Layer Architecture

The requirement for separation plays a fundamental role in defining the typical architecture for a data warehouse system, as shown in Figure 1-3. Although it is typically called a *two-layer architecture* to highlight a separation between physically available sources and data warehouses, it actually consists of four subsequent data flow stages (Lechtenbörger, 2001):

1. **Source layer**   A data warehouse system uses heterogeneous sources of data. That data is originally stored to corporate relational databases or *legacy*[1] databases, or it may come from information systems outside the corporate walls.

2. **Data staging**   The data stored to sources should be extracted, cleansed to remove inconsistencies and fill gaps, and integrated to merge heterogeneous sources into one common schema. The so-called *Extraction, Transformation, and Loading tools (ETL)* can merge heterogeneous schemata, extract, transform, cleanse, validate, filter, and load source data into a data warehouse (Jarke et al., 2000). Technologically speaking, this stage deals with problems that are typical for distributed information systems, such as inconsistent data management and incompatible data structures (Zhuge et al., 1996). Section 1.4 deals with a few points that are relevant to data staging.

3. **Data warehouse layer**   Information is stored to one logically centralized single repository: a data warehouse. The data warehouse can be directly accessed, but it can also be used as a source for creating *data marts*, which partially replicate data warehouse contents and are designed for specific enterprise departments. *Meta-data repositories* (section 1.6) store information on sources, access procedures, data staging, users, data mart schemata, and so on.

4. **Analysis**   In this layer, integrated data is efficiently and flexibly accessed to issue reports, dynamically analyze information, and simulate hypothetical business scenarios. Technologically speaking, it should feature aggregate data navigators, complex query optimizers, and user-friendly GUIs. Section 1.7 deals with different types of decision-making support analyses.

The architectural difference between *data warehouses* and *data marts* needs to be studied closer. The component marked as a data warehouse in Figure 1-3 is also often called the *primary data warehouse* or *corporate data warehouse*. It acts as a centralized storage system for

---

[1]The term *legacy system* denotes corporate applications, typically running on mainframes or minicomputers, that are currently used for operational tasks but do not meet modern architectural principles and current standards. For this reason, accessing legacy systems and integrating them with more recent applications is a complex task. All applications that use a nonrelational database are examples of legacy systems.

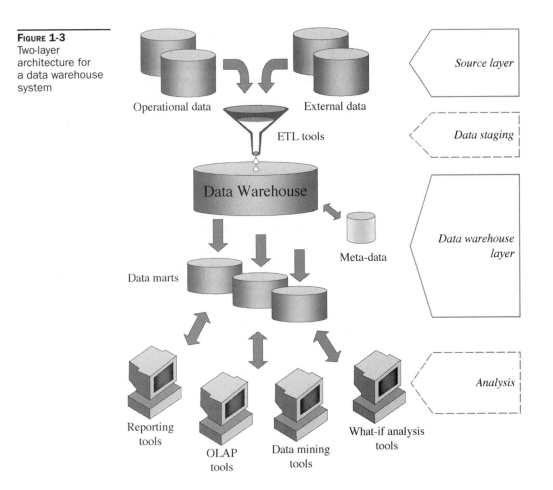

FIGURE 1-3
Two-layer
architecture for
a data warehouse
system

Operational data   External data

Source layer

ETL tools

Data staging

Data Warehouse

Meta-data

Data warehouse
layer

Data marts

Analysis

Reporting
tools

OLAP
tools

Data mining
tools

What-if analysis
tools

all the data being summed up. Data marts can be viewed as small, local data warehouses replicating (and summing up as much as possible) the part of a primary data warehouse required for a specific application domain.

Data Marts

A *data mart* is a subset or an aggregation of the data stored to a primary data warehouse. It includes a set of information pieces relevant to a specific business area, corporate department, or category of users.

The data marts populated from a primary data warehouse are often called *dependent*. Although data marts are not strictly necessary, they are very useful for data warehouse systems in midsize to large enterprises because

- they are used as building blocks while incrementally developing data warehouses;
- they mark out the information required by a specific group of users to solve queries;
- they can deliver better performance because they are smaller than primary data warehouses.

Sometimes, mainly for organization and policy purposes, you should use a different architecture in which sources are used to directly populate data marts. These data marts are called *independent* (see section 1.3.4). If there is no primary data warehouse, this streamlines the design process, but it leads to the risk of inconsistencies between data marts. To avoid these problems, you can create a primary data warehouse and still have independent data marts. In comparison with the standard two-layer architecture of Figure 1-3, the roles of data marts and data warehouses are actually inverted. In this case, the data warehouse is populated from its data marts, and it can be directly queried to make access patterns as easy as possible.

The following list sums up all the benefits of a two-layer architecture, in which a data warehouse separates sources from analysis applications (Jarke et al., 2000; Lechtenbörger, 2001):

- In data warehouse systems, good quality information is always available, even when access to sources is denied temporarily for technical or organizational reasons.

- Data warehouse analysis queries do not affect the management of transactions, the reliability of which is vital for enterprises to work properly at an operational level.

- Data warehouses are logically structured according to the multidimensional model, while operational sources are generally based on relational or semi-structured models.

- A mismatch in terms of time and granularity occurs between OLTP systems, which manage current data at a maximum level of detail, and OLAP systems, which manage historical and summarized data.

- Data warehouses can use specific design solutions aimed at performance optimization of analysis and report applications.

NOTE *A few authors use the same terminology to define different concepts. In particular, those authors consider a data warehouse as a repository of integrated and consistent, yet operational, data, while they use a multidimensional representation of data only in data marts. According to our terminology, this "operational view" of data warehouses essentially corresponds to the reconciled data layer in three-layer architectures.*

1.3.3   Three-Layer Architecture

In this architecture, the third layer is the *reconciled data layer* or *operational data store*. This layer materializes operational data obtained after integrating and cleansing source data. As a result, those data are integrated, consistent, correct, current, and detailed. Figure 1-4 shows a data warehouse that is not populated from its sources directly, but from reconciled data.

The main advantage of the reconciled data layer is that it creates a common reference data model for a whole enterprise. At the same time, it sharply separates the problems of source data extraction and integration from those of data warehouse population. Remarkably, in some cases, the reconciled layer is also directly used to better accomplish some operational tasks, such as producing daily reports that cannot be satisfactorily prepared using the corporate applications, or generating data flows to feed external processes periodically so as to benefit from cleaning and integration. However, reconciled data leads to more redundancy of operational source data. Note that we may assume that even two-layer architectures can have a reconciled layer that is not specifically materialized, but only virtual, because it is defined as a consistent integrated view of operational source data.

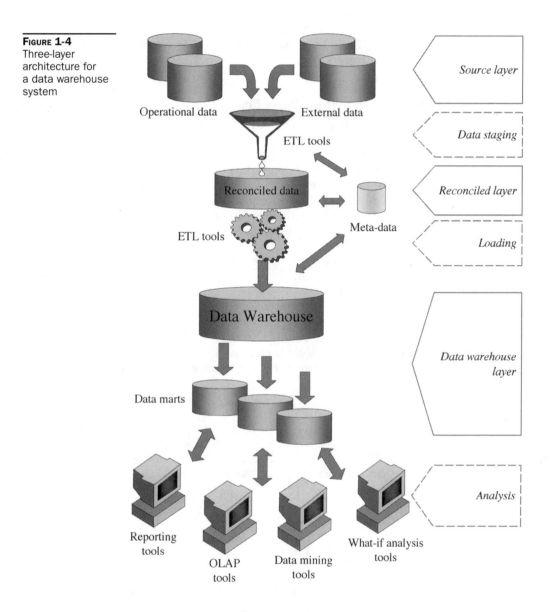

FIGURE 1-4
Three-layer
architecture for
a data warehouse
system

Operational data   External data

ETL tools

Reconciled data

ETL tools

Meta-data

Data Warehouse

Data marts

Reporting
tools

OLAP
tools

Data mining
tools

What-if analysis
tools

Source layer

Data staging

Reconciled layer

Loading

Data warehouse
layer

Analysis

Finally, let's consider a supplementary architectural approach, which provides a comprehensive picture. This approach can be described as a hybrid solution between the single-layer architecture and the two/three-layer architecture. This approach assumes that although a data warehouse is available, it is unable to solve all the queries formulated. This means that users may be interested in directly accessing source data from aggregate data (*drill-through*). To reach this goal, some queries have to be rewritten on the basis of source data (or reconciled data if it is available). This type of architecture is implemented in a prototype by Cui and Widom, 2000, and it needs to be able to go dynamically back to the source data required for queries to be solved (*lineage*).

NOTE *Gupta, 1997a; Hull and Zhou, 1996; and Yang et al., 1997 discuss the implications of this approach from the viewpoint of performance optimization, and in particular view materialization.*

1.3.4   An Additional Architecture Classification

The scientific literature often distinguishes five types of architecture for data warehouse systems, in which the same basic layers mentioned in the preceding paragraphs are combined in different ways (Rizzi, 2008).

In *independent data marts architecture*, different data marts are separately designed and built in a nonintegrated fashion (Figure 1-5). This architecture can be initially adopted in the absence of a strong sponsorship toward an enterprise-wide warehousing project, or when the organizational divisions that make up the company are loosely coupled. However, it tends to be soon replaced by other architectures that better achieve data integration and cross-reporting.

The *bus architecture*, recommended by Ralph Kimball, is apparently similar to the preceding architecture, with one important difference. A basic set of *conformed dimensions* (that is, analysis dimensions that preserve the same meaning throughout all the facts they belong to), derived by a careful analysis of the main enterprise processes, is adopted and shared as a common design guideline. This ensures logical integration of data marts and an enterprise-wide view of information.

In the *hub-and-spoke architecture*, one of the most used in medium to large contexts, there is much attention to scalability and extensibility, and to achieving an enterprise-wide view

FIGURE 1-5
Independent data
marts architecture

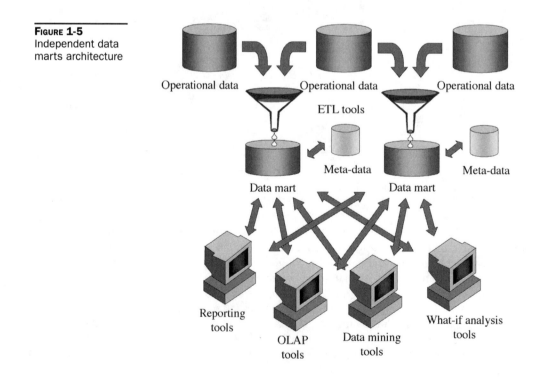

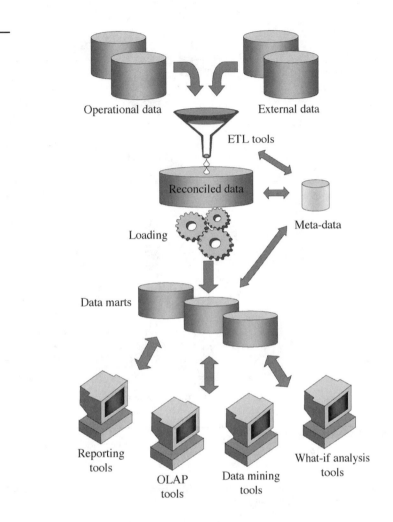

FIGURE 1-6
Hub-and-spoke
architecture

of information. Atomic, normalized data is stored in a reconciled layer that feeds a set of data marts containing summarized data in multidimensional form (Figure 1-6). Users mainly access the data marts, but they may occasionally query the reconciled layer.

The *centralized architecture*, recommended by Bill Inmon, can be seen as a particular implementation of the hub-and-spoke architecture, where the reconciled layer and the data marts are collapsed into a single physical repository.

The *federated architecture* is sometimes adopted in dynamic contexts where preexisting data warehouses/data marts are to be noninvasively integrated to provide a single, cross-organization decision support environment (for instance, in the case of mergers and acquisitions). Each data warehouse/data mart is either virtually or physically integrated with the others, leaning on a variety of advanced techniques such as distributed querying, ontologies, and meta-data interoperability (Figure 1-7).

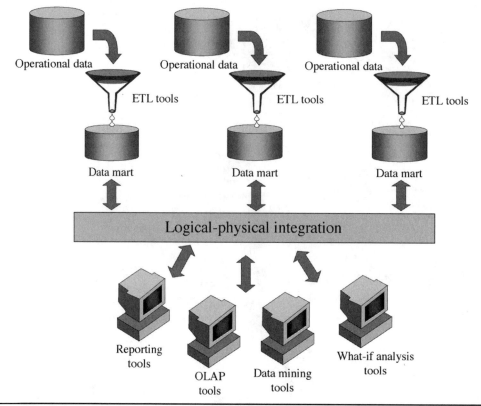

FIGURE 1-7   Federated architecture

The following list includes the factors that are particularly influential when it comes to choosing one of these architectures:

- The amount of interdependent information exchanged between organizational units in an enterprise and the organizational role played by the data warehouse project sponsor may lead to the implementation of enterprise-wide architectures, such as bus architectures, or department-specific architectures, such as independent data marts.

- An urgent need for a data warehouse project, restrictions on economic and human resources, as well as poor IT staff skills may suggest that a type of "quick" architecture, such as independent data marts, should be implemented.

- The minor role played by a data warehouse project in enterprise strategies can make you prefer an architecture type based on independent data marts over a hub-and-spoke architecture type.

- The frequent need for integrating preexisting data warehouses, possibly deployed on heterogeneous platforms, and the pressing demand for uniformly accessing their data can require a federated architecture type.

1.4 Data Staging and ETL

Now let's closely study some basic features of the different architecture layers. We will start with the data staging layer.

The data staging layer hosts the ETL processes that extract, integrate, and clean data from operational sources to feed the data warehouse layer. In a three-layer architecture, ETL processes actually feed the reconciled data layer—a single, detailed, comprehensive, top-quality data source—that in its turn feeds the data warehouse. For this reason, the ETL process operations as a whole are often defined as *reconciliation*. These are also the most complex and technically challenging among all the data warehouse process phases.

ETL takes place once when a data warehouse is populated for the first time, then it occurs every time the data warehouse is regularly updated. Figure 1-8 shows that ETL consists of four separate phases: *extraction* (or *capture*), *cleansing* (or *cleaning* or *scrubbing*), *transformation*, and *loading*. In the following sections, we offer brief descriptions of these phases.

NOTE *Refer to Jarke et al., 2000; Hoffer et al., 2005; Kimball and Caserta, 2004; and English, 1999 for more details on ETL.*

The scientific literature shows that the boundaries between cleansing and transforming are often blurred from the terminological viewpoint. For this reason, a specific operation is not always clearly assigned to one of these phases. This is obviously a formal problem, but not a substantial one. We will adopt the approach used by Hoffer and others (2005) to make our explanations as clear as possible. Their approach states that cleansing is essentially aimed at rectifying data *values*, and transformation more specifically manages data *formats*.

Chapter 10 discusses all the details of the data-staging design phase. Chapter 3 deals with an early data warehouse design phase: *integration*. This phase is necessary if there are heterogeneous sources to define a schema for the reconciled data layer, and to specifically transform operational data in the data-staging phase.

1.4.1 Extraction

Relevant data is obtained from sources in the extraction phase. You can use *static extraction* when a data warehouse needs populating for the first time. Conceptually speaking, this looks like a snapshot of operational data. *Incremental extraction*, used to update data warehouses regularly, seizes the changes applied to source data since the latest extraction. Incremental extraction is often based on the log maintained by the operational DBMS. If a timestamp is associated with operational data to record exactly when the data is changed or added, it can be used to streamline the extraction process. Extraction can also be source-driven if you can rewrite operational applications to asynchronously notify of the changes being applied, or if your operational database can implement triggers associated with change transactions for relevant data.

The data to be extracted is mainly selected on the basis of its quality (English, 1999). In particular, this depends on how comprehensive and accurate the constraints implemented in sources are, how suitable the data formats are, and how clear the schemata are.

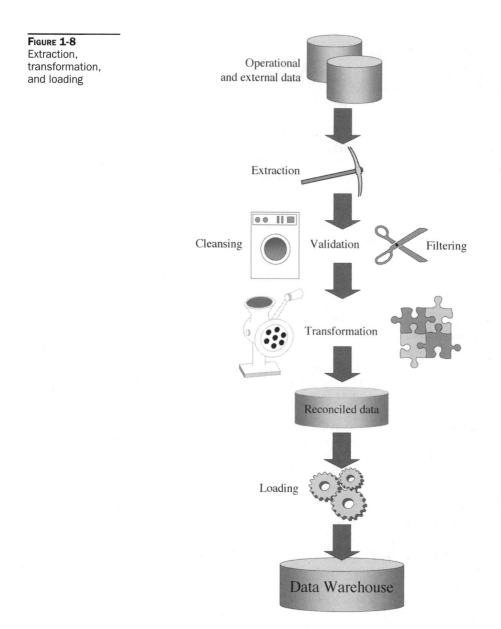

Figure 1-8
Extraction, transformation, and loading

1.4.2 Cleansing

The cleansing phase is crucial in a data warehouse system because it is supposed to improve data quality—normally quite poor in sources (Galhardas et al., 2001). The following list includes the most frequent mistakes and inconsistencies that make data "dirty":

- **Duplicate data** For example, a patient is recorded many times in a hospital patient management system

- **Inconsistent values that are logically associated**   Such as addresses and ZIP codes
- **Missing data**   Such as a customer's job
- **Unexpected use of fields**   For example, a `socialSecurityNumber` field could be used improperly to store office phone numbers
- **Impossible or wrong values**   Such as 2/30/2009
- **Inconsistent values for a single entity because different practices were used**   For example, to specify a country, you can use an international country abbreviation (I) or a full country name (Italy); similar problems arise with addresses (Hamlet Rd. and Hamlet Road)
- **Inconsistent values for one individual entity because of typing mistakes**   Such as Hamet Road instead of Hamlet Road

In particular, note that the last two types of mistakes are very frequent when you are managing multiple sources and are entering data manually.

The main data cleansing features found in ETL tools are *rectification* and *homogenization*. They use specific dictionaries to rectify typing mistakes and to recognize synonyms, as well as *rule-based cleansing* to enforce domain-specific rules and define appropriate associations between values. See section 10.2 for more details on these points.

1.4.3   Transformation

Transformation is the core of the reconciliation phase. It converts data from its operational source format into a specific data warehouse format. If you implement a three-layer architecture, this phase outputs your reconciled data layer. Independently of the presence of a reconciled data layer, establishing a mapping between the source data layer and the data warehouse layer is generally made difficult by the presence of many different, heterogeneous sources. If this is the case, a complex integration phase is required when designing your data warehouse. See Chapter 3 for more details.

The following points must be rectified in this phase:

- *Loose texts may hide valuable information.* For example, BigDeal LtD does not explicitly show that this is a Limited Partnership company.
- *Different formats can be used for individual data.* For example, a date can be saved as a string or as three integers.

Following are the main transformation processes aimed at populating the reconciled data layer:

- *Conversion* and *normalization* that operate on both storage formats and units of measure to make data uniform
- *Matching* that associates equivalent fields in different sources
- *Selection* that reduces the number of source fields and records

When populating a data warehouse, normalization is replaced by *denormalization* because data warehouse data are typically denormalized, and you need *aggregation* to sum up data properly.

FIGURE 1-9
Example of
cleansing and
transforming
customer data

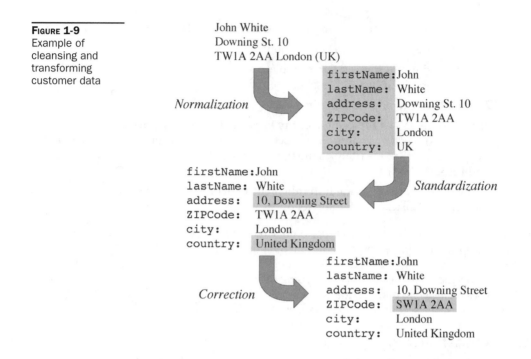

Cleansing and transformation processes are often closely connected in ETL tools. Figure 1-9 shows an example of cleansing and transformation of customer data: a field-based structure is extracted from a loose text, then a few values are standardized so as to remove abbreviations, and eventually those values that are logically associated can be rectified.

1.4.4   Loading

Loading into a data warehouse is the last step to take. Loading can be carried out in two ways:

- **Refresh**   Data warehouse data is completely rewritten. This means that older data is replaced. Refresh is normally used in combination with static extraction to initially populate a data warehouse.

- **Update**   Only those changes applied to source data are added to the data warehouse. Update is typically carried out without deleting or modifying preexisting data. This technique is used in combination with incremental extraction to update data warehouses regularly.

1.5 Multidimensional Model

The data warehouse layer is a vitally important part of this book. Here, we introduce a data warehouse key word: *multidimensional*. You need to become familiar with the concepts and terminology used here to understand the information presented throughout this book, particularly information regarding conceptual and logical modeling and designing.

Over the last few years, multidimensional databases have generated much research and market interest because they are fundamental for many decision-making support applications, such as data warehouse systems. The reason why the multidimensional model is used as a paradigm of data warehouse data representation is fundamentally connected to its ease of use and intuitiveness even for IT newbies. The multidimensional model's success is also linked to the widespread use of productivity tools, such as spreadsheets, that adopt the multidimensional model as a visualization paradigm.

Perhaps the best starting point to approach the multidimensional model effectively is a definition of the types of queries for which this model is best suited. Section 1.7 offers more details on typical decision-making queries such as those listed here (Jarke et al., 2000):

- *"What is the total amount of receipts recorded last year per state and per product category?"*
- *"What is the relationship between the trend of PC manufacturers' shares and quarter gains over the last five years?"*
- *"Which orders maximize receipts?"*
- *"Which one of two new treatments will result in a decrease in the average period of admission?"*
- *"What is the relationship between profit gained by the shipments consisting of less than 10 items and the profit gained by the shipments of more than 10 items?"*

It is clear that using traditional languages, such as SQL, to express these types of queries can be a very difficult task for inexperienced users. It is also clear that running these types of queries against operational databases would result in an unacceptably long response time.

The multidimensional model begins with the observation that the factors affecting decision-making processes are enterprise-specific *facts*, such as sales, shipments, hospital admissions, surgeries, and so on. Instances of a fact correspond to *events* that occurred. For example, every single sale or shipment carried out is an event. Each fact is described by the values of a set of relevant *measures* that provide a quantitative description of events. For example, sales receipts, amounts shipped, hospital admission costs, and surgery time are measures.

Obviously, a huge number of events occur in typical enterprises—too many to analyze one by one. Imagine placing them all into an *n*-dimensional space to help us quickly select and sort them out. The *n*-dimensional space axes are called *analysis dimensions*, and they define different perspectives to single out events. For example, the sales in a store chain can be represented in a three-dimensional space whose dimensions are products, stores, and dates. As far as shipments are concerned, products, shipment dates, orders, destinations, and terms & conditions can be used as dimensions. Hospital admissions can be defined by the department-date-patient combination, and you would need to add the type of operation to classify surgery operations.

The concept of dimension gave life to the broadly used metaphor of *cubes* to represent multidimensional data. According to this metaphor, events are associated with cube cells and cube edges stand for analysis dimensions. If more than three dimensions exist, the cube is called a *hypercube*. Each cube cell is given a value for each measure. Figure 1-10 shows an intuitive representation of a cube in which the fact is a sale in a store chain. Its analysis dimensions are *store*, *product* and *date*. An event stands for a specific item sold in a specific store on a specific date, and it is described by two measures: the *quantity* sold and the *receipts*. This figure highlights that the cube is *sparse*—this means that many events did not actually take place. Of course, you cannot sell every item every day in every store.

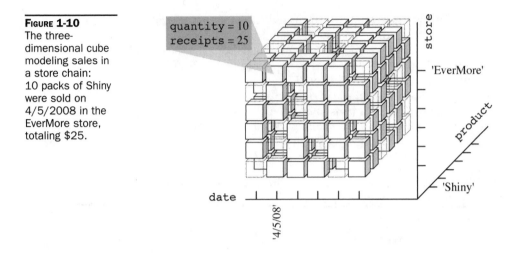

FIGURE 1-10
The three-dimensional cube modeling sales in a store chain: 10 packs of Shiny were sold on 4/5/2008 in the EverMore store, totaling $25.

If you want to use the relational model to represent this cube, you could use the following relational schema:

```
SALES(store, product, date, quantity, receipts)
```

Here, the underlined attributes make up the primary key and events are associated with tuples, such as <'EverMore', 'Shiny', '04/05/08', 10, 25>. The constraint expressed by this primary key specifies that two events cannot be associated with an individual store, product, and date value combination, and that every value combination *functionally determines* a unique value for `quantity` and a unique value for `receipts`. This means that the following functional dependency[2] holds:

$$\text{store, product, date} \rightarrow \text{quantity, receipts}$$

To avoid any misunderstanding of the term *event*, you should realize that the group of dimensions selected for a fact representation singles out a unique event in the multidimensional model, but the group does not necessarily single out a unique event in the application domain. To make this statement clearer, consider once again the sales example. In the application domain, one single *sales* event is supposed to be a customer's purchase of a set of products from a store on a specific date. In practice, this corresponds to a sales receipt. From the viewpoint of the multidimensional model, if the sales fact has the `product`, `store`, and `date` dimensions, an event will be the daily total amount of an item sold in a store. It is clear that the difference between both interpretations depends on sales

---

[2]The definition of functional dependency belongs to relational theory. Given relation schema R and two attribute sets $X = \{a_1 \ldots, a_n\}$ and $Y = \{b_1 \ldots, b_m\}$, X is said to *functionally determine* Y ($X \rightarrow Y$) if and only if, for every legal instance r of R and for each pair of tuples t_1, t_2 in r, $t_1[X] = t_2[X]$ implies $t_1[Y] = t_2[Y]$. Here $t[X/Y]$ denotes the values taken in t from the attributes in X/Y. By extension, we say that a functional dependency holds between two attribute sets X and Y when each value set of X always corresponds to a single value set of Y. To simplify the notation, when we denote the attributes in each set, we drop the braces.

receipts that generally include various items, and on individual items that are generally sold many times every day in a store. In the following sections, we use the terms *event* and *fact* to make reference to the granularity taken by events and facts in the multidimensional model.

Normally, each dimension is associated with a *hierarchy* of aggregation levels, often called *roll-up hierarchy*. Roll-up hierarchies group aggregation level values in different ways. Hierarchies consist of levels called *dimensional attributes*. Figure 1-11 shows a simple example of hierarchies built on the `product` and `store` dimensions: products are classified into types, and are then further classified into categories. Stores are located in cities belonging to states. On top of each hierarchy is a fake level that includes all the dimension-related values. From the viewpoint of relational theory, you can use a set of functional dependencies between dimensional attributes to express a hierarchy:

$$\text{product} \rightarrow \text{type} \rightarrow \text{category}$$
$$\text{store} \rightarrow \text{city} \rightarrow \text{state}$$

In summary, a *multidimensional* cube hinges on a *fact* relevant to decision-making. It shows a set of *events* for which numeric *measures* provide a quantitative description. Each cube axis shows a possible analysis *dimension*. Each dimension can be analyzed at different detail levels specified by hierarchically structured *attributes*.

The scientific literature shows many formal expressions of the multidimensional model, which can be more or less complex and comprehensive. We'll briefly mention alternative terms used for the multidimensional model in the scientific literature and in commercial tools.

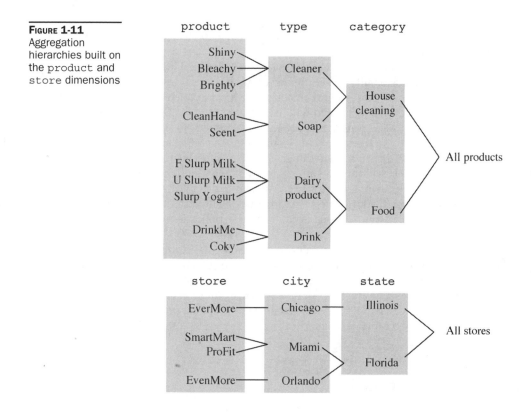

FIGURE 1-11
Aggregation hierarchies built on the `product` and `store` dimensions

The *fact* and *cube* terms are often interchangeably used. Essentially, everyone agrees on the use of the term *dimensions* to specify the coordinates that classify and identify fact occurrences. However, entire hierarchies are sometimes called *dimensions*. For example, the term *time dimension* can be used for the entire hierarchy built on the date attribute. Measures are sometimes called *variables*, *metrics*, *properties*, *attributes*, or *indicators*. In some models, dimensional attributes of hierarchies are called *levels* or *parameters*.

NOTE *The main formal expressions of the multidimensional model in the literature were proposed by Agrawal et al., 1995; Gyssens and Lakshmanan, 1997; Datta and Thomas, 1997; Vassiliadis, 1998; and Cabibbo and Torlone, 1998.*

The information in a multidimensional cube is very difficult for users to manage because of its quantity, even if it is a concise version of the information stored to operational databases. If, for example, a store chain includes 50 stores selling 1000 items, and a specific data warehouse covers three-year-long transactions (approximately 1000 days), the number of potential events totals $50 \times 1000 \times 1000 = 5 \times 10^7$. Assuming that each store can sell only 10 percent of all the available items per day, the number of events totals 5×10^6. This is still too much data to be analyzed by users without relying on automatic tools.

You have essentially two ways to reduce the quantity of data and obtain useful information: *restriction* and *aggregation*. The cube metaphor offers an easy-to-use and intuitive way to understand both of these methods, as we will discuss in the following paragraphs.

1.5.1   Restriction

Restricting data means separating part of the data from a cube to mark out an analysis field. In relational algebra terminology, this is called making *selections* and/or *projections*.

The simplest type of selection is *data slicing*, shown in Figure 1-12. When you slice data, you decrease cube dimensionality by setting one or more dimensions to a specific value. For example, if you set one of the sales cube dimensions to a value, such as store='EverMore', this results in the set of events associated with the items sold in the EverMore store. According to the cube metaphor, this is simply a plane of cells—that is, a data slice that can be easily displayed in spreadsheets. In the store chain example given earlier, approximately 10^5 events still appear in your result. If you set two dimensions to a value, such as store='EverMore' and date='4/5/2008', this will result in all the different items sold in the EverMore store on April 5 (approximately 100 events). Graphically speaking, this information is stored at the intersection of two perpendicular planes resulting in a line. If you set all the dimensions to a particular value, you will define just one event that corresponds to a point in the three-dimensional space of sales.

Dicing is a generalization of slicing. It poses some constraints on dimensional attributes to scale down the size of a cube. For example, you can select only the daily sales of the food items in April 2008 in Florida (Figure 1-12). In this way, if five stores are located in Florida and 50 food products are sold, the number of events to examine changes to $5 \times 50 \times 30 = 7500$.

Finally, a *projection* can be referred to as a choice to keep just one subgroup of measures for every event and reject other measures.

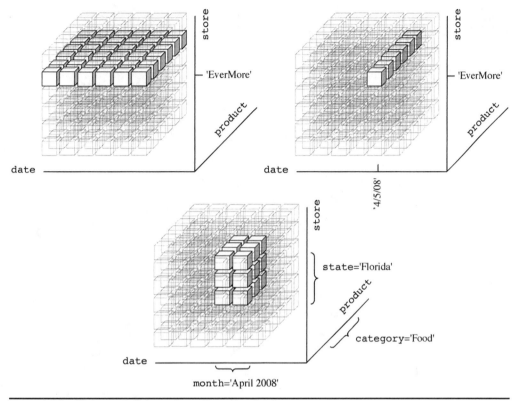

FIGURE 1-12   Slicing and dicing a three-dimensional cube

1.5.2   Aggregation

Aggregation plays a fundamental role in multidimensional databases. Assume, for example, that you want to analyze the items sold monthly for a three year period. According to the cube metaphor, this means that you need to sort all the cells related to the days of each month by product and store, and then merge them into one single macrocell. In the aggregate cube obtained in this way, the total number of events (that is, the number of macrocells) is $50 \times 1000 \times 36$. This is because the granularity of the time dimensions does not depend on days any longer, but now depends on months, and 36 is the number of months in three years. Every aggregate event will then sum up the data available in the events it aggregates. In this example, the total amount of items sold per month and the total receipts are calculated by summing every single value of their measures (Figure 1-13). If you further aggregate along time, you can achieve just three events for every store-product combination: one for every year. When you completely aggregate along the time dimension, each store-product combination corresponds to one single event, which shows the total amount of items sold in a store over three years and the total amount of receipts.

Figure 1-13
Time hierarchy
aggregation of the
quantity of items
sold per product
in three stores.
A dash shows that
an event did not
occur because no
item was sold.

	EverMore	EvenMore	SmartMart
1/1/2007	–	–	–
1/2/2007	10	15	5
1/3/2007	20	–	5
....	....	....	....
1/1/2008	–	–	–
1/2/2008	15	10	20
1/3/2008	20	20	25
....	....	....	....
1/1/2009	–	–	–
1/2/2009	20	8	25
1/3/2009	20	12	20
....	....	....	....

	EverMore	EvenMore	SmartMart
January 2007	200	180	150
February 2007	180	150	120
March 2007	220	180	160
....	....	....	....
January 2008	350	220	200
February 2008	300	200	250
March 2008	310	180	300
....	....	....	....
January 2009	380	200	220
February 2009	310	200	250
March 2009	300	160	280
....	....	....	....

	EverMore	EvenMore	SmartMart
2007	2,400	2,000	1,600
2008	3,200	2,300	3,000
2009	3,400	2,200	3,200

	EverMore	EvenMore	SmartMart
Total	9,000	6,500	7,800

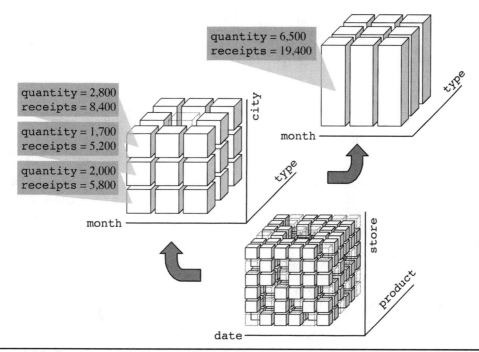

FIGURE 1-14 Two cube aggregation levels. Every macro-event measure value is a sum of its component event values.

You can aggregate along various dimensions at the same time. For example, Figure 1-14 shows that you can group sales by month, product type, and store city, and by month and product type. Moreover, selections and aggregations can be combined to carry out an analysis process targeted exactly to users' needs.

1.6 Meta-data

The term *meta-data* can be applied to the data used to define other data. In the scope of data warehousing, meta-data plays an essential role because it specifies source, values, usage, and features of data warehouse data and defines how data can be changed and processed at every architecture layer. Figures 1-3 and 1-4 show that the meta-data repository is closely connected to the data warehouse. Applications use it intensively to carry out data-staging and analysis tasks.

According to Kelly's approach, you can classify meta-data into two partially overlapping categories. This classification is based on the ways system administrators and end users exploit meta-data. System administrators are interested in *internal meta-data* because it defines data sources, transformation processes, population policies, logical and physical schemata, constraints, and user profiles. *External meta-data* is relevant to end users. For example, it is about definitions, quality standards, units of measure, relevant aggregations.

Meta-data is stored in a meta-data repository which all the other architecture components can access. According to Kelly, a tool for meta-data management should

- allow administrators to perform system administration operations, and in particular manage security;
- allow end users to navigate and query meta-data;
- use a GUI;
- allow end users to extend meta-data;
- allow meta-data to be imported/exported into/from other standard tools and formats.

As far as representation formats are concerned, Object Management Group (OMG, 2000) released a standard called *Common Warehouse Metamodel (CWM)* that relies on three famous standards: *Unified Modeling Language (UML)*, *eXtensible Markup Language (XML)*, and *XML Metadata Interchange (XMI)*. Partners, such as IBM, Unisys, NCR, and Oracle, in a common effort, created the new standard format that specifies how meta-data can be exchanged among the technologies related to data warehouses, business intelligence, knowledge management, and web portals.

Figure 1-15 shows an example of a dialog box displaying external meta-data related to hierarchies in MicroStrategy Desktop of the MicroStrategy 8 tool suite. In particular,

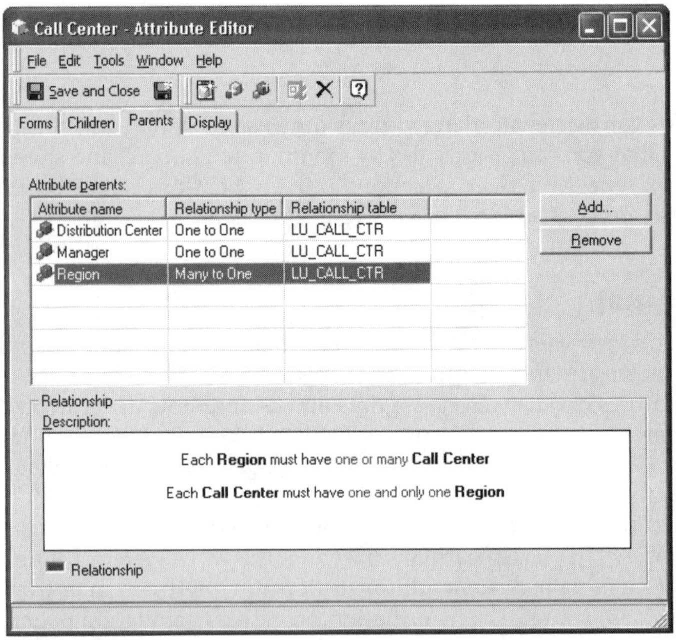

FIGURE 1-15
Accessing hierarchy meta-data in MicroStrategy

this dialog box displays the Calling Center attribute parent attributes. Specifically, it states that a calling center refers to a distribution center, belongs to a region, and is managed by a manager.

NOTE *See Barquin and Edelstein, 1996; Jarke et al., 2000; Jennings, 2004; and Tozer, 1999, for a comprehensive discussion on meta-data representation and management.*

1.7 Accessing Data Warehouses

Analysis is the last level common to all data warehouse architecture types. After cleansing, integrating, and transforming data, you should determine how to get the best out of it in terms of information. The following sections show the best approaches for end users to query data warehouses: *reports*, *OLAP*, and *dashboards*. End users often use the information stored to a data warehouse as a starting point for additional business intelligence applications, such as what-if analyses and data mining. See Chapter 15 for more details on these advanced applications.

1.7.1   Reports

This approach is oriented to those users who need to have regular access to the information in an almost static way. For example, suppose a local health authority must send to its state offices monthly reports summing up information on patient admission costs. The layout of those reports has been predetermined and may vary only if changes are applied to current laws and regulations. Designers issue the queries to create reports with the desired layout and "freeze" all those in an application. In this way, end users can query current data whenever they need to.

A *report* is defined by a query and a layout. A query generally implies a restriction and an aggregation of multidimensional data. For example, you can look for the monthly receipts during the last quarter for every product category. A layout can look like a table or a chart (diagrams, histograms, pies, and so on). Figure 1-16 shows a few examples of layouts for the receipts query.

A reporting tool should be evaluated not only on the basis of comprehensive report layouts, but also on the basis of flexible report delivery systems. A report can be explicitly run by users or automatically and regularly sent to registered end users. For example, it can be sent via e-mail.

Keep in mind that reports existed long before data warehouse systems came to be. Reports have always been the main tool used by managers for evaluating and planning tasks since the invention of databases. However, adding data warehouses to the mix is beneficial to reports for two main reasons: First, they take advantage of reliable and correct

FIGURE 1-16
Report layouts:
table (top),
line graph (middle),
3-D pie graphs
(bottom)

Receipts (K$)	Oct. 2008	Sep. 2008	Aug. 2008
Clothes	80	100	50
Food	20	40	10
Furniture	50	5	10
Perfumes	25	35	20
House cleaning	15	20	5
Free time	60	50	20

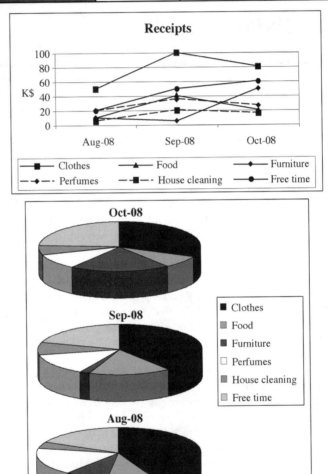

results because the data summed up in reports is consistent and integrated. In addition, data warehouses expedite the reporting process because the architectural separation between transaction processing and analyses significantly improves performance.

1.7.2   OLAP

OLAP might be the main way to exploit information in a data warehouse. Surely it is the most popular one, and it gives end users, whose analysis needs are not easy to define beforehand, the opportunity to analyze and explore data interactively on the basis of the multidimensional model. While users of reporting tools essentially play a passive role, OLAP users are able to start a complex analysis session actively, where each step is the result of the outcome of preceding steps. Real-time properties of OLAP sessions, required in-depth knowledge of data, complex queries that can be issued, and design for users not familiar with IT make the tools in use play a crucial role. The GUI of these tools must be flexible, easy-to-use, and effective.

An OLAP session consists of a *navigation path* that corresponds to an analysis process for facts according to different viewpoints and at different detail levels. This path is turned into a sequence of queries, which are often not issued directly, but differentially expressed with reference to the previous query. The results of queries are multidimensional. Because we humans have a difficult time deciphering diagrams of more than three dimensions, OLAP tools typically use tables to display data, with multiple headers, colors, and other features to highlight data dimensions.

Every step of an analysis session is characterized by an *OLAP operator* that turns the latest query into a new one. The most common operators are roll-up, drill-down, slice-and-dice, pivot, drill-across, and drill-through. The figures included here show different operators, and were generated using the MicroStrategy Desktop front-end application in the MicroStrategy 8 tool suite. They are based on the V-Mall example, in which a large virtual mall sells items from its catalog via phone and the Internet. Figure 1-17 shows the attribute hierarchies relevant to the sales fact in V-Mall.

The *roll-up* operator causes an increase in data aggregation and removes a detail level from a hierarchy. For example, Figure 1-18 shows a query posed by a user that displays

FIGURE 1-17
Attribute hierarchies in V-Mall; arrows show functional dependencies

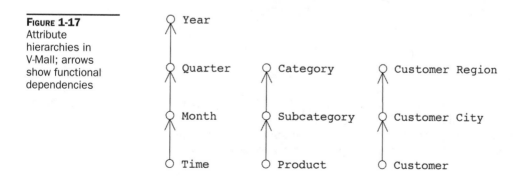

| Month | Metrics | Revenue | | | | | | |
	Customer Region	Northeast	Mid-Atlantic	Southeast	Central	South	Northwest	Southwest
Jan 2005		$160,155	$518,405	$81,381	$322,294	$98,001	$103,368	$298,730
Feb 2005		$170,777	$491,628	$80,399	$314,466	$91,222	$114,341	$373,645
Mar 2005		$200,434	$611,424	$129,102	$382,946	$123,038	$147,472	$351,602
Apr 2005		$194,811	$502,241	$93,654	$357,188	$90,663	$124,824	$304,416
May 2005		$169,998	$462,364	$117,780	$300,389	$79,999	$117,506	$311,123
Jun 2005		$202,477	$559,466	$109,979	$309,683	$115,318	$117,008	$373,526
Jul 2005		$194,490	$577,515	$105,099	$332,300	$92,730	$103,494	$369,380
Aug 2005		$203,085	$599,761	$118,805	$410,885	$119,178	$131,148	$384,555
Sep 2005		$241,992	$625,517	$122,261	$415,763	$75,655	$124,974	$364,651
Oct 2005		$217,477	$641,340	$137,925	$382,321	$89,679	$124,276	$337,489
Nov 2005		$238,004	$708,036	$156,525	$457,105	$116,478	$156,466	$386,399
Dec 2005		$273,721	$774,372	$154,139	$479,729	$119,113	$143,753	$414,983
Jan 2006		$215,786	$662,632	$125,238	$392,922	$91,791	$122,235	$343,027
Feb 2006		$253,128	$711,937	$123,725	$415,742	$97,309	$137,589	$391,277
Mar 2006		$253,564	$704,652	$135,180	$430,143	$112,459	$144,659	$406,956
Apr 2006		$255,352	$710,402	$126,717	$426,423	$113,233	$140,976	$395,924
May 2006		$231,766	$676,205	$130,981	$440,813	$107,277	$136,043	$377,349
Jun 2006		$290,534	$769,788	$123,743	$507,166	$125,631	$131,549	$439,321
Jul 2006		$247,683	$811,060	$145,955	$448,939	$113,683	$128,113	$415,251
Aug 2006		$252,313	$719,509	$125,944	$427,188	$108,987	$153,966	$421,310
Sep 2006		$288,772	$801,819	$148,023	$539,406	$112,784	$149,236	$419,878
Oct 2006		$307,610	$710,458	$163,254	$450,006	$105,218	$144,906	$440,856
Nov 2006		$284,671	$800,941	$157,117	$505,952	$118,552	$163,560	$470,591
Dec 2006		$310,775	$891,543	$170,207	$575,086	$120,228	$155,409	$534,680

| Quarter | Metrics | Revenue | | | | | | |
	Customer Region	Northeast	Mid-Atlantic	Southeast	Central	South	Northwest	Southwest
2005 Q1		$531,366	$1,621,457	$290,882	$1,019,706	$312,261	$365,181	$1,023,977
2005 Q2		$567,286	$1,524,070	$321,413	$967,260	$285,981	$359,339	$989,065
2005 Q3		$639,567	$1,802,793	$346,165	$1,158,948	$287,563	$359,616	$1,118,587
2005 Q4		$729,202	$2,123,749	$448,589	$1,319,154	$325,269	$424,495	$1,138,871
2006 Q1		$722,478	$2,079,221	$384,143	$1,238,807	$301,559	$404,483	$1,141,260
2006 Q2		$777,651	$2,156,394	$381,441	$1,374,402	$346,141	$408,567	$1,212,593
2006 Q3		$788,768	$2,332,388	$419,923	$1,415,533	$335,455	$431,315	$1,256,439
2006 Q4		$903,056	$2,402,942	$490,578	$1,531,044	$343,998	$463,874	$1,446,127

Figure 1-18 Time hierarchy roll-up

monthly revenues in 2005 and 2006 for every customer region. If you "roll it up," you remove the month detail to display quarterly total revenues per region. Rolling-up can also reduce the number of dimensions in your results if you remove all the hierarchy details. If you apply this principle to Figure 1-19, you can remove information on customers and display yearly total revenues per product category as you turn the three-dimensional table

Category	Year	Metrics Customer Region 	Revenue Northeast	Mid-Atlantic	Southeast	Central	South	Northwest	Southwest
Books	2005		$416,183	$316,104	$36,517	$207,850	$137,502	$19,062	$187,368
	2006		$534,932	$401,908	$42,027	$239,806	$138,683	$22,655	$183,275
Electronics	2005		$1,860,172	$6,517,723	$1,226,825	$3,719,752	$915,633	$1,434,575	$3,625,191
	2006		$2,403,311	$8,253,620	$1,451,397	$4,631,259	$999,611	$1,615,848	$4,298,985
Movies	2005		$112,560	$138,611	$118,179	$153,556	$119,566	$27,060	$362,858
	2006		$148,785	$188,567	$147,445	$203,547	$145,434	$35,878	$463,470
Music	2005		$78,507	$99,631	$25,528	$383,911	$38,373	$27,933	$95,083
	2006		$104,925	$126,851	$35,215	$485,174	$43,424	$33,860	$110,689

Category	Year	Metrics	Revenue
Books	2005		$1,320,585
	2006		$1,563,287
Electronics	2005		$19,299,870
	2006		$23,654,030
Movies	2005		$1,032,391
	2006		$1,333,126
Music	2005		$748,966
	2006		$940,136

Figure 1-19   Roll-up removing customer hierarchy

into a two-dimensional one. Figure 1-20 uses the cube metaphor to sketch a roll-up operation
with and without a decrease in dimensions.

The *drill-down* operator is the complement to the roll-up operator. Figure 1-20 shows that
it reduces data aggregation and adds a new detail level to a hierarchy. Figure 1-21 shows an
example based on a bidimensional table. This table shows that the aggregation based
on customer regions shifts to a new fine-grained aggregation based on customer cities.

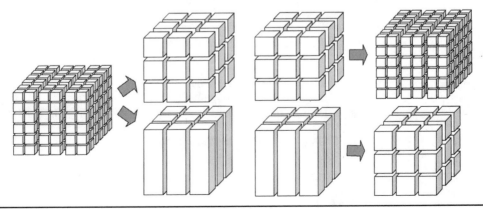

Figure 1-20   Rolling-up (left) and drilling-down (right) a cube

Metrics Customer Region Quarter	Revenue Northeast	Mid-Atlantic	Southeast	Central	South	Northwest	Southwest
2005 Q1	$531,366	$1,621,457	$290,882	$1,019,706	$312,261	$365,181	$1,023,977
2005 Q2	$567,286	$1,524,070	$321,413	$967,260	$285,981	$359,339	$989,065
2005 Q3	$639,567	$1,802,793	$346,165	$1,158,948	$287,563	$359,616	$1,118,587
2005 Q4	$729,202	$2,123,749	$448,589	$1,319,154	$325,269	$424,495	$1,138,871
2006 Q1	$722,478	$2,079,221	$384,143	$1,238,807	$301,559	$404,483	$1,141,260
2006 Q2	$777,651	$2,156,394	$381,441	$1,374,402	$346,141	$408,567	$1,212,593
2006 Q3	$788,768	$2,332,388	$419,923	$1,415,533	$335,455	$431,315	$1,256,439
2006 Q4	$903,056	$2,402,942	$490,578	$1,531,044	$343,998	$463,874	$1,446,127

Metrics Customer City Quarter	Revenue Addison	Akron	Albany	Albert City	Alexandria	Allentown	Anderson	Annapolis	Arden	Arlington Heights	Arlington	Artesia	A:
2005 Q1	$7,713	$30,140	$4,626	$6,686	$29,042	$4,579	$1,948	$40,066	$23,341	$10,481		$10,922	$1
2005 Q2	$15,903	$48,029	$8,959	$2,088	$17,590	$7,268	$2,416	$42,764	$21,026	$7,514	$1,695	$2,984	$
2005 Q3	$10,091	$30,510	$5,763	$11,380	$26,389	$10,195	$568	$51,650	$25,132	$10,784	$3,796	$8,701	$
2005 Q4	$12,425	$48,588	$10,939	$10,463	$28,016	$10,426	$3,412	$67,515	$28,398	$14,692		$9,975	$1
2006 Q1	$7,256	$26,183	$7,998	$5,603	$35,959	$10,273	$2,732	$50,121	$26,351	$7,276	$1,593	$6,208	$1
2006 Q2	$10,411	$49,540	$6,065	$5,670	$25,166	$6,992	$1,377	$68,198	$27,556	$16,755	$3,420	$6,656	$1
2006 Q3	$10,325	$38,414	$9,108	$7,760	$33,170	$16,978	$821	$69,858	$33,579	$10,235	$4,319	$7,636	$1
2006 Q4	$16,613	$49,133	$13,137	$10,637	$30,344	$13,875	$747	$48,305	$32,842	$13,311	$6,176	$9,191	$1

Figure 1-21   Drilling-down customer hierarchy

In Figure 1-22, the drill-down operator causes an increase in the number of table dimensions after adding customer region details.

Slice-and-dice is one of the most abused terms in data warehouse literature because it can have many different meanings. A few authors use it generally to define the whole OLAP navigation process. Other authors use it to define selection and projection operations based on data. In compliance with section 1.5.1, we define *slicing* as an operation that reduces the

Metrics Year Category	Revenue 2005	2006
Books	$1,320,585	$1,563,287
Electronics	$19,299,870	$23,654,030
Movies	$1,032,391	$1,333,126
Music	$748,966	$940,136

Metrics Customer Region Year Category	Revenue Northeast 2005	2006	Mid-Atlantic 2005	2006	Southeast 2005	2006	Central 2005	2006	South 2005	2006	Nort 2
Books	$416,183	$534,932	$316,104	$401,908	$36,517	$42,027	$207,850	$239,806	$137,502	$138,683	$
Electronics	$1,860,172	$2,403,311	$6,517,723	$8,253,620	$1,226,825	$1,451,397	$3,719,752	$4,631,259	$915,633	$999,611	$1,4
Movies	$112,560	$148,785	$138,611	$188,567	$118,179	$147,445	$153,556	$203,547	$119,566	$145,434	$
Music	$78,507	$104,925	$99,631	$126,851	$25,528	$35,215	$383,911	$485,174	$38,373	$43,424	$

Figure 1-22   Drilling-down and adding a dimension

FIGURE 1-23
Slicing (above)
and dicing (below)
a cube

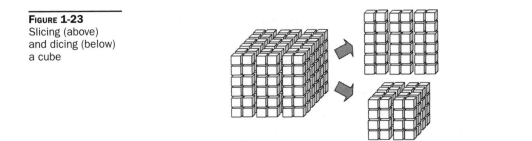

number of cube dimensions after setting one of the dimensions to a specific value. *Dicing* is an operation that reduces the set of data being analyzed by a selection criterion (Figure 1-23). Figures 1-24 and 1-25 show a few examples of slicing and dicing.

The *pivot* operator implies a change in layouts. It aims at analyzing an individual group of information from a different viewpoint. According to the multidimensional metaphor, if you pivot data, you rotate your cube so that you can rearrange cells on the

		Metrics	Revenue						
		Customer							
		Region	Northeast	Mid-Atlantic	Southeast	Central	South	Northwest	Southwest
Category	Year								
Books	2005		$416,183	$316,104	$36,517	$207,850	$137,502	$19,062	$187,368
	2006		$534,932	$401,908	$42,027	$239,806	$138,683	$22,655	$183,275
Electronics	2005		$1,860,172	$6,517,723	$1,226,825	$3,719,752	$915,633	$1,434,575	$3,625,191
	2006		$2,403,311	$8,253,620	$1,451,397	$4,631,259	$999,611	$1,615,848	$4,298,985
Movies	2005		$112,560	$138,611	$118,179	$153,556	$119,566	$27,060	$362,858
	2006		$148,785	$188,567	$147,445	$203,547	$145,434	$35,878	$463,470
Music	2005		$78,507	$99,631	$25,528	$383,911	$38,373	$27,933	$95,083
	2006		$104,925	$126,851	$35,215	$485,174	$43,424	$33,860	$110,689

Report Filter (Local Filter):
Year = 2006

	Metrics	Revenue						
	Customer							
	Region	Northeast	Mid-Atlantic	Southeast	Central	South	Northwest	Sout
Category								
Books		$534,932	$401,908	$42,027	$239,806	$138,683	$22,655	$1
Electronics		$2,403,311	$8,253,620	$1,451,397	$4,631,259	$999,611	$1,615,848	$4,2
Movies		$148,785	$188,567	$147,445	$203,547	$145,434	$35,878	$4
Music		$104,925	$126,851	$35,215	$485,174	$43,424	$33,860	$1

FIGURE 1-24   Slicing based on the `Year='2006'` predicate

Subcategory	Metrics Revenue									
Customer City	Addison	Akron	Albany	Albert City	Alexandria	Allentown	Anderson	Annapolis	Arden	Arlir Heig
Art & Architecture	$253	$365	$1,506	$279	$268	$1,960		$407	$282	
Business	$198	$357	$719	$75	$134	$1,225	$8	$304	$184	
Literature	$92	$116	$277	$54	$66	$503		$137	$128	
Books - Miscellaneous	$216	$95	$830	$120	$73	$605	$4	$233	$71	
Science & Technology	$363	$943	$3,271	$578	$491	$2,547		$834	$366	
Sports & Health	$220	$153	$416	$165	$128	$1,476		$409	$204	
Audio Equipment	$4,782	$32,192	$2,982	$4,318	$36,458	$7,303	$4,430	$77,591	$17,397	$
Cameras	$7,671	$39,381	$5,810	$3,898	$12,045	$8,124	$405	$33,744	$11,840	$
Computers	$1,531	$14,810	$1,935	$3,022	$7,967	$3,354		$5,097	$7,087	$
Electronics - Miscellaneous	$4,667	$25,861	$5,289	$5,979	$25,484	$4,821	$130	$9,533	$11,923	$
TV's	$9,027	$34,635	$5,013	$3,500	$33,432	$4,930		$46,933	$32,527	$
Video Equipment	$7,422	$10,078	$5,540	$2,479	$5,500	$7,470	$540	$55,552	$35,723	$
Action	$108	$302	$204	$134	$256	$259	$25	$859	$117	
Comedy	$308	$520	$355	$195	$204	$261		$361	$216	
Drama	$424	$548	$225	$243	$313	$399		$511	$415	
Horror	$339	$196	$141	$195	$188	$372		$261	$184	
Kids / Family	$361	$277	$236	$213	$235	$460	$11	$744	$323	
Special Interests	$700	$670	$353	$289	$179	$695		$816	$288	
Alternative	$1,077	$236	$114	$484	$234	$139		$365	$173	$
Country	$1,169	$336	$310	$576	$206	$123	$43	$283	$288	
Music - Miscellaneous	$1,193	$364	$167	$494	$254	$281	$18	$410	$132	$
Pop	$541	$286	$231	$392	$139	$178	$26	$350	$173	
Rock	$1,184	$324	$202	$490	$161	$341	$14	$285	$127	
Soul / R&B	$760	$225	$182	$1,496	$223	$293	$23	$463	$159	$

Report Filter (Local Filter):
(Year = 2006) And (Category = Electronics) And (Revenue > 80) And ({Customer Region} = Northwest)

Subcategory	Metrics Revenue					
Customer City	Bellevue	Bothell	Caldwell	Cheyenne	Coulee City	E
Audio Equipment	$9,945	$23,211	$2,531	$2,347	$30,857	$
Cameras	$31,245	$5,613	$5,592	$1,240	$11,250	$
Computers	$12,751	$4,771	$1,443	$713	$8,181	
Electronics - Miscellaneous	$13,940	$29,072	$3,722	$2,444	$16,254	$
TV's	$40,652	$9,788	$3,990	$1,871	$10,846	$
Video Equipment	$36,423	$26,363	$3,543	$3,947	$5,480	$

Figure 1-25   Selection based on a complex predicate

basis of a new perspective. In practice, you can highlight a different combination of dimensions (Figure 1-26). Figures 1-27 and 1-28 show a few examples of pivoted two-dimensional and three-dimensional tables.

The term *drill-across* stands for the opportunity to create a link between two or more interrelated cubes in order to compare their data. For example, this applies if you calculate

Figure 1-26
Pivoting a cube

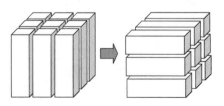

Category	Year	Metrics	Revenue
Books	2005		$1,320,585
	2006		$1,563,287
Electronics	2005		$19,299,870
	2006		$23,654,030
Movies	2005		$1,032,391
	2006		$1,333,126
Music	2005		$748,966
	2006		$940,136

	Metrics	Revenue	
	Year	2005	2006
Category			
Books		$1,320,585	$1,563,287
Electronics		$19,299,870	$23,654,030
Movies		$1,032,391	$1,333,126
Music		$748,966	$940,136

FIGURE 1-27   Pivoting a two-dimensional table

an expression involving measures from two cubes (Figure 1-29). Figure 1-30 shows an example in which a sales cube is drilled-across a promotions cube in order to compare revenues and discounts per quarter and product category.

Most OLAP tools can perform *drill-through* operations, though with varying effectiveness. This operation switches from multidimensional aggregate data in data marts to operational data in sources or in the reconciled layer.

In many applications, an intermediate approach between static reporting and OLAP is broadly used. This intermediate approach is called *semi-static reporting*. Even if a semi-static report focuses on a group of information previously set, it gives users some margin of freedom. Thanks to this margin, users can follow a limited set of navigation paths. For example, this applies when you can roll up just to a few hierarchy attributes. This solution is common, because it provides some unquestionable advantages. First, users need less skill to use data models and analysis tools than they need for OLAP. Second, this avoids the risk that occurs in OLAP of achieving inconsistent analysis results or incorrect ones because of any misuse of aggregation operators. Third, if you pose constraints on the analyses allowed, you will prevent users from unwillingly slowing down your system whenever they formulate demanding queries.

		Metrics Customer Region	Revenue						
Category	Year		Northeast	Mid-Atlantic	Southeast	Central	South	Northwest	Southwest
Books	2005		$416,183	$316,104	$36,517	$207,850	$137,502	$19,062	$187,368
	2006		$534,932	$401,908	$42,027	$239,806	$138,683	$22,655	$183,275
Electronics	2005		$1,860,172	$6,517,723	$1,226,825	$3,719,752	$915,633	$1,434,575	$3,625,191
	2006		$2,403,311	$8,253,620	$1,451,397	$4,631,259	$999,611	$1,615,848	$4,298,985
Movies	2005		$112,560	$138,611	$118,179	$153,556	$119,566	$27,060	$362,858
	2006		$148,785	$188,567	$147,445	$203,547	$145,434	$35,878	$463,470
Music	2005		$78,507	$99,631	$25,528	$383,911	$38,373	$27,933	$95,083
	2006		$104,925	$126,851	$35,215	$485,174	$43,424	$33,860	$110,689

	Metrics Customer Region Year	Revenue Northeast 2005	2006	Mid-Atlantic 2005	2006	Southeast 2005	2006	Central 2005	2006	South 2005	2006	Nort 2
Category												
Books		$416,183	$534,932	$316,104	$401,908	$36,517	$42,027	$207,850	$239,806	$137,502	$138,683	$
Electronics		$1,860,172	$2,403,311	$6,517,723	$8,253,620	$1,226,825	$1,451,397	$3,719,752	$4,631,259	$915,633	$999,611	$1,4
Movies		$112,560	$148,785	$138,611	$188,567	$118,179	$147,445	$153,556	$203,547	$119,566	$145,434	$
Music		$78,507	$104,925	$99,631	$126,851	$25,528	$35,215	$383,911	$485,174	$38,373	$43,424	$

FIGURE 1-28   Pivoting a three-dimensional table

FIGURE 1-29
Drilling across
two cubes

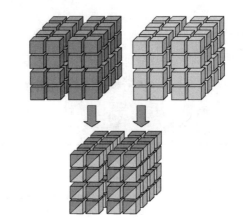

1.7.3 Dashboards

Dashboards are another method used for displaying information stored to a data warehouse. The term *dashboard* refers to a GUI that displays a limited amount of relevant data in a brief and easy-to-read format. Dashboards can provide a real-time overview of the trends for a specific phenomenon or for many phenomena that are strictly connected with each other. The term is a visual metaphor: the group of indicators in the GUI are displayed like a car dashboard. Dashboards are often used by senior managers who need a quick way to view information. However, to conduct and display very complex analyses of phenomena, dashboards must be matched with analysis tools.

Today, most software vendors offer dashboards for report creation and display. Figure 1-31 shows a dashboard created with MicroStrategy Dynamic Enterprise. The literature related to dashboard graphic design has also proven to be very rich, in particular in the scope of enterprises (Few, 2006).

Category / Quarter	Metrics Revenue 2005 Q1	2005 Q2	2005 Q3	2005 Q4	2006 Q1	2006 Q2	2006 Q3	2006 Q4
Books	$319,767	$313,339	$336,862	$350,617	$348,483	$387,849	$407,392	$419,563
Electronics	$4,448,112	$4,299,411	$4,918,673	$5,633,676	$5,411,499	$5,714,783	$5,999,174	$6,528,576
Movies	$228,108	$232,201	$264,471	$307,611	$299,531	$326,270	$334,143	$373,182
Music	$168,843	$169,462	$193,234	$217,427	$212,438	$228,289	$239,112	$260,298

Category	Quarter 2005 Q1 Metrics Discount	Revenue	2005 Q2 Discount	Revenue	2005 Q3 Discount	Revenue	2005 Q4 Discount	Revenue	2006 Q1 Discount	Re
Books	$ 0	$319,767	$ 10,845	$313,339	$ 9,497	$336,862	$ 18,279	$350,617	$ 0	
Electronics	$ 0	$4,448,112	$ 150,366	$4,299,410	$ 143,395	$4,918,673	$ 302,884	$5,633,675	$ 0	$5
Movies	$ 0	$228,108	$ 8,025	$232,201	$ 7,948	$264,471	$ 16,649	$307,611	$ 0	
Music	$ 0	$168,843	$ 6,143	$169,462	$ 5,563	$193,234	$ 11,047	$217,427	$ 0	

FIGURE 1-30 Drilling across the sales cube (`Revenue` measure) and the promotions cube (`Discount` measure)

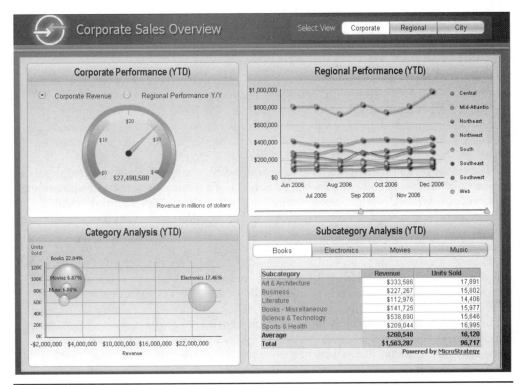

FIGURE 1-31   An example of dashboards

Keep in mind, however, that dashboards are nothing but performance indicators behind GUIs. Their effectiveness is due to a careful selection of the relevant measures, while using data warehouse information quality standards. For this reason, dashboards should be viewed as a sophisticated effective add-on to data warehouse systems, but not as the primary goal of data warehouse systems. In fact, the primary goal of data warehouse systems should always be to properly define a process to transform data into information.

1.8 ROLAP, MOLAP, and HOLAP

These three acronyms conceal three major approaches to implementing data warehouses, and they are related to the logical model used to represent data:

- *ROLAP* stands for *Relational OLAP*, an implementation based on relational DBMSs.
- *MOLAP* stands for *Multidimensional OLAP*, an implementation based on multidimensional DBMSs.
- *HOLAP* stands for *Hybrid OLAP*, an implementation using both relational and multidimensional techniques.

The idea of adopting the relational technology to store data to a data warehouse has a solid foundation if you consider the huge amount of literature written about the relational model, the broadly available corporate experience with relational database usage and management, and the top performance and flexibility standards of relational DBMSs (RDBMSs). The expressive power of the relational model, however, does not include the concepts of dimension, measure, and hierarchy, so you must create specific types of schemata so that you can represent the multidimensional model in terms of basic relational elements such as attributes, relations, and integrity constraints. This task is mainly performed by the well-known *star schema*. See Chapter 8 for more details on star schemata and star schema variants.

The main problem with ROLAP implementations results from the performance hit caused by costly join operations between large tables. To reduce the number of joins, one of the key concepts of ROLAP is *denormalization*—a conscious breach in the third normal form oriented to performance maximization. To minimize execution costs, the other key word is *redundancy,* which is the result of the materialization of some derived tables (*views*) that store aggregate data used for typical OLAP queries.

From an architectural viewpoint, adopting ROLAP requires specialized *middleware,* also called a *multidimensional engine,* between relational back-end servers and front-end components, as shown in Figure 1-32. The middleware receives OLAP queries formulated by users in a front-end tool and turns them into SQL instructions for a relational back-end application with the support of meta-data. The so-called *aggregate navigator* is a particularly important component in this phase. In case of aggregate views, this component selects a view from among all the alternatives to solve a specific query at the minimum access cost.

In commercial products, different front-end modules, such as OLAP, reports, and dashboards, are generally strictly connected to a multidimensional engine. Multidimensional engines are the main components and can be connected to any relational server. Open source solutions have been recently released. Their multidimensional engines (Mondrian, 2009) are disconnected from front-end modules (JPivot, 2009). For this reason, they can be more flexible

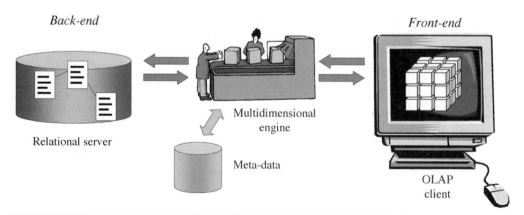

Figure 1-32   ROLAP architecture

than commercial solutions when you have to create the architecture (Thomsen and Pedersen, 2005). A few commercial RDBMSs natively support features typical for multidimensional engines to maximize query optimization and increase meta-data reusability. For example, since its 8*i* version was made available, Oracle's RDBMS gives users the opportunity to define hierarchies and materialized views. Moreover, it offers a navigator that can use meta-data and rewrite queries without any need for a multidimensional engine to be involved.

Different from a ROLAP system, a MOLAP system is based on an ad hoc logical model that can be used to represent multidimensional data and operations directly. The underlying multidimensional database physically stores data as arrays and the access to it is positional (Gaede and Günther, 1998). *Grid-files* (Nievergelt et al., 1984; Whang and Krishnamurthy, 1991), *R*-trees* (Beckmann et al., 1990) and *UB-trees* (Markl et al., 2001) are among the techniques used for this purpose.

The greatest advantage of MOLAP systems in comparison with ROLAP is that multidimensional operations can be performed in an easy, natural way with MOLAP without any need for complex join operations. For this reason, MOLAP system performance is excellent. However, MOLAP system implementations have very little in common, because no multidimensional logical model standard has yet been set. Generally, they simply share the usage of optimization techniques specifically designed for sparsity management. The lack of a common standard is a problem being progressively solved. This means that MOLAP tools are becoming more and more successful after their limited implementation for many years. This success is also proven by the investments in this technology by major vendors, such as Microsoft (Analysis Services) and Oracle (Hyperion).

The intermediate architecture type, *HOLAP*, aims at mixing the advantages of both basic solutions. It takes advantage of the standardization level and the ability to manage large amounts of data from ROLAP implementations, and the query speed typical of MOLAP systems. HOLAP implies that the largest amount of data should be stored in an RDBMS to avoid the problems caused by sparsity, and that a multidimensional system stores only the information users most frequently need to access. If that information is not enough to solve queries, the system will transparently access the part of the data managed by the relational system. Over the last few years, important market actors such as MicroStrategy have adopted HOLAP solutions to improve their platform performance, joining other vendors already using this solution, such as Business Objects.

1.9 Additional Issues

The issues that follow can play a fundamental role in tuning up a data warehouse system. These points involve very wide-ranging problems and are mentioned here to give you the most comprehensive picture possible.

1.9.1   Quality

In general, we can say that the *quality* of a process stands for the way a process meets users' goals. In data warehouse systems, quality is not only useful for the level of data, but above all for the whole integrated system, because of the goals and usage of data warehouses. A strict quality standard must be ensured from the first phases of the data warehouse project.

Defining, measuring, and maximizing the quality of a data warehouse system can be very complex problems. For this reason, we mention only a few properties characterizing *data quality* here:

- **Accuracy**   Stored values should be compliant with real-world ones.
- **Freshness**   Data should not be old.
- **Completeness**   There should be no lack of information.
- **Consistency**   Data representation should be uniform.
- **Availability**   Users should have easy access to data.
- **Traceability**   Data can easily be traced data back to its sources.
- **Clearness**   Data can be easily understood.

Technically, checking for data quality requires appropriate sets of metrics (Abelló et al., 2006). In the following sections, we provide an example of the metrics for a few of the quality properties mentioned:

- **Accuracy and completeness**   Refers to the percentage of tuples not loaded by an ETL process and categorized on the basis of the types of problem arising. This property shows the percentage of missing, invalid, and nonstandard values of every attribute.
- **Freshness**   Defines the time elapsed between the date when an event takes place and the date when users can access it.
- **Consistency**   Defines the percentage of tuples that meet business rules that can be set for measures of an individual cube or many cubes and the percentage of tuples meeting structural constraints imposed by the data model (for example, uniqueness of primary keys, referential integrity, and cardinality constraint compliance).

Note that corporate organization plays a fundamental role in reaching data quality goals. This role can be effectively played only by creating an appropriate and accurate *certification* system that defines a limited group of users in charge of data. For this reason, designers must raise senior managers' awareness of this topic. Designers must also motivate management to create an accurate certification procedure specifically differentiated for every enterprise area. A board of corporate managers promoting data quality may trigger a virtuous cycle that is more powerful and less costly than any data cleansing solution. For example, you can achieve awesome results if you connect a corporate department budget to a specific data quality threshold to be reached.

An additional topic connected to the quality of a data warehouse project is related to documentation. Today most documentation is still nonstandardized. It is often issued at the end of the entire data warehouse project. Designers and implementers consider documentation a waste of time, and data warehouse project customers consider it an extra cost item. Software engineering teaches that a standard system for documents should be issued, managed, and validated in compliance with project deadlines. This system can ensure that different data warehouse project phases are correctly carried out and that all analysis and implementation points are properly examined and understood. In the medium and long term, correct documents increase the chances of reusing data warehouse projects and ensure project know-how maintenance.

NOTE *Jarke et al., 2000 have closely studied data quality. Their studies provide useful discussions on the impact of data quality problems from the methodological point of view. Kelly, 1997 describes quality goals strictly connected to the viewpoint of business organizations. Serrano et al., 2004, 2007; Lechtenbörger, 2001; and Bouzeghoub and Kedad, 2000 focus on quality standards respectively for conceptual, logical, and physical data warehouse schemata.*

1.9.2   Security

Information security is generally a fundamental requirement for a system, and it should be carefully considered in software engineering at every project development stage from requirement analysis through implementation to maintenance. Security is particularly relevant to data warehouse projects, because data warehouses are used to manage information crucial for strategic decision-making processes. Furthermore, multidimensional properties and aggregation cause additional security problems similar to those that generally arise in statistic databases, because they implicitly offer the opportunity to infer information from data. Finally, the huge amount of information exchange that takes place in data warehouses in the data-staging phase causes specific problems related to network security.

Appropriate management and auditing control systems are important for data warehouses. Management control systems can be implemented in front-end tools or can exploit operating system services. As far as auditing is concerned, the techniques provided by DBMS servers are not generally appropriate for this scope. For this reason, you must take advantage of the systems implemented by OLAP engines. From the viewpoint of users profile–based data access, basic requirements are related to hiding whole cubes, specific cube slices, and specific cube measures. Sometimes you also have to hide cube data beyond a given detail level.

NOTE *In the scientific literature there are a few works specifically dealing with security in data warehouse systems (Kirkgöze et al., 1997; Priebe and Pernul, 2000; Rosenthal and Sciore, 2000; Katic et al., 1998). In particular, Priebe and Pernul propose a comparative study on security properties of a few commercial platforms. Ferrandez-Medina et al., 2004 and Soler et al., 2008 discuss an approach that could be more interesting for designers. They use a UML extension to model specific security requirements for data warehouses in the conceptual design and requirement analysis phases, respectively.*

1.9.3   Evolution

Many mature data warehouse implementations are currently running in midsize and large companies. The unstoppable evolution of application domains highlights dynamic features of data warehouses connected to the way information changes at two different levels as time goes by:

- **Data level**   Even if measured data is naturally logged in data warehouses thanks to temporal dimensions marking events, the multidimensional model implicitly assumes that hierarchies are completely static. It is clear that this assumption is not very realistic. For example, a company can add new product categories to its catalog and remove others, or it can change the category to which an existing product belongs in order to meet new marketing strategies.

- **Schema level**   A data warehouse schema can vary to meet new business domain standards, new users' requirements, or changes in data sources. New attributes and measures can become necessary. For example, you can add a subcategory to a product hierarchy to make analyses richer in detail. You should also consider that the set of fact dimensions can vary as time goes by.

Temporal problems are even more challenging in data warehouses than in operational databases, because queries often cover longer periods of time. For this reason, data warehouse queries frequently deal with different data and/or schema versions. Moreover, this point is particularly critical for data warehouses that run for a long time, because every evolution not completely controlled causes a growing gap between the real world and its database representation, eventually making the data warehouses obsolete and useless.

As far as changes in data values are concerned, different approaches have been documented in scientific literature. Some commercial systems also make it possible to track changes and query cubes on the basis of different temporal scenarios. See section 8.4 for more details on dynamic hierarchies. On the other hand, managing changes in data schemata has been explored only partially to date. No commercial tool is currently available on the market to support approaches to data schema change management.

The approaches to data warehouse schema change management can be classified in two categories: *evolution* (Quix, 1999; Vaisman et al., 2002; Blaschka, 2000) and *versioning* (Eder et al., 2002; Golfarelli et al., 2006a). Both categories make it possible to alter data schemata, but only versioning can track previous schema releases. A few approaches to versioning can create not only "true" versions generated by changes in application domains, but also alternative versions to use for what-if analyses (Bebel et al., 2004).

The main problem that has not been solved in this field is the creation of techniques for versioning and data migration between versions that can flexibly support queries related to more schema versions. Furthermore, we need systems that can semiautomatically adjust ETL procedures to changes in source schemata. In this direction, some OLAP tools already use their meta-data to support an impact analysis aimed at identifying the full consequences of any changes in source schemata.

CHAPTER

Data Warehouse System Lifecycle

Data warehouse systems have gained popularity as companies from the most varied industries realize how useful these systems can be. A large number of these organizations, however, lack the experience and skills required to meet the challenges involved in data warehousing projects. In particular, a lack of a methodological approach prevents data warehousing projects from being carried out successfully. Generally, methodological approaches are created by closely studying similar experiences and minimizing the risks for failure by basing new approaches on a constructive analysis of the mistakes made previously.

This chapter considers a few methodological approaches mentioned in the literature that describe how best to manage data warehouse lifecycles. This chapter also defines our methodological approach to a data mart project. We will use this approach as a reference point in following chapters.

2.1 Risk Factors

2600 years ago, a Chinese strategist used to say "Know your enemy!" The same advice is valuable here. Before you study methodological approaches, you need to be familiar with the major risk factors and frequent causes for failure of data warehousing projects. Risks can be divided into four groups:

- *Risks related to project management.* A data warehousing project involves all company levels and implies enterprise-specific policies and organizational phases. A factor that frequently interferes with data warehousing projects is the need for information exchange to be shared between a company's departments. Managers often reluctantly meet this need because they "might lose their power" and the flaws in their conduct might be revealed (Vassiliadis, 2000). Other frequent causes for failure are related to scopes, sponsoring, and goals of data warehouse systems. In particular, many data warehousing projects in small and midsize enterprises are nipped in the bud because project managers cannot convincingly report estimates of costs and benefits.

- *Risks related to technology*. The technological solutions used for designing, implementing, accessing, and maintaining data warehouse systems are rapidly evolving. The architecture suggested should be able to keep up with new standards. The problems that frequently occur are poor scalability of architectures in terms of data volumes and number of users; lack of expandability to implement new technological solutions, components, or applications; insufficient technical skills of implementers about data warehouse-specific software tools; and inefficient management of meta-data exchange between every component.

- *Risks related to data and design*. These risk factors depend on the quality of the data supplied and the project carried out. In particular, consider the risk of achieving low quality results because of source instability and unreliability or because users did not properly specify their requirements. Another frequent cause for failure results from the inability to provide users with high added value when delivering initial prototypes. This undermines the reputation of the whole project.

- *Risks related to organization*. Last, but not least, this kind of failure is due to (a) the inability to involve end users, to interest them in the current project, and to make them support it; (b) difficulties found in radically changing business culture to make it aware of the role played by information; and (c) users' inability to take advantage of the results achieved because of their consolidated organization's practices.

CAUTION *On the whole, a high risk for data warehousing projects to be unsuccessful exists because of users' great expectations. In today's business culture, many believe that data warehousing should be some kind of panacea that is able to rectify all organizational mistakes and fill the gaps of business information systems. On the contrary, in reality, a successful project largely depends on its source data quality and on far-sighted, helpful, dynamic company personnel.*

2.2 Top-Down vs. Bottom-Up

When you consider methodological approaches, their top-down structures or bottom-up structures play a basic role in creating a data warehouse. Both structures deeply affect the data warehouse lifecycle.

If you use a top-down approach, you will have to analyze global business needs, plan how to develop a data warehouse, design it, and implement it *as a whole*. This procedure is promising: it will achieve excellent results because it is based on a global picture of the goal to achieve, and in principle it ensures consistent, well integrated data warehouses. However, a long story of failure with top-down approaches teaches that:

- high-cost estimates with long-term implementations discourage company managers from embarking on these kind of projects;

- analyzing and bringing together *all* relevant sources is a very difficult task, also because it is not very likely that they are all available and stable at the same time;

- it is extremely difficult to forecast the specific needs of every department involved in a project, which can result in the analysis process coming to a standstill;

- since no prototype is going to be delivered in the short term, users cannot check for this project to be useful, so they lose trust and interest in it.

In a bottom-up approach, data warehouses are incrementally built and several data marts are iteratively created. Each data mart is based on a set of facts that are linked to a specific company department and that can be interesting for a user subgroup (for example, data marts for inventories, marketing, and so on). If this approach is coupled with quick prototyping, the time and cost needed for implementation can be reduced so remarkably that company managers will notice how useful the project being carried out is. In this way, that project will still be of great interest.

The bottom-up approach turns out to be more cautious than the top-down one and it is almost universally accepted. Naturally the bottom-up approach is not risk-free, because it gets a partial picture of the whole field of application. We need to pay attention to the first data mart to be used as prototype to get the best results: this should play a very strategic role in a company. In fact, its role is so crucial that this data mart should be a reference point for the whole data warehouse. In this way, the following data marts can be easily added to the original one. Moreover, it is highly advisable that the selected data mart exploit consistent data already made available.

Figure 2-1 shows an example in a hospital. DM1 stands for the first data mart implemented; it is designed for hospital tasks to be collected and monitored. Then other data marts are added: DM2 is a data mart for the accounting department; DM3 is a data mart for the department of epidemiology; DM4 is a data mart for hospital personnel; and DM5 is a data mart for the purchasing department.

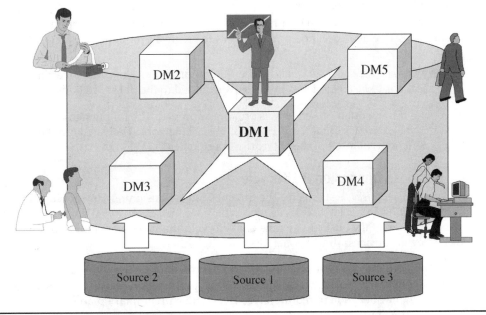

FIGURE 2-1   Bottom-up design of a data warehouse for a hospital

Figure 2-2
Data warehouse
system lifecycle

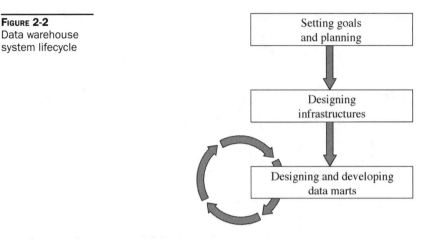

Figure 2-2 shows the basic phases of the lifecycle for a data warehouse system to be developed on the basis of a bottom-up approach (Mattison, 2006). The following section examines those basic phases.

1. *Setting goals and planning*. This preliminary phase involves preparatory work. It is based on a feasibility study aimed at setting system goals, properties, and size estimates; at selecting an approach to build the data warehouse; and at estimating costs and added value. Additionally, a risk and expectation analysis and a team competence examination should be done to deal with organizational issues. In this way, you can define an implementation plan for this data warehousing project and submit it to top management.

2. *Designing infrastructures*. This phase analyzes and compares architecture solutions and assesses existing technology and tools to create a preliminary plan of the whole system.

3. *Designing and developing data marts*. Every iteration causes a new data mart and new applications to be created and progressively added to the data warehouse system.

The general framework outlined here is broadly approved. The following paragraphs cover two specific examples of methods based on this framework. They are both the result of design experiences collected in the enterprise-specific field.

2.2.1   Business Dimensional Lifecycle

Business Dimensional Lifecycle stands for the time needed for designing, developing, and implementing data warehouse systems as reported by Kimball et al., (1998). Figure 2-3 shows the current structure of the business dimensional lifecycle after a 20-years long evolution. We will quickly review business dimensional lifecycle phases here.

1. The phase for *project planning* includes the definition of system goals and properties, an assessment of the impact on organizational practices, an estimate of costs and benefits, the allocation of required resources, and a preliminary plan for the project to be carried out.

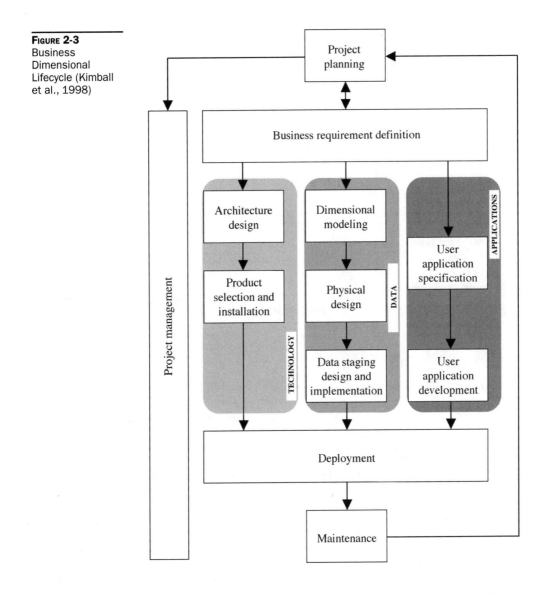

Figure 2-3
Business
Dimensional
Lifecycle (Kimball
et al., 1998)

2. The phase for *business requirement definition* plays a vital role in making sure that designers properly and fully understand users' needs, to maximize the benefits and the profitability of the system under construction. At this stage, designers should detect key factors of decision-making processes and turn them into design specifications. The definition of requirements creates three parallel tracks, each consisting of different phases: *data*, *technology*, and *application*.

3. The first phase of the data track is *dimensional modeling*. At this stage, user requirements and an analysis of operational sources should lead to the definition of data structures in a data warehouse. The final result is a set of logical schemata and a set of relationships with source schemata. The subsequent phase of the data

track is *physical design*. It mainly deals with the issues of logical schemata to be optimized and implemented into the selected DBMS, such as indexing and partitioning. Eventually, the phase for *designing and developing data staging* includes all the issues linked with data extraction, transformation, loading, and, last but not least, quality.

4. The technology track includes an *architecture design* that is based on the current technical specifications for business information systems and performance requirements set forth by users. This track also shows a phase for *product selection and installation* to study and assess usable hardware platforms; DBMSs; Extraction, Transformation, and Loading tools (ETL); and additional data analysis tools available on the market.

5. If you follow the application track, you can collect the specifications for the applications that will provide end users with data access. You can also assess the need for reports to be created, interactive navigation of data, and automatic knowledge extraction (*user application specification* phase). The analysis tools selected in the product selection phase should be set up and configured accordingly (*user application development* phase).

6. The *deployment* phase involves all the tracks previously mentioned and leads to the system startup.

7. The deployment phase does not mean that a system lifecycle comes to its end. A system needs continuous *maintenance* to provide users with support and training.

8. *Project management* should be accurate in every data warehouse lifecycle phase. This allows you to keep tasks in sync, to monitor current project conditions, and to check that the design team is closely collaborating with users.

2.2.2 Rapid Warehousing Methodology

Rapid Warehousing Methodology is an iterative and evolutionary approach to managing data warehousing projects. This approach, created by SAS Institute, a leader in the statistical analysis industry, divides potentially large projects into smaller, much less risky subprojects, called *builds*. Each build takes advantage of the data warehouse environments developed during previous builds. It expands them to add new features and evolves them. In this way, each build can make previous data warehouse environments keep on meeting users' ever-changing needs. As time goes by, this approach ensures that users will still be interested and involved in projects, and it lays the foundation for successful long-term projects.

Figure 2-4 shows all the phases of this approach, which are briefly examined in the following section.

1. **Assessment** This phase mostly corresponds to Kimball's planning phase and it aims at ascertaining whether an enterprise is ready to undertake a data warehousing project and setting goals, risks, and benefits.

2. **Requirements** This phase corresponds to Kimball's business requirement definition and end user application specification, and it gathers analysis, project, and architecture specifications for the system.

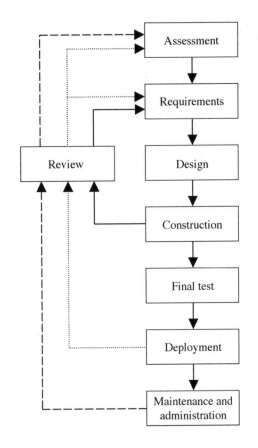

3. **Design**   The design phase focuses on one project build at a time. The analysis specifications are refined to generate logical and physical data designs and a data-staging design. Implementation tools are also selected at this stage.

4. **Construction and final test**   One data warehouse is implemented and populated with the data extracted from data sources. Front-end applications are developed and tested.

5. **Deployment**   The system is delivered and started up after properly training its end users.

6. **Maintenance and administration**   This phase is as long as the whole data warehouse system lifecycle. Maintenance and administration can implement additional features, upgrade the data warehouse architecture to meet new needs, and check data for quality.

7. **Review**   Each build includes three review processes: implementation check, post-deployment check (to make sure that an organization is properly prepared to take advantage of a data warehouse), and a final check for costs and benefits to be assessed.

2.3 Data Mart Design Phases

The preceding paragraphs highlighted that each single data mart design plays a crucial role when building data warehouses on the basis of a bottom-up approach. This process becomes more and more difficult because it requires design techniques that are completely different from those used for conventional operational databases.

To design a data mart, use the following methodological approach, which consists of seven phases, as shown in Table 2-1. The following sections offer a short description of each phase. See specific chapters for detailed information.

Figure 2-5 shows a functional overview of basic information flows of a standard case. This overview does not include the user application and ETL implementation phase, because these mainly depend on the tools and languages used. For this reason, this book does not deal with them. Section 2.4 shows that the order of the design phases depends on the design approach that specific needs and circumstances suggest adopting. Section 2.5 not only provides a brief description of data mart testing and major difficulties, but it also offers a few general hints on how to test a data mart.

Phase	Input	Output	People Involved
Analysis and reconciliation of data sources	Operational source schemata	Reconciled schema	Designer, data processing center staff
Requirement analysis	Strategic goals	Requirement specifications, preliminary workload	Designer, end users
Conceptual design	Reconciled schema, requirement specification	Fact schemata	Designer, end users
Workload refinement, validation of conceptual schemata	Fact schemata, preliminary workload	Workload, data volume, validated fact schemata	Designer, end users
Logical design	Fact schemata, target logical model, workload	Logical data mart schema	Designer
Data-staging design	Source schemata, reconciled schema, logical data mart schema	ETL procedures	Designer, database administrators
Physical design	Logical data mart schema, target DBMS, workload	Physical data mart schema	Designer

TABLE 2-1   Seven Phases of the Design of a Data Mart

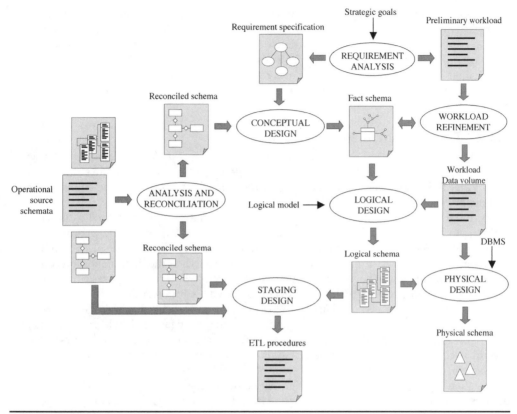

FIGURE 2-5   Seven-phase design: A functional view

2.3.1   Analysis and Reconciliation of Data Sources

This design phase requires that you define and document the *reconciled schema*, that is, the schema of the reconciled data layer used to feed your data mart. You should

- analyze and understand available source schemata (*inspection*);
- transform them to discover useful relationships previously unexpressed (*normalization*), if necessary;
- select which groups of data can be useful for the purposes of decision-making processes in the specific business area to which your data mart is devoted;
- assess data quality;
- if multiple data sources are to be used, you should homogenize and integrate their schemata to determine common features and remove every inconsistency (*integration*).

This phase involves a data warehouse designer and data processing center staff. Generally, data processing center staff members are the only ones who can assign a meaning to schemata and records that are often hardly understandable. In addition, their familiarity with the fields of application is essential for schema normalization. Operational database documentation is often very poor or completely lacking. Because of this, this phase often results in the longest and most difficult one: it can take even 50 percent of the total time devoted to a whole project.

Chapter 3 is devoted to the analysis and reconciliation phase of data sources. After dealing with the topics of data source inspection and normalization, we will focus on a more complex topic: integration.

2.3.2 Requirement Analysis

Designers collect, filter, and document end user requirements in the requirement analysis phase to select relevant information to be represented in compliance with the strategic goals. After this phase, you can obtain specifications for the facts to be modeled, as well as preliminary guidelines for the workload.

As mentioned in section 1.5, facts are concepts of primary importance in the decision-making process. A fact is a phenomenon that dynamically occurs in an enterprise; each fact occurrence is called an event. End users are essentially responsible for the selection of facts. Designers help end users to carry out this critical task based on the documentation collected in the previous phase of analysis and source reconciliation. Each fact requires a historical interval—that is, the time frame that the events stored are supposed to cover.

You should express a preliminary workload in a "pseudo-natural" language. Workloads should specify the major measures and aggregations for every fact. This will give designers the opportunity to define dimensions and measures for conceptual design. Of course, you should select the minimum information synthesis level matched to the workload assessment. The minimum information synthesis level stands for the *granularity* in fact representation. Granularity plays a crucial role in the success of an entire project because it defines how flexible data mart queries are. Granularity is the result of a compromise between the system feedback speed and the maximum level of query detail. If this does not slow system response time, you should use a higher granularity value than the one required by end users, because this results in more flexible and easy-to-use data marts.

Chapter 4 deals with the most frequent problems experienced in requirement analysis and also suggests a specific approach based on a graphical *goal-oriented* formalism.

2.3.3 Conceptual Design

Even if the sequence of the conceptual, logical, and physical design phases is apparently similar to that used for creating operational databases, we should point out that the design process of data marts is different, because data mart workloads are different.

According to our approach, a conceptual design implies that the user requirements of the previous phase are exploited to create a conceptual schema for a data mart on the basis of a reconciled schema. Chapter 5 broadly describes the conceptual model adopted, the so-called *Dimensional Fact Model*. This model includes a *fact schema* to be created for every fact of primary importance for users. A fact schema can graphically represent all multidimensional model concepts, such as facts, measures, dimensions, and hierarchies. It can also include a set of advanced constructs that can accurately represent different conceptual shades distinguishing the most complex real-world scenarios.

Chapter 6 provides more details on the problems with creating a fact schema based on the reconciled layer and on user requirements. In particular, this chapter shows how to extract a preliminary conceptual schema automatically from the functional dependencies of the reconciled schema. The structure of the preliminary conceptual schema is then modified and adjusted to user requirements.

The resulting group of fact schemata is the conceptual schema for your data mart. Chapter 13 describes how effectively useful the association of fact schemata to a set of glossaries integrating fact schema definitions can be for managing and documenting projects. This chapter also introduces a bus matrix and an overlap matrix that can successfully sum up the existing relationships between different fact schemata.

2.3.4 Workload Refinement and Validation of Conceptual Schemata

After the conceptual design phase, you should refine the workload that was expressed in a preliminary phase. To do this, you should represent your queries directly in the conceptual schema. This allows you to check for all the expected queries to be actually feasible and leads to the validation of the conceptual schema obtained from the previous phase.

Chapter 7 introduces an easy-to-use language to denote multidimensional queries in fact schemata. It also deals with the problem of setting data volumes. Data volumes are fundamental for the following logical and physical design phases.

2.3.5 Logical Design

The essential requirement for logical design is naturally the selection of a logical model to act as a reference framework: this means that you should opt for Relational OLAP (ROLAP) or Multidimensional OLAP (MOLAP) implementations. We will mainly focus on ROLAP implementations in the following chapters because a wide range of standard project solutions are available for the relational model.

After you set a basic logical schema on the basis of the so-called *star schema*, the technique that mostly affects performance is the so-called *view materialization*. *Vertical and horizontal fragmentation* of views can be helpful, too. Both techniques are driven by the workload expected for a data mart and by the data volume estimate. Chapter 8 describes the logical models used in data warehouse systems. Chapter 9 deals with the topics of logical design based on fact schemata.

2.3.6 Physical Design

The most important problem of the physical design phase is the selection of the indexes to optimize performance. Having chosen to adopt the relational model is not sufficient in this phase, you must also choose the specific DBMS on which your data mart will be implemented. Workload and data volume also play an essential role for physical design. While Chapter 11 deals with the main types of indexes used for data warehouse applications, Chapter 12 describes some physical design techniques for relational DBMSs.

2.3.7 Data-Staging Design

This phase expects designers, end users, and database administrators to collaborate and make all the significant decisions on the population process of the reconciled layer, if it exists, and data marts. The time intervals for regularly updating data marts from data sources fall into this group of significant decisions. Chapter 10 deals with the major points of data-staging design.

2.4 Methodological Framework

The approaches to designing data marts, as described in the scientific literature, can be essentially divided into two categories (Winter and Strauch, 2003).

- *Data-driven* or *supply-driven* approaches design data marts on the basis of a close operational data source analysis. User requirements show designers which groups of data, relevant for decision-making processes, should be selected and how to define data structures on the basis of the multidimensional model.

- *Requirement-driven* or *demand-driven* approaches begin with the definition of information requirements of data mart users. The problem of how to map those requirements into existing data sources is addressed at a later stage when appropriate ETL procedures are implemented.

A prototype of the first approach category dates back to 1992, when Inmon first announced that a data warehouse development should be driven by data as opposed to the requirement-driven development used for operational systems (Inmon, 2005). Further data-driven approaches were suggested by Hüsemann et al., 2000; Golfarelli et al., 1998; and Moody and Kortink, 2000. These articles show that conceptual design takes root in operational source schemata as a result of the specification of measures, the selection of facts, and the classification of operational entities, respectively.

Data-driven approaches have one major advantage: the ETL design is extremely streamlined because every single information piece stored in a data mart is directly associated with one or more source attributes. In particular, an initial conceptual schema for data marts can be algorithmically derived from the reconciled layer—that is, it strictly depends on data source structures. This causes the time required for data-driven conceptual design to be roughly proportional to the complexity of data sources. An additional advantage of data-driven approaches is that the resulting data marts are quite stable in time, because they are rooted in source schemata that change less frequently than requirements expressed by end users. However, those approaches make user requirements play a minor role when it comes to specifying information contents to carry out an analysis; this problem is particularly serious when users ask for complex performance indicators to be computed. Furthermore, data-driven approaches provide designers with limited support when facts, dimensions, and measures need to be determined. Finally, they are poorly enforceable if you cannot rely on an in-depth knowledge of operational sources in the conceptual design phase.

As far as requirement-driven approaches are concerned, consider the one suggested by Prakash and Gosain (2003) as an example. It is a *goal-oriented* approach based on the goal–decision–information model. On the contrary, Bruckner et al., (2001) suggested a *process-oriented* approach, with three different perspectives with increasing levels of detail. Each perspective is linked to a specific requirement *template*. It is recommended that requirements be iteratively and incrementally collected on the basis of use cases. An additional approach is based on a technique consisting of many steps for the requirement analysis phase (Winter and Strauch, 2003). Two different phases are included in this approach: an "as-is" analysis aimed at describing data existing in data sources, and a "to-be" analysis that examines information needs of decision-makers and intersects them with operational data.

Requirement-driven approaches make users' wishes play a leading role. They are usually much appreciated by users, who feel actively involved in the design process. Unfortunately, requirement-driven approaches are typically more time-expensive than data-driven approaches, because users often do not have a clear and shared understanding of business goals and processes. Designers are then required to have strong leadership and meeting facilitation qualities to properly grab and integrate the different points of view. In addition, requirement-driven approaches require that designers make great efforts in the data-staging design phase.

An additional problem with these approaches is that facts, measures, and hierarchies are drawn directly from the specifications provided by users, and only at a later stage can designers check for the information required to be actually available in operational databases. This solution runs the risk of undermining customers' confidence in designers and in the advantage gained by data marts on the whole. In particular, designers propose solutions to end users that perfectly meet their needs at the beginning of the design phase, but a few users' analyses cannot be offered due to the lack of specific operational data. As a matter of fact, this problem is not as serious as it seems. If a reporting system is already available, users should be accustomed to requesting only the analyses for which all the essential data are made available.

On the basis of a case study, List et al., (2002) make an interesting comparison between data-driven and requirement-driven approaches. They conclude that the techniques based on data and those based on requirements are actually complementary and can be implemented in parallel to achieve an optimal design. As a result, it is not surprising how widespread mixed approaches are in the scientific literature. Mixed approaches are driven by requirements and data. This means that they examine operational data sources to shape hierarchies, and, at the same time, requirements play a fundamental role in restricting the analysis-specific research field and in selecting facts, dimensions, and measures (Bonifati et al., 2001; Luján-Mora and Trujillo, 2003; Giorgini et al., 2008).

In the following chapters, we'll introduce our methodological framework for designing a data mart. This framework can be adjusted to circumstances and design needs to support data-driven, requirement-driven, or mixed approaches. In the following paragraphs, we propose three realistic scenarios for designing data marts. We also match each scenario with its methodological reference framework for arranging the design phases described in section 2.3.

2.4.1   Scenario 1: Data-Driven Approach

Within the data-driven approach, data sources are particularly significant for modeling data marts. For this reason, the data source analysis and reconciliation phase is the first phase, as shown in Figure 2-6. Under this condition, you can analyze requirements and create a conceptual schema of your data mart without losing sight of the features of actually available data. In this way, you can obtain a set of specifications that are consistent with your data.

The user requirement analysis phase is closely connected to the conceptual design phase within this approach. This means that the activities performed in the requirement analysis phase, such as specifying dimensions, are completed in the conceptual design phase when they trigger operations that specify structures of conceptual schemata. It is important to remember that this connection between phases shows that it is possible and suitable to

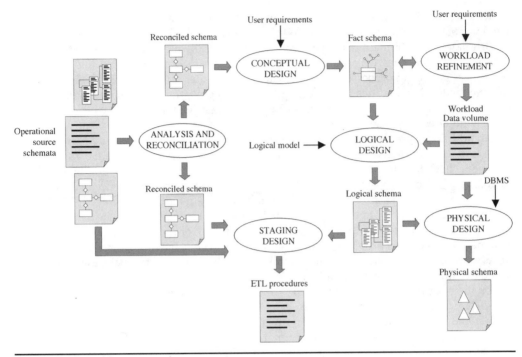

FIGURE 2-6   Data-driven approach

conduct a requirement analysis *at the same time as* a conceptual design after opting for a data-driven methodological approach. Chapter 6 shows how an initial conceptual schema for your data mart can be extracted from a reconciled schema if you apply a simple algorithm. Some project decisions, such as those dealing with hierarchy structures, must not only reflect users' expectations, but hinge on that initial schema as well. As a result, if you adopt a data-driven approach, our methodological framework allows the user requirement analysis phase to be informally completed by taking advantage of the specifications of requirement *glossaries* instead of formal schemata (see section 4.2 for more information).

At the end of the conceptual design phase is a workload refinement phase followed by a logical design phase. Data-staging design and physical design can occur at the same time.

The following are the prerequisites for the successful adoption of the data-driven approach:

- An *in-depth knowledge* of data sources to populate data marts should be available or it should be achieved at a reasonable price and in the short term.
- Data source schemata should show a good level of *normalization*.
- Data source schemata should not be too *complex*.

When your architecture includes a reconciled layer, you can amply meet these requirements: normalization and in-depth knowledge are obtained at the end of the reconciliation process. If your data sources are reduced to one single, small, well-designed database, you can achieve the same result after accurately completing the inspection phase.

Our experience in design shows that the data-driven approach, if applicable, is better than other approaches, because it gives you the opportunity to reach your project goals within a very short time. On the one hand, conceptual design can be automatically carried out to some extent, as previously mentioned; on the other hand, data-staging design is streamlined because data mapping between data sources and data marts is the "free-of-charge" result of conceptual design.

2.4.2   Scenario 2: Requirement-Driven Approach

The requirements expressed by end users are the driving force of the design phase in this approach. In this case, we suggest that you adopt formalisms that are suitable for requirement specifications, such as the expressive formalism proposed in section 4.3. Then the collected requirements should be turned into a conceptual schema, as described in section 6.5. In this case, the conceptual design phase is particularly critical, because you cannot take advantage of the detailed knowledge of operational data to extract structural relationships among the bits of information to be represented in your data mart.

After completing the conceptual design phase, the subsequent phases are the same as those in the preceding scenario, as shown in Figure 2-7. However, the data-staging design will have to carry a heavy burden because of a poor source analysis, and you will have to manually extract all the relationships among data mart data and operational data sources.

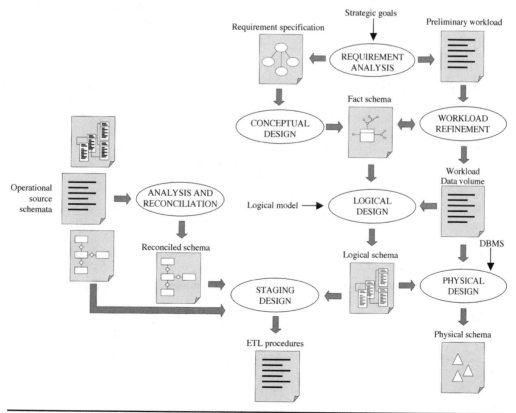

FIGURE 2-7   Requirement-driven approach

We think that this approach is the most difficult one to perform. It also produces results that become obsolete quickly, especially if requirements reflect the personal viewpoints of users and do not adequately express the corporate culture and working procedures. Still, this is your only alternative approach if you cannot conduct any preliminary, detailed source analysis (for example, when an ERP system is used to feed your data mart), or if sources are represented by legacy systems with such complexity that it is not recommended that you explore and normalize them, and as a result you do not think it appropriate to create the reconciled layer.

2.4.3   Scenario 3: Mixed Approach

In medio stat virtus: Virtue stands in the middle. It is almost too easy to state that a mixed approach to design is the most sensible compromise. The requirement and source analyses are conducted at the same time: the requirement analysis formally specifies project requirements and the source analysis results in a reconciled layer drawing (Figure 2-5). The conceptual design phase is semiautomatically carried out, as described in scenario 1, but requirements are used to reduce its complexity beforehand. Section 6.4 provides a detailed description of how to carry out this process.

The sequence of the subsequent phases remains unchanged in this case, too. There is a low level of complexity for data-staging design, as described in scenario 1.

The mixed approach teams the easy conditions of data-driven approaches with the guarantees of requirement-driven approaches. It is advisable that you use a mixed approach when the reconciled layer extension and complexity are remarkable. The costs for more accurate and formal requirement analyses are balanced by a quicker conceptual design process.

2.5 Testing Data Marts

The test phase aims at checking for data marts to be properly created and for user requirements to be fulfilled. This test checks functionality, performance, robustness, and usability—just to mention a few major factors. The techniques proposed by software engineering literature to test software systems can be successfully applied to the field of business intelligence, too. For this reason, you can consult typical reference books (such as Beizer, 1990; Mayers, 2004) for learning standard techniques and approaches. In the following paragraphs, we discuss specifically how to apply these techniques to data warehouse systems.

First of all, the chance to perform an effective test depends on the completion and accuracy of documentation in terms of collected requirements and project description. In other words, if you did not specify what you want from your system at the beginning, you cannot expect to get it right later. Testers should also be able to check for the behavior of the implemented system to be consistent with the expectations of the design phase. Currently no standardized documentation exists for data warehousing projects. See Chapter 13 for more details on this point.

The test phase is part of the data warehouse lifecycle for all practical purposes. It also acts in synergy with design. For this reason, you have to plan and arrange the test phase at the beginning of your project when you can specify which type of tests you want to perform, which data set needs to be tested, and which service level you expect.

The formal arrangement of the test phase is nearly taken for granted if your system implementation is outsourced. However, if your own company implements your system, it will tend to use an informal approach, which turns out to be less effective as a whole.

You should not mix testing and application debugging, a task generally performed by implementers who often tend to take some hypotheses for granted and do not eliminate them even when they should. For example, this is the case in system usage modes or results expected in specific reports. For this reason, tests should always be carried out by technicians who are different from system implementers. Furthermore, they should involve a very large number of end users who generally are so familiar with application domains that they can determine even the slightest abnormality in data.

It is naturally clear that incorrect results in online analytical processing (OLAP) analyses are the most difficult to detect in data warehouse systems. They can be caused by faulty ETL procedures as well as an incorrect data aggregation and selection method used in front-end tools or in meta-knowledge. Some faults are not due to your data warehouse system; instead, they result from the data quality of your operational system. This condition can be detected only if you directly query your operational sources.

Data warehouse systems are particularly suitable for tests to be carried out in a modular fashion. Specifically, a test process can be separately carried out for back-end components, mainly ETL processes, and front-end components, such as OLAP, reporting, or dashboard environments. Under these conditions, the test phase can take place before the project end to avoid the delays and deadlines that can force testers to perform their tasks in a hurry or announce successful test results for those components that do not even meet minimum requirements.

The group of testers can find it difficult to check thoroughly for a system to be correct, and a comprehensive test is very demanding in terms of time and costs. For these reasons, tests often result in sample tests, but this practice is very dangerous. Sample tests are not recommended for life-critical systems or for systems in which one fault can be very demanding in terms of costs and time for systems to be restored. On the contrary, sample tests are suitable for data warehouse systems. As a result, we can distinguish between *alpha test* and *beta test* phases. The alpha test is conducted on a sample basis as soon as the system (or part of it) is completed. This results in the system being deployed to every user or to a specific subgroup of users. The beta test is conducted by end users. While they regularly access the system, they also check for proper system operation in its application field.

The test phase should include multiple types of tests that differ in granularity as well as in features to be checked. We propose the following major test types:

- **Unit test**   Defines a set of test cases, each including its test data, of every single application component. In particular, analysis sessions for every single cube need to be planned. As far as ETL processes are concerned, the functional test mainly consists of defining a group of tests checking for correct ETL flows.

- **Integration test**   Checks the general and integrated operation of all the system components. This is an essential test because unit tests do not exclude failures due to interacting units. In particular, you need to plan analysis sessions that involve multiple cubes (drill-across queries) and take advantage of different application components. For example, this is the case when your dashboard data is exported into an OLAP analysis, or when you check for single-sign-on policies to be set up properly after switching from reporting mode to OLAP mode.

- **Architecture test**   Checks for the system implementation to be compliant with the specifications of the architectural schema.

- **Usability test**   Checks how easy it is to understand, learn, and use applications. End user participation is essential for this type of test. Normally it checks for interfaces and operating modes to comply with the specifications supplied. It can also include a few analysis sessions with end users. An integral part of this type of tests checks for every report to be suitably represented and commented to avoid any misunderstanding about the real meaning of data.

- **Safety test**   Checks for the proper operation of hardware and software mechanisms used to implement a safe system. In this scope, it is particularly important to check for user profiles to be properly set up.

- **Error simulation test**   Checks that main application error conditions are properly managed. In this scope, ETL-flow tests are particularly important because they must check for procedures to be able to manage incoming or incomplete data. This type of test needs to adopt a "white box technique": the specification of test cases has to consider the real structure of the implemented code and error conditions expected to be managed.

- **Performance test (workload test)**   Checks that software meets efficiency requirements. Typically a workload test for ETL components checks for operational data processing time of a specific hardware configuration to be compatible with the time frames expected for data-staging processes. A workload test for an OLAP component submits a group of concurrent queries to a system and checks for the time needed to process those queries. Performance tests imply a preliminary specification of the standard workload in terms of number of concurrent users, types of queries, and data volume. For this reason, you should not mix these tests with stress tests, in which you apply progressively heavier workloads than the standard loads to evaluate system stability.

- **Fault-tolerance test**   Checks how robust the system actually is. The test simulates errors in one or more components and evaluates the system response to errors under standard and overload operating conditions. For example, you can cut off the power supply while an ETL process is in progress or you can set a database offline while an OLAP session is in progress to check for restore policies' effectiveness.

A very real problem for frequently updated systems concerns time and costs needed to check for new components and new add-on features to be compatible with the operation of the whole system. In this case, the term *regression test* defines the testing activities performed to make sure that any change applied to the system does not jeopardize the quality of preexisting, already tested features. Testing the whole system many times dramatically impacts time and costs needed for implementation. For this reason, test procedures should be as automatic as possible. In this way, the regression test just restarts all the available test procedures and then it (automatically, if possible) checks for the new results to be consistent with the previous ones. If test procedures cannot be automatically performed, the regression test will necessarily be sketchier.

NOTE *Section 13.2.7 offers a few hints on how to document test activities.*

Analysis and Reconciliation of Data Sources

As mentioned in previous chapters, data warehouse data is extracted from a set of sources storing operational data. Data sources can have different technological solutions for their management, such as database management systems (DBMSs), spreadsheets, file systems, and so on; different representation models, such as the relational model, the object-oriented model, flat file, and so on; and different data semantics. In this chapter, the term *local source schema* refers to the conceptual schema that describes the data stored in a source without regard to the models and technological solutions implemented. This means that we will focus on the representation of the application domain that can be equally achieved using relational databases, spreadsheets, or generic files, even though those solutions have different expressive potentials: local source schemata result from the analysis of relations and constraints in relational databases, from the analysis of cell relationships in spreadsheets, and from the analysis of file records in flat files.

Data sources can show strong relationships or can be completely independent. The domains described by data sources can be separate or overlapping. The data mart designer's primary goal is to improve as much as possible his or her knowledge of data sources in the source analysis phase. In this way, the designer can determine those concepts significant for the data warehousing projects and detect the most suitable data sources to populate the data warehouses.

The data source analysis in itself is insufficient for creating the prerequisites for the data mart design phases that follow, because it will mostly highlight a series of inconsistencies and flaws that absolutely need to be solved before moving on. In particular, one of the fundamental data warehousing concepts is *integrated data*; it gives you the opportunity to derive consistent, error-free information. Achieving this ambitious result needs a *reconciliation* process that involves *integrating*, *cleansing*, and *transforming* data to create a reconciled database. This process can be very demanding in terms of time and resources.

Remember that the integration phase is based on the intensional features of data sources. This means that the phase deals with the consistency of schemata that describe the data sources. Data cleansing and transformation processes are based on extensional concepts, instead. This means that those phases directly involve actual data.

Figure 3-1 shows a set of ovals representing the phases required for designing the reconciled layer. As you can see, data source schemata supply information to the analysis and reconciliation processes that generate a set of meta-data. The meta-data does not only model the reconciled schema, but the relationships (*mappings*) between the reconciled schema and the source schema attributes, as well. The cleansing and transformation design phases create the Extraction, Transformation, and Loading (ETL) procedures to populate your data mart; to this end, they exploit meta-data information and some data samples of sources to assess the quality of information resources. Even though the overall process consists of three closely related phases, we focus on the analysis and reconciliation phase in this chapter because it is essential for the definition of the reconciled layer, which is the starting point for conceptual design. Chapter 10 offers a description of the remaining two phases involved in the data-staging design.

We will adopt the three-layer architecture proposed in Section 1.3.3 and use it as our reference model. This approach assumes that the reconciled data layer—that is, an integrated version of selected portions of the source operational databases—should be existing and materialized. The goal of the data integration and cleansing phases is to create the reconciled data layer. After this stage, both reconciled data and schema are consistent and error-free.

It's very important that reconciled schemata be created in two-layer architectures, too—even if they are not materialized. This condition proves that data mart designers have definitively gained accurate knowledge of their operational systems, which is essential for data marts to be properly populated—in this case, directly from data sources. However, we prefer the three-layer approach because a direct data feed to our data mart is too complex a task to be performed all-at-once, as an elementary, non-decomposable task. It should be decomposed into simpler tasks. An intermediate stage facilitates the tasks of the project management team, makes data-staging and cleansing easier, and prevents the integrated conceptual source schemata from being implicitly coded in ETL procedures.

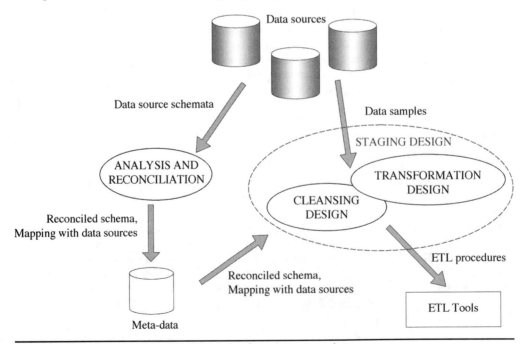

FIGURE 3-1 Three-phase reconciled layer design from data source layer

Let's closely study the analysis and reconciliation phase to identify the required activities. The general picture is very complex due to the large number of potential combinations that depend on the variables involved. A conceptual schema, or just the logical one, may be available for every data source. Both schemata can show varied formalisms. There can be one or more data sources. Source schemata can be mutually consistent or very heterogeneous and inconsistent. To break free from this hard task safely, you must carefully and precisely plan a list of actions to take. Figure 3-2 shows in detail the reconciliation and analysis phase of Figure 3-1. It outlines the necessary procedures for the most complex case, in which multiple inconsistent sources are only described by their logical schemata—even defined by different formalisms. In this case, you should first *inspect* and *normalize* all the local schemata to generate a set of comprehensive, locally consistent, conceptual schemata. Then you should go on to the *integration* phase, resulting in a globally consistent conceptual schema. Eventually, you should exploit this schema to logically design your reconciled schema and establish a mapping between the reconciled schema and the logical schemata of data sources.

TIP   *Even though the relationship between data is logically established, it is highly advisable to use conceptual formalisms for integration because they ensure a better understanding of concepts and allow you to write better documentation.*

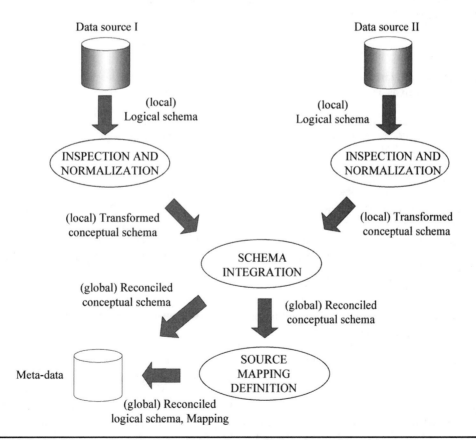

FIGURE 3-2   Design steps forming the analysis and reconciliation phase of two data sources

Under easier conditions than the preceding ones, you could skip unnecessary steps. For example, if only a single data source is available, you'd just need to inspect and normalize your local schema. The resulting normalized local schema will coincide with the global reconciled schema, and you will use it as the starting point for the subsequent phase aimed at defining a mapping between the global reconciled schema and your sources.

Conceptual schemata of sources are definitely the main results of analysis. They must be expressed by the same formalism applied to every source. If conceptual schemata are not available, you should apply reverse engineering to logical schemata of sources. To do this, you can use specific tools, such as ERwin ERX by Logic Works, GroundWorks by Cayenne Software for the Entity-Relationship model (ERM), and IBM Rational Rose for Unified Modeling Language (UML). The most widespread formalism for real-world cases is absolutely the ERM. Nevertheless, the academic community supports more complex data models that are able to represent information on data dependencies, void values, and support other semantic features to provide a greater knowledge of data sources.

3.1 Inspecting and Normalizing Schemata

Apart from any integration process, designers should get an in-depth knowledge of their data sources before going on to the data mart conceptual design phase. To do this, they should perform the following tasks:

- **Inspection**   A close investigation of local schemata to understand completely the field of application.

- **Normalization**   An attempt to rectify local schemata to model the application domain as accurately as possible.[1]

NOTE *The inspection and normalization processes must be completed even if only a single data source is available. For this reason, they cannot be considered part of the integration process. If more data sources are available, both processes need to be repeated for every local schema.*

Designers should collaborate with the experts of the application domain, such as data processing center staff, managers, and so on, in this analysis phase. They should also check for local schemata to be comprehensive and try to find any relationships accidentally excluded—for example, the explicit representation of functional dependencies previously skipped and new relationships between entities. These processes can bring about changes in a local schema to adjust it to specific data warehousing project needs.

The changes applied to local schemata should not add new concepts, but they must explicitly clarify all the concepts that can be extracted from the data stored in operational sources. Consider the example shown in Figure 3-3, which represents two potential changes to be applied to the Entity-Relationship schema modeling a specific company's production. In this scope, the first change can be applied because the productCode→categoryCode functional dependency is true even if it is not represented in this diagram, and the BELONGS TO association cardinality can be checked using source data. The other change, however,

---

[1]We use the term *normalization* in this context even if we do not necessarily apply it to relational schemata, because this task generally causes local schemata to include additional functional dependencies previously left out.

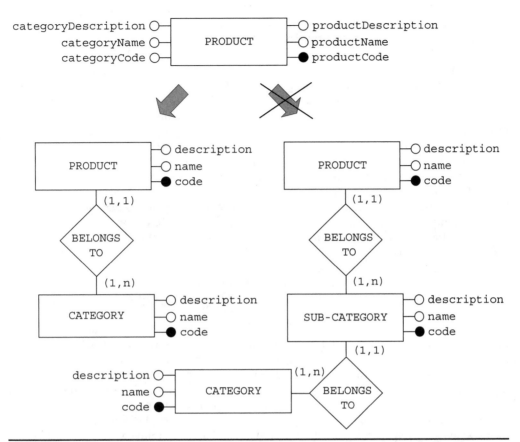

FIGURE 3-3 Applicable and inapplicable changes in the source inspection and normalization phase

cannot be applied because the operational data does not contain the information required to represent explicitly any product subcategory. If you want to highlight the classification of products into subcategories in your data mart, you should find a data source containing subcategory information and consequently integrate it .

In addition to applying necessary changes, designers must also detect any portions of local schemata that are not useful for their data marts. For example, management information on business staff or information on operating expenses of distribution chain stores are not significant in the scope of a sales data mart.

3.2 The Integration Problem

Researchers have been studying integration since the 1980s. This ongoing study has highlighted the integration problems with many data sources, such as relational databases, object-oriented databases, and semi-structured sources (Jarke et al., 2000); it has proposed new approaches to coping better with those integration problems (Batini et al., 1986); and it has defined a series of formalisms able to express relevant information (Blanco et al., 1994; Calvanese et al., 1998; Garcia-Solaco et al., 1995). More recently, researchers have focused more and more attention on ontology-based integration techniques (Wache et al., 2001).

Researchers are currently focusing on the automation of the integration process. Most systems available, such as The Stanford-IBM Manager of Multiple Information Sources (TSIMMIS) (Chawathe et al., 1994), Garlic (Carey et al., 1995), Sqirrel (Hull and Zhou, 1996), and Mediator Environment for Multiple Information Sources (MOMIS) (Beneventano et al., 2000), should still be considered as research prototypes rather than commercial applications despite their recent technical breakthroughs. Clio by IBM (Miller et al., 2001) makes an exception. It is a semi-automatic tool that supports transformation and integration of heterogeneous databases. Clio gives users the opportunity to define mappings between relational schemata and XML diagrams, but it can also infer these mappings so that users need only validate them. Clio interprets these mappings to create queries that transform and integrate source data to fit them to target data. Those queries can ultimately be used to populate data marts or create virtual views and tables in federated databases.

The tools mentioned here take advantage of conceptual techniques that are difficult to implement manually. For this reason, we promote an approach based on the guidelines of the 20-year-long study conducted in the field of heterogeneous databases that best meet enterprise specific needs.

Integrating a set of heterogeneous data sources, such as relational databases, data files, and legacy sources, means detecting any relationships between the concepts represented in local schemata and solving the conflicts found to create one single global schema, whose elements can be mapped onto local schema elements.

If each data source modeled independent, separate, real-world portions, there would be no problem with integration, and designers' tasks would be remarkably easier. This means that it would take just a local schema analysis to understand which enterprise-specific parts a data source models. Unfortunately, this cannot be put into practice, because every organization is a consistent universe in which business units take part in common processes, sharing all their actors or part of them. For example, the product concept is involved both in warehousing processes and in business-management processes. The latter should also include the employee concept. Finally, it is very likely that the employee concept is viewed in different ways in business management and project management processes.

Computerizing information systems[2] is an incremental, evolutionary process that results in a mosaic of several tiles and adds to those differences in viewpoints. Each component takes advantage of the most popular technological solutions currently in use for computerizing processes. These components also attempt to be as compatible as possible with preexisting components, if necessary. In the end, consider that modeling and implementation errors can occur, because no sophisticated system is completely error-free. All these points provide a clearer picture of how complex this situation is.

The integration phase should not only highlight differences in representing concepts common to multiple local schemata, but it should also identify a group of semantic relationships between a set of objects in one schema and a different set of objects in another schema (*interschema properties*). These features are not explicitly modeled in local schemata and can be detected only after conducting joint analyses.

To handle the concepts represented by data sources, you must apply only one formalism to set the constructs that can be used and the expressive potential. If there are schemata with

---

[2]We would like to emphasize that the concept of *information systems* is independent from the concept of *information technology (IT) systems*: Information systems represent the amount of information managed to monitor business organizations. IT systems refer to a part of the information system controlled by computer-based equipment.

different formalisms (Entity-Relationship schemata, UML schemata, relational schemata, object-oriented schemata, XML Document Type Definitions [DTD], and so on), you should opt for just one formalism and rewrite all the schemata involved in the integration process, accordingly.

TIP *The formalism that ensures top expressive potential should be preferred. In this way, loss of information will not occur during the conversion process. Nevertheless, many designers opt for the formalism common to most schemata or for the one with which they are more familiar, trading off higher expressive power for lower design effort.*

In the following sections, we list the main causes for problems needing resolution in the integration phase. To be as clear as possible, we use the ERM as a reference point. We adopt the original ERM notation, where boxes and diamonds represent entities and relationships, respectively; relationships are annotated with their minimum and maximum cardinalities; and identifiers are denoted by black circles. Of course, these remarks are not dependent on the specific formalism that we will adopt.

3.2.1 Different Perspectives

User groups' points of view on application domain objects may greatly vary, depending on the points relevant for the tasks users have to perform. For example, Figure 3-4 shows how to model the appointment of an employee to a department. The left-hand modeling includes the project in which the employee is involved. This modeling could be suitable for a database used for business organization chart management. The right-hand modeling does not include this concept because it is not relevant.

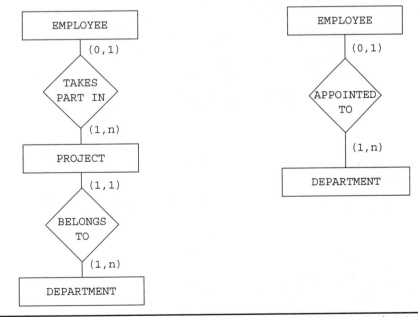

FIGURE 3-4 Two different perspectives for modeling the appointment of employees to departments (Batini et al., 1986)

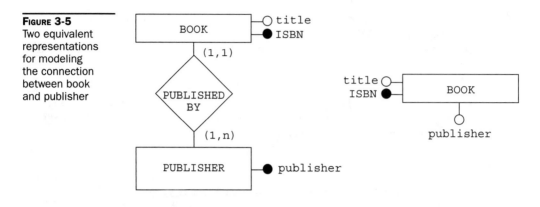

FIGURE 3-5
Two equivalent
representations
for modeling
the connection
between book
and publisher

3.2.2 Equivalent Modeling Constructs

Every modeling formalism can use many different construct combinations to represent individual concepts. For example, Figure 3-5 shows two schemata modeling the relationship between a book and its publishing house. The right-hand side schema uses just one attribute, but the left-hand side one aims at emphasizing the same concept creating the PUBLISHER entity.

Note that this case is merely syntactically different: both modeling representations are perfectly equivalent. On the contrary, a new concept is added in the example of Figure 3-4 in the preceding section: the concept of project, causing the expressive potential of the whole schema to change.

3.2.3 Incompatible Specifications

When specifications are incompatible, this means that different schemata modeling the same application domain include different, contrasting concepts. This often happens because schemata were created at different times, so they reflect different versions of the application domain. Differences can also be due to incorrect design decisions that involve names, data types, and integrity constraints. For example, both modeling representations shown in Figure 3-6 could be the result of an error because it is very unlikely that a professor is not allowed to teach more than one course at the same time (on the left) or that he is required to teach more than one course (on the right).

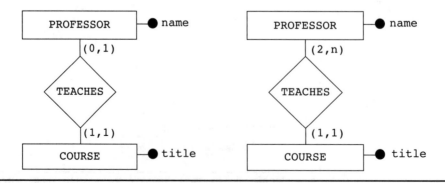

FIGURE 3-6 Two unlikely modeling representations for the association between university professor and courses

As mentioned, you must also consider that enterprises evolve as time goes by. For this reason, the assumptions previously made could now no longer be true. For example, a salary management software application compiled before the Euro currency was launched could use integers to store amounts of money. After the Euro launch, you would need to take advantage of floating-point attributes.

3.2.4   Common Concepts

Here we'll define the semantic relationship between common concepts that are modeled in different ways in separate schemata. Four types of relationships exist between separate representations R_1 and R_2 for the same concept:

- **Identity**   When you use the same constructs and you model the concept from the same point of view with no specification mistake—in other words, when R_1 and R_2 exactly coincide.

- **Equivalence**   When R_1 and R_2 are not exactly the same because different, yet equivalent, constructs are used and neither specification mistakes nor different perspectives exist. To quote Rissanen's (1977) definition of *equivalence*:

> **Equivalence Between Schemata**
> Two schemata R_1 and R_2 are equivalent if their instances can have a one-to-one association.

  Note that equivalent schemata imply that the extensional level always includes two different, yet equivalent, groups of data storing the same information. For example, Figure 3-5 shows schemata that are equivalent. Figure 3-7 shows two possible instances of the schemata that are compliant with the previous definition.

- **Compatibility**   When R_1 and R_2 are neither identical nor equivalent, but the constructs used and designers' view points are comparable. For example, Figure 3-4 shows compatible schemata. In particular, even if the schemata are not equivalent (the schema on the left-hand side is more expressive and also models employees' participation in projects), they are not incompatible because you can immediately understand that employees are assigned either to 0 or to 1 department, and that one or more employees are assigned to a department after navigating the PROJECT entity.

- **Incompatibility**   When R_1 and R_2 are incomparable because of inconsistent specifications. This means that the set of objects in the real world modeled by R_1 denies the set of objects in the real world modeled by R_2. Figure 3-6 shows incompatible schemata because the scenarios expected for professors are conflicting: on the one hand, professors cannot teach more than one course, and on the other hand, they should teach at least two courses.

All the previous scenarios generate conflicting results except for the identity relationship. Solving those conflicts is the main goal of the integration phase.

> **Conflict**
> A *conflict* between two representations R_1 and R_2 for the same concept occurs every time both representations are not identical.

BOOK

ISBN	title	publisher
123445	DFM	McGraw-Hill
4354543	Apparently Logical	Read All
4566454	The Right Measure	Not Only Books
.....	.....	.....

PUBLISHER

publisher
McGraw-Hill
Read All
Not Only Books
.....

BOOK

ISBN	title	publisher
123445	DFM	McGraw-Hill
4354543	Apparently Logical	Read All
4566454	The Right Measure	Not Only Books
.....	.....	.....

FIGURE 3-7　Two instances for the equivalent schemata shown in Figure 3-5

3.2.5　Interrelated Concepts

As you complete the integration phase, many different yet interrelated concepts will be part of the same schema. Under this condition, they will create new relationships that you could not infer previously. These relationships are called *interschema properties* and they should be explicitly identified and represented. For example, Figure 3-8 shows the association between PUBLISHER and AUTHOR entities that could not be highlighted in the source schemata.

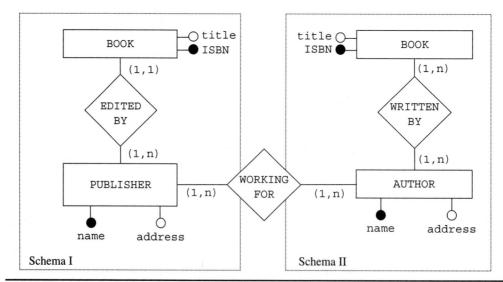

FIGURE 3-8　An interschema property of PUBLISHER and AUTHOR entities

3.3 Integration Phases

Solving all the problems discussed so far and properly representing the features that emerge after integrating local schemata implies a complex set of tasks. To manage those tasks properly, you need to adopt a methodological approach. Many approaches proposed in the scientific literature agree on the sequence of steps to take. The following list sums up those steps (Batini et al., 1986):

- Preintegration
- Schema comparison
- Schema alignment
- Merging and restructuring schemata

3.3.1   Preintegration

The preintegration phase thoroughly analyzes data sources and leads to the definition of the general integration standards. The main decisions to make concern the following:

- **Parts of schemata to be integrated**   Not all operational data is useful for decision-making purposes. For this reason, some parts of the source schemata can be scrapped beforehand.

- **Integration strategy**   You should assign a priority to schema integration steps. Figure 3-9 shows a few solutions: the integration techniques can be divided into *n-ary* and *binary* techniques. The integration process of *n*-ary techniques involves more than two schemata at the same time. The integration process of binary techniques always involves pairs of schemata. Binary techniques are also called *ladder* techniques when new schemata are integrated into a current schema.

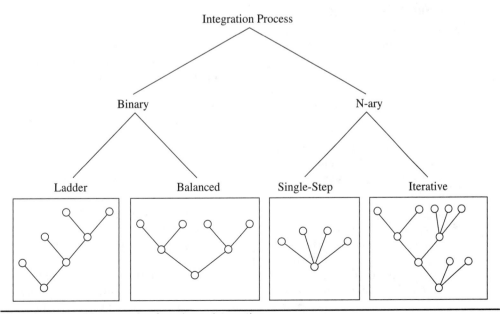

FIGURE 3-9 Possible strategies for schema integration

Most approaches proposed by the scientific literature prefer binary techniques, because they make every integration process step easier, thanks to the small number of concepts involved at the same time. Nevertheless, the researchers supporting *n*-ary techniques state that every concept can be analyzed in detail, because all the information is made available if various schemata are integrated at the same time. Furthermore, *n*-ary techniques reduce the total amount of comparisons between concepts because each concept is processed only once. If you use a binary ladder technique, you can prioritize your source schemata and decide in which order they will be analyzed and added to your reconciled schema. You can begin with data sources that are the information system core so that their integration will outline your reconciled schema. Then you can go on to integrating parts of minor schemata that can be added to your starting structure. When you adopt this approach, you should opt for the partially reconciled schema version that already complies with the most important source schemata in order to solve any conflicts.

TIP *When you have to opt for a strategy to adopt, schema complexity and number play a very influential role: N-ary techniques can be very helpful when the whole process is not very complex. If this is not the case, you should generally use binary ladder techniques, because they make the integration process easier and their guideline meets the standards that we suggest in this book: To design data warehouses you should adopt a bottom-up approach and create iteratively new data marts. Every time you create a new data mart, you will have a new integration phase that leads to the analysis of new data sources.*

During the data source analysis, designers will also have to check the quality standards of source data (percentage of wrong data, percentage of missing data, validation check for database consistency, and so on), because quality can affect the decisions on the integration strategy.

3.3.2   Schema Comparison

This phase consists of a comparison analysis of schemata. Its goal is to discover relationships and conflicts in schemata. The effectiveness of the schema comparison phase depends on designers' knowledge of a specific application domain and information source structures. However accurate the analysis phase can be, designers must collaborate with the data processing center staff and end users to dispel any doubts about the concepts being modeled. The type of conflicts that can be detected and easily linked to the problems listed in section 3.2 belong to the following categories (Batini; Reddy et al., 1994):

- **Heterogeneity conflicts**   These conflicts point out inconsistencies due to the usage of formalisms with different expressive power in source schemata. If the same formalism has been used for modeling all source schemata, no heterogeneity conflicts can occur.

- **Name conflicts**   These conflicts are due to different terms used in various data sources because of different perspectives adopted by designers. Two main name conflicts occur: *homonymies* and *synonymies*. In homonymies, the same term stands for two different concepts. In synonymies, two equivalent representations of the same concept are marked with different terms. If a comparison of the concepts with the same names in different schemata is necessary to determine the homonymies, an in-depth knowledge of the application domain is required to detect synonymies.

Figure 3-10 shows a few examples of these types of conflicts. Both schemata in the upper part of the figure show the EQUIPMENT. In the left-hand schema, this term means scientific equipment, such as PCs, printers, plotters, and so on. In the right-hand schema, this term could also mean building furniture. Of course, the reconciled schema should suitably distinguish both concepts. The lower part of the figure shows that the CUSTOMER and PURCHASER entities turn out to be synonyms. They are likely to make reference to the same real-word concept. Both entities should be unified in the reconciled schema to avoid useless duplicates. To document this type of conflict properly, you can take advantage of data dictionaries where relationships can be stored (Navathe and Kerschberg, 1986).

- **Semantic conflicts**   These conflicts occur when two source schemata model the same part of the real world at different abstraction and detail levels. For example, Figures 3-4 and 3-11 show pairs of schemata that are semantically conflicting. The detail level applied to local schemata is different in both cases. As a result, the set of information to be represented changes, too. If you study this case closely, you can infer that a semantic conflict could occur between both schemata shown in Figure 3-4 depending on the interpretation of the "Department Appointment" concept. A possible interpretation is that an employee is appointed to the department to which the project that he is working on, belongs. In this case, the APPOINTED TO association of the right-hand schema is obviously the result of the transitive combination of TAKES PART IN and BELONGS TO.

FIGURE 3-10
Examples of
synonymies
and homonymies
(Batini)

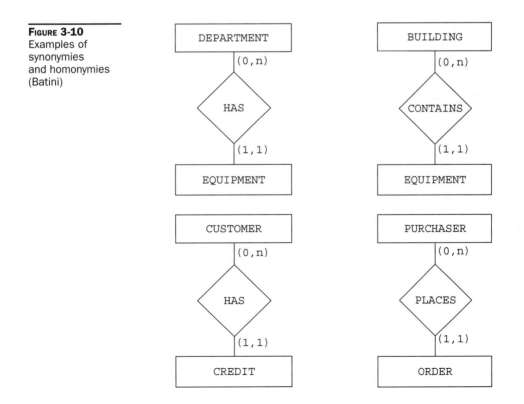

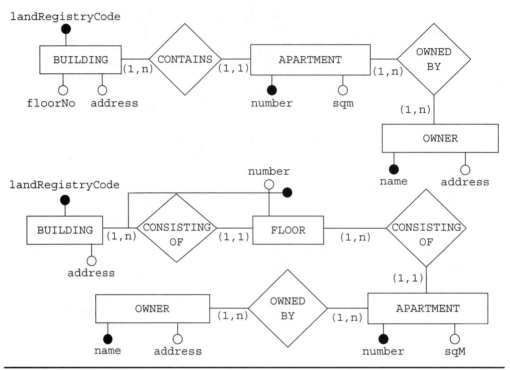

FIGURE 3-11 Two schemata in semantic conflict: they model a common part of the application domain at different abstraction levels.

For this reason, a semantic conflict results. An additional possible interpretation is that the appointment of an employee to a department does not depend on his/her participation in projects. For example, John can be appointed to the X department even if he takes part in a project of the Y department. If this is the case, the information represented by both schemata is completely complementary and there is no conflict. It is clear that designers can dispel their doubts about the previous interpretations only after discussing those points with an application domain expert or inspecting data stored in both databases.

- **Structural conflicts** These conflicts are caused by different options for modeling the same concepts or by the application of different integrity constraints. Specifically, structural conflicts can be classified into four categories: *Type conflicts* occur when two different constructs are used to model the same concept. For example, consider how the Publisher concept is modeled in Figure 3-5. *Dependency conflicts* occur when two or more concepts are interrelated with different dependencies in separate schemata. For example, the left-hand side of Figure 3-12 shows that a wedding

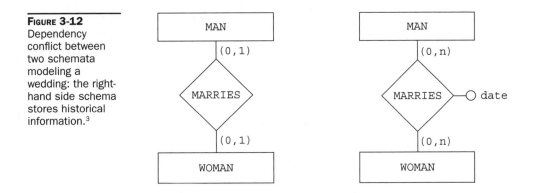

FIGURE 3-12
Dependency conflict between two schemata modeling a wedding: the right-hand side schema stores historical information.[3]

between a man and a woman is defined by a one-to-one association, and the right-hand side of this figure shows that the wedding is defined by a one-to-many association to keep track of historical information. *Key conflicts* occur when different attributes in separate schemata are used to identify the same concept. For example, people could be identified on the basis of their Social Security numbers or progressive numbering. *Behavior conflicts* occur when you take different actions to delete/edit data on the same concept in separate schemata. For example, information on a customer is deleted from a schema if the customer has no pending orders, but another schema still stores the customer's information for future use.

NOTE *Identifying relationships and conflicts requires an in-depth knowledge of the semantics of all the elements involved. For this reason, the features of operational schemata should be accurately documented using powerful formalisms.*

3.3.3   Schema Alignment
The goal of the schema alignment phase is to solve any conflicts found in the preceding step. To do this, you should apply *transformation primitives* to source schemata. Transformation primitives typically deal with changes in names, attribute types, functional dependencies, and existing constraints applied to schemata. Consider the example shown in Figure 3-4. If a semantic conflict occurs, the right-hand schema is changed and the Project concept is added to it so that this schema is identical to the one on the left-hand side. Conflicts cannot always be solved, however, because they may stem from basic inconsistencies of the source databases (see Figure 3-6). If this is the case, you should agree on a solution with end users who should provide accurate feedback on the most reliable interpretation of real-world facts.

---

[3]To make this example easier, we intentionally skipped the case of a man who repeatedly marries the same woman.

As mentioned, in case of doubt, you should opt for the transformations that give priority to schemata playing a vital role in your future data mart. In this case, the binary ladder technique is the best strategy to adopt, provided that you start integration from the most important schemata, that will become the core of your reconciled schema.

From this phase onward, designers should define and take note of the mappings between source schema and reconciled schema elements.

3.3.4   Merging and Restructuring Schemata

The final phase merges all the aligned schemata into a single reconciled schema. The most widespread approach to merging overlaps common concepts to connect them to all the remaining ones from local schemata. After this operation, you should complete further transformation processes to improve the reconciled schema structure. To do this, check for the following properties:

- **Completeness**   After overlapping source schemata, additional interschema properties may emerge. For this reason, designers should closely study the schema built so far to determine new properties that can be explicitly recorded by adding new associations and generalization hierarchies.

- **Minimality**   When you overlap many schemata, you may incur redundant concepts. This means that some concepts may be duplicated or be mutually derived in reconciled schemata, even if their representation in source schemata is unique. For example, Figure 3-13 shows that a generalization between TECHNICAL MANAGER and EMPLOYEE is redundant and can be deleted. Cyclic relationships between concepts and derived attributes are often additional sources of redundancy.

- **Readability**   Improving the readability of schemata streamlines the design phases that follow. Even if it is difficult to quantify the readability differences between two schemata, the qualitative meaning of this term is comparatively easy to understand. Figure 3-14 shows an example by Batini that involves two equivalent schemata. It is easy to establish that the schema in the lower part of the figure is easier to understand because the relationships between its concepts are better arranged.

Figure 3-13
Schema with redundant inclusion dependency

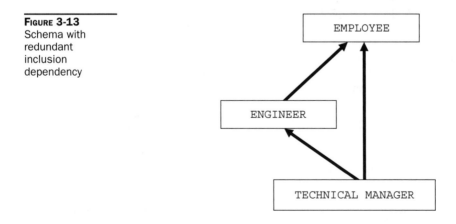

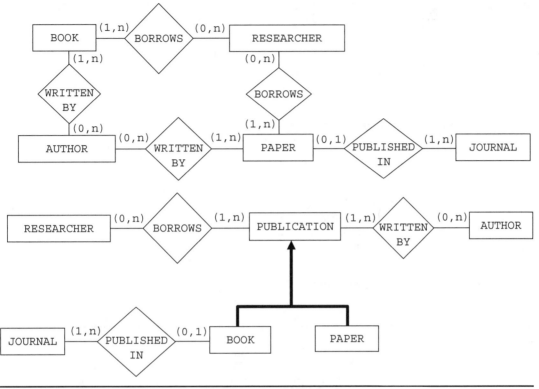

FIGURE 13-14   Two equivalent schemata with different readability levels

3.4 Defining Mappings

The result of the source schema analysis targeted to integration consists of two elements: the reconciled schema where the conflicts between local schemata are solved and the set of relationships between the source schema and reconciled schema elements. Chapter 10 will show that those relationships are necessary in the data-staging design phase to define the procedures used by ETL tools to migrate data from source layer into the reconciled layer.

The approach usually adopted to establish the relationship between both architecture layers expects global schemata to be represented on the basis of source schemata; this approach is called *Global-As-View (GAV)*. Specifically, each concept of your reconciled schema should be related to a view whose meaning is explained by source schema concepts (Levy, 2000). The procedures followed to define those relationships affect the methods to issue the queries used by ETL tools for data loading. If the GAV approach is adopted, every global schema concept will be replaced with the views defining it in term of local schema concepts. Halevy (2000) offers a description of this operation, called *unfolding*. The easy query expression is paid back in terms of reconciled schema expandability. In particular, if you add a new source, this will cause you to apply changes to all the global schema concepts that exploit that source.

Figure 3-15 shows two GAV mappings in the scope of an order database. We use the relational formalism and SQL to define relationships. If the integration process were

---

FIGURE 3-15   GAV mapping for an order database; primary keys are underlined.

```
// DB1 Warehouse
ORDERS_2001(keyO, keyC, orderDate, employee)
CUSTOMER(keyC, name, address, town, county, state)
. . . . . . . . . . . . . . .

// DB2 Management
CUSTOMER(keyC, VATRegNo, name, phone, billing)
INVOICES(keyI, date, keyC, amount, VAT)
ORDER_HISTORY_2000(keyO, keyC, orderDate, employee)
. . . . . . . . . . . . . . .

CREATE VIEW CUSTOMER AS
SELECT  C1.keyC, C1.name, C1.address, C1.town, C1.county,
        C1.state, C2.VATRegNo, C2.phone, C2.billing
FROM    DB1.CUSTOMER AS C1, DB2.CUSTOMER AS C2
WHERE   C1.keyC = C2.keyC;

CREATE VIEW ORDERS AS
SELECT * FROM DB1.ORDERS_2001
UNION
SELECT * FROM DB2.ORDER_HISTORY_2000;
```

---

completed using the ERM, you would naturally have to carry out the logical design of the reconciled schema that was created before mapping data sources.[4] The upper part of this figure shows two fragments of the local schemata of warehouse and business management databases. The lower part shows the customer and order concepts used in the reconciled schema. The customer view of the reconciled schema sorts out all the information from both local schemata by customer. The order view gathers all the specific information from the warehouse database for current year orders and from the business management database for previous year orders.

Note that a few authors have proposed diametrically opposed approaches. They suggest that the expression of global schemata should not depend on sources, whose concepts can be defined as views of global schemata (Calvanese et al., 1999). This approach is called *Local-As-View (LAV)* and does not expect any view definition to describe reconciled schema concepts directly. For this reason, this approach requires very complex transformation processes, generally called *query rewriting* (Abiteboul et al., 1995; Qian, 1996; Ullman, 1997), to understand which source schema elements should be taken into account to re-create specific global schema concepts. Nevertheless, the LAV approach streamlines reconciled schema extensibility and maintenance processes. For example, if you add a new source to a system, this will require just the definition of a new view of the global schema. As a result, you do not need to change your global schema. Refer to Ullman for an accurate comparison of both approaches.

---

[4]Prototyping tools designed for processing the integration phase automatically are based on conceptual formalisms that provide suitable languages to specify relationships directly.

CHAPTER 4

User Requirement Analysis

A collaboration of designers and end users occurs in the project planning phase. This collaboration aims at specifying goals and limitations of the data warehouse system, assessing priorities, and evaluating the added value. After setting these priorities, designers can begin building a single data mart. After investigating the available information resources in the data source analysis and reconciliation phase, it is now time to approach end users again to get more accurate information.

The user requirement analysis phase attempts to collect end user needs for data mart applications and usage. This phase holds a strategic significance for designing data marts, because it influences almost every decision made during the project. It plays an essential role in defining conceptual schemata of data, data-staging designs, requirements for data analysis applications, data warehouse system architectures, training course plans, instructions for data warehouse system maintenance, and upgrades.

Unfortunately, the user requirement analysis phase often delivers ambiguous, incomplete, and short-lived requirements in data warehousing projects because

- these are long-term projects and it is difficult to get and arrange every requirement from the beginning;

- the information requirements of data warehouse applications are difficult to explain because decision-making processes have very flexible structures, are poorly shared across large organizations, are guarded with care by managers, and may greatly vary as time goes by to keep up with new business process evolution;

- decision-making process requirements frequently make reference to a set of information that is not available in a suitable format and needs to be derived from data sources.

Imprecise requirements can cause a remarkable percentage of data warehousing projects to be unable to fulfill users' expectations or even to be successful.

As mentioned in Chapter 2, we propose two different approaches to user requirement analysis in this chapter. Section 4.2 describes the first approach—an informal approach that requires glossaries to support designers in the conceptual design phase. It fits perfectly into a data-driven design framework that emphasizes deriving data mart schemata from operational source schemata. Section 4.3 describes the second approach, a formal approach based on Tropos formalism for user requirement analysis. This approach documents the needs of users more accurately. On the one side, it clears the way for requirement-driven design frameworks that are practicable in case of a limited knowledge of operational sources. But it also clears the way for mixed-design frameworks, bringing user requirements and operational schema-bound constraints together to create data mart conceptual schemata. Golfarelli (2009) provides a comprehensive survey and comparison of the approaches to user requirement analysis in data warehousing.

Section 4.1 paves the way for both approaches and offers a few guidelines to arrange interviews for requirement elicitation. In the final part of this chapter, we discuss additional types of requirements that play an important role in data warehousing projects, even if they do not directly affect the conceptual schemata of data marts.

4.1 Interviews

The main "sources" from which to draw requirements are the future data mart end users—the so-called *business users*. The entire data warehousing project hinges on business users. Sometimes interviews can be difficult and fruitless because of the differences in the language used by designers and end users, and because of end users' distorted understanding of data warehousing projects. Because end user satisfaction depends on how accurately the system meets their needs, it is fundamental that designers carefully manage the analysis phases.

As far as the technical know-how is concerned, information system administrators and/or data processing center staff will be a point of reference for designers. In particular, the requirements that need to be collected are mainly about various constraints on data warehouse systems. Those requirements will play a vital role in ensuring that the performance level is optimal and the integration with previous information systems is as smooth as possible.

Kimball et al., (1998) stated that two basic procedures can be used to conduct user requirement analysis: *interviews* and *facilitated sessions*. Interviews are conducted either with single users or small, homogenous groups. They offer the advantage that everyone can actively participate, and they generally result in a very detailed list of specifications. Facilitated sessions involve large, heterogeneous groups led by a facilitator, who is in charge of setting up a common language for all the interviewees. They can be very helpful because they encourage creative brainstorming. Sessions aimed at setting general priorities typically follow interviews focusing on detail specifications. The following points from Kimball list the main preliminary activities involved in interviews:

- **Pre-interview research**   The goal is to raise awareness among the interviewees on business issues that are typical for a specific application domain. You can also read a company's annual report and strategic initiatives, analyze the reports currently in use, and study main competitors. Furthermore, it is essential that you analyze previous data warehousing projects to understand why they were unsuccessful.

- **Interviewee selection**   Working with the business management, you should select a representative sample of end users to derive a wide-ranging set of information on the analysis needs in the data mart–specific application field.

- **Interview question development**   These are not exactly questionnaires, but more appropriately guidelines to follow. Of course, they should vary by interviewees' job functions and levels.

- **Interview scheduling**   We recommend that the first meeting be arranged with the project sponsor. Then users in the middle of the organizational hierarchy can be interviewed.

- **Interviewee preparation**   This activity involves a meeting to clarify interview goals and plans to all the users potentially impacted by this project.

After these activities have been accomplished, you can start interviewing. You can ask three types of questions (Table 4-1 shows their advantages and disadvantages):

- **Open-ended questions**   Such as *What do you think of data source quality?* and *What are the key objectives your unit has to face?*

- **Closed questions**   Such as *Are you interested in sorting out purchases by hour?* and *Do you want to receive a sales report every week?*

- **Evidential questions**   Such as *Could you please give me an example of how you calculate your business unit budget?* and *Could you please describe the issues with poor data quality that your business unit is experiencing?*

Questions Asking For	Advantages	Disadvantages
Open-ended answers	They give the interviewer the opportunity to learn participants' vocabulary that proves their educational level, attitudes, and opinions. Answers are rich in details. They allow the interviewer to explore new possibilities that were not found in the interview preparation phase. They get interviewees more involved.	Their answers can be long and rich in useless details. They can result in digressions diverting from the interview goals. They can be very time-demanding. They can make interviewees think that the interviewer is not well-trained.
Closed answers	They shorten the interview time. They make various interviewees' answers comparable. They allow interviewees to focus on relevant elements.	They can sound boring to interviewees. They do not allow interviewer to begin a real dialog with interviewees. They assume that the interviewer has already guessed key factors.
Evidential answers	They allow interviewer to understand interviewees' knowledge level. They show the interviewer's interest in understanding the interviewees' opinions.	They can make interviewees nervous because the questions are probing.

TABLE 4-1   Advantages and Disadvantages of Three Types of Questions (Kendall & Kendall, 2002).

Essentially, interviews can be organized in two ways, as shown in Figure 4-1 (Kendall and Kendall, 2002):

- **Pyramid-shaped**   Interviews follow an inductive approach. The interviewer starts with very detailed questions (frequently closed questions). Then the interviewer broadens topics, asking open questions for generic answers. This type of interview allows the interviewer to overcome skeptical interviewees' reluctance, because it does not initially get interviewees deeply involved.

FIGURE 4-1
Pyramid-shaped
and funnel-shaped
approaches for
interviews

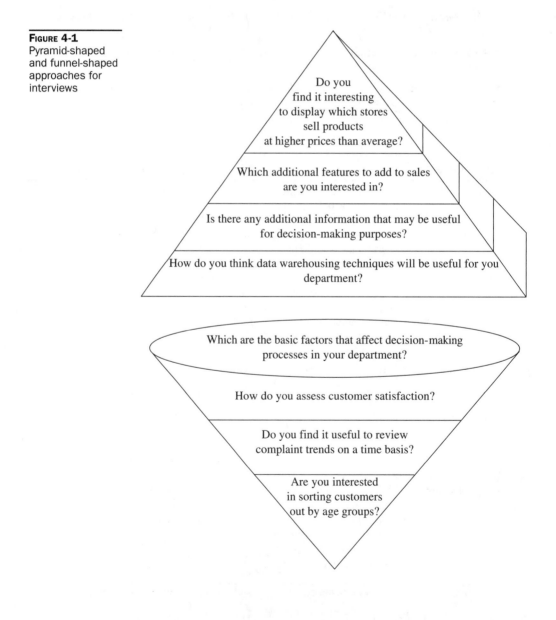

Job	Key Questions
Manager	What are the enterprise goals? How do you rate your company's success? What are the main company problems now? How do you think a better exchange of information could improve your company's conditions?
Department manager	What are the goals of your department? How do you rate your department's success? Describe the people involved in your field. Does any bottleneck to data access exist? Which routine analyses do you conduct? Which analysis would you like to conduct? At what detail level would you like information to be displayed? How much historical information do you need?
IT staff	What are the main features of main data sources available? Which tools do you use to analyze data? How do you manage ad hoc analysis requests? What are the main quality issues with data?

TABLE 4-2   Questions Typically Asked of Interviewees Performing Different Enterprise Jobs (Kimball et al., 1998)

- **Funnel-shaped**   Interviews follow a deductive approach. The interviewer starts with very general questions and then asks specific questions to narrow interview topics. This approach is useful if interviewees are excited or too deferential, because general questions (generally open) cannot have "wrong" answers, and as a result interviewees feel better.

Table 4-2 shows examples of a few questions typical of interviews that can be asked of interviewees performing different enterprise jobs.

4.2 Glossary-based Requirement Analysis

In this section, we describe an informal approach to user requirement analysis. It is based on simple *glossaries of requirements*. You should remember that this approach is normally part of a data-driven design framework.

In 2001, Lechtenbörger proposed a user requirement analysis approach based on glossaries. He suggested that a *derivation table* and a *usage table* should be first created. Both tables should list the attributes for data mart modeling. The derivation table establishes every attribute relationship with operational sources by specifying a reconciled schema attribute or a procedure for values to be extracted. The usage table links textual descriptions to attributes and specifies attribute roles, such as analysis dimension and/or measure. Attribute roles are based on users' specifications on workload. Note that attributes can play both roles if queries use them to select/aggregate and to quantify events. Then a table listing all the existing functional dependencies between attributes should be created. Finally, he suggests a *structure table* should be created that specifies whether attributes should be modeled as dimensions, or attributes linked to dimensions, or measures.

The approach that we propose expects the user requirement analysis to be focused on facts and their workload. User requirement analysis is conducted simultaneously with conceptual design in data-driven design frameworks. Processing important requirements, such as hierarchy requirements, hinges on preliminary conceptual schemata that are automatically derived from operational source schemata. For this reason, more details on those requirements are discussed in Chapter 6.

4.2.1   Facts

The essential piece of information designers should be able to seize concerns the *facts* for modeling. Facts are concepts on which data mart end users base their decision-making process. Each fact describes a category of events taking place in enterprises.

It is almost mandatory for facts to show dynamic features—this means that the events described by facts should make reference to a time frame. Almost nothing is absolutely and completely static, neither in nature nor in business. Reference time frames and the ability to feel changes are mainly based on a matter of scale. Not only will dynamic features help data mart designers to define facts for data marts, but specific application fields and the type of analyses in which users are interested also play a central role. In addition, a fact may be relevant for a specific data mart, but it cannot be relevant for other data marts. For example, consider a business agent assigned to a specific region. Obviously, this assignment may vary as time goes by because of the regular staff turnover planned by appropriate business policies. For this reason, dynamic features certainly exist even if periodic assignments may occur only after longer intervals. Should agents assigned to specific regions be considered as a fact? There is no absolute right answer to this question. However, you could provide a sensible answer based on data mart users' interest. If you design a sales data mart, then the assignments of commercial agents will not likely be considered as a fact. Though an analysis of the sales sorted out by geographic areas and commercial agents is useful to provide better insight into business performance, there is no point in analyzing every assignment in detail. On the contrary, an analysis of assignments and staff turnover will play a central role when managing a staff data mart. These assignments should be then viewed as facts.

Table 4-3 shows a list of examples of relevant facts for a few data marts in different application fields because no formula can reliably identify the facts to be modeled. You may find comfort in the following point: Even if many doubts can be raised when you manage data mart projects, end users generally have a very clear view of the fact sets they want to analyze in their data marts right from the start.

When designers select facts, they should pay attention to the insights gained into operational sources in the preceding analysis and reconciliation phases. To be more precise, the selected facts should be present in reconciled schemata. In borderline cases, users may also find it essential to model a data mart fact about which existing sources provide almost no information. In such a case, designers and users should be aware that basic data for every event is required for data mart population. Furthermore, they should realize that the data must be manually input during every population session at regular intervals. Alternatively, designers can edit one of the source operational schemata and applications for database management to add the required information. However, this alternative is more theoretical than functional and would sound appalling to any information system administrator.

Application Field	Data Mart	Facts
Business, manufacturing	Supplies	Purchases, stock inventory, distribution
	Production	Packaging, inventory, delivery, manufacturing
	Demand management	Sales, invoices, orders, shipments, complaints
	Marketing	Promotions, customer retention, advertising campaigns
Finance	Banks	Checking accounts, bank transfers, mortgage loans, loans
	Investments	Securities, stock exchange transactions
	Services	Credit cards, bill payment through standing orders
Health service	Division	Admissions, discharges, transfers, surgical operations, diagnosis, prescriptions
	Accident & emergency	Admissions, tests, discharges
	Epidemiology	Diseases, outbreaks, treatments, vaccinations
Transportation	Goods	Demand, supply, transport
	Passengers	Demand, supply, transport
	Maintenance	Operations
Telecommunications	Traffic management	Network traffic, calls
	Customer relationship management	Customer retention, complaints, services
Tourism	Demand management	Ticketing, car rental, stays
	Customer relationship management	Frequent flyers, complaints
Management	Logistics	Transport, stocks, handling
	Human resources	Hiring, resignation, firing, transfers, advancement, premiums
	Budgeting	Commercial budget, marketing budget
	Infrastructure	Purchases, works

TABLE 4-3   Typical Facts of Different Application Fields

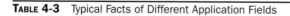

Finding out the facts is not enough. Designers should also arrange a set of additional information for each fact. First of all, designers should attempt to have clear ideas on fact dimensions and measures. To do this, they can take advantage of the documentation on

their reconciled layer. It is particularly important to focus on the dimensions of a fact, because this leads to the definition of fact *granularity*—the highest detail level for data to be represented in a data mart.

CAUTION *Selecting a granularity level for fact representation is the result of a delicate compromise between two opposite needs. On the one side is the need for maximum usage flexibility, which implies the same granularity level as operational sources. On the other side is the need for top performance, which implies a concise synthesis of data.*

The following examples of granularity may further clarify the concept. In the health care industry, users and designers frequently talk about dimensions suitable for patients when they conduct requirement analyses. Health care managers are likely to insist on the ability to follow every patient's medical history events. This means that a patient identifier, such as taxpayer's Social Security numbers or health care provider ID, should be added to dimensions. However, designers are likely to attempt to convince health care managers that the most suitable context for queries about individual patients is not a data warehouse, but an operational database. A sensible compromise that proves optimal in real-world applications sorts out patients by age groups, towns of residence, and gender. This means that three dimensions are required: `patientAge`, `patientTownOfResidence`, and `patientGender`.

As opposed to the preceding example of dimensions, assessing measures to quantify each fact plays only a preliminary and guiding role. A detailed specification of the measures to link to facts can be easily postponed to the following conceptual design phase (see section 6.1.7), as can attribute hierarchies with roots in dimensions. Even if you can derive the attributes generally used for aggregation from preliminary workloads, you can create the draft structures of hierarchies in the conceptual design phase as you navigate functional dependencies represented in reconciled schemata. The subsequent process of hierarchy adjustment is still part of the requirement phase in principle, because it is based on users' specifications. Nevertheless, since it requires concepts and formalisms not discussed so far, it will be analyzed in section 6.1.3.

Last, but not least, one of the most important features of data warehouses is the representation of historical data, as mentioned in Chapter 1. For this reason, every fact needs a *historical interval* to be defined—that is, a period of time covered by the events stored in a data mart. The values of this interval typically range from three to five years. However, this is not a precise formula: very dynamic application domains can need only a one-year history, but it can take a history of more than five years to support very complex decision-making processes.

Table 4-4 shows an example of the requirement glossary that a data mart designer can create to manage supplies and sales for a supermarket chain in this phase. This is not much different from Lechtenbörger's usage table (2001). Note that no relationship between the

Fact	Dimensions	Measures	History
STOCK INVENTORY	product, date, warehouse	stocked quantity	1 year
SALES	product, date, store	sold quantity, receipts, discount	5 years
ORDER LINES	product, date, supplier	ordered quantity, receipts, discount	3 years

TABLE 4-4   Example of User Requirement Glossary

facts, the dimensions, and the measures found on the one side and the operational source schemata on the other side has been created yet. Those relationships will be established during conceptual design, when reconciled schemata will be studied under a new light to reveal the basic structure of a multidimensional schema.

To conclude this section, we emphasize that the automatic tools applying conceptual design algorithms give designers the opportunity to improve requirement analyses. Those tools help designers get a clear idea of the maximum potential that data marts are going to develop. But designers can also investigate specifications from a more realistic point of view as they carry out conceptual designs.

4.2.2   Preliminary Workload

The identification of facts, dimensions, and measures is strictly connected to the identification of *preliminary workloads*. This process essentially collects a set of users' specifications on analysis queries a data mart is going to issue frequently. In addition to information gathered through direct interaction with users, valuable information can become available after an accurate examination of reports currently used by an enterprise. It is important to clarify that this kind of information is absolutely preliminary. Users are asked for more details in the workload refinement phase after the conceptual design phase. The workload refinement phase aims at validating the conceptual schema created by designers and at laying the foundations of a functional logical and physical design. See section 7.1.5 for more details.

In this phase, a workload can be expressed in natural language, which will be useful in helping designers dispel their doubts about fact granularity and relevant measures. Furthermore, it can also be beneficial in coping with aggregation—namely regarding how hierarchies should be built on dimensions and which operators should be used for measure aggregation. For example, consider the workload shown in Table 4-5 and linked to the facts listed in Table 4-4. The information that this workload shows to designers is summed up by the following list.

Fact	Query
STOCK INVENTORY	What is the average quantity of each product made available monthly in every warehouse? Which product stocks ran out at least once last week at the same time in every warehouse? What's the daily trend of all the stocks grouped by product type?
SALES	What's the total amount per product sold last month? What are the daily receipts per store? What are the receipts per product category of a specific store on a specific day? What is the annual report of receipts per state per product?
ORDER LINES	What's the total amount of goods ordered from a specific supplier every year? What's the daily total amount ordered last month for a specific product type? What's the best discount given by each supplier last year and grouped by product category?

TABLE 4-5   An Example Preliminary Workload

As far as the STOCK INVENTORY fact is concerned,

- the hierarchy built on the product dimension must include at least the type attribute;
- the time hierarchy must include at least the day, week, and month attributes;
- the stocked quantity measure is added when aggregating along the hierarchies of warehouses and products;
- the average and minimum values of the stocked quantity measures are calculated when aggregating along the time hierarchy.

As far as the SALES fact is concerned,

- the hierarchy built on the product dimension must include at least the type and category attributes;
- the hierarchy built on the store dimension must include at least the state attribute;
- the time hierarchy must include at least the day, month, and year attributes;
- the sold quantity measure is added when aggregating along the hierarchies of stores and time;
- the receipts measure is added when aggregating along every hierarchy.

As far as the ORDER LINES fact is concerned,

- the hierarchy built on the product dimension must include at least the type and category attributes;
- the time hierarchy must include at least the day, month, and year attributes;
- the receipts measure is added when aggregating along the hierarchies of warehouses and products;
- the maximum value of the discount measure is calculated when aggregating along the hierarchies of time and products;
- the ordered quantity measure is added when aggregating along the hierarchies of products and time.

When it comes to attributes within hierarchies, note that hierarchies built on dimensions, which are common to different facts (the product dimension in the previous example), should be *completely* shared by facts, according to the *conformed dimensions principle*. For this reason, the type and category attributes are likely to be part of the hierarchy of products in all three facts shown by the preceding example. See section 5.2.4 for more details.

When it comes to assessing aggregation operators, their importance is due to the need to represent in a conceptual schema of a data mart how measures can be aggregated along hierarchies. Sections 6.1.7 and 9.1.7 show how the selection of the aggregation operators to be used dramatically affects the logical and conceptual design phases, respectively. See also section 5.2.9 for our considerations on *additivity*.

One more point regarding workloads involves the definition of temporal scenarios of queries affecting dynamic features of hierarchies (the so-called *slowly-changing dimensions* by Kimball, 1998). Without going into too much confusing detail, here's a small example that's used in section 5.4.3. Assume that users showed their interest in the sales fact with the `product`, `date`, and `store` dimensions, and that the preliminary workload includes a query for the total amount of sales in 2008. Each sale should be ascribed to sales managers, as sales manager is an attribute in the store hierarchy. This means that one person is in charge of sales for each store. Moreover, assume that sales managers change progressively due to staff turnover as time goes by. If Smith, former sales manager of EverMore, was replaced by Johnson in June 2008 to be assigned to EverMore2, what's the aggregation for the sales in 2008? In particular, should the sales carried out in EverMore until the end of June be attributed to Smith, the previous sales manager of this store, or to Johnson, the current sales manager? Or should neither be credited? Any interpretation of this query generates a different temporal scenario. In this phase, the main goal of designers is to understand which scenario users are interested in. Section 8.4 shows that logical design options may vary accordingly.

4.3 Goal-oriented Requirement Analysis

This section explains how the user requirement analysis for a data mart can be formally conducted using appropriate language in the scope of a mixed or requirement-driven design framework.

The first example of this approach was proposed by Bonifati et al., in 2001. According to their proposal, a goal-oriented approach should be used to design a data mart. Requirement analyses should be based on the goals of decision-makers in enterprises. *Abstraction sheets* are used to analyze their goals separately. The considerations on how goals and enterprise-specific activities are interrelated are written in natural language and added to those sheets.

NOTE *In the scope of requirement-driven design, other approaches to requirement analysis have been written by Bruckner et al., 2001; Prakash and Gosain, 2003; Paim and Castro, 2003; and Mazón et al., 2007a.*

The approach that we propose is based on the Tropos formalism, and it can be used for requirement-driven design frameworks or mixed ones (Giorgini et al., 2008). This approach adopts two different perspectives to conduct requirement analyses: decision-making modeling and organizational modeling. Decision-making modeling focuses on the requirements of enterprise decision-makers. This is the so-called *to-be analysis* according to the terminology of Winter and Strauch (2003). Organizational modeling hinges on stakeholders—the actors who take part in managing an enterprise. The organizational modeling plays a primary role in detecting facts and supporting the data-driven component of this approach (*as-is analysis*). The resulting diagrams relate enterprise-specific goals to facts, dimensions, and measures. These diagrams are then used for the conceptual design phase. If you adopt a requirement-driven design framework, you can directly turn the user requirement model created by Tropos into a conceptual schema that should be mapped onto data sources. (See section 6.5 for more details.) In a mixed design framework, the user requirements represented by Tropos play an active role in determining the part of operational schemata that designers should analyze, and in selecting facts, dimensions, and measures. (See section 6.4 for more details.)

In the following sections, we focus on a real-world case study conducted at the University of Trento, Italy, to provide more information on this approach. This case study addresses a business intelligence system in the banking industry. In particular, our focus involves the analysis of bank transactions (transaction number, transaction amount, internal and external automated teller machine transactions, and so on).

4.3.1   Introduction to Tropos

Tropos (Bresciani et al., 2004) is an agent-oriented methodology for software development. It is based on the *i* modeling framework* by Yu (1995), and it has two main features. First, the Tropos methodology is based on *agent* and *goal* concepts used to back every development stage, from analysis to implementation. Second, the early requirement analysis prior to design requirement specification plays a crucial role.

The main reason for managing the early requirement analysis phase is the need to develop a comprehensive, conceptual approach to model and analyze those processes involving multiple members—both people and software systems—and their specific intentions. In this way, you can establish a connection between functional and nonfunctional requirements of the system being developed and main stakeholders and stakeholders' intentions. Tropos manages four software development stages:

- **Early requirement analysis**   Closely studies organizations to understand problems arising in them.

- **Design requirement analysis**   Systems are described within their operating environments along with their foremost functions and features.

- **Architectural design**   The global system architecture is defined in terms of subsystems connected with each other by data, controls, and additional dependencies.

- **Working plan**   A detailed description of every software module behavior.

The Tropos methodology was successfully adopted in many application domains ranging from requirement analysis to process reengineering. In the following sections, we mention just a tiny part of the notation of the Tropos methodology that applies to requirement analysis for data marts.

- **Actors**   An actor stands for a business stakeholder. More precisely, an actor can model a physical or software *agent* (for example, Smith); a *role*, an abstraction of the behavior of one or more agents under given conditions (for example "sales analyst"); or a *position*, a set of roles generally played by individual agents (for example, "marketing manager"). Circles are used to graphically represent actors.

- **Strategic dependencies**   A strategic dependency is an agreement between two actors, such that one of them depends on the other to meet the agreement obligations. This agreement can consist of a goal to reach, a task to perform, or a resource to make available. In this scope, you should be mainly interested in agreements for *goals*, represented as ovals.

- **Actor diagram**   The actor diagram is a graph of actors bound by strategic dependencies. It is used to describe how actors depend on each other.

- **Rationale diagram**   This is used to represent the logical and rational bases ruling the relationships of actors with other actors. It looks like a bubble, where the goals of a given actor are analyzed and dependencies on the other actors are clarified. Goals can be divided into subgoals using the AND semantics (every subgoal must be reached) or the OR semantics (any one of those subgoals must be reached). Positive or negative contributions between goals are represented by arrows. Intuitively, a positive/negative contribution means that reaching the G goal encourages/discourages actors to reach/from reaching a new goal (G'). The + and ++ / – and – – marks are used to rate the value of contributions.

In the early requirement analysis phase for a general software system, an analyst identifies the stakeholders of a domain, models them within an actor diagram, and shows how they depend on each other to reach their goals. On the basis of those dependencies, analysts can answer *why*, *what*, and *how* questions on system features. The answers to *why* questions connect features to stakeholders' needs, preferences, and goals. Then analysts draw a rationale diagram per actor to adjust means to ends for every goal.

In the early requirement analysis phase for data marts, you should consider two different points of view: First, modeling organization environments for future data marts plays an important role (*organizational modeling*). This activity results in an actor diagram and a rationale diagram for every stakeholder. Then analysts should arrange rationale diagrams for decision-makers—main actors in the decision-making process—to collect functional and nonfunctional data mart–specific requirements (*decision-making modeling*). In the following sections, we study both points of view more closely with reference to our case study.

It is interesting how highly scalable this approach proves to be. In this regard, the association of an actor diagram with many rationale diagrams is fundamental to cope with complex application domains. Precisely, a detailed requirement analysis is based on rationale diagrams, whose complexity depends on the difficulty of each actor's decision-making tasks, but the complexity is not directly proportional to the size of the domain. Domain size in terms of stakeholder number directly affects actor diagrams, which never get overwhelmingly complex because they are represented at a higher abstraction level.

As to notation, we need to introduce a few concepts to apply the Tropos approach to data warehousing:

- **Facts**   From the standpoint of organizational modeling, a fact models a group of events taking place when an actor reaches a goal. From the standpoint of decision-making modeling, facts are properly considered as potential analysis items. Rectangles connected to goals graphically mark facts in diagrams.

- **Attributes**   An attribute is a field that is given a value to record a fact after reaching a goal. Small diamonds connected to goals graphically mark attributes in diagrams.

- **Dimensions**   A dimension is a property of a fact. This property describes an analysis coordinate of its specific fact. Dimensions can help decision-makers gain a different perspective on facts to reach an analysis goal. Small circles connected to goals graphically mark dimensions in diagrams.

- **Measures**   A measure is a numerical property of a fact. A measure specifies a quantitative feature of a fact, and it is relevant for the purposes of the decision-making process. Small squares connected to goals graphically mark measures in diagrams.

Table 4-6 lists all the marks used in diagrams.

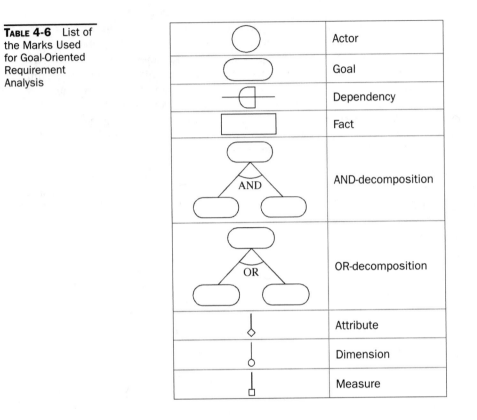

TABLE 4-6 List of the Marks Used for Goal-Oriented Requirement Analysis

4.3.2 Organizational Modeling

When you model organizations, you should follow a three-phase process. Each phase consists of an iterative process whose inputs are the diagrams resulting from the previous phase.

1. **Goal analysis**   Actor and rationale diagrams are drawn.
2. **Fact analysis**   Rationale diagrams are extended as facts are identified.
3. **Attribute analysis**   Rationale diagrams are further extended to specify the attributes connected to facts.

4.3.2.1 Goal Analysis

When you analyze goals, first create a representation of organization-relevant stakeholders, including internal and external actors and actors' social dependencies. To do this, create an actor diagram. The actors in the diagram should represent agents, roles, and positions in your organization.

Figure 4-2 shows a fraction of the actor diagram for our case study. The Customer actor depends on the Bank actor to reach the use bank services goal and depends on the ATM actor to reach the automatic money withdrawal goal. The Bank actor depends on ATM to reach the provide ATM services goal.

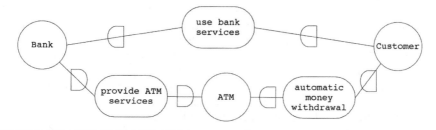

Figure 4-2   Actor diagram for the case study; circles and ovals mark actors and their goals, respectively.

The second step consists of studying every actor's goal more closely to draw a rationale diagram per actor (Giorgini et al., 2003). The goal analysis phase is completed as soon as all the goals relevant for every actor are specified and all the dependencies between actors are set.

Figure 4-3 shows part of the rationale diagram for the bank and focuses on three goals: gain new customers, manage loans, and provide customers with services.

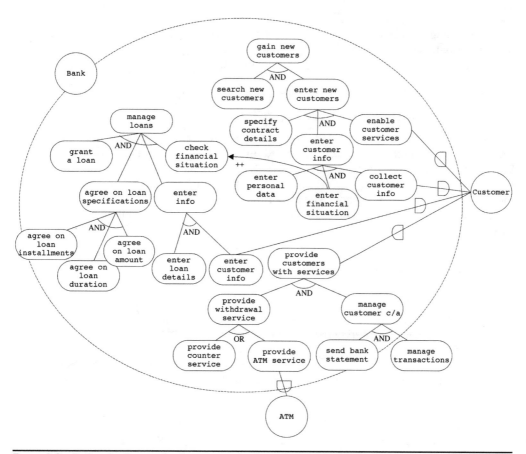

Figure 4-3   Rationale diagram for the Bank actor from the standpoint of organizational modeling

A few goals are internal and other goals are the result of the social dependencies structured in the previous actor diagram. For example, the manage loans and the gain new customers goals are internal goals of the Bank actor, and the provide customers with services goal is created to comply with the use bank services dependency set for the Customer actor.

Now goals can be AND-decomposed or OR-decomposed so that contribution relationships between goals can be detected. The gain new customers goal is AND-decomposed into the search new customers and the enter new customers goals. The enter new customers goal is in its turn AND-decomposed into the specify contract details, the enter customer info, and the enable customer services goals. The enter customer info is further broken down into the collect customer info, the enter personal data, and the enter financial situation goals. At this stage, you can discover new dependencies. For example, the Bank actor depends on its customers in order to collect their data.

Now you can conduct an analysis similar to the previous one to examine the manage loans goal AND-decomposed into the enter info (concerning specific loans), the check financial situation, the agree on loan specifications, and the grant a loan goals. Note that the check financial situation goal gets a positive contribution from the enter financial situation goal. This means that the stored data concerning each customer's financial situation obviously helps the bank check on the financial situation of a customer before granting a loan. The provide customers with services goal is AND-decomposed into the manage customer c/a and the provide withdrawal service goals. The latter is OR-decomposed into the provide counter service and provide ATM service goals.

4.3.2.2   Fact Analysis

The fact analysis phase aims at identifying all the facts relevant for organizations. Analysts explore rationale diagrams for every actor and link facts to goals to make rationale diagrams become more comprehensive.

Figure 4-4 shows an extended rationale diagram for the bank. This diagram hinges on the manage transactions goal. For example, the transactions, the debits, the withdrawals, and the POS payments facts are respectively joined to the manage transactions, the manage c/a debits, the manage withdrawals, and the manage POS payments goals.

4.3.2.3   Attribute Analysis

Attribute analysis aims at identifying all the attributes that are given a value when facts are recorded. First of all, analysts should closely study the extended rationale diagrams created in the previous phase. Then they should explore all the goal subgraphs to make rationale diagrams become more comprehensive and establish relationships between goals and the attributes required by goals. In this phase, note that attributes are mentioned without specifying any detail on the roles they play, such as dimensions or measures. More precisely, those attributes are simply data matched to the appropriate goals from the standpoint of organizational modeling.

In Figure 4-4, if you analyze the subgraph of the manage POS payments goal to which the POS payments fact is matched, you can add the POS value date, the POS date, the POS description, the POS c/a, the POS amount, and the POS card code attributes.

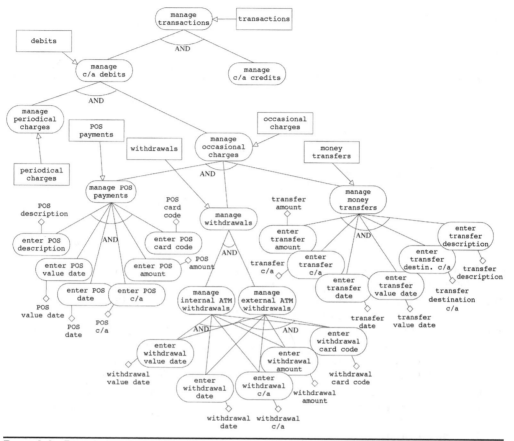

FIGURE 4-4 Extended rationale diagram for the Bank actor from the standpoint of organizational modeling

4.3.3 Decision-making Modeling

After the organizational modeling phase, our approach requires an additional type of analysis oriented to the goals of decision-makers—the main actors in the decision-making process. First, identify every decision-maker. Then stick to a four-step analysis procedure for every one of them:

1. **Goal analysis** Leads to rationale diagrams
2. **Fact analysis** Specifies facts in order to create extended rationale diagrams
3. **Dimensional analysis** Adds dimensions to extended rationale diagrams
4. **Measure analysis** Adds measures to extended rationale diagrams

4.3.3.1 Goal Analysis

The goal analysis phase initially examines actor diagrams for decision-makers just as in organizational modeling. After identifying decision-makers, you should study their dependencies. Then the goals matched to each decision-maker can be decomposed and

FIGURE 4-5
Rationale
diagram for the
`Financial
promoter`
decision-maker
from the
standpoint of
decision-making
modeling

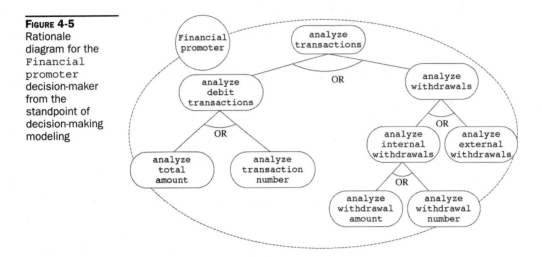

closely studied to draw a rationale diagram. Those goals can be completely different from those detected in the organizational modeling phase. They are an integral part of the decision-making process and may not be involved in a business operating process.

Figure 4-5 shows a rationale diagram for the `Financial promoter` decision-maker, and it hinges on the `analyze transactions` goal. The `analyze transactions` goal is OR-decomposed into the `analyze debit transactions` and the `analyze withdrawals` goals that are decomposed in turn. The `analyze debit transactions` goal is OR-decomposed into the `analyze total amount` and the `analyze transaction number` goals. The `analyze withdrawals` goal is OR-decomposed into the `analyze internal withdrawals` and the `analyze external withdrawals` goals.

4.3.3.2   Fact Analysis

Analysts should extend rationale diagrams just as in organizational modeling as they identify facts and match those facts to decision-makers' goals. Facts stand for business events that take place dynamically in an organization. They are usually imported from the extended rationale diagrams created in the organizational modeling phase, because decision-makers' goals are often connected to information flow from the business operating processes. For this reason, organization activity-related facts play a vital role in reaching decision-making goals. For example, Figure 4-6 shows how to join the `transactions` fact, which was detected in the organizational modeling phase, to the `analyze transactions` goal. Sometimes analysts can also add new facts as they directly analyze rationale diagrams of decision-makers.

4.3.3.3   Dimensional Analysis

In this phase, each fact is connected to those dimensions that decision-makers consider essential for every decision-making goal to be reached. Figure 4-6 shows that dimensions are connected to the goals matched to a fact. For example, the `c/a` and the `month` dimensions are specified to reach the `analyze total amount` goal.

4.3.3.4   Measure Analysis

Next, analysts should connect a set of measures to every fact previously identified. For example, Figure 4-6 shows that the `average amount` and the `total amount` measures are identified for the `analyze total amount` fact.

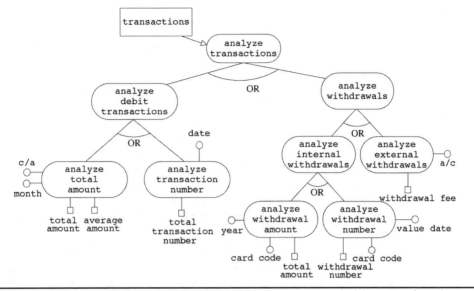

Figure 4-6 Extended rationale diagram for the `Financial promoter` decision-maker from the standpoint of decision-making modeling

Now you can consider the documentation on requirements as complete. Note that organizational modeling leads to representing the main business data on which operating processes are based so that you can draw a general map of the most relevant attributes that should be in your operational database. Decision-making modeling sums up the role played by user requirement glossaries (see Table 4-4) and by preliminary workload descriptions (see Table 4-5) in glossary-based requirement analysis. Sections 6.4 and 6.5 show how the drawn diagrams can find their application in the scope of the mixed approach and the requirement-driven approach, respectively.

4.4 Additional Requirements

The specifications on facts and preliminary workload are crucial for the conceptual design of our data mart. However, additional specifications are equally significant for the following project phases, and designers should collect them from end users and information system administrators.[1] Those specifications concern the following:

- **Logical and physical design** Chapters 9 and 12 show that logical and physical design are related to a set of constraints posed by data warehouse designers and corporate IT staff in close collaboration. For example, those constraints are related to the space freed up to optimize data mart performance by means of materialized views (see section 9.2) and indexes (see section 12.2).

---

[1]Other methodological approaches classify a few of these specifications in the infrastructure planning and design phase. Nevertheless, we discuss them in this chapter to emphasize that users and information system administrators actively take part in drawing up those specifications.

- **Data-staging design**   The main topic to be discussed in this regard is connected to the frequency of data staging. End users and operational database administrators should take part in this decision. End users should specify the minimum update frequency for the information they need. Administrators should provide information on operating requirements related to operational sources. (*Is there any time during a day or a week for the source to be offline or be working at low capacity? How long is this time frame?*) Typically, frequency values for data staging range from a day to a week. Special real-time applications can also require hourly updates.

- **Data quality**   Designers should record end user expectations concerning data quality, especially in terms of data accuracy and freshness—the latter is tightly connected to the frequency of data staging discussed above. The IT staff should bring to the forefront the main quality problems in data sources. This helps designers setting criteria and thresholds to discard faulty data during ETL. In addition, senior managers should start sketching a reliable corporate workflow to ensure data quality certification.

- **Data warehouse architecture**   The collaboration with corporate IT staff is vital to making crucial decisions on architecture implementation, such as number of layers, independent or dependent data marts, and reconciled layer materialization. In particular, database administrators are very familiar with the difficulties and bottlenecks due to their information system architecture and business organization.

- **Data analysis applications**   After investigating the types of queries end users expect to issue to their data marts and the analytic reports IT staff members are usually required to draw up, you can get useful tips on the analysis tool features to consider. In particular, it can be useful to specify a small number of data mart user groups, each characterized by a class of queries, level of IT skills, and tools oriented to reporting or multidimensional analysis (OLAP). See section 7.1.6 for more details on this point.

- **Startup schedule**   The schedule to start up a data warehouse system needs to be decided with support from database administrators who provide their technical expertise and with end users to ensure their complete collaboration.

- **Training schedule**   It is fundamentally important that users be carefully and promptly trained so that enterprise-related skills and know-how can be properly updated and help pave the way for a new data warehouse system to be welcomed. Designers should arrange for a training schedule and should also organize follow-up sessions for user groups with different skill levels and analysis needs, as necessary.

5 CHAPTER

Conceptual Modeling

While it is now universally recognized that a data mart is based on a multidimensional view of data, there is still no agreement on how to implement its conceptual design from user requirements. However, it is well known that an accurate conceptual design is the fundamental requirement for the construction of a well-documented database that completely meets requirements. Use of the Entity-Relationship model (ERM) is quite widespread throughout companies as a conceptual tool for standard documentation and design of relational databases. Many efforts are made to use it in design of nonrelational systems as well (Fahrner and Vossen, 1995). However, it is oriented to queries that follow associations among data rather than summarize the data, so it turns out to be a bad choice in the case of data marts. According to Kimball (1996), Entity-Relationship schemata "cannot be understood by users nor be navigated usefully by DBMS software. Entity-Relationship schemata cannot be adopted as the basis for enterprise data warehouses."

The ERM is actually expressive enough to represent the majority of concepts necessary for data mart modeling. However, the basic ERM is not able to accurately highlight the distinctive features of the multidimensional model. For this reason, its use for data mart modeling proves to be not very intuitive. Additionally, the use of the ERM in this context is not very efficient from the notational viewpoint, as the examples clearly show in the following sections.

In many cases, designers base their data mart designs on the logical level—that is, they directly define *star schemata* that are the standard implementation of the multidimensional model in relational systems. (See Chapter 8 for more details on star schemata.) A star schema is nothing but a relational schema; it contains only the definition of a set of relations and integrity constraints. Using star schemata as a support for conceptual design equates to designing a relational database without first designing an Entity-Relationship schema. Or, worse still, it is tantamount to starting to create a complex software from the coding phase without any static, dynamic, or functional design schema. This practice generally leads to rather discouraging results from the viewpoint of responsiveness to requirements, ease of maintenance, and reuse. In the case of data warehouses, star schemata make things worse because they are almost completely denormalized and do not properly code those functional dependencies on which the definition of hierarchies is based.

For all of these reasons, current literature has proposed different original approaches to multidimensional modeling, some of which are based on ERM extensions, others on Unified Modeling Language (UML) extensions. Table 5-1 lists the main models proposed so far and shows whether each one is defined as a conceptual or logical model and whether it is associated with a design methodology. It also specifies whether the conceptual models are based on the ERM or UML, or if they are ad hoc models. The remainder of this paragraph briefly outlines the conceptual models considered the most representative and aims at highlighting their similarities in expressive power.

Figure 5-1 shows a class diagram for analysis of purchase orders (Luján-Mora et al., 2006). It uses an object-based formalism, more precisely a UML extension. Purchase orders play the role of facts. A UML class, whose attributes are the fact measures, models purchase orders. The dimensions are the supplier, the date, and the item ordered. Both the dimensions and different levels of aggregation describing them are represented as classes. Aggregations (represented in UML by small diamonds) connect the facts and the dimensions, and many-to-one associations link the different levels of aggregation.

On the contrary, the model used in Figure 5-2 is an extension of the ERM (Franconi, 1999). The schema in the example analyzes the calls made through a telephone company. Here, the fact is called *target* and the measures *properties*. You can represent relevant aggregations (*aggregate entities*) and use the specialization hierarchies of the ERM to list the values of one level of aggregation.

Model	Level	Methodology
Abelló et al. (2006)	Conceptual (UML)	No
Agrawal et al. (1995)	Logical	No
Cabibbo and Torlone (1998)	Logical	Yes
Datta and Thomas (1997)	Conceptual (ad hoc)	No
Franconi and Sattler (1999)	Conceptual (ERM)	No
Golfarelli et al. (1998)	Conceptual (ad hoc)	Yes
Gyssens and Lakshmanan (1997)	Logical	No
Hüsemann et al. (2000)	Conceptual (ad hoc)	Yes
Li and Wang (1996)	Logical	No
Luján-Mora et al. (2006)	Conceptual (UML)	Yes
Nguyen et al. (2000)	Conceptual (UML)	No
Pedersen and Jensen (1999)	Conceptual (ad hoc)	No
Sapia et al. (1998)	Conceptual (ERM)	No
Tryfona et al. (1999)	Conceptual (ERM)	No
Tsois et al. (2001)	Conceptual (ad hoc)	No
Vassiliadis (1998)	Conceptual (ad hoc)	No

TABLE 5-1   Approaches to Multidimensional Modeling

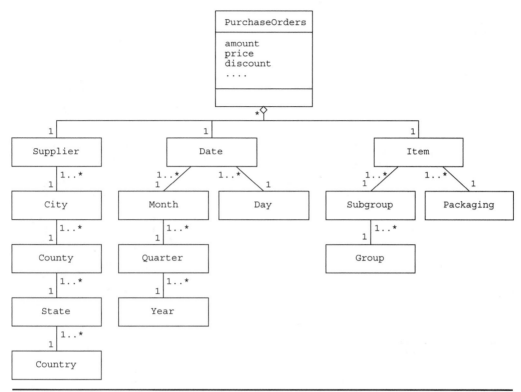

Figure 5-1 A UML class diagram for purchase order analysis (Luján-Mora, 2006)

Finally, Figure 5-3 shows a *fact schema* for the analysis of checking accounts (Hüsemann et al., 2000). In addition to facts, dimensions, and measures, nonusable attributes for the aggregation (*property attributes*), *optional attributes,* and *alternative aggregation paths* are represented. Specifically, the extensional meaning of the alternative aggregation path in Figure 5-3 is that either a value of profession or a value of branch is linked with a value of customerId.

The remainder of the chapter describes in depth the Dimensional Fact Model, proposed by Golfarelli, Maio, and Rizzi in 1998 and constantly enriched and refined during the following ten years to optimally fit the variety of modeling situations that may be faced in real projects. We will present basic concepts and more advanced constructs in sections 5.1 and 5.2, respectively. Section 5.3 deals with extensional properties and defines aggregation semantics. Section 5.4 tackles specific features tied to the representation of time. Section 5.5 shows how to overlap fact schemata. Section 5.6 proposes a formalization of the intensional and extensional properties of the model.

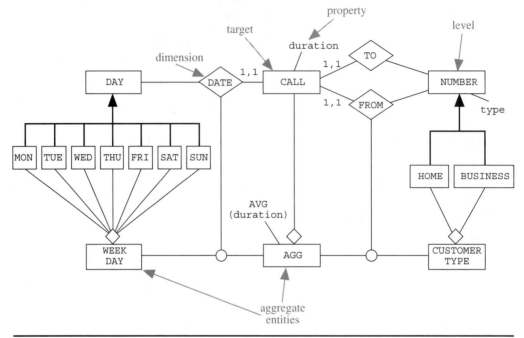

FIGURE 5-2   An ERM–based conceptual schema for phone call analysis (Franconi and Sattler, 1999)

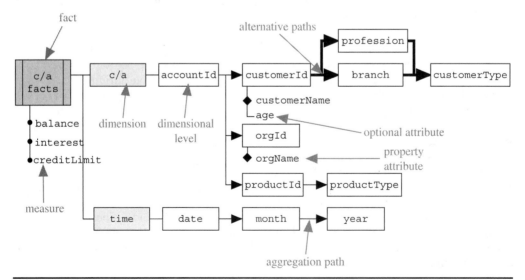

FIGURE 5-3   A fact schema for the analysis of checking accounts (Hüsemann et al., 2000)

5.1 The Dimensional Fact Model: Basic Concepts

The *Dimensional Fact Model (DFM)* is a conceptual model created specifically to function as data mart design support. It is essentially graphic and based on the multidimensional model. The goals of the DFM are to

- lend effective support to conceptual design;
- create an environment in which user queries may be formulated intuitively;
- make communication possible between designers and end users with the goal of formalizing requirement specifications;
- build a stable platform for logical design;
- provide clear and expressive design documentation.

These characteristics make the DFM an optimal candidate for use in real application contexts. In particular, we prefer this model to others presented in the preceding paragraph because we consider its graphic formalism particularly simple, expressive, and appropriate for communication between designers and end users. Moreover, the availability of a semiautomatic technique to obtain conceptual schemata from operational source schemata facilitates the designer's work, especially when conceptual design is implemented within a design tool.

The conceptual representation generated by the DFM consists of a set of *fact schemata*. Fact schemata basically model facts, measures, dimensions, and hierarchies.

> **Fact**
> A *fact* is a concept relevant to decision-making processes. It typically models a set of events taking place within a company.

Examples of facts in the commercial domain are sales, shipments, purchases, and complaints. In the healthcare industry, some interesting examples are admissions, discharges, transfers, surgeries, and access to emergency services. In the financial industries, stock exchange transactions, checking account and credit card balances, contract creation, loan disbursement, and the like are considered facts, as are flights, car rentals, and nights' stay in the tourism industry.

It is essential that a fact have dynamic properties or evolve in some way over time. Indeed, few of the concepts represented in a database are completely static. Even the association between cities and states can change if state boundaries are modified. For this reason, the distinction between facts and other concepts must be based on the average frequency of change or on the specific interests of users. For example, the assignment of a new sales manager to a department occurs less frequently than the promotion of a product. While the association between promotions and products is a good candidate to be modeled as a fact, the association between sales managers and departments generally is not, unless users are interested in monitoring the transfers of sales managers to find out the correlations between department managers and how much that department sells. See section 5.4.3 for a more in-depth discussion on the dynamic properties of fact schemata.

> **Measure**
> A *measure* is a numerical property of a fact and describes a quantitative fact aspect that is relevant to analysis.

For example, each sale is measured by the number of units sold, the unit price, and the total receipts. The reason why measures must preferably be numeric is that they are generally used to make calculations. A fact can also have no measures, as in the case when you might be interested in recording only the *occurrence* of an event. In this case, the fact schema is said to be *empty*. Section 5.3.5 discusses some specific features of empty schemata.

> ### Dimension
> A *dimension* is a fact property with a finite domain and describes an analysis coordinate of the fact.

A fact generally has more *dimensions* that define its minimum representation granularity. Typical dimensions for the sales fact are products, stores, and dates. In this case, the basic information that can be represented is product sales in one store in one day. At this level of granularity, it is not possible to distinguish between sales made by different employees or at different times of day. Because facts are generally dynamic, a fact schema will almost certainly have at least one temporal dimension whose granularity can vary from the minute to the month (more probably, the day or week).

The connection between measures and dimensions is expressed at the extensional level (that is, at a data level rather than at a schema level) by the event concept we informally define here, while referring you to its formal properties in section 5.6.3.

> ### Primary Event
> A *primary event* is a particular occurrence of a fact, identified by one n-ple made up of a value for each dimension. A value for each measure is associated with each primary event.

In reference to sales for example, a possible primary event records that 10 packages of Shiny detergent were sold for total sales of $25 on 10/10/2008 in the SmartMart store. As this example shows, dimensions are normally used to identify and select primary events.

On the basis of the concepts introduced so far, you can design a simple fact schema for sales in this chain of stores. Figure 5-4 shows that a fact is represented by a box that displays the fact name along with the measure names. Small circles represent the dimensions, which are linked to the fact by straight lines.

A fact expresses a many-to-many association between dimensions. For this reason, the Entity-Relationship schema corresponding to a fact schema consists mainly of an *n*-ary

Figure 5-4
A simple fact
schema for sales

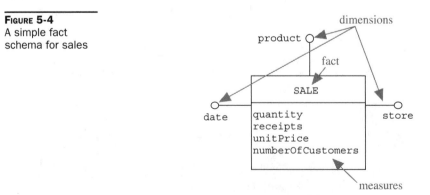

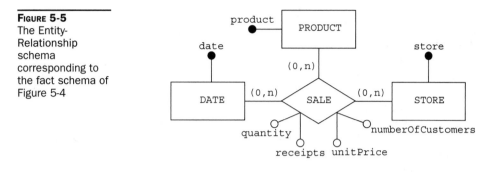

FIGURE 5-5
The Entity-Relationship schema corresponding to the fact schema of Figure 5-4

relationship, which models the fact, among entities that model dimensions. The measures are attributes of this relationship. Figure 5-5 shows the Entity-Relationship schema corresponding to the fact schema of Figure 5-4. Clearly, though the ERM is expressive enough to show facts, dimensions, and measures, it does not represent these concepts as first-class citizens.

Note that some multidimensional models in the literature are focused on the symmetrical treatment of dimensions and measures (Agrawal et al., 1995; Gyssen and Lakshmanan, 1997). This is an important result from the viewpoint of uniformity in the logical model and flexibility of online analytical processing (OLAP) operators. Despite that, we believe that you should distinguish between measures and dimensions at the conceptual level, because this enables logical design to be aimed more at reaching the efficiency required by data warehouse applications.

Before defining what a hierarchy means, we should introduce the concept of dimensional attribute.

Dimensional Attribute
The general term *dimensional attributes* stands for the dimensions and other possible attributes, always with discrete values, that describe them.

For example, a product is described by its type, by the category to which it belongs, by its brand, and by the department in which it is sold. Then `product`, `type`, `category`, `brand`, and `department` will be dimensional attributes. The relationships among the dimensional attributes are expressed by hierarchies.

Hierarchy
A *hierarchy* is a directed tree[1] whose nodes are dimensional attributes and whose arcs model many-to-one associations between dimensional attribute pairs. It includes a dimension, positioned at the tree's root, and all of the dimensional attributes that describe it.

---

[1]Graph theory reminds us that a *tree* is an acyclic connected graph (Berge, 1985). A directed tree is a tree with a *root* or a node called v_0 from which you can reach all the other nodes via directed paths. Within a directed tree, only one directed path connects the v_0 root to each of the other v_i nodes. Given a node called v, into which an arc called a enters and from which $b, c, d \ldots$ arcs exit, we will call the node from which a exits the *parent* of v and the nodes into which $b, c, d \ldots$ enter the *children* of v. In addition to its parent, the *predecessors* of v are the parents of its parent and so on. In addition to its children, the *descendants* of v are the children of its children and so on.

Do not confuse the term *hierarchy* used in this context with the identical term used in Entity-Relationship modeling, where it refers to specialization links between entities (IS-A hierarchies). In the multidimensional modeling context, *hierarchy* refers instead to associative links of different kinds in a way that is not dissimilar to aggregation hierarchies in object-oriented models. For example, in the `product` dimension hierarchy you will have an arc from `product` to `type` to express the type of each product, an arc from `product` to `brand` to express its brand, an arc from `category` to `type` to express the fact that all the drink type products belong to the food category, an arc from `category` to `department` to express the fact that all of the food category products are sold in the food department, and so on. In relational terminology, each arc in a hierarchy models a *functional dependency* between two attributes:

$$\text{product} \rightarrow \text{type, product} \rightarrow \text{brand,}$$
$$\text{type} \rightarrow \text{category, category} \rightarrow \text{department}$$

Because the transitive property applies to functional dependencies, each directed path inside a hierarchy represents in turn a functional dependency between the start and end attributes. For example, `product`→`type` and `type`→`category` imply `product`→`category`.

Figure 5-6 shows how you may add hierarchies built on dimensions to enhance the fact schema of Figure 5-4. Dimensional attributes are represented by circles and are connected by lines that mark the hierarchy arcs and express functional dependencies. For example, the city where a store is located defines the state to which that store belongs. Hierarchies are structured like trees with their roots in dimensions. For this reason, you should not explicitly show arc directions as each one of them is implicitly oriented in a direction moving away from the root.

Figure 5-6 shows a typical temporal hierarchy that ranges from `date` to `year`. A fact can include more than one temporal hierarchy modeling different dynamic properties. For example, a shipments fact schema may include a hierarchy built on the shipping date and one built on the order date. Other frequently used hierarchies are geographical hierarchies,

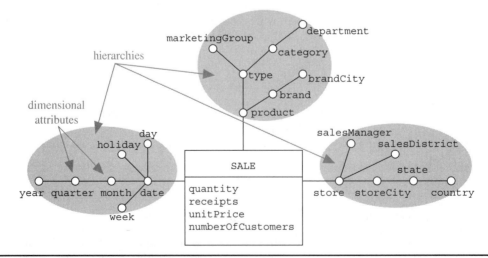

Figure 5-6   Enhanced fact schema for sales

hierarchies related to company organization charts, and part-component hierarchies. Figure 5-6 shows an example of geographical hierarchy as one built on the store dimension.

NOTE *All of the attributes and measures within a fact schema must have different names. You can differentiate similar names, if you qualify them with the name of the dimensional attribute that comes before them in hierarchies (for example,* storeCity *and* brandCity*).*

The convention proposed by Kimball et al., (1998) provides for each name to be built from three components: an *object* (client, product, city...), a *classification* (average, total, date, description...), and a *qualifier* (start, primary...). For example, you may then have a checkingAccountStartDate or a primaryProductDescription.

The available functional dependencies establish many-to-one associations between the values of a dimension and those of each dimensional attribute in the corresponding hierarchy. For example, a many-to-one association exists between products and product types (a product is of one type, a type identifies a product set). As a result, each n-ple of values within any set of dimensional attributes is associated with a set of value n-ples within the dimensions, or with a set of primary events. This makes it possible to use hierarchies to define the way you can aggregate primary events and effectively select them for decision-making processes. While the dimension in which a hierarchy takes root defines its finest aggregation granularity, the other dimensional attributes correspond to a gradually increasing granularity. This concept is set out in the definition of secondary events as we informally propose here.

Secondary Events

Given a set of dimensional attributes (generally belonging to separate hierarchies), each n-ple of their values identifies a *secondary event* that aggregates all of the corresponding primary events. Each secondary event is associated with a value for each measure that sums up all the values of the same measure in the corresponding primary events.

For example, sales can be grouped according to the category of products sold, to the month when sales were made, to the city in which stores are located, or according to any combination of those. Let's choose storeCity, product, and month as dimensional attributes for our aggregation. The n-ple (storeCity: 'Miami', product: 'Shiny', month: '10/2008') identifies a secondary event that aggregates all of the Shiny product sales in October 2008 in Miami stores. In other words, it aggregates all of the primary events corresponding to the n-ples where the product value is Shiny, the value of store is any store in Miami, and the value of date ranges from 10/01/2008 to 10/31/2008. The value of the receipts measure in this secondary event will be expressed as total receipts related to the sales it aggregates. See section 5.3 for an in-depth discussion on complex problems connected to aggregations.

Now we can make a quick comparison with the Entity-Relationship schema corresponding to the fact schema in Figure 5-6, which is shown in Figure 5-7. Note that each dimensional attribute (dimensions included) corresponds to an entity, which has that attribute as an identifier. Also note that a many-to-one relationship represents each arc in the hierarchies. From this viewpoint, the hierarchy notation adopted in fact schemata can be interpreted as a simplification of the Entity-Relationship notation, where the representation of relationships is simplified (their names and their multiplicity, which is always many-to-one, are not shown) and where just an identifier is shown for each entity.

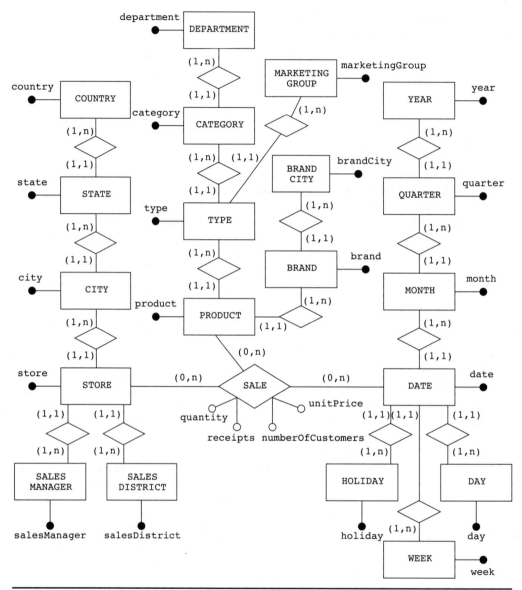

FIGURE 5-7   Entity-Relationship schema corresponding to the fact schema of Figure 5-6

5.2 Advanced Modeling

The concepts introduced in this paragraph, along with their corresponding graphic constructs, are descriptive and cross-dimensional attributes; convergences; shared, incomplete, and recursive hierarchies; multiple and optional arcs; and additivity (Rizzi, 2006). Although they are not necessary in the simplest and most common modeling conditions, they do prove very useful to best express the multitude of conceptual nuances that characterize actual scenarios. In particular, we will show that the introduction of some constructs generally makes hierarchies no longer mere trees, but graphs.

5.2.1   Descriptive Attributes

Many times, we find that it is important to give additional information on a dimensional attribute in a hierarchy, although it may not be very interesting to use this information as aggregation criteria. For example, users may find it useful to know the address of each store, but they may hardly want to sort out sales by store address. Descriptive attributes represent this type of information in fact schemata.

A *descriptive attribute* is functionally determined by a dimensional attribute of a hierarchy and specifies a property of this attribute. Descriptive attributes often are tied to dimensional attributes by one-to-one associations and do not actually add useful levels of aggregation. Sometimes, they have domains with continuous values, so they cannot be used for aggregation at all. Some examples are a store's address and telephone number as well as product weight.

Descriptive attributes are always the "leaves" of hierarchies.[2] Figure 5-8 shows that horizontal lines mark them graphically in the DFM. Figure 5-9 shows the representation of the fact schema of Figure 5-8 according to the ERM. Note that you can model descriptive attributes as attributes of the entities corresponding to dimensional attributes.

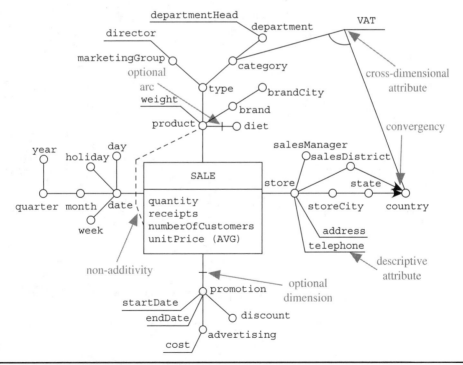

FIGURE 5-8   Complete fact schema for sales

---

[2]A tree *leaf* is a node without any children.

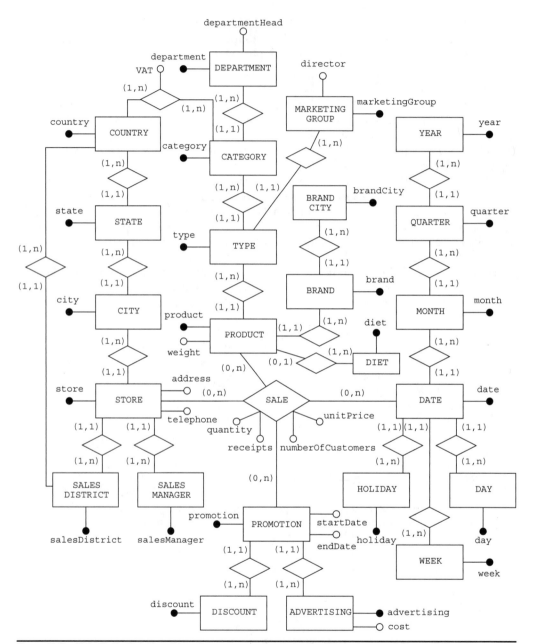

Figure 5-9   This Entity-Relationship schema corresponds to the fact schema of Figure 5-8.

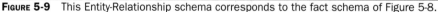

A descriptive attribute can also be directly connected to a fact if it describes primary events, but it is neither possible nor interesting to use it to identify single events or even to make calculations (otherwise, it would be a dimension or a measure, respectively). For example, consider Figure 5-10, which shows the fact schema for shipments. The order, shipping, and

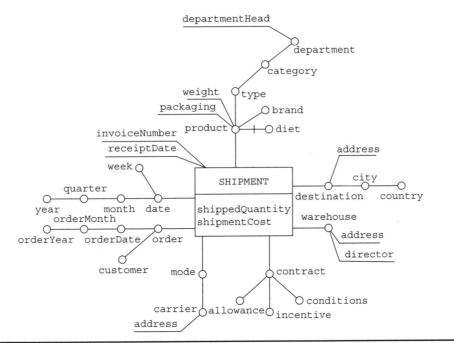

Figure 5-10   Fact schema for shipments

receipt dates must be represented. While it is useful to define the order and shipping dates as dimensions and build two different temporal hierarchies on them, you should probably not represent the receipt date as a dimension as well. However, representing a date as a measure causes problems because the only applicable aggregation operators would be MAX and MIN. For this reason, you can accurately represent the receipt date as a descriptive attribute of the SHIPMENT fact. Keep in mind that in order to correctly link a descriptive attribute directly to the fact, you will have to give it a single value for each primary event. In the case of shipments, the representation adopted for receiptDate would not be correct if separate shipments received by a customer on different dates could be made for the same order and the same product.

5.2.2   Cross-Dimensional Attributes

A *cross-dimensional attribute* is a dimensional or descriptive attribute whose value is defined by the combination of two or more dimensional attributes, possibly belonging to different hierarchies. For example, if a product's value added tax (VAT) depends both on the product category and on the country where the product is sold, you can use a cross-dimensional attribute to represent it. Figure 5-8 shows this example joining the arcs that define a product's VAT with a circular arc. Figure 5-9 shows that the equivalent Entity-Relationship representation involves a VAT association between the COUNTRY and CATEGORY entities. Figure 5-11 gives another example showing DFM modeling for the animal sighting fact. Here, the area and the species attributes jointly define the residentPopulation attribute that gives an estimate of the number of specimens of each animal species who live in each area.

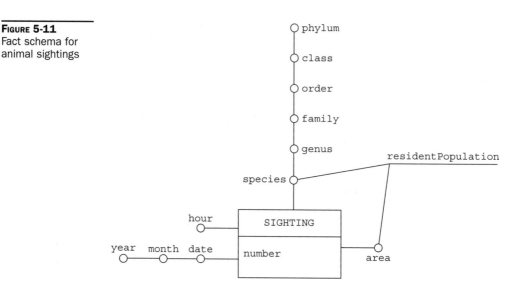

5.2.3   Convergence

The concept of *convergence* deals with the structure of hierarchies. In particular, hierarchies may not be real trees because two or more distinct directed paths may connect two specific dimensional attributes on the condition that each one of them still represents a functional dependency. Look at the example of the `store` geographical hierarchy in Figure 5.8. Stores are grouped into cities, which in turn are grouped into states belonging to countries. Assume that stores are also grouped into sales districts and that no inclusive relationship exists between districts and states. Assume also that each district is nevertheless part of exactly one country—the same country to which the store city belongs. If this is the case, each store belongs to one country alone, independent of the path followed:

store→storeCity→state→country or
store→salesDistrict→country

Two or more arcs belonging to the same hierarchy and ending at the same dimensional attribute mark convergences in fact schemata. If a convergence exists, a tree structure can no longer define arc directions uniquely. Figure 5-8 shows that you have to add arrows to converging arcs. On the corresponding Entity-Relationship schema of Figure 5-9, the convergence could be modeled by adding an explicit constraint stating that the association cycle between the STORE, STATE, CITY, COUNTRY, and SALES DISTRICT entities is redundant.

If there are apparently similar attributes, this does not always result in a convergence. For example, look at the `brandCity` attribute in the `product` dimension, which represents the city where products in one brand are manufactured, and at the `storeCity` attribute in the `store` dimension. Both city attributes obviously have different meaning and must be represented separately because a product manufactured in one city may also be sold in other cities.

FIGURE 5-12
Redundant
convergence (left)
and its correct
representation
(right)

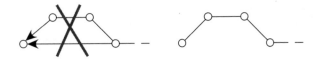

Finally, look at Figure 5-12. Note that a hierarchy like this, in which one of the alternate paths does not include intermediate attributes, does not have a reason to exist. The convergence is completely obvious in virtue of the transitive property holding for functional dependencies.

5.2.4   Shared Hierarchies

Entire portions of hierarchies are frequently replicated two or more times in fact schemata. Temporal hierarchies are a classic example. Two or more date-type dimensions with different meanings can easily exist in the same fact, and you may need to build a month-year hierarchy on each one of them. Another example is a geographical hierarchy built on all the `city` attributes in a schema. Figure 5-8 shows that two exist in the sales fact schema: `storeCity` and `brandCity`. All of the attributes in a fact schema must have distinct names to avoid ambiguity. This would force you to qualify your attribute names and strain your notation uselessly: this would then result in `brandState`, `brandCountry`, `storeState`, and `storeCountry`.

For this reason, we introduce an abbreviated graphic notation that emphasizes the sharing of your hierarchies and allows you to adopt ad hoc logical design solutions (see section 9.1.3). Figure 5-13 shows an example of a fact schema in which the fact consists of

FIGURE 5-13
Shared hierarchy
and roles in the
phone calls fact
schema and
equivalent schema
without shared
hierarchies

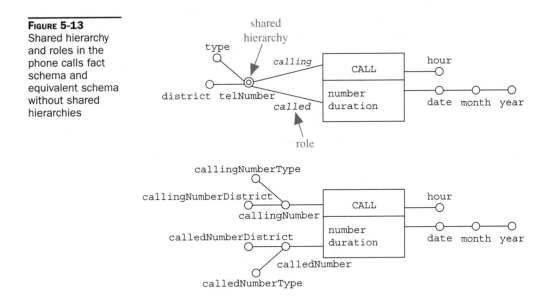

Figure 5-14

Shared hierarchies
and roles in the
shipments fact
schema

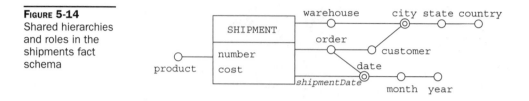

telephone calls made with the number calling, number called, date, and hour of the call as dimensions. A double circle represents and emphasizes the first attribute to be shared (telNumber). It should always be implicitly clear that all descendants of shared attributes are shared, too. If one or more descendants of the shared attributes should not be shared in turn, you would then need to represent those hierarchies separately.

When hierarchies are shared starting from their dimensions, you need to add a *role* that specifies its significance to each incoming arc (calling and called in Figure 5-13). Figure 5-14 shows the case of city. Here, you can instead omit the role as its parents implicitly define it (the *warehouse* city, the *customer* city).

5.2.5   Multiple Arcs

Hierarchies most commonly include attributes connected to their parents by to-one associations. However, it may be useful or even necessary to also include attributes that can take multiple values for each single value of their parent attributes.

Look at the fact schema that models book sales in a bookstore. Its dimensions are date and book. It would certainly be interesting to aggregate and select sales on the basis of book authors. However, it would not be accurate to model author as a dimensional child attribute of book because many different authors can write many books. Figure 5-15 shows the notation that we suggest. It graphically requires you to double the arc from book to author. In general, the meaning of a multiple arc that goes from an attribute called *a* to an attribute called *b* is that a many-to-many association exists between *a* and *b*. In other words, a single value you give to *a* can correspond to many values of *b*, and vice versa. Section 5.3.4 will show you that you need to give each multiple arc a coefficient that defines a *weight* for this many-to-many association so that aggregation can be consistently defined along hierarchies that also include multiple arcs.

A multiple arc may enter a dimension rather than any dimensional attribute. For instance, in the healthcare industry, if you wanted to model a fact related to hospital admissions, relevant dimensions could be admission dates, admitted patient identifications, and the departments into which the admission occurred. As a matter of fact, you would find it useful to be able to aggregate and select admissions on the basis of the diagnoses issued.

Figure 5-15

Fact schema for
book sales

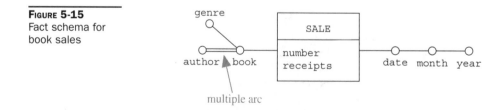

FIGURE 5-16
Fact schema for
hospital
admissions

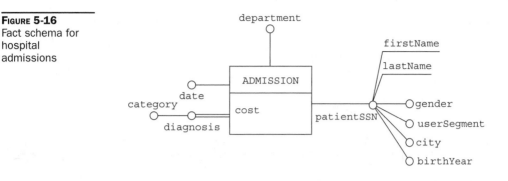

But multiple diagnoses often correspond to a single admission, each one belonging to a
category. Figure 5-16 shows that you can turn the start arc in the `diagnosis` dimension
into a multiple arc to model this scenario in that fact schema. As discussed in section 5.3.4,
when a multiple arc enters a dimension, the semantics of aggregation becomes more complex.

5.2.6   Optional Arcs

Optionality is used to model scenarios for which an association represented in a fact schema
is not defined for a subset of events. Optional arcs are marked with a dash. If *r* is the
optional arc, it is worth singling out two remarkable cases: (1) *r* determines a dimensional
attribute called *a*, and (2) *r* determines a dimension called *d*. In case (1), if *b* is the
dimensional attribute that determines *a* through *r*, the meaning of optionality is that *a* and
all the possible descendents in its hierarchy may be undefined for one or more values of *b*.
For example, Figure 5-8 shows the `diet` attribute in the sales fact schema. This attribute is
given a value (such as cholesterol-free, gluten-free, or sugar-free) only for food. Its value is
null for the other products. Note that the minimum multiplicity of the association from
PRODUCT to DIET is 0 rather than 1 in the Entity-Relationship representation of Figure 5-9.
In case (2), we state that the *d* dimension is optional—that is, some primary events exist that
are identified only by the other dimensions. For example, the `promotion` dimension in the
sales schema is optional. This means that the value of `promotion` will be 'No promotion'
for some product-store-date combinations.

When two or more optional arcs exit from the same attribute, you can specify their
coverage—that is, establish a relationship between the different options involved. In a similar
way to the coverage of specialization hierarchies in the ERM, two parameters, independent of
each other, can characterize the coverage of a set of optional arcs. Let *a* then be a dimensional
attribute from which optional arcs exit, traveling toward the $b_1, \ldots, b_m$ child attributes:

- The coverage is *total* if a value of at least one of the children is linked to each value
  of *a*. If, instead, values of *a* exist for which all of the children are undefined, the
  coverage is called *partial*.

- The coverage is *disjoint* if you have a value for at most one of the children
  corresponding to each value of *a*. If, instead, values of *a* exist linking to values of
  two or more children, the coverage is called *overlapping*.

Altogether, you have four types of coverage, marked with T-D, T-O, P-D, and P-O.
Figure 5-17 shows an example of optionality marked with its coverage. With three types

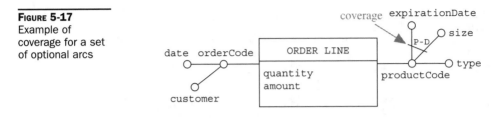

FIGURE 5-17
Example of
coverage for a set
of optional arcs

of products (food, clothing, and household), coverage proves to be partial and disjoint because `expirationDate` and `size` are defined only for food and clothing, respectively.

5.2.7 Incomplete Hierarchies

Let $a_1 \ldots, a_n$ be a sequence of attributes that form a path in a fact schema hierarchy (for example, `city`, `county`, `state`, `country`). We have so far implicitly taken for granted that each value of a_1 corresponds to a specific value of each one of the other path attributes. In the example, this is certainly true for every American city. However, this assumption may be wrong, and it quite frequently is—think of the cases of two countries: the United Kingdom and Vatican City. State breakdown is not defined for the United Kingdom. In the Vatican's case, county and city breakdown are not even defined (Figure 5-18).

An *incomplete hierarchy* is one in which one or more levels of aggregation prove missing in some instances (because they are not known or defined). Figure 5-19 shows that we can mark all of the attributes whose values may be missing with a dash to distinguish an incomplete hierarchy graphically. To designate this type of hierarchy in the literature, the term *ragged hierarchy* is sometimes used (Niemi et al., 2001). Each level of aggregation has precise and consistent semantics, but different instances may have different lengths because one or more levels are missing, making the parent-child relationships among the levels not uniform. For example, the parent of 'Orange' belongs on the `state` level and the parent of 'Norfolk' on the `country` level.

It is important that you understand the difference between an incomplete hierarchy and an optional arc. In incomplete hierarchies, one or more attribute values for certain hierarchy instances *in any hierarchy position* (the start and end attributes included) are missing. If we use an optional arc, we instead model the fact that the value of an attribute *and the values of all the attribute descendents* are missing. If only the end attribute of a hierarchy is missing, both approaches to modeling are completely equivalent (see Figure 5-20).

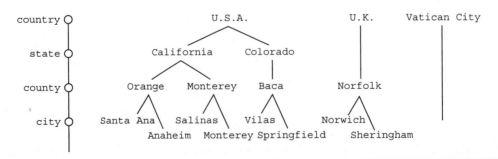

FIGURE 5-18   Irregular breakdown into states and counties

FIGURE 5-19
Incomplete
geographic
hierarchy

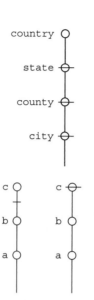

FIGURE 5-20
Two equivalent
modeling options
for a hierarchy

5.2.8 Recursive Hierarchies

Unlike incomplete hierarchies, parent-child relationships among the levels in *recursive* (or *unbalanced*) *hierarchies* are consistent, but their instances can have different lengths. For example, think of a company organization chart that maps a reporting structure of employees. Figure 5-21 shows the hierarchy of employee roles if some branches in the organizational chart have different lengths. Although those parent-child relationships are consistent throughout the two branches, their levels of aggregation are not equivalent from the conceptual viewpoint: the president's administrative assistant and the chief executive officer have quite different responsibilities.

Figure 5-22 shows how the DFM represents a recursive hierarchy. In this fact schema, each employee's work hours are measured daily on various projects sorted out by activity type. Each employee has a role, and more than one employee may hold a role. It is interesting to model hierarchy relationships among employees as implied in the company organization chart. The loop-back in `employee` emphasizes that you cannot distinguish the various levels of aggregation semantically at the fact schema level.

FIGURE 5-21
Role hierarchy in
an unbalanced
company
organization chart

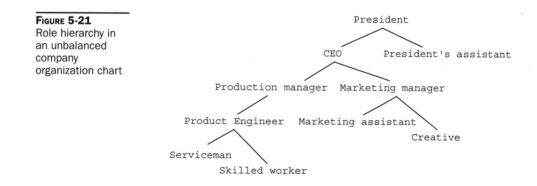

Figure 5-22
Recursive hierarchy
for a company
organization chart

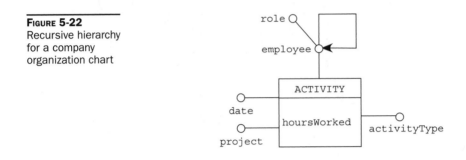

5.2.9   Additivity

Aggregation requires the definition of a suitable operator to compose the measure values that mark primary events into values to be assigned to secondary events. From this viewpoint, measures can be classified into three categories (Lenz and Shoshani, 1997):

- *Flow Measures* refer to a timeframe, at the end of which they are evaluated cumulatively. Some examples are the number of products sold in a day, monthly receipts, and yearly number of births.

- *Level Measures* are evaluated at particular times. Some examples are the number of products in inventory and the number of inhabitants in a city.

- *Unit Measures* are evaluated at particular times but are expressed in relative terms. Some examples are product unit price, discount percentage, and currency exchange.

The usable operators for aggregating different types of measures along temporal and nontemporal hierarchies are shown in Table 5-2.

Additivity

A measure is called *additive* along a dimension when you can use the SUM operator to aggregate its values along the dimension hierarchy. If this is not the case, it is called *non-additive*. A non-additive measure is *non-aggregable* when you can use no aggregation operator for it.

Table 5-2 clearly shows a general rule: flow measures are additive along all the dimensions, level measures are non-additive along temporal dimensions, and unit measures are non-additive along all the dimensions.

An example of an additive flow measure in the sales schema is `quantity`. The quantity sold in a month is the sum of quantities sold every day in a month. Figure 5-23 shows an example of a non-additive level measure. The inventory level is not additive along `date`, but it is additive along the other dimensions. An example of a non-additive unit measure is

		Temporal Hierarchies	Nontemporal Hierarchies
Table 5-2 Valid Aggregation Operators for Three Types of Measures (Lenz, 1997)	Flow Measures	SUM, AVG, MIN, MAX	SUM, AVG, MIN, MAX
	Level Measures	AVG, MIN, MAX	SUM, AVG, MIN, MAX
	Unit Measures	AVG, MIN, MAX	AVG, MIN, MAX

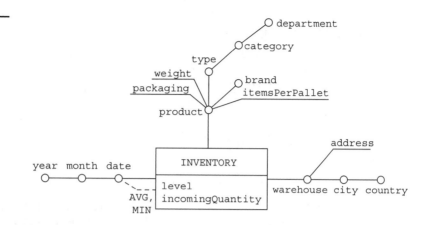

Figure 5-23
Fact schema for
an inventory

unitPrice in the sales schema (Figure 5-8). In any case, you can use other operators, such as AVG, MAX, and MIN, to aggregate those non-additive measures. For example, it makes sense to average unitPrice for more than one product, store, and date.

On the contrary, you cannot intrinsically aggregate non-aggregable measures for conceptual reasons. For example, look at the numberOfCustomers measure in the sales fact schema (Figure 5-8). This measure is estimated for a certain product, store, and day, counting the number of sale receipts issued on that day in that store, which refer to that product. Totaling or averaging the number of customers for two or more products would lead to an inconsistent result, because the same sales receipt may also include other products. Then numberOfCustomers is non-aggregable along the product dimension (while it is additive along date and store). In this case, it is non-aggregable because the association between sales receipts and products is many-to-many instead of many-to-one. You cannot aggregate the numberOfCustomers measure consistently along the product dimension, no matter the aggregation operator adopted, unless event granularity is set to a finer level.

Additivity is the most frequent case. So in order to simplify graphic notation in the DFM, you should explicitly represent only the exceptions. Figure 5-8 shows that a measure connects to the dimensions along which it is non-additive via a dashed line labeled with the usable aggregation operators. If a measure shows the same type of additivity on all of the dimensions, you can mark the aggregation operator on its side. If the total amount of non-additivity were such that it reduced schema readability, you should adopt a matrix representation. Table 5-3 shows the equivalent additivity matrix for the fact schema of Figure 5-8.

	product	date	store	promotion
quantity	SUM	SUM	SUM	SUM
receipts	SUM	SUM	SUM	SUM
numberOfCustomers	–	SUM	SUM	SUM
unitPrice	AVG	AVG	AVG	AVG

Table 5-3 Additivity Matrix of the Sales Fact Schema

5.3 Events and Aggregation

In this paragraph, we abandon the intensional DFM level and move on to the extensional level in order to return to the concept of the event, the basis of aggregation. In other words, we'll now describe the instances that populate fact schemata.

We have already shown how a *primary event*, the basic unit that can represent information in a fact schema, corresponds to a specific fact occurrence, which you can clearly identify if you give each dimension a value. We will call a primary event *coordinate* the n-ple of dimension values that identifies it. Each measure takes exactly one value in a primary event. For example, the

$$\alpha' = (\text{product: 'CleanHand', store: 'EverMore', date: '5/5/08'})$$

coordinate in the fact schema example in Figure 5-6 defines a single primary event that represents the CleanHand soap sales in the EverMore store on May 5, 2008. The measure values of this event could be: quantity: 20, receipts: 80, unitPrice: 4, numberOfCustomers: 3.

A *cube* is a set of primary events associated with different coordinates. However, *not every possible coordinate corresponds to a primary event*. In other words, cubes are generally quite sparse, and just a small percentage of coordinates actually define events. For example, a few products are sold every day in all the stores. We postpone the discussion on how to evaluate sparsity to Chapter 7, where we deal with fundamental questions on workload and data volume.

The shades of meaning in missing events can vary from one fact schema to the other. There is no event in the sales schema of Figure 5-6 because a product in a certain store on a certain date remained unsold. In the shipments schema of Figure 5-10, a missing event means that a specific warehouse did not ship a specific product from an order on a certain date to a specific destination. In the telephone calls schema of Figure 5-13, it means that at a certain time on a certain day, two telephone numbers were not connected. In the hospital admissions schema of Figure 5-16, it means that on a specific day, a patient was not admitted to a specific department. In the inventory schema of Figure 5-23, it means that a warehouse ran out of product supplies on a specific day.

Generally speaking, the meaning of missing events depends on the existing relationship between primary events and transactions in operational database sources. Typically, the information modeled in a fact schema sums up data in operational databases. This means that each primary event summarizes one or more transactions that actually occurred in an application domain in a unit of time. If this is the case, that fact schema is said to be a *lossy-grained fact schema*. The sales schema is an example of a lossy-grained schema, because each sales event modeled in that schema sums up all the sales of one product on the same day at the same store. If this is not the case, event representation granularity in fact schemata coincides with that of operational databases. We would then say that this kind of fact schema is a *lossless-grained schema*. An example of a lossless-grained schema is the one that exploits the date, department, and patient dimensions to model admissions to a hospital, if we assume that the same patient cannot be admitted twice on the same day into the same department.

Based on this distinction, we can say the following:

- In a lossy-grained fact schema, an event is missing because its measures would have irrelevant values—typically equal to zero. For instance, this applies to sales, telephone calls, and inventory.

- In a lossless-grained fact schema, an event is missing because it did not occur in the application domain. For instance, this applies to admissions and shipments.

After a careful examination, we can conclude that some relevant pieces of information may not be represented in lossy-grained schemata. Look at the sales, for example. If a missing event shows that a product is still unsold, how can you represent that a product is or is not for sale in a store on a certain day? From the conceptual viewpoint, the best thing to do is to place a new empty *coverage schema* with product, date, and store dimensions next to the sales schema. Each coverage schema event should represent that a specific product was actually for sale at a specific store on a certain date. This empty schema corresponds to the *coverage table* defined by Kimball (1996). To compare it with the sales schema, see section 5.5 on overlapping procedures that allow you to answer queries such as which products for sale are still unsold?

As a matter of fact, you could also use only the sales schema if you created an event that corresponds to each product *for sale* on one day in one store and use those events whose measures are null, to explicitly represent the products still unsold. It is clear that this solution leads to a remarkable amount of wasted space if the number of unsold products is high.

As we mentioned, often you cannot analyze data at the maximum level of detail; and this results in the need for primary events to be aggregated along different abstraction levels. According to OLAP terminology, aggregation is called *roll-up* and group-by set is the key concept used to define it.

> ### Group-by Set
> A *group-by set* is any subset of dimensional attributes in a fact schema that does not contain two attributes related by a functional dependency. The group-by set that includes only and all of the dimensions of a fact is said to be its *primary group-by set*. All of the others are called *secondary group-by sets* and identify potential ways to aggregate primary events.

The primary group-by set for the sales fact schema of Figure 5-6 is G_0 = {product, store, date}. Some examples of secondary group-by sets are shown here:

G_1 = {product, state, quarter}
G_2 = {type, brand, store, month, day}
G_3 = {country, date}
G_4 = {year}
G_5 = { }

Note that no attributes appear for one or more hierarchies in some of these group-by sets. For example, no attributes appear for the product hierarchy in G_3 and no attributes are present for the product and store hierarchies in G_4. The G_5 group-by set is an extreme case. It has no hierarchies, and we can call it the *empty group-by set*. The {product, category, date} attribute set is not a group-by set, since product→category.

It is fundamental to note that the set of all possible group-by sets in a fact schema are linked by a partial order relationship called *roll-up*.

> **Roll-up Order**
> Given two group-by sets called G_i and G_j and belonging to the set of all the possible group-by sets in a fact schema, we say that $G_i \leq G_j$ when $G_j \to G_i$—that is, when a b attribute exists in G_j for each a attribute of G_i such that b belongs to the same hierarchy as a and $a \to b$.

For example, the following relationships between group-by sets hold:

$$\{year\} \leq \{type, quarter\} \leq \{product, quarter\} \leq \{product, store, date\}$$
$$\{state\} \leq \{type, brand, store, month, day\} \leq \{product, store, date\}$$

A maximum element, corresponding to the primary group-by set of the fact schema, and a minimum element, corresponding to the empty group-by set, always exist in roll-up orders. Additionally, for each pair of group-by sets, both a superior (*sup*) and an inferior (*inf*) group-by sets always exist in roll-up orders. From the algebraic viewpoint, roll-up characterizes a lattice. Figure 5-24 shows a small fragment of the roll-up lattice for the sales schema of Figure 5-6. In real-world applications, it is easy to imagine that the entire lattice can be huge.

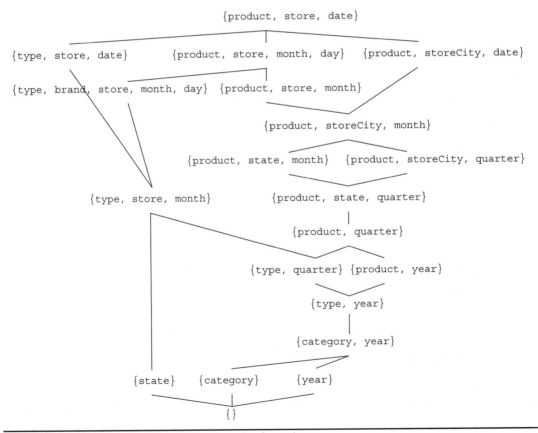

FIGURE 5-24 A part of the roll-up lattice for the sales fact schema

A coordinate of a group-by set G is an n-ple of values of the dimensional attributes in G. We already showed an example of a coordinate α' of the sales primary group-by set G_0. Some examples of coordinates of the G_1 and G_3 secondary group-by sets are respectively:

$\alpha'' = (\text{product: 'CleanHand', state: 'Texas', quarter: 'II, 2007')}$
$\alpha''' = (\text{country: 'France', date: '5/5/2008')}$

We recall that each dimension value exactly determines one value for each attribute in its hierarchy by means of functional dependencies. In this way, each coordinate of the primary group-by set determines one coordinate of each secondary group-by set, and vice versa, one coordinate of a secondary group-by set corresponds to a set of coordinates of the primary group-by set.

Each coordinate α of a given secondary group-by set uniquely identifies a secondary event that aggregates all the primary events identified by the coordinates of the primary group-by set corresponding to α. For example, the secondary event identified by the α''' coordinate of the G_3 group-by set aggregates the primary events related to the sales of all products on May 5, 2008, along the French stores. The empty group-by set G_5 has one single secondary event that aggregates *all* the primary events.

Each secondary event then expresses a value for each measure. In order to define *how* to calculate the value of each measure for secondary events, we need to specify aggregation semantics. We provide a gradual solution for this requirement in the following paragraphs. We begin with the simplest case and then introduce new situations to outline the global framework for advanced constructs of the DFM.

5.3.1 Aggregating Additive Measures

Measures are additive along all the dimensions under the simplest (luckily most common) conditions. If this is the case, the value of a measure m for a secondary event can be calculated by summing the values of m in all the corresponding primary events.

It is well known that the associative property holds for the SUM operator. Thanks to this property, you can also calculate the sum of a set of values as the total of their partial sums. As a result, the measure values of the secondary events for the G' group-by set can also be calculated by summing the measure values of the secondary events for any G'' secondary group-by set such that $G' \leq G''$. Section 9.2 shows that this has important consequences on logical design because it makes it possible to answer a query using aggregate views at different levels of aggregation.

Table 5-4 shows the values of the quantity measure in the primary events of a sales fact schema with the product and quarter dimensions. The events are represented within a two-dimensional matrix, as they would be in an OLAP tool. Each event is indexed by its coordinate, which is represented by the values of its attributes (quarter and product in Table 5-4). In relation to the values of the coordinate attributes, the values of other relevant attributes in the same hierarchy are also shown (the year of a quarter, the type and category of a product), as defined by the functional dependencies. Tables 5-5, 5-6, and 5-7 show the corresponding aggregations for different group-by sets. The SUM is used as an aggregation operator. Note that the {category, year} aggregation can be equivalently obtained from any of the three other aggregations thanks to the associative property of the SUM operator. Section 5.3.2 will show that you cannot always apply this property when you use other aggregation operators.

category	type	product	2007				2008			
			I'07	II'07	III'07	IV'07	I'08	II'08	III'08	IV'08
House cleaning	Cleaner	Shiny	100	90	95	90	80	70	90	85
		Bleachy	20	30	20	10	25	30	35	20
		Brighty	60	50	60	45	40	40	50	40
	Soap	CleanHand	15	20	25	30	15	15	20	10
		Scent	30	35	20	25	30	30	20	15
Food	Dairy product	F Slurp Milk	90	90	85	75	60	80	85	60
		U Slurp Milk	60	80	85	60	70	70	75	65
		Slurp Yogurt	20	30	40	35	30	35	35	20
	Drink	DrinkMe	20	10	25	30	35	30	20	10
		Coky	50	60	45	40	50	60	45	40

TABLE 5-4 Primary Events of the Sales Cube

category	2007				2008			
	I'07	II'07	III'07	IV'07	I'08	II'08	III'08	IV'08
House cleaning	225	225	220	200	190	185	215	170
Food	240	270	280	240	245	275	260	195

TABLE 5-5 The {category, quarter} Group-by Set Secondary Events

5.3.2 Aggregating Non-additive Measures

If a measure can be aggregated using *the same aggregation operator along all of the dimensions,* even though the operator is not the SUM (for example AVG or MAX), the preceding instructions still apply. You can apply the operator to the values of measure *m* in all the

TABLE 5-6 The {type, year} Group-by Set Secondary Events

category	type	2007	2008
House cleaning	Cleaner	670	605
	Soap	200	155
Food	Dairy product	750	685
	Drinks	280	290

TABLE 5-7 The {category, year} Group-by Set Secondary Events

category	2007	2008
House cleaning	870	760
Food	1030	975

primary events to calculate the measure values for each secondary event. However, we should add that not all aggregation operators show the same useful associative property holding for sums. From this viewpoint, Gray and others (1997) classified aggregation operators into three groups:

- **Distributive**   Calculating aggregates from partial aggregates
- **Algebraic**   Requiring the usage of additional information in the form of a finite number of *support measures* to correctly calculate aggregates from partial aggregates
- **Holistic**   Calculating aggregates from partial aggregates only via an infinite number of support measures

Some examples of distributive operators are the previously mentioned SUM operator, as well as the MIN and MAX operators; the considerations made in the preceding paragraph apply to these operators. Some examples of algebraic operators are the average, the standard deviation, and the barycenter operators. If you add all the required support measures to every secondary event, you can still calculate secondary events from other more fine-grained secondary events.

Let's look at the case of the AVG operator. Generally, it is clear that the average of partial averages of a set of values is different from the average of the same set. Tables 5-8, 5-9, and 5-10 show examples of the `unitPrice` measure of `SALE`. The AVG operator can be used to aggregate `unitPrice` along all the dimensions. It is apparent that there is no way to obtain

category	type	product	year	2009			
			quarter	I'09	II'09	III'09	IV'09
House cleaning	Cleaner	Shiny		2	2	2.2	2.5
		Bleachy		1.5	1.5	2	2.5
		Brighty		–	3	3	3
	Soap	CleanHand		1	1.2	1.5	1.5
		Scent		1.5	1.5	2	–

TABLE 5-8   Primary Events of the Sales Cube: A Dash Stands for the Unsold Items in a Quarter

category	type	year	2009			
		quarter	I'09	II'09	III'09	IV'09
House cleaning	Cleaner		1.75	2.17	2.40	2.67
	Soap		1.25	1.35	1.75	1.50
	Average:		1.50	1.76	2.08	2.09

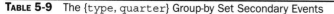

TABLE 5-9   The {`type`, `quarter`} Group-by Set Secondary Events

	year	2009			
	quarter	I'09	II'09	III'09	IV'09
category					
House cleaning		1.50	1.84	2.14	2.38

TABLE 5-10 The {category, quarter} Group-by Set Secondary Events

the proper aggregation by `category` and `quarter` (Table 5-10) from the aggregation by `type` and `quarter` (Table 5-9) unless you add a new measure that counts the number of primary events that make up each secondary event. COUNT is the support measure for AVG. See section 9.1.9 for more details of the impacts on logical design.

Some examples of holistic operators are median and rank. Secondary events must be calculated from primary events because they cannot use a finite number of support measures to calculate aggregates from partial aggregates.

Things get more complex when *different* operators are used to aggregate a measure along different dimensions. For example, Figure 5-23 shows the `level` measure in the INVENTORY fact schema. The MIN operator is used to aggregate `level` along the `date` dimension, and the SUM operator is used to aggregate it along the `warehouse` dimension. Table 5-11 shows some primary events with reference to a single product. Tables 5-12 and 5-13 show the secondary events obtained by aggregating along only one dimension. If you instead have to aggregate simultaneously along *both* dimensions (for example, by month

month		March 2009								
	date	3/1/09	3/2/09	3/3/09	3/4/09	3/5/09	3/6/09	3/7/09	3/8/09	3/9/09
city	warehouse									
Paris	Défense	10	10	8	4	20	20	15	15	12
	Élysée	5	4	4	4	2	2	2	10	10
	Reuilly	14	14	14	12	20	20	20	20	16
Lyon	Villette	4	2	2	2	10	10	10	8	8
	Ainay	4	20	20	15	15	12	12	10	9

TABLE 5-11 Primary Events in the Inventory Schema

month		March 1999								
	date	3/1/09	3/2/09	3/3/09	3/4/09	3/5/09	3/6/09	3/7/09	3/8/09	3/9/09
city										
Paris		29	28	26	20	42	42	37	45	38
Lyon		8	22	22	17	25	22	22	18	17

TABLE 5-12 The {date, city} Group-by Set Secondary Events

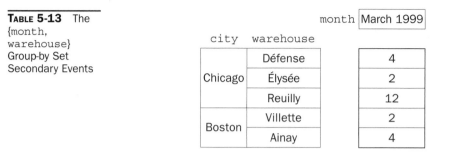

TABLE 5-13 The {month, warehouse} Group-by Set Secondary Events

	month	March 1999

city	warehouse	
Chicago	Défense	4
	Élysée	2
	Reuilly	12
Boston	Villette	2
	Ainay	4

and city), this causes a problem. Will each secondary event have to be calculated as the minimum of the sums or as the sum of the minimums? It is obvious that the results obtained in both cases are generally different! In practice, you must choose a *priority order* for dimensions to decide which aggregation should come first. Note that in the specific example of Table 5-11, the result of the aggregation by month and city would have seemed to be independent of the application order of operators if we had used the AVG operator instead of MIN to aggregate along date. As a matter of fact, this applies only because *no primary events are missing*. If this is not the case, results still depend on the operator priority order.

To conclude this section, we would like to consider the case of *derived measures*, whose values can be calculated from other measures in the same schema. For example, the receipts = unitPrice × quantity measure is derived from the unitPrice and quantity measures. If a derived measure is additive, as in the case of receipts, you can calculate the aggregation from partial aggregations (the annual receipts are the sum of monthly receipts). However, you cannot calculate the aggregation from aggregations of its component measures. For instance, you cannot multiply the amount of items sold in a year by the average unit price during the same year to calculate annual receipts accurately!

5.3.3 Aggregating with Convergence and Cross-dimensional Attributes

A convergence in a fact schema is completely transparent to the goals of aggregation. For example, if we look at the hierarchy built on the store dimension of Figure 5-8, including a convergence based on country, we can immediately note that the aggregation along country is clearly defined because the convergence results in each store corresponding precisely to a country. In addition to that, you can calculate secondary events of any group-by set that includes country from the events of any more fine-grained group-by set that includes either storeCity, state, or salesDistrict.

If your fact schema includes a cross-dimensional attribute, you should use similar reasoning to check for aggregation semantics. Figure 5-25 shows a simplified sales schema. Here, the category and country parents jointly define the VAT cross-dimensional attribute. Each primary event is associated with a product and a store, and, consequently, a category and a country. For this reason, the secondary events of the group-by sets that include VAT are uniquely defined because the VAT value for each primary event is clearly defined. Figure 5-26 sums up the substantial difference between convergence and cross-dimensional attributes from the viewpoint of roll-up relationships between group-by sets.

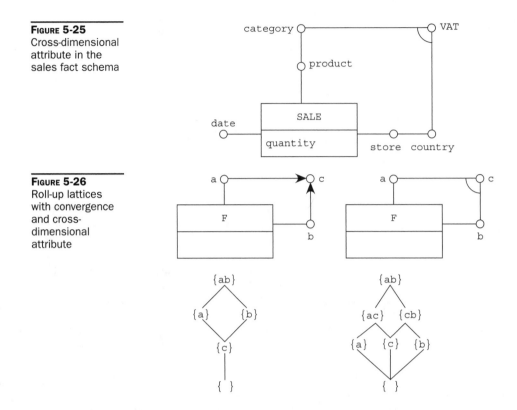

FIGURE 5-25
Cross-dimensional attribute in the sales fact schema

FIGURE 5-26
Roll-up lattices with convergence and cross-dimensional attribute

5.3.4 Aggregating with Optional or Multiple Arcs

If an optional arc exists between two attributes called a and b in a hierarchy, at least one value of the domain of a corresponds to an undefined value of b. As a result, if G is the primary group-by set and G' is a secondary group-by set that includes b, a corresponding coordinate of G' does not exist for some coordinate(s) of G. Conceptually, you can solve this problem if you use a fictitious 'No Value' value to expand the domain of b that you can give to b every time it is undefined. Using this expanded domain, roll-up is defined for all the coordinates. For all of the secondary group-by sets including b or one of its descendants in the hierarchy, the optional arc then results in a set of fictitious secondary events that group all the primary events excluded from the normal roll-up—that is, those primary events for which b equals 'No Value'.

For example, look at the `diet` attribute in the sales schema (Figure 5-8), linked to `product` via an optional arc. Tables 5-14 and 5-15 show an example of aggregation where the dash means 'No Value'.

Things get more difficult for a fact schema that includes a multiple arc. Look at Figure 5-15, which shows the book sales schema in which a multiple arc links `book` and `author`. In particular, relevant queries are those that group sales by `book` or `author`. Table 5-16 shows the `number` measure of some primary events related to a certain date, and Table 5-17 shows the corresponding secondary events grouped by date and author. Note immediately that totaling all partials of the various authors would lead to an inaccurate result (an estimated total of 37 books sold against the 30 actually sold) when you calculate secondary events grouped by date. For this reason, it is not correct here to exploit the distributive property of the SUM operator, even though the `number` measure is additive along the `book` dimension.

TABLE 5-14
Primary Events in
the Sales Schema

date 1/2/09

diet	type	product	
–	Dairy product	Slurp Milk	30
Cholesterol		Slim Yogurt	15
–		Fatty Yogurt	20
Cholesterol	Sweets	Strict Cake	10
Macrobiotics		Ghandi Cake	5

TABLE 5-15 The
{diet, date}
Group-by Set
Secondary Events

date 1/2/09

diet	
–	50
Cholesterol	25
Macrobiotics	5

Now let's associate each book-author pair with a weight ranging from 0 to 1 that expresses the relevance of that pair. Table 5-18 shows a potential weight distribution, assuming that the contribution of different authors to each book they write is equal. If you total a *weighted* sum of the sales contributions for every single book to calculate the secondary events grouped by {author, date}, you will obtain the results shown in Table 5-19. From those results, you can easily infer that the use of weights restores the distributive property of the SUM operator if the weights are normalized for every book—that is, if the sum of the weights for each book is equal to 1.

Now let's examine the case in which the multiple arc enters a dimension, as shown in the hospital admissions schema of Figure 5-16. Here, more than one diagnosis is associated with

date 1/2/09

genre	author	book	
Technical	Golfarelli, Rizzi	Facts & Crimes	3
	Golfarelli	Sounds Logical	5
Current affairs	Rizzi	The Right Measure	10
	Golfarelli, Rizzi	Facts, How and Why	4
Science Fiction	Golfarelli	The 4th Dimension	8
		Total:	30

TABLE 5-16   Primary Events in the Bookseller Schema

TABLE 5-17 The
{author, date}
Group-by Set
Secondary Events

date 1/2/09

author	
Golfarelli	20
Rizzi	17
Total:	37

TABLE 5-18
Multiple Arc
Weights Between
`book` and `author`

	Golfarelli	Rizzi
Facts & Crimes	0.5	0.5
Sounds Logical	1	0
The Right Measure	0	1
Facts, How and Why	0.5	0.5
The 4th Dimension	0	0

TABLE 5-19   The
`{author, date}`
Group-by Set
Weighted
Secondary Events

date 1/2/09

author

Golfarelli	16.5
Rizzi	13.5

Total: 30

each admission. In particular, the aggregation semantics seems to be rather confusing. More than one coordinate (each one with a different diagnosis) corresponds to one primary event (an admission). And, vice versa, a coordinate of the {diagnosis, date, department, patientSSN} primary group-by set does not define a primary event, but a fraction of it (the "contribution" a single diagnosis makes to the admission). To evaluate the aggregation semantics, we suggest that you first transform the fact schema into an equivalent schema. To do this, you can stick to two procedures described in the following paragraphs. Section 9.1.4 shows how both procedures generate just as many logical design solutions.

Figure 5-27 shows the first equivalent schema. Here, we introduce the fictitious diagnosisGroup dimension with a domain of all the diagnosis combinations linked to admissions. This transformed schema is largely similar to that of book sales, where the multiple arc enters a dimensional attribute. Using a multiple arc weight allows the admission cost to be distributed over the different diagnoses, as required by the application domain, so that significant aggregates can be obtained for single diagnoses and for single categories. Table 5-20 shows the cost measure of a set of primary events related to one department and one date, and Table 5-21 shows the weights of the multiple arc.

The second schema of Figure 5-28 has been obtained from the original one of Figure 5-16 by using the ADMISSION PER DIAGNOSIS fact rather than the arc entering diagnosis in order to model the multiplicity of the association between admissions and diagnoses.

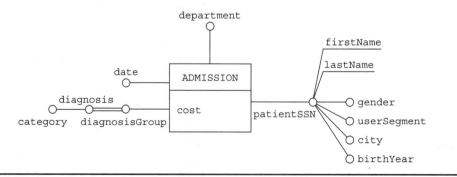

FIGURE 5-27   Equivalent fact schema for admissions

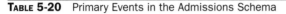

patient	Johnson	Smith
	1,000	–
	–	2,000

diagnosis	diagnosisGroup
Cardiopathy, Hypertension, Asthma	G1
Fracture, Asthma	G2

TABLE 5-20   Primary Events in the Admissions Schema

TABLE 5-21
Multiple Arc
Weights Between
diagnosisGroup
and diagnosis

	G1	G2
Cardiopathy	0.5	0
Hypertension	0.3	0
Asthma	0.2	0.3
Fracture	0	0.7

To achieve this result, we reduced the fact granularity. The diagnosis dimension is now a normal "single" dimension, and each primary event no longer corresponds to an entire admission, but to the "portion" of an admission that you can assign to a single diagnosis. We will briefly describe this operation as the diagnosis attribute *push-down*. Table 5-22 shows the costPerDiagnosis measure of the primary events that instance this schema. Note that the admissions costs have been weighted according to the weights listed in Table 5-21 to calculate the partial costs in primary events.

5.3.5   Empty Fact Schema Aggregation

A fact schema is said to be *empty* if it does not have any measures. If this is the case, primary events only record the *occurrence* of events in an application domain. For example, Figure 5-29 shows a fact schema in the university domain. Here, each primary event shows that a student attended a specific course during a specific semester.

The information each secondary event represents in an empty fact schema is normally the *number* of primary events corresponding to it, computed by the COUNT[3] aggregation operator. In other words, you can assume that an empty fact schema is described by an

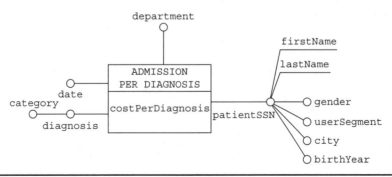

FIGURE 5-28   Equivalent fact schema for admissions resulting from the diagnosis attribute push-down

[3]The COUNT aggregation operator is distributive, even if the operator that enables the calculation of a COUNT aggregate from the partial aggregates is not COUNT itself but rather SUM.

Table 5-22
Primary Events in
the Admissions
Schema after
Pushing Down the
`diagnosis`
Attribute

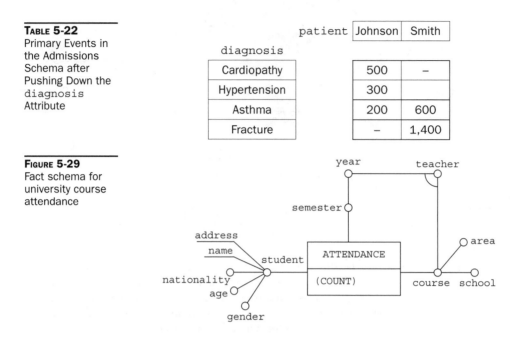

diagnosis	patient	Johnson	Smith
Cardiopathy		500	–
Hypertension		300	
Asthma		200	600
Fracture		–	1,400

Figure 5-29
Fact schema for
university course
attendance

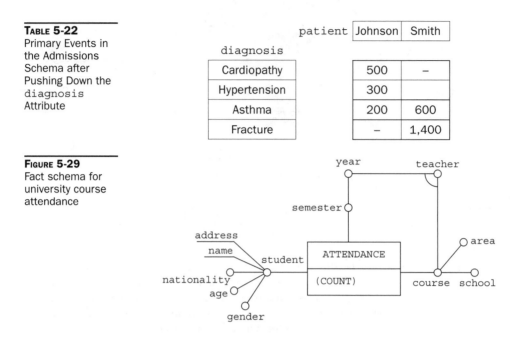

implicit integer measure that equals 1 if the event occurred or 0 otherwise, and that the SUM operator aggregates the events. Then, the (`course`: 'Database Design', `gender`: 'F') coordinate defines the secondary event that shows the total number of female students that took the Database Design course.

An additional approach to aggregation is actually also possible. In this approach, the information each secondary event carries is linked to the *existence* of the corresponding primary events. In order to explain this concept, we can assume that you have an implicit Boolean measure, which is TRUE if an event has occurred or FALSE if the event has not occurred. Then you may use both the AND and OR operators for aggregation with universal and existential semantics, respectively. The secondary event defined by the (`student`: 'Will Smith', `area`: 'Databases', `school`: 'Engineering') coordinate can then mark that Smith took *at least one course* on databases in the School of Engineering (OR operator), or alternatively that he took *all of the courses* on databases in the School of Engineering (AND operator).

Table 5-24 compares the different aggregation options based on the simple example of Table 5-23.

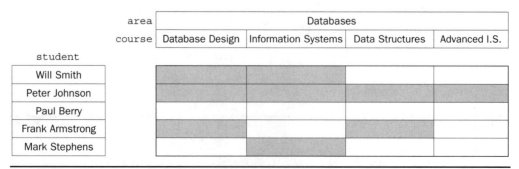

area		Databases		
course	Database Design	Information Systems	Data Structures	Advanced I.S.
student				
Will Smith	▓▓▓	▓▓▓		
Peter Johnson	▓▓▓	▓▓▓	▓▓▓	▓▓▓
Paul Berry				
Frank Armstrong	▓▓▓		▓▓▓	
Mark Stephens		▓▓▓		

Table 5-23   Primary Events (in Gray) in the Course Attendance Schema for Engineering

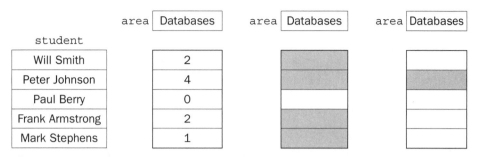

Table 5-24   The {student, area} Group-by Set Secondary Events Using the COUNT (Left), OR (Middle), AND (Right) Operators for Aggregation

5.3.6   Aggregating with Functional Dependencies among Dimensions

One or more functional dependencies may occur between the dimensions in a fact schema. For example, a specific store sells each product on a certain date through at most one promotion in the sales schema of Figure 5-8. A date, product, store→promotion functional dependency then exists. In the admissions schema (Figure 5-27), we may reasonably assume that a patient cannot be admitted twice on the same day. For this reason we have patientSSN, date→department, diagnosisGroup. In the attendance schema of Figure 5-29, if a student attends each course at most once, we have student, course→ semester.

Unlike what occurs in standard relational databases, a functional dependency in a fact schema does not generate serious anomalies, and you should not then necessarily avoid it. From the aggregation viewpoint, the immediate result is that the association between coordinates of some pairs of group-by sets is one-to-one rather than many-to-one. In the case of sales, this happens for all group-by sets that include date, store, and product. You may note the effects of these conditions when OLAP operators query that schema. If events are being analyzed by date, store, and product, the application of roll-up and drill-down operators along the promotion hierarchy will not modify the query result, because one promotion value will be determined at most and you will not be able to execute any significant aggregation.

To conclude, you should note that a fact schema where the $a_1 \ldots, a_m$ dimensions determine the $a_{m+1} \ldots, a_n$ dimensions is equivalent to a schema where $a_1 \ldots, a_m$ are the only dimensions and $a_{m+1} \ldots, a_n$ are included as cross-dimensional attributes jointly determined by the dimensions. It is nevertheless more useful to represent $a_{m+1} \ldots, a_n$ as dimensions, if you want to give more importance to their role in aggregation.

5.3.7   Aggregating along Incomplete or Recursive Hierarchies

Hierarchies in the fact schemata are at times irregular when their occurrence results in missing values for one or more attributes (incomplete hierarchies) and/or when the actual hierarchy length varies from occurrence to occurrence (recursive hierarchies), as mentioned in sections 5.2.7 and 5.2.8. From the aggregation viewpoint, this obviously has quite considerable effects.

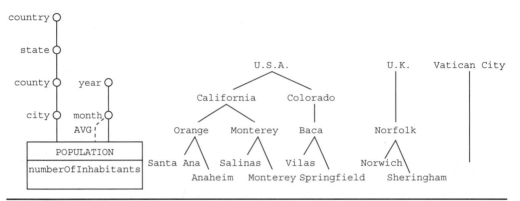

FIGURE 5-30 Irregular breakdown into states and counties

We first discuss the case of incomplete hierarchies and make reference to the geographic hierarchy example shown in Figure 5-30. If a fact expresses the number of inhabitants per city as a result of a census, Table 5-25 shows some examples of specific primary events.

Because states are not defined for the United Kingdom and for Vatican City, primary events can be aggregated by `state` after balancing hierarchies in three different ways, depending on user preferences and decision-making process features. More specifically, data about the cities that cannot be grouped to states can be

1. completely summed up in a single value labeled 'Other', as shown in Table 5-26 (*balancing by exclusion*);

2. shown at the coarsest aggregation level, among those finer than `state`, for which a value is defined—`county` in the example of Table 5-27 (*downward balancing*);

3. shown at the finest aggregation level, among those coarser than `county`, for which a value is defined—`country` in the example in Table 5-28 (*upward balancing*).

TABLE 5-25
Primary Events in the Census Schema

month	Jan 09

country	state	county	city	
USA	California	Orange	Santa Ana	353,184
			Anaheim	346,823
		Monterey	Salinas	148,350
			Monterey	30,641
	Colorado	Baca	Vilas	110
			Springfield	1,562
UK		Norfolk	Norwich	121,600
			Sheringham	7,143
		Essex	Epping	11,047
			Tilbury	12,091
Vatican City				800

TABLE 5-26 The {month, state} Group-by Set Secondary Events in the Population Schema with Balancing by Exclusion (We Assumed for Simplicity that No Other Cities Are Present)		

	month	Jan 09
state		
California		878,998
Colorado		1,672
Other		152,681

TABLE 5-27 The {month, state} Group-by Set Secondary Events in the Population Schema with Downward Balancing		

	month	Jan 09
state		
California		878,998
Colorado		1,672
Norfolk		128,743
Essex		23,138
Vatican City		800

We deal with logical design of different types of balancing in section 9.1.6. Here, we would like to draw your attention to two of their features:

- Balancing by exclusion fails to meet the classic roll-up semantics, which requires that each progressive step in aggregation causes more than one group to collapse into a single group. When you roll up from state to country in the geographic hierarchy, the group labeled with 'Other' is broken down into two groups: UK and Vatican City, respectively.

- You cannot always apply all three balancing solutions that we proposed. For example, Table 5-27 shows that we could not downward balance the Vatican City row because there is no defined city for this country.

Aggregation semantics change slightly with regard to recursive hierarchies. Unlike other hierarchies, you are not supposed to use a fixed number of distinguishable aggregation levels to characterize them. Look at the example of Figure 5-22. The example fact represents the activities carried out around projects. Table 5-29 shows some primary

TABLE 5-28 The {month, state} Group-by Set Secondary Events in the Population Schema with Upward Balancing		

	month	Jan 09
state		
California		878,998
Colorado		1,672
UK		151,881
Vatican City		800

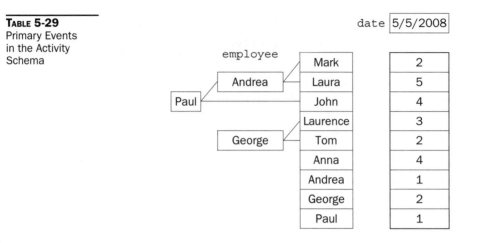

Table 5-29
Primary Events in the Activity Schema

date 5/5/2008

employee		hours
	Mark	2
Andrea	Laura	5
Paul	John	4
	Laurence	3
George	Tom	2
	Anna	4
	Andrea	1
	George	2
	Paul	1

events related to a specific project and a specific activity type. As you can see, each employee works a specific number of hours on a specific day. Additionally, reporting relationships of varying length exist between employees, as the recursive hierarchy models.

When there is no explicit subdivision in levels of aggregation with specific semantics, the only way to aggregate primary events to secondary events is recursively. Table 5-30 shows secondary events at the first level of recursion. The total number of hours worked links to each employee and to possible other employees that report directly to each one of them (the "children" in the hierarchy). For example, we allocate 6 hours to Paul, calculated by totaling 1 hour he worked, 1 hour Andrea worked, and 4 hours John worked. At the second level of recursion—Table 5-31 shows its secondary events—we calculate instead the total hours per employee and those of their "grandchildren." The hours worked and assigned to Paul then become 13. The result at subsequent levels of recursion remains unchanged because the hierarchies in the example have a maximum length of 3.

See section 9.1.7 for an explanation on logical design solutions for recursive hierarchies.

Table 5-30
Secondary Events in the Activity Schema at the First Level of Recursion

date 5/5/2008

employee	hours
Mark	2
Laura	5
John	4
Laurence	3
Tom	2
Anna	4
Andrea	8
George	7
Paul	6

TABLE 5-31	date	5/5/2008

Secondary Events in the Activity Schema at the Second Level of Recursion

employee

Mark	2
Laura	5
John	4
Laurence	3
Tom	2
Anna	4
Andrea	8
George	7
Paul	13

5.4 Time

Time is commonly understood as a key factor in data warehousing systems, since the decision process often relies on computing historical trends and on comparing snapshots of the enterprise taken at different moments. In the following discussion, we collect some notes regarding temporal dimensions in fact schemata and their semantics.

5.4.1   Transactional vs. Snapshot Schemata

Kimball (1996) introduced two basic paradigms for representing inventory-like information in a data warehouse: the *transactional model*, where each increase and decrease in the inventory level is recorded as an event, and the *snapshot model*, where the current inventory level is periodically recorded. A similar characterization is proposed by Bliujute et al. (1998), who distinguish between *event-oriented data* such as sales, inventory transfers, and financial transactions, and *state-oriented data* such as unit prices, account balances, and inventory levels. In this section, we generalize these paradigms to define a classification of facts based on the conceptual role given to events (Golfarelli and Rizzi, 2007).

We start by observing that, in general terms, the facts to be monitored for decision support fall into two broad categories according to the way they are collected and measured in the application domain. *Flow facts* are monitored by collecting their occurrences during a time interval and are cumulatively measured at the end of that period; examples of flow facts are orders, invoices, sales, shipments, enrollments, phone calls, and so on. *Stock facts* are monitored by periodically sampling and measuring their state; examples of stock facts are those measuring the price of a share or the water level of a river.

Depending on the nature of the monitored fact and on the expected workload, two types of fact schemata can be built whose events have different semantics:

- A *transactional fact schema* is one for which each event may either record a single transaction or summarize a set of transactions that occur during the same time interval. In this case, most measures are flow measures (see section 5.2.9)—that is, they are cumulatively evaluated at the end of each time interval and are additive along all dimensions.

Figure 5-31
Transactional (top)
and snapshot
(bottom) fact
schemata

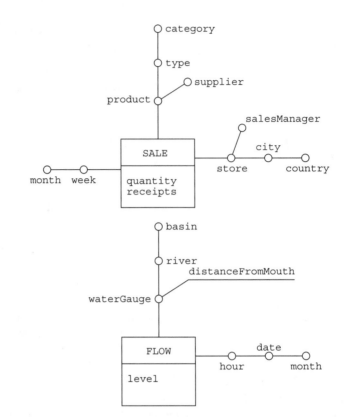

- A *snapshot fact schema* is one whose events correspond to periodical snapshots of the fact. Its measures are mostly stock measures (see section 5.2.9)—that is, they refer to an instant in time and are evaluated at that instant, so they are non-additive along temporal dimensions (that is, their values cannot be summed when aggregating along time, while, for instance, they can be averaged).

For a flow fact, a transactional fact schema is typically the most natural choice. For the sales fact, for instance, a subset of events of the transactional fact schema in Figure 5-31 might be those reported in Table 5-32, each representing the total quantity of a product sold in a store during a week.

On the other hand, for some flow facts, both transactional and snapshot schemata can be reasonably used. This is true, for instance, for the stock inventory fact, for which a transactional fact schema and a snapshot schema are depicted in Figure 5-32. The two schemata are clearly identical, except for the meaning of their measures. A sample set of

Table 5-32
Events for the
Transactional SALE
Fact Schema

store	week	product	quantity
SmartMart	10/1/2008	CD-R	100
SmartMart	10/1/2008	DVD+R	20
SmartMart	10/1/2008	CD-RW	80
SmartMart	10/8/2008	DVD+R	25

FIGURE 5-32
Transactional (top)
and snapshot
(bottom) fact
schemata for the
stock inventory
fact

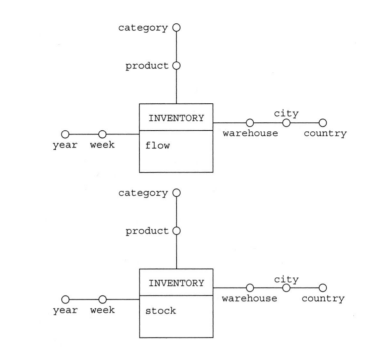

inventory events for the transactional solution is shown in Table 5-33: each event records the net flow of items of one product over a week within one warehouse. Table 5-34 shows how the same events could be represented within a snapshot solution: here each event records, on a specific date, the *total* number of items of a product available in a warehouse.

The choice of one solution or another for a flow fact depends first of all on the expected workload, and in particular on the relative weight of queries asking for flow and stock information, respectively. For instance, the current inventory level for LCD TVs in Austin, Texas, can be obtained in the transactional solution by summing up all pertinent events, which may be costly, while in the snapshot solution it is sufficient to read a single event (the most recent one). On the other hand, consider a query asking for the net flow of LCD TVs in

TABLE 5-33
Events for the
Transactional
INVENTORY
Fact Schema

week	product	warehouse	flow
10/1/2008	LCD TV	Austin	+20
10/8/2008	LCD TV	Austin	−5
10/15/2008	LCD TV	Austin	+3

TABLE 5-34
Events for the
Snapshot
INVENTORY Fact
Schema

week	product	warehouse	stock
10/1/2008	LCD TV	Austin	20
10/8/2008	LCD TV	Austin	15
10/15/2008	LCD TV	Austin	18

	hour	waterGauge	level
TABLE 5-35 Events for the Snapshot FLOW Fact Schema	9:00 a.m., Jan.7, 2008	Westminster Bridge	8.0
	10:00 a.m., Jan.7, 2008	Westminster Bridge	8.4
	11:00 a.m., Jan.7, 2008	Westminster Bridge	7.9

Austin during a specific week. While in the transactional solution this query is answered by reading one event, in the snapshot solution the result must be computed as the difference between the values of `quantity` registered in two consecutive weeks.

Differently from flow facts, stock facts naturally conform to the snapshot solution; for instance, a sample set of events for the river flow fact in Figure 5-31 is reported in Table 5-35: like in the transactional solution applied to a flow fact, each event records the exact value of the measurement. In principle, adopting a transactional solution for a stock fact is still possible, although not recommended. In fact, it would require disaggregating the (stock) measurements made in the application domain into a net flow to be registered, which implies that, before each new event can be registered, the current stock level must be computed by aggregating all previous events.

In conclusion, *a transactional fact schema is the best solution if, in the application domain, events are measured as in- and out-flows*. It should not be adopted when events are measured in the form of stock levels. *A snapshot fact schema is the best solution if, in the application domain, events are measured as stock levels*, but it can also be adopted when events are measured as flows. In general, the best choice also depends on the core workload expected for the fact.

5.4.2   Late Updates

The meaning commonly given to the time dimension in fact schemata is the so-called *valid time* (Tansel et al., 1993), which stands for the moment when an event occurs in the business world. *Transaction time* is the time at which a database stores an event; it is not typically given importance in data marts because it is not considered as important for decision support. However, this is not always true, as you will see in the following sections.

One of the underlying assumptions in data marts is that, once an event has been registered, it is never modified, so that the only possible writing operation consists in appending new events as they occur. While this is acceptable for a wide variety of domains, some applications call for a different behavior. In particular, the values of one or more measures for a specific event may change over a period of time, longer than the refresh interval, to be finally consolidated only *after* the event has been registered for the first time in the data mart. This typically happens when the early measurements made for events may be subject to errors or when events inherently evolve over time.

As an example for this discussion, consider an educational data mart in which a fact models the enrollment of students to university courses. Figure 5-33 shows a possible fact schema. Each primary event records the number of students in a specific city that registered for a specific course for a specific academic year on a specific date. An enrollment is completed and sent to the education secretary and then recorded as an event in the data mart only when the enrollment fee is paid. If you think of the delays tied to bank payment management and transmissions, it is not at all uncommon that the secretary receives payment notification more than a month *after* the actual enrollment date.

In this context, if you still wish to draw decision-makers' attention to the actual scenario of the current phenomenon at the right time, you should update past events with each

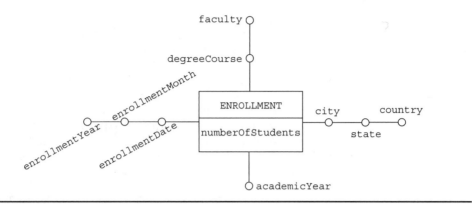

FIGURE 5-33   Fact schema for student enrollments

population cycle to reflect new data entered. We will call this type of operation *late update*, as it may imply registration of more than one measure for the same event. See section 10.4 for the implications of the population procedure.

The usage of valid time only is no longer enough to attain full query expressivity and flexibility when you have to deal with late updates:

1. It is the decision-maker's responsibility to justify his or her decisions. This requires the ability to trace precise information available at the time when decisions are made. If old events are replaced by their new versions, past decisions can no longer be justified.

2. In some scenarios, accessing only information from current versions is not enough to ensure the accuracy of analyses. A typical case comes from those queries that compare the advancement status of a phenomenon in progress and past statuses of that phenomenon. Because the data recorded for the phenomenon in progress are not yet consolidated, their comparison with past, already consolidated data is conceptually inaccurate.

Now look at the enrollments example. Figure 5-34 shows a possible flow of data the secretary received over an interval of six days for a specific combination of cities, academic years, and courses. We have distinguished two temporal coordinates: the *registration date*,

FIGURE 5-34
Number of enrollments by city, course and academic year.

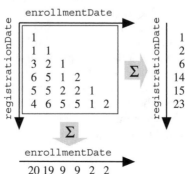
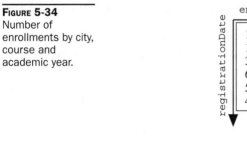

the date when the secretary receives notification of payment, and the *enrollment date*, the date to which a payment refers. Each matrix cell records the number of enrollments received on a specific date related to the date in which they were actually completed.

This example helps us to understand that two different temporal coordinates can be distinguished for all of the facts potentially affected by late updates. The first temporal coordinate refers to the time when each event actually took place and coincides with valid time as we previously mentioned. The second temporal coordinate refers instead to the time when a measurement for an event was received and recorded to a data mart; this coordinate coincides with the transaction time. As in the case of operational databases, you do not necessarily have to maintain both coordinates, because this mainly depends on the workload type. In particular, we can distinguish three types of queries:

- **Up-to-date queries**   Only require currently valid measurements for the events. For example, look at the ENROLLMENT fact. We can ask, In which months do students tend by preference to enroll in a certain course? To answer this query accurately, you must use the most updated data available on the number of enrollments per date of enrollment. This means the data shown along the enrollmentDate axis at the bottom of Figure 5-34. You do not have to record any transaction time to answer up-to-date queries because they just use the valid time.

- **Rollback queries**   Require, for each event, the measurement that was valid at a time *t*. For example, you may find it interesting to examine the current trend of total number of enrollments per faculty, compared with that of the previous year. If you answer this query on the basis of enrollment date when you compare the current data (still partial) with past data (already consolidated), you could erroneously infer that enrollments are declining this year. Instead, if the average delay of payment receipt shows no change from previous years, you can base an accurate comparison on the population date (the registrationDate axis on the right in Figure 5-34). It is clear that the valid time alone is no longer enough to support this type of query and it becomes essential to model transaction time as well.

- **Historical queries**   Require more than one measurement be made at different times for each event. An example of a historical query is a query that defines the daily distribution of the number of enrollments received on a certain enrollment date. As in the previous case, you should also explicitly represent the transaction time here.

Depending on whether late updates occur, and on the composition of expected workload, two main types of conceptual design solutions can be envisaged for a fact: *monotemporal*, where only valid time is modeled as a dimension, and *bitemporal*, where both valid and transaction time are modeled as dimensions.

Monotemporal solutions are commonly implemented for facts that either are not subject to late updates or are only required to support up-to-date queries. They are the simplest solutions: updates are done by physically overwriting the measurements taken at previous times for the same event, so that one single measurement (the most recent one) is kept in the database for each event. The transaction times of measurements are not represented and no trace is left of past measurements, so only up-to-date queries are supported, and, in case of late updates, accountability is not guaranteed. For instance, the schema of the monotemporal

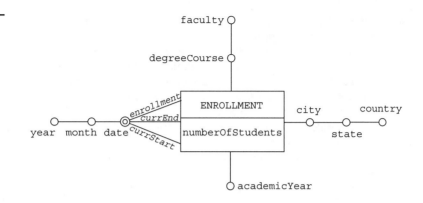

FIGURE 5-35
Bitemporal fact
schema for
enrollments

solution for the enrollment facts is exactly the one already shown in Figure 5-33, where the only temporal dimension is `enrollmentDate` (valid time).

Conversely, bitemporal solutions are the most comprehensive solutions that can be adopted when late updates might occur, and they allow all three types of queries to be accurately answered. For each population cycle, new update measurements for previous events may be added, and their transaction time is traced; no overwriting of previous measurements is carried out, so nothing is lost. A bitemporal fact schema for enrollments is shown in Figure 5-35; the shared temporal hierarchy enables the modeling of valid time (`enrollmentDate`) and transaction time (in the form of a currency interval [`currencyStart`, `currencyEnd`]). A sample set of events is depicted in Table 5-36.

The interested reader is referred to Golfarelli and Rizzi (2007) for a deeper analysis of the issues arising in the presence of late updates and a more detailed description of the possible conceptual design solutions for transactional and snapshot fact schemata.

5.4.3   Dynamic Hierarchies

Up to this point, we have hypothesized that the only dynamic component described in a fact schema may be the fact itself and its events. We have attributed an exclusively static nature to hierarchies. This is evidently not completely true. Slowly, sales managers rotate among various departments. Each month, new products are added to those already for sale, product categories change, and their attribution to products changes. Sales districts may be modified or a store may be moved from one district to another. We should clarify that only the dynamic properties at the extensional level—that is, the dynamic properties of hierarchy instances—will be considered in this paragraph. We will not be concerned about possible

enrollmentDate	currencyStart	currencyEnd	degreeCourse	academicYear	numberOfStudents
Oct. 21, 2008	Oct. 27, 2008	Oct. 31, 2008	Elec. Eng.	08/09	5
Oct. 21, 2008	*Nov. 1, 2008*	*Nov. 4, 2008*	*Elec. Eng.*	*08/09*	*13*
Oct. 21, 2008	*Nov. 5, 2008*	*–*	*Elec. Eng.*	*08/09*	*11*
Oct. 22, 2008	Oct. 27, 2008	Nov. 4, 2008	Elec. Eng.	08/09	2
Oct. 22, 2008	*Nov. 5, 2008*	*–*	*Elec. Eng.*	*08/09*	*6*
Oct. 23, 2008	Oct. 23, 2008	–	Elec. Eng.	08/09	3

TABLE 5-36   Events for the ENROLLMENTS Schema with Late Updates in Italics

modifications that alter the structure of hierarchies, such as the addition of a new attribute to a hierarchy or the addition of a new dimension, which are not considered routine phenomena, but rather extraordinary events connected to data mart maintenance.

On the conceptual level, the representation of dynamic properties in hierarchies is strictly bound to their impact on queries. When you use a dynamic hierarchy, you can actually distinguish four different temporal scenarios in the event analysis, as proposed first by SAP Business Warehouse. To discuss those scenarios, we will make reference to the following example. Assume that on 1/1/08, the sales manager for the EverMore store changed from Smith to Johnson, and that a new store, EverMore2, opened with Smith as manager. Consider the possibilities:

- **Today-for-yesterday**   All the events are analyzed according to the hierarchies' current configuration. In the example, we attribute EverMore store sales before 2008 as well as the more recent ones to Johnson, while we attribute EverMore2 store sales to Smith. This approach proves interesting if Johnson also becomes responsible for past sales.

- **Yesterday-for-today**   All of the events are analyzed according to the configuration the hierarchies had at a previous time. In the example, we attribute all EverMore store sales to Smith and we do not consider EverMore2 store sales.

- **Today-or-yesterday**   Each event is analyzed according to the configuration the hierarchies had at the time when the event occurred. For this reason, we attribute the EverMore store sales prior to 2008 and all of the EverMore2 store sales to Smith, and we attribute EverMore store sales from 2008 onward to Johnson.

- **Today-and-yesterday**   Only the events referring to the hierarchy instances that remain unchanged are considered. Sales in neither of the two stores are then considered.

In the example, the dynamic properties involve an arc in a hierarchy—the arc expressing the association between `store` and `salesManager`—because instances of the corresponding association vary. However, dynamic attributes are very frequent as well. For example, the name of a product category or store may change over time. Let's assume then that the EverMore store changes its name to EvenMore on 1/1/09. We may then describe the four scenarios as follows:

- **Today-for-yesterday**   We attribute all of the store's sales (even those prior to 2009) to EvenMore.

- **Yesterday-for-today**   We attribute all store sales (even those from 2009 forward) to EverMore.

- **Today-or-yesterday**   We attribute the sales prior to 2009 to EverMore and those from 2009 forward to EvenMore.

- **Today-and-yesterday**   The store's sales are not considered.

From the viewpoint of conceptual modeling, it is important to note that you should not also consider as dynamic the creation of a new value in the attribute domain (for example,

Attributes/Arcs	Today-for-Yesterday	Yesterday-for-Today	Today-or-Yesterday	Today-and-Yesterday
store			×	
store – salesManager			×	×
store – salesDistrict			×	
type – marketingGroup	×	×	×	×
category – department			×	

TABLE 5-37   Table of Dynamic Properties of the Sales Schema

a new product for sale or a newly opened store) or the consequent creation of a new instance for all of the associations regarding it (the new product must be associated with a type and brand, the new store to a city and to a sales district). All logical design solutions act uniformly as far as the addition of new values is concerned (section 8.4).

It is useful to mark the analysis scenarios of interest to the user for each arc and attribute. We will assume by default that the only scenario of interest is *today-or-yesterday*. If some attributes or arcs require different scenarios, you can prepare a table to list them. Table 5-37 shows how to perform this task with reference to the sales fact schema of Figure 5-8. Section 8.4 discusses how the logical design solution to be adopted depends on the specific combination of scenarios required by users.

5.5 Overlapping Fact Schemata

Separate fact schemata represent different facts in the DFM. However, part of the queries may require a comparison of the measures from two or more facts correlating to each other. In OLAP terminology, these are called *drill-across queries*. For example, next to the sales fact schema can be a fact schema that models the shipments sent with the `quantityShipped` and `cost` measures, and the `product`, `date`, `warehouse`, and `customer` dimensions. In that case, users may find it interesting to compare quantities sold with those shipped for the same dates and products.

In this section, we will discuss the ways you can combine two or more fact schemata into a new schema to use for drill-across queries. For simplicity of notation, we will denote two dimensional attributes that belong to different fact schemata but share the same semantics and have non-disjoint domains with the same name.

> **Comparable Fact Schemata**
> Two fact schemata are *comparable* when they have at least one group-by set (not the empty one) in common.

Obviously, two schemata are comparable when they share at least one dimensional attribute. Some examples of comparable schemata are SALE (Figure 5-8), SHIPMENT (Figure 5-10), and INVENTORY (Figure 5-23). They have the majority of dimensional attributes in their hierarchies based on date and product in common. Additionally, SHIPMENT and INVENTORY have the warehouse attribute in common. In particular, the group-by sets common to SALE and SHIPMENT are {product, date} plus all of the others lower than them in the roll-up order.

Naturally, the main problem with determining comparability in real-world cases lies in identifying common attributes. Even though universal methods to resolve this do not exist, we list some criteria for you to follow, with differing levels of effectiveness according to the scenario:

- Having non-disjoint domains is a necessary condition so that two attributes can correspond. Unfortunately, this criterion is difficult to follow if you extract attribute domains from underlying operational schemata, because the majority of attributes will be defined on the basis of standard primitive data types.

- Determining pairs of attributes with the same name in both source fact schemata can be useful to suggest correspondence if the designer selected names consistently in the conceptual design phase.

- According to design rules commonly adopted, hierarchies built on the same dimension in distinct fact schemata within the same data mart should be identical (the so-called *conformed dimensions*). In cases like this, you can immediately define a correspondence.

After defining common attributes, you can overlap two comparable schemata to create a resulting schema.

Reducing Hierarchies

Given a hierarchy *h* and a subset *R* of its dimensional attributes, the *reduction* of *h* to *R* is a set of hierarchies that include all and only the attributes in *R* linked to each other via functional dependencies transitively derived from those in *h*.

Figure 5-36 shows an example of reduction. On the left is a hierarchy with the a dimension. On the right are two hierarchies obtained after reducing to the c, e, g, i, and l

FIGURE 5-36
Reducing a
hierarchy to
a subset of
attributes

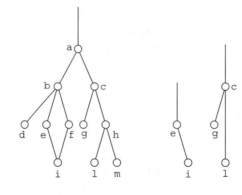

attributes, respectively. For example, note that you can transitively derive the c→l functional dependency in the result from c→h and h→l in the initial hierarchy.

> **Overlapping Compatible Fact Schemata**
> Two comparable fact schemata are called *compatible* when reductions of their hierarchies to common attributes are equal. *Overlapping* two compatible fact schemata results in an *overlapped fact schema* in which (1) hierarchies are the common reduction of the hierarchies in source fact schemata; (2) measures are the union of the measures in source fact schemata; (3) each attribute domain is an intersection of the corresponding attribute domains in source fact schemata.

Compatibility between two fact schemata implies that the functional dependencies they contain are all mutually consistent. It is easy to verify that the SALE, INVENTORY, and SHIPMENT schemata are compatible. For example, two fact schemata are incompatible if one of them contains the $a_i{\rightarrow}a_j$ dependency and the other has the $a_j{\rightarrow}a_i$ dependency. As a matter of fact, both functional dependencies could theoretically coexist. This implies that a one-to-one association exists between a_i and a_j. In our context, though, the fact that the same attributes are in separate hierarchies in inverse order probably means that a design error occurred in one of both schemata (Golfarelli et al., 1998).

Figure 5-37 shows how to overlap INVENTORY and SHIPMENT. You can use the resulting overlapped schema to compare quantities shipped and those warehoused for each product. See section 7.1.2 for a detailed discussion on drill-across queries on overlapped schemata.

We repeat that hierarchies are widely shared between more than one fact schemata in the majority of cases. And in many cases, they will even be identical (conformed hierarchies—for example the product hierarchy). In other cases, a hierarchy dimension will coincide with a dimensional attribute from another hierarchy (for example, a hierarchy rooted in the customer dimension in the complaints fact schema will probably coincide with the subhierarchy rooted in customer from the order hierarchy in the shipments schema). Figure 5-38 shows an example of conformed hierarchies.

FIGURE 5-37
Overlapping the
INVENTORY and
SHIPMENT
schemata

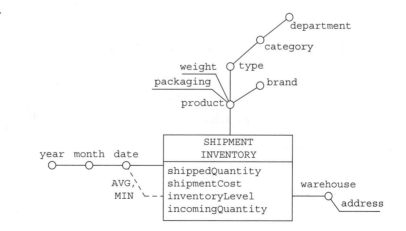

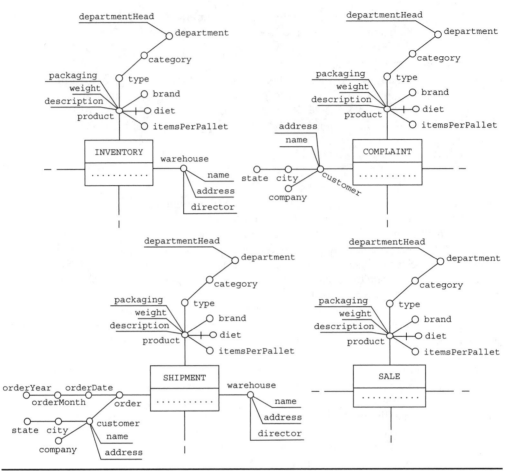

FIGURE 5-38   Conformed hierarchies

5.6 Formalizing the Dimensional Fact Model

In this section we discuss how to formalize the extensional and intensional properties of the DFM. Section 5.6.1 introduces the metamodel of a fact schema for readers familiar with UML. Sections 5.6.2 and 5.6.3 show how to formalize the basic concepts of the DFM. We have excluded advanced constructs of DFM on purpose to simplify this explanation.

5.6.1   Metamodel

Figure 5-39 shows the UML metamodel of the DFM. We suggest you read one of the many texts on this subject (for example, Arlow and Neustadt, 2005) for an explanation of the syntax used in this figure.

FIGURE 5-39
UML metamodel
of the DFM

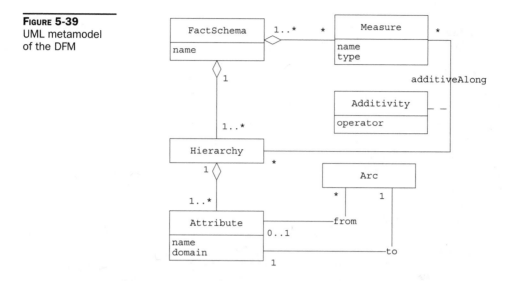

5.6.2   Intensional Properties

Hierarchy
A *hierarchy h* is a pair $(A, \leq_h)$ where

- *A* is a finite set of *dimensional attributes*;
- $\leq_h$ is a partial order based on the attributes of *A* where one and only one maximum element always exists and is called a *dimension*.

Semantics of the partial order are that $a_i \leq_h a_j$ when $a_j \rightarrow a_i$.
Looking at Figure 5-6, the product hierarchy can be described as follows:

$$A = \{\text{product, type, category, department,}$$
$$\text{marketingGroup, brand, brandCity}\}$$

Figure 5-40 shows the Hasse diagram that illustrates the partial order for the product hierarchy. The `product` attribute is the dimension.

FIGURE 5-40
Hasse diagram
showing the partial
order of attributes
in the product
hierarchy

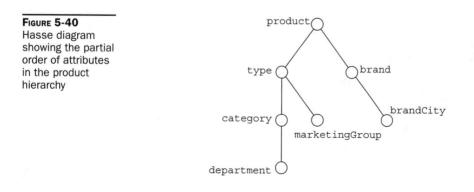

Fact Schema

We define a *fact schema F* as a pair (*H*, *M*) in which

- *H* is a finite set of hierarchies
- *M* is a finite (possibly empty) set of *measures*

If *n* is the number of hierarchies in *H*, we say that *F* is *n-dimensional*. Additionally, we will denote the set of all the attributes in the hierarchies and the set of the measures in *F* with *Attr(F)* and *Meas(F)*, respectively.

The sales fact schema in Figure 5-6 includes three hierarchies: one with the product dimension (shown in Figure 5-40), one with the store dimension, and one with the date dimension (both shown in Figure 5-41). The measures are quantity, receipts, unitPrice, and numberOfCustomers.

Group-by Set

Let *F* be a fact schema. We define a *group-by set* of *F* as any subset of attributes, $G \subseteq Attr(F)$, such that for each pair of attributes a_i and a_j, contained in *G* from the same hierarchy *h*, neither $a_i \leq_h a_j$ nor $a_j \leq_h a_i$ holds.

The $\{a_1 \ldots, a_n\}$ group-by set including all of the dimensions of *F* is called the primary *group-by set* of *F* and marked with *Gbs(F)*. All of the others are called *secondary group-by sets* and identify possible ways to aggregate events, as we mentioned in section 5.3.

Roll-up Order

Given fact schema *F*, we define a partial *roll-up* order $\leq$ on the set of all possible group-by sets of *F* as follows: $G_i \leq G_j$ if and only if $G_j \rightarrow G_i$.

According to the roll-up order definition, it is $G_i \leq G_j$ when, for each attribute a_j from hierarchy *h* contained in G_j, either G_i includes an attribute a_i such that $a_i \leq_h a_j$, or no attribute from *h* is part of G_i.

FIGURE 5-41
Store and date
hierarchies,
assuming that the
allocation of stores
to districts does
not depend on the
cities to which
stores belong

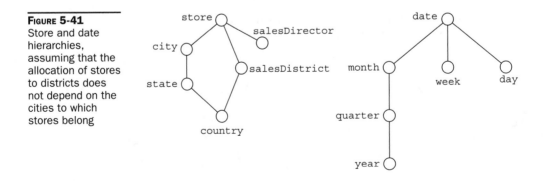

5.6.3 Extensional Properties

Hierarchy Instance

Given a hierarchy $h = (A, \leq_h)$, an *instance* of h is a pair (D, L) where

- D is the set of domains $Dom(a_i)$ of the attributes in A; each domain is the (countable) set of values that the attribute can be given;

- L is a family of *roll-up functions* that map each value of $Dom(a_j)$ into a value of $Dom(a_i)$ for each pair of a_i and a_j attributes such that $a_i \leq_h a_j$:

$$up_{a_i}^{a_j} : Dom(a_j) \mapsto Dom(a_i)$$

Consider this example:

$Dom(\texttt{city}) = \{$'Abbyville', 'Auburn', 'Pushmataha', 'Jackson', 'Castlewood', 'Deckers'$\}$
$Dom(\texttt{state}) = \{$'Kansas', 'Oklahoma', 'Colorado'$\}$
$up_{\texttt{state}}^{\texttt{city}}$ ('Abbyville') = 'Kansas'

You should actually define a roll-up function only for the immediately adjacent pairs of attributes in the partial order. You may transitively compose the function for the other pairs. Given the a_1, a_2, and a_3 attributes such that $a_1 \leq_h a_2 \leq_h a_3$, it would actually be

$$up_{a_1}^{a_3}(\cdot) = up_{a_1}^{a_2}\left(up_{a_2}^{a_3}(\cdot)\right)$$

If two or more separate paths exist in the $\leq_h$ order that join two attributes a_i and a_j, we assume that the $up_{a_i}^{a_j}$ roll-up functions obtained from composing roll-up functions along the different paths are identical to enable an accurate aggregation. In the stores hierarchy in Figure 5-41, country and store are connected by two paths that include salesDistrict on the one side and city and state on the other side. For this reason, it should result in this:

$$up_{\texttt{country}}^{\texttt{salesDistrict}}\left(up_{\texttt{salesDistrict}}^{\texttt{store}}(\cdot)\right) = up_{\texttt{country}}^{\texttt{state}}\left(up_{\texttt{state}}^{\texttt{city}}\left(up_{\texttt{city}}^{\texttt{store}}(\cdot)\right)\right)$$

Coordinate

Given a fact schema $F = (H, M)$, an instance of each hierarchy in H and a group-by set $G = \{a_1 \ldots, a_v\}$, a *coordinate* of G is a function that maps each $a_i \in G$ attribute into a value of $Dom(a_i)$. We will mark with $Dom(G)$ the set of possible coordinates of G:

$$Dom(G) = Dom(a_1) \times \ldots \times Dom(a_v)$$

Now you can define an instance of a fact as a function that associates the coordinates of the primary group-by set with primary events.

> ### Cube and Primary Event
> Given a fact schema $F = (H, M)$ with $M = \{m_1, \ldots, m_s\}$, and given an instance of each hierarchy in H, a *cube* instance of F is a partial function that maps from the coordinates of $Gbs(F)$ to the measure domains of M:
>
> $$c : Dom(Patt(F)) \mapsto Dom(m_1) \times \ldots \times Dom(m_s)$$
>
> Each specific n-ple of measure values determined is called a *primary event*.

A primary event is a basic cell of information defined by a coordinate of the primary group-by set. A value for each measure in the fact schema is associated with each primary event. Let $a_1, \ldots, a_n$ be the dimensions of fact schema F and c be a cube instance of F. We will mark the primary event corresponding to the $\alpha = (a_1 : \alpha_1 \ldots, a_n : \alpha_n) \in Dom(a_1) \times \ldots \times Dom(a_n)$ coordinate with $c(\alpha)$.

In the sales example, a cube may be then defined as follows:

c (product:'Shiny', store:'EverMore', date:'4/5/07') = (quantity:10, receipts:25)
c (product:'Shiny', store:'EverMore', date:'4/7/07') = (quantity:20, receipts:50)
c (product:'Scent', store:'EverMore', date:'4/5/07') = (quantity:5, receipts:10)
c (product:'Scent', store:'SmartMart', date:'4/8/07') = (quantity:10, receipts:20)

Given two group-by sets G_i and G_j such that $G_i \leq G_j$, the functional dependency between G_j and G_i and the roll-up functions in F allow each coordinate α_j of G_j to be mapped into exactly one coordinate α_i of G_i. Each coordinate of G_i corresponds to a set of coordinates of G_j. You may then extend the roll-up function definition to map from one group-by set domain to another:

$$up_{G_i}^{G_j} : Dom(G_j) \mapsto Dom(G_i) \text{ such that } up_{G_i}^{G_j}(\alpha_j) = \alpha_i$$

For example,

$$up_{\{category, state\}}^{\{type, city\}} (\text{'Drink', 'Los Angeles'}) = (\text{'Food', 'California'})$$

(We have omitted the attribute names that define the coordinates to simplify notation, as the subscript and superscript group-by sets of the roll-up function already express them.)

If G_j includes more attributes from the same hierarchy, the constraint on unique compositions of roll-up functions among attributes ensures a clear definition of roll-up functions among coordinates; here's an example:

$$up_{\{country\}}^{\{salesDistrict, city\}} (\text{'NorthIllinois', 'Chicago'}) = (\text{'USA'})$$

A hierarchy may be present in G_j, but not in G_i:

$$up_{\{type, year\}}^{\{product, state, quarter\}} (\text{'CleanHand', 'Colorado', 'II 2007'}) = (\text{'Soap', '2007'})$$

Here we use the $up_{\{type, year\}}^{\{product, state, quarter\}}$ roll-up function to map all the coordinates of the {product, state, quarter} group-by set and related to soap-type products, to the four quarters of 2000 and to *all* the stores into the (type:'Soap', year:'2007') coordinate.

As a last example, think of the specific case of a roll-up function that maps into the empty group-by set. The coordinates of the empty group-by set do not exist strictly because no attributes are displayed in the empty group-by set. Conventionally, you may assume that one fictitious coordinate exists, to which all of the coordinates of any group-by set G correspond via the $up_{\{\}}^{G}$ roll-up function.

Now let there be a secondary group-by set $G \leq Gbs(F)$. The roll-up function that associates a set of coordinates of $Gbs(F)$ with each coordinate of G enables the aggregation of primary events of cube c by group-by set G. You then obtain an aggregation c' where the measure values for each coordinate sum up those in the coordinates of c corresponding via the roll-up function.

Aggregation and Secondary Events

Let F be a fact schema and let $G \leq Gbs(F)$. Let c be a cube instance of F. The *aggregation* of c by G is a function c' that maps from the coordinates of G to the measure domains of $Meas(F)$:

$$c' : Dom(G) \mapsto Dom(m_1) \times \ldots \times Dom(m_s)$$

This is defined as follows,

$$c'(\alpha').m_i = \underset{\alpha \,:\, up_G^{Gbs(F)}(\alpha) = \alpha'}{\Omega_i} c(\alpha).m_i$$

where α is a generic coordinate of $Gbs(F)$, α' is a generic coordinate of G, and Ω_i is an aggregation operator for measure m_i. Each n-ple of the measure values defined is called a *secondary event*.

CHAPTER

Conceptual Design

Chapter 5 described a conceptual model for data marts, which should be used to create a set of fact schemata. In this chapter, we discuss how to build a conceptual schema for a data mart in order to meet user requirements and be consistent with operational source schemata.

Chapter 2 already pointed out that three fundamental methodological approaches can be taken to data mart design: the data-driven approach, the requirement-driven approach, and the mixed approach. Their differences are based on the relevance given to the source database analysis and the end-user requirement analysis phases. Opting for one of those approaches dramatically affects the way conceptual design will be carried out:

- The *data-driven approach* defines the conceptual schema for a data mart in relation to the structure of an operational data source—typically, your reconciled database. This helps you skip the complex task of linking them at a later stage. Moreover, you can almost automatically derive a preliminary conceptual schema for your data mart from your data source schema. When you analyze user requirements, this gives you the immediate opportunity to have a precise idea of the maximum performance potential of your data mart, and then to discuss specifications more realistically.

- In a *requirement-driven approach*, there is more room for a user requirement analysis because no detailed information on data sources is available or sources are too complex to be investigated. The resulting specifications become the foundations for a conceptual schema of a data mart. Virtually, this means that designers have to be able to manipulate their interviews with users to extract (i) very precise instructions about facts to be represented; (ii) measures defining those facts; and (iii) hierarchies for those facts to be usefully aggregated. Designers will deal with the resulting conceptual schemata linked to operational data sources only at a later stage.

- In a *mixed approach*, user requirements play an active role in imposing limits on complexity of data source analysis. The in-depth requirements analysis is formally performed as in the requirement-based approach. The results of requirement analysis guide the algorithm that obtains a draft structure of fact schemata from data source schemata as in the data-driven approach.

In this chapter, we will examine conceptual design with reference to these three approaches.

In the data-driven approach, it is extremely interesting to study how you can derive your conceptual schema from those schemata that define a relational database. This is because the majority of the operational databases created over the last decade are based on the relational model. Our methodology may be applied to conceptual Entity-Relationship schemata (see section 6.1) or relational logical schemata (see section 6.2) along with minor changes. Naturally, conceptual Entity-Relationship schemata are more expressive than relational logical schemata. For this reason, they are generally considered as a better design resource. However, companies often provide Entity-Relationship schemata that are incomplete and inaccurate. Very often, the only accessible documentation consists of logical schemata of databases if no careful investigation is carried out.

Companies are increasingly considering the Internet as an integral part of their business and communications plans. Moreover, a large part of web data is stored in eXtensible Markup Language (XML) format. For this reason, it is important that you can integrate XML data into your data warehousing systems. Section 6.3 shows how a data mart conceptual schema can be derived from schemata defining XML sources. The material presented is discussed in Golfarelli and others (2001).

NOTE   *See Atzeni et al., 1999 for a more detailed discussion on the Entity-Relationship model (ERM). See Cabibbo and Torlone, 1998; Hüsemann et al., 2000; and Song et al., 2007 for other approaches to conceptual design from the Entity-Relationship source schemata. Jones and Song (2005) discuss an interesting approach to conceptual design based on the application of relevant design patterns. Other work relevant to XML sources and semantic web contexts is presented in Vrdoljak et al., 2003; Jensen et al., 2001; and Romero and Abelló, 2007.*

Section 6.4 gives a detailed description of the mixed approach to conceptual design that is only partially different from the data-driven approach. Finally, section 6.5 provides more details on the main instructions for the requirement-driven approach to conceptual design.

6.1 Entity-Relationship Schema-based Design

Data-driven Conceptual Design
The technique used for the Dimensional Fact Model (DFM)–compliant conceptual design of a data mart based on an operational source Entity-Relationship schema includes the following steps:

1. *Define facts.*
2. For each fact:
    a. *Build an attribute tree*
    b. *Prune and graft the attribute tree*
    c. *Define dimensions*
    d. *Define measures*
    e. *Create a fact schema*

First, select relevant facts from your source schema (step 1). Then, create your *attribute tree* in semi-automatic mode (step 2.a). This is a transitional structure that is useful for delimiting the area relevant to your fact schema in order to eliminate all the irrelevant attributes and modify dependencies that link these (step 2.b), and to define measures and dimensions (steps 2.c and 2.d). The attribute tree is also very important because it links your data mart and source schema. This link acts as a key for the data-staging process. Then it is relatively simple to translate your attribute tree into a fact schema (step 2.e). Note that step 2.a is based on the application of an algorithm; steps 2.c, 2.d, and 2.e are based on the objective properties of attributes; and steps 1 and 2.b require an in-depth knowledge of the corporate business model. For this reason, designers must pay much greater attention to the last two steps.

Every step in this method will be described with reference to the sales example. Figure 6-1 shows a simplified Entity-Relationship schema for this example. Each instance of the SALE relationship represents the sale of a specific product listed on a specific sale receipt. The unitPrice attribute relates to SALE rather than PRODUCT because product prices can vary over time. The identifier of SALES DISTRICT is the pair consisting of the districtNum attribute and the COUNTRY entity identifier. Note that there is a redundant cycle involving the STORE, CITY, STATE, COUNTRY, and SALES DISTRICT entities. However, the cycle involving PRODUCT and CITY through STORE and BRAND is not redundant because the city where a product of a particular brand is produced is usually different from the cities where those products are sold.

6.1.1   Defining Facts

Facts are concepts of key importance for a decision-making process. They typically correspond to events dynamically occurring in a company.

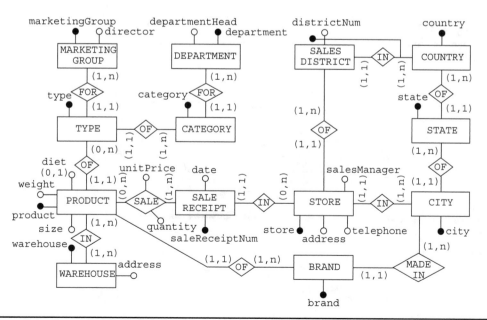

FIGURE 6-1 Conceptual Entity-Relationship schema for the sales operational database

In an Entity-Relationship schema, a fact may correspond either to an entity or an n-ary relationship, R, between the $E_1, E_2..., E_n$ entities. In the latter case, in the interests of simplicity, you can transform R into an entity (*reification* process). To do this, add a new entity called F and replace each branch of R with a binary relationship (R_i) between F and E_i. If you mark the minimum and maximum cardinality level, at which an entity E participates in a relationship A, with $min(E, A)$ and $max(E, A)$,[1] respectively, you get this:

$$min(F, R_i) = max(F, R_i) = 1, min(E_i, R_i) = min(E_i, R), max(E_i, R_i) = max(E_i, R), i = 1..., n$$

The attributes of the R relationship become attributes of F. The identifier of F is the combination of the identifiers of $E_i, i = 1..., n$. Figure 6-2 shows the reification process applied to a ternary relationship.

TIP *Those entities that represent frequently updated archives, such as SALE, are good candidates for fact definition, but those entities that represent structural domain properties corresponding to almost static archives, such as STORE and CITY, are not.*

As a matter of fact, this common sense rule must not be applied too literally. This is because the borderline between what should be a fact and what should not depends largely on the application domain and the type of analysis users wish to carry out. Consider the example in which shop assistants in a supermarket are assigned to different departments. If each assistant is assigned only to one department at any time, is it correct to classify this relationship as a fact? If users want to pay attention to the sales made by each assistant, both assistants and departments will be modeled as hierarchy attributes. A functional dependency will model shop assistant assignments to a specific supermarket department. On the contrary,

FIGURE 6-2
Reification of the R
relationship

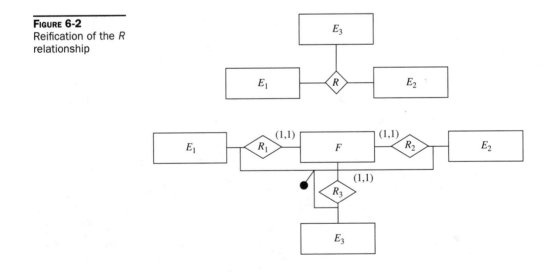

---

[1]Typically, $min(E, A) \in \{0, 1\}$ and $max(E, A) \in \{1, n\}$.

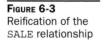

FIGURE 6-3
Reification of the
SALE relationship

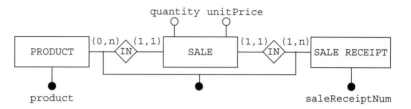

if users are more interested in studying assistants transferred from a supermarket department to another one, then you should introduce a new fact to emphasize dynamic properties of the assignments to specific departments. Note that the choice between one or the other design solution does not necessarily depend on how often assistant assignments change.

Each fact identified in a source schema becomes the root of a different fact schema. In the following sections, we will focus on one single fact that corresponds to an entity possibly deriving from a reification process. The most relevant fact for the analysis is the sales of a product in the sales example. At a conceptual level, the sales fact is represented by the SALE relationship, reified into the SALE entity, as shown in Figure 6-3.

It is important to note that different entities can sometimes be candidates for expressing an individual fact. If this is the case, we suggest you should always choose as a fact the entity to build an attribute tree that includes as many attributes as possible. Section 6.2.2 will give an example to clarify this concept.

6.1.2   Building Attribute Trees

> **Attribute Trees**
> Given a relevant part of an Entity-Relationship source schema and one of its entities F classified as a fact, an *attribute tree* is the tree that meets the following requirements:
>
> - Each node corresponds to a source schema attribute (simple or composite).
> - The root corresponds to the identifier of the F entity.
> - For each node v, the corresponding attribute functionally determines all the attributes corresponding to the descendants of v.

You can automatically build the attribute tree corresponding to F if you run an algorithm that recursively navigates functional dependencies expressed by identifiers and to-one relationships in your source schema. Each time you examine an entity E, you should create a new node v corresponding to the E identifier, and then you should add a child node to v for every attribute of E. These also include all the individual attributes that make up the E identifier, if it is composite. Every time you find a relationship R with a maximum cardinality of 1 from the E entity to another entity G, you should add a child for the G identifier and all the children for the attributes of R to the v node. Then you should repeat this procedure for the G entity. The entity from which this process is triggered is the one you chose as the fact, F.

Figure 6-4 shows the basic features of the algorithm that builds the attribute tree in pseudo-code. Figure 6-5 shows an example of the control flow for the `translate` procedure and it gives a step-by-step explanation on how to build an attribute tree branch for the sales example. Figure 6-6 shows the resulting tree.

FIGURE 6-4 Pseudo-code for the attribute tree-building algorithm

---

```
root=newNode(ident(F)); // ident(F) is the identifier of F
// the tree root is labeled with the identifier
// of the entity set as a fact
translate(F, root);

procedure translate(E, v):
// E is the current entity of the source schema,
// v is the current node of the tree
{   for each attribute a∈E such that a≠ident(E)
        addChild(v, newNode(a));
        // adds the a child to the v node
    for each entity G linked to E by an R relationship s.t. max(E, R)=1
    {   for each b∈R attribute
            addChild(v, newNode(b));
            // adds the b child to the v node
        next=newNode(ident(G));
        // creates a new node with the name of the identifier of G ...
        addChild(v, next);
        // ... adds it to v as a child ...
        translate(G, next);
        // ... and triggers the recursion
    }
}
```

FIGURE 6-5 Operating flow of the `translate` procedure for the sales example

---

```
root=newNode(product+saleReceiptNum)

translate(E=SALE, v=product+saleReceiptNum):
    addChild(product+saleReceiptNum, quantity);
    addChild(product+saleReceiptNum, unitPrice);
    for G=SALE RECEIPT:
        addChild(product+saleReceiptNum, saleReceiptNum);
        translate(SALE RECEIPT, saleReceiptNum);
    for G=PRODUCT:
        addChild(product+saleReceiptNum, product);
        translate(PRODUCT, product);

translate(E=SALE RECEIPT, v=saleReceiptNum):
    addChild(saleReceiptNum, date);
    for G=STORE:
        addChild(saleReceiptNum, store);
        translate(STORE, store);
```

```
translate(E=STORE, v=store):
    addChild(store, address);
    addChild(store, telephone);
    addChild(store, salesManager);
    for G=DISTRICT:
        addChild(store, districtNum+country);
        translate(DISTRICT, districtNum+country);
    for G=CITY:
        addChild(store, city);
        translate(CITY, city);

translate(E=DISTRICT, v=districtNum+country):
    addChild(districtNum+country, districtNum);
    for G=COUNTRY:
        addChild(districtNum+country, country);
        translate(COUNTRY, country);

translate(E=COUNTRY, v=country)
```

Naturally, the need to duly pay attention to many specific elements, for which you must check your source schema, makes your algorithm operations more complex than this. In the following paragraphs we will make a few remarks and give you some guidelines to manage those elements.

Your source schema may contain a many-to-one relationship cycle. For example, one part may be made up of many other parts. If this is the case, the `translate` procedure loops forever and attempts to build an infinite branch in the attribute tree. Two solutions are possible at the conceptual level. The first solution involves the use of a recursive hierarchy to show that the height of the hierarchy is generally unlimited. With this solution you can have instances of hierarchies of different heights, but bear in mind that the logical modeling of recursive hierarchies inevitably involves complexity and performance problems. See sections 5.2.8 and 9.1.7 for more details on conceptual and logical modeling of recursive hierarchies. The second solution is very often preferred. This solution stops the loop cycle after a specific number of iterations determined by the relationship relevance in your application domain. Figure 6-7 shows a simplified schema for the transfer of personnel within a company. There is a many-to-one relationship in this schema involving the EMPLOYEE, the DEPARTMENT, and the DIVISION entities. There are three cycles because you can reach DEPARTMENT twice directly from TRANSFER, chosen as a fact, and a third

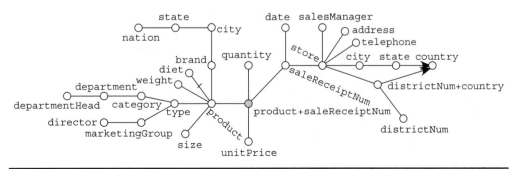

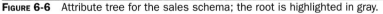

FIGURE 6-6 Attribute tree for the sales schema; the root is highlighted in gray.

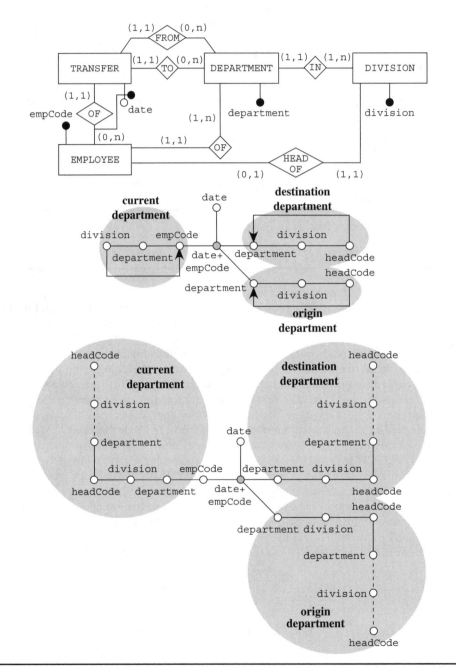

FIGURE 6-7 Entity-Relationship schema for the personnel transfers and two possible corresponding attribute trees

time from EMPLOYEE. Figure 6-7 shows two possible attribute trees. In the first tree, we used three recursive hierarchies for modeling. In the second tree, for each department r_1, we chose to stop the cycle at the r_2 department to which the r_1 manager belongs, because we assumed that the r_2 division coincides with the r_1 division.

While you are exploring a cyclic schema, you may happen to reach an individual E entity twice while you go down different paths. In this way, you generate two homologous nodes called v' and v'' in your tree. If each instance of F precisely determines one instance of E, regardless of the path followed, you can have the v' and v'' nodes coinciding in a single node called v. In this way, you create a convergence. The same applies to each pair of homologous children of v' and v''. If this is not the case, v' and v'' must be left separate. After creating the fact schema, you can opt for a shared hierarchy construct. Figure 6-7 shows an example of the inappropriate conditions for a convergence because the origin and destination departments must be separate. The sales example shows the correct conditions for convergence instead, because the country attribute can be reached either from districtNum or from state.

To-many relationships ($max(E, R) > 1$) and multiple attributes in the source Entity-Relationship schema are not automatically inserted in trees. These may give rise to cross-dimensional attributes or multiple arcs that designers will frame manually in fact schemata at the end of the conceptual design phase. See section 6.1.8 for more details on cross-dimensional attributes or multiple arcs.

It is important to show whether an optional link exists between attributes in one hierarchy. To do this, you can use a hyphen in those arcs that correspond to optional relationships ($min(E, R) = 0$) or optional attributes in your Entity-Relationship schema. In the sales example, this applies to the diet attribute.

If you carry out a reification process (section 6.1.1), you can turn an n-ary relationship in your Entity-Relationship schema into n binary relationships. Most n-ary relationships have a maximum multiplicity that is greater than 1 for all their branches. If this is the case, they define n one-to-many binary relationships that you can not insert into attribute trees. Figure 6-8 gives an example of this point. On the contrary, a branch of an n-ary relationship, whose maximum multiplicity is equal to 1, defines a one-to-one relationship in a reified schema. In this case, you can insert it in your tree. Figure 6-9 shows an example of this point. You can reach TEAM twice from MATCH. Remember that you can always replace an n-ary relationship with a maximum multiplicity of 1 for one branch in your Entity-Relationship schema with $n - 1$ equivalent binary relationships without the need for reification.

Specialization Entity-Relationship hierarchies are equivalent to optional one-to-one relationships between super-entities and sub-entities, and they may be treated as such in the algorithm. Alternatively, if a hierarchy exists between the E super-entity and the $E_1, ..., E_n$ sub-entities, you can merely add a child to the node corresponding to the E identifier. This child allows you to discriminate between different sub-entities, and it actually corresponds to an attribute with n possible values. Figure 6-10 shows both solutions and makes reference to the order line example. Note that the specialization attributes of the sub-entities are optional in the second solution that includes the productType discriminator.

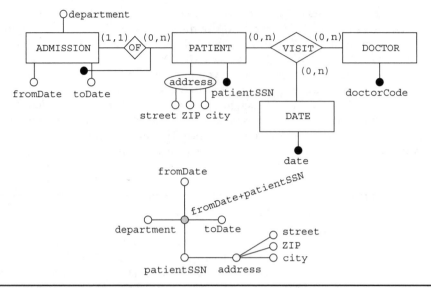

Figure 6-8   Entity-Relationship schema for hospital admissions and the corresponding attribute tree

A composite attribute called *c* of the Entity-Relationship schema consists of simple attributes, such as $a_1 \ldots, a_m$. It is inserted in the attribute tree as a *c* node with children $a_1 \ldots, a_m$. See the address example in Figure 6-8. Then you can graft *c* or prune its children, as mentioned in section 6.1.3. Figure 6-11 shows that composite identifiers can also be treated in the same way.

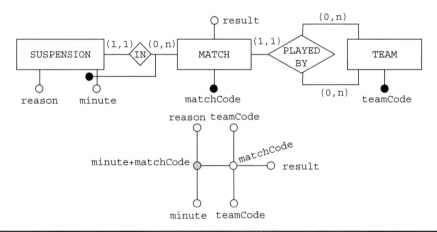

Figure 6-9   Entity-Relationship schema for suspensions in football matches and the corresponding attribute tree

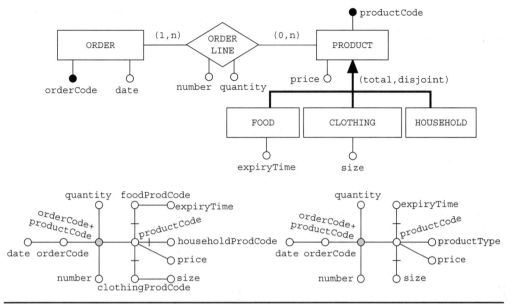

FIGURE 6-10 Entity-Relationship schema for the order line example and two solutions for the attribute tree

6.1.3 Pruning and Grafting Attribute Trees

Generally, not all the attributes in the tree are relevant to the data mart. For example, a customer's fax number can hardly be useful for decision-making purposes. For this reason, trees have to be manipulated to delete unnecessary levels of detail.

FIGURE 6-11
Entity-Relationship schema for the telephone calls and the corresponding attribute tree

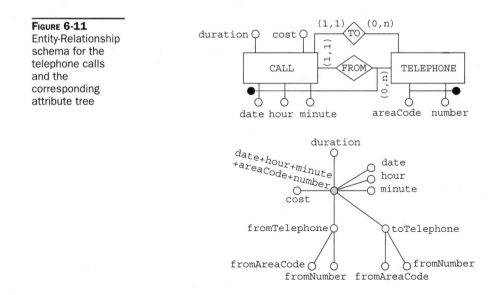

FIGURE 6-12
Attribute tree (top),
pruning (left) and
grafting (right)

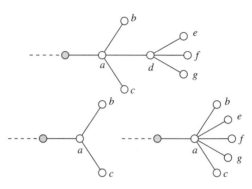

To *prune* node v, you should remove the entire sub-tee rooted in v. The attributes that you remove will not be included in your fact schema, so they can not be used for data aggregation. *Grafting* is used when you need to retain the descendants of a node in your tree, although that node shows information that is not relevant. To graft node v, whose parent is called v', you should link all the children of v directly to v' and then remove v. As a result, the aggregation level corresponding to v will be lost, but the levels corresponding to its descendants will not.

Figure 6-12 shows examples of pruning and grafting. Figure 6-13 shows how you can transform the attribute tree in the sales example, if you graft saleReceiptNum and prune state, districtNum, and size.

When you graft an optional node, all of its children become optional. If you prune or graft an optional node v with a parent called v', you can add to v' a new child b corresponding to a Boolean attribute to express optionality. For this reason, the value of b is TRUE for every value of v' for which a value of v exists. Figure 6-14 shows an example of this: The check-in attribute is Boolean. It was added to the tree when the optional ticketNumber (CHECK-IN) attribute was pruned. Its value is TRUE only for those tickets whose passengers have checked in.

If you prune or graft a root child that corresponds to an attribute included in the identifier of the entity chosen as a fact, this makes fact granularity more coarse-grained than your source schema. Moreover, if the node you graft has more than one child, this potentially leads to an increase in the number of dimensions in your fact schema. Figure 6-6 shows

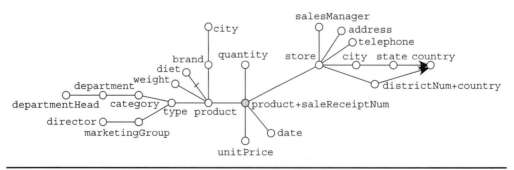

FIGURE 6-13   The attribute tree for sales after pruning and grafting

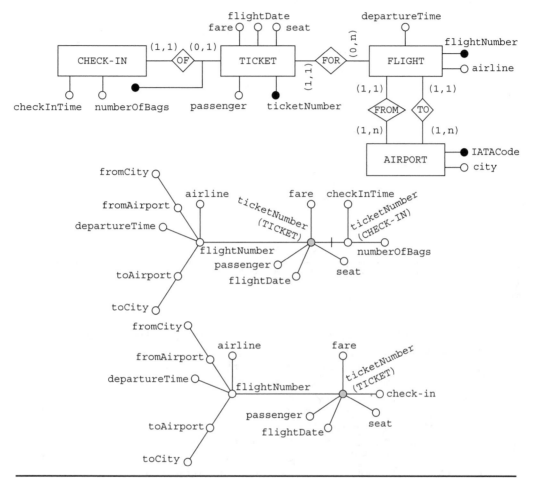

FIGURE 6-14 Entity-Relationship schema for airline ticketing and the attribute tree before and after pruning the optional `ticketNumber(CHECK-IN)` attribute

a sales example: Grafting `saleReceiptNum` changes the granularity of sales. Before grafting, a separate sales event existed for each product item listed on each sale receipt. After grafting, all the sales related to a single product and to the sale receipts issued by an individual store on a single date are aggregated and become one single event. Before grafting, the potential dimensions were `product` and `saleReceiptNum`. After grafting, the potential dimensions become `product`, `date`, and `store`.

In this phase, you should think of how to deal with composite identifiers. Now look at Figure 6-15: The E entity in the Entity-Relationship schema has a composite identifier (it consists of the internal $a_1 \ldots, a_m$ attributes and the external $b_1 \ldots, b_t$ attributes). The algorithm described in section 6.1.2 translates E into the $c = a_1 + \ldots + a_m + b_1 + \ldots + b_t$ node with the $a_1 \ldots, a_m$ children (the $b_1 \ldots, b_t$ children will be added when the entity they identify is translated).

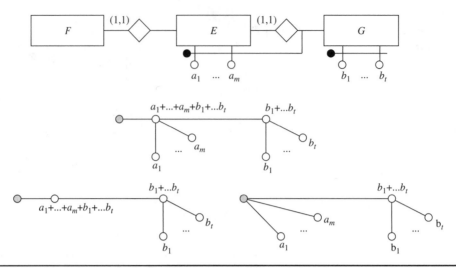

Figure 6-15   Managing composite identifiers: source schema, attribute tree, pruning (left), and grafting (right)

You can achieve two possible results. If you have to leave the granularity of E unchanged in your fact schema, you can retain the c node and prune one or more of its children. For example, you can retain the `districtNum+country` node because you need to aggregate by individual sales districts, but you can prune `districtNum` because this is not a significant aggregation. Otherwise, you can graft c to remove it and retain all or some of its children if the aggregation expressed by E is too fine grained.

To conclude this section, we must emphasize that you may need to manipulate your attribute trees further. In particular, you may need to make radical modifications to the structure of your trees by replacing the parent of a specific node. This is the same as adding or deleting a functional dependency, depending on whether the new parent is a descendant or a predecessor of the original parent, respectively. Figure 6-16 shows how the structure of a hierarchy changes when you modify functional dependencies. The left-hand tree shows the $a{\to}b$, $b{\to}c$, and the $a{\to}c$ functional dependencies—you can use transitivity to infer the third functional dependency from $a{\to}b$ and $b{\to}c$. The right-hand tree shows only $a{\to}b$ and $a{\to}c$.

In practice, you should add a functional dependency if this is not displayed in the source schema but is inherent to the application domain. On the contrary, you could also find it useful to delete a functional dependency if you want an attribute that is not a direct root child to become a dimension or measure. However, you should remember that this particular operation introduces a functional dependency between dimensions. For example, if you do not want to sacrifice the information from the sale receipt but you also want to have a time dimension in the sales fact, you can delete the functional dependency between `saleReceiptNum` and `date`. Figure 6-17 shows the tree you can obtain. In this tree, you can choose as dimensions `product`, `saleReceiptNum`, and `date`; the resulting fact schema will clearly have a functional dependency between the `saleReceiptNum` and the `date` dimensions.

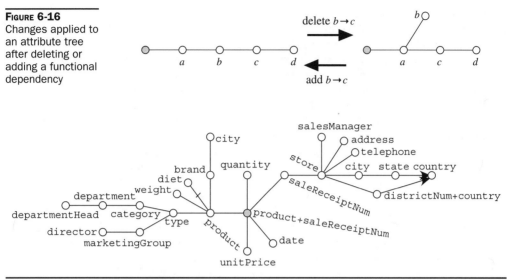

FIGURE 6-16
Changes applied to an attribute tree after deleting or adding a functional dependency

FIGURE 6-17 An alternative sales attribute tree

6.1.4 One-to-One Relationships

A one-to-one relationship may be seen as a special case of a many-to-one relationship. For this reason, a one-to-one relationship can be inserted in attribute trees. Despite this, if you issue an online analytical processing (OLAP) query to drill down a one-to-one association, this does not add any further useful detail. As a result, we suggest the following solutions:

- When the node determined by a one-to-one association in the attribute tree has relevant descendants, you can graft it out to remove it.

- When the node determined by a one-to-one association does not have any relevant descendants, you can represent it as a descriptive attribute.

When a one-to-one association exists, you can sometimes find it useful to invert both its end nodes. This can be helpful when (i) a relation key is not a mnemonic code so you do not need to include it in your data mart, and (ii) one of the relation attributes is a description field that can act as an alternate key. In this case, you can switch both attributes and then prune the code attribute. Figure 6-18 shows an example of this point.

6.1.5 Defining Dimensions

Dimensions define how you can significantly aggregate events for decision-making processes. They must be selected from the root child nodes of the attribute tree and may correspond to discrete attributes or value ranges of discrete or continuous attributes.

FIGURE 6-18
Switching and pruning attributes in one-to-one associations

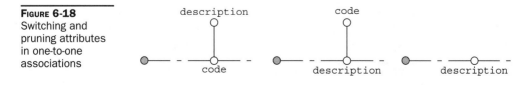

Selecting dimensions is crucial for design because it defines the granularity of primary events. Each primary event "sums up" all the instances of *F* corresponding to a combination of dimension values. If all the attributes making up the identifier of *F* are chosen as dimensions, each primary event will correspond to an instance of *F* (lossless-grained fact schema). Otherwise, you can prune or graft one or more attributes identifying *F* so that each primary event can correspond to multiple instances (lossy-grained fact schema).

In the sales example, we have chosen the `date`, `store`, and `product` attributes as dimensions. The granularity of primary events is coarser than that of the `SALE` source schema entity because we grafted the `saleReceiptNum` node, a child of the root.

Figure 6-19 shows an interesting example of how to choose granularity. It shows part of the Entity-Relationship schema relating to the admissions of a patient and the attribute tree associated with admissions. Data warehousing in the health industry faces the classic dilemma of keeping or losing patient granularity. The left-hand tree in the figure shows that we retained the `patientSSN` node. For this reason you may use it as a dimension, together with `fromDate`, `toDate`, and `department`. On the contrary, we grafted the `patientSSN` node and pruned `firstName` and `surname` to sacrifice the granularity of individual patients in the right-hand tree. Now the dimensions become `fromDate`, `toDate`, `department`, `gender`, `userSegment`, `city`, and `yearOfBirth`. The last dimension is of course obtained from `dateOfBirth`. Figure 6-20 shows the fact schemata that you can obtain for both cases after selecting your measures. The first schema is lossless-grained. The second schema is lossy-grained. The second schema might seem to have a higher number of primary events than the first one because it has more dimensions. But the opposite is true. When the department and admission date values are equal, all the patients born in the same year, of the same gender, resident in the same city, and belonging to the same user segment are classified into a single event in the second schema. The first schema, instead, classifies them as different events.

One particular feature of the choice of dimensions requires a separate discussion. Let us consider the airline ticketing case of Figure 6-14. Here, the identifier of the *F* entity chosen as

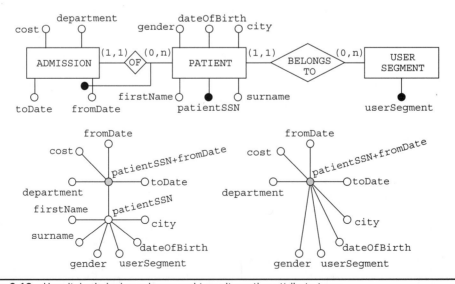

FIGURE 6-19 Hospital admission schema and two alternative attribute trees

FIGURE 6-20
Fact schemata
corresponding to
the trees in
Figure 6-19

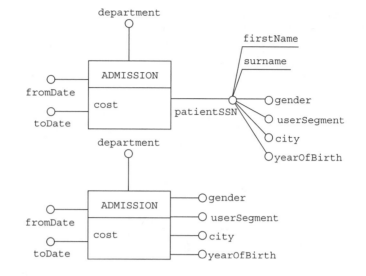

a fact is simple—that is, it consists of a single attribute k. If the granularity of each single instance of F is not relevant, you can choose the dimensions among the children of the root, as we previously mentioned. Figure 6-37, later in this chapter, shows an example of a ticketing fact schema with the `flightNumber`, `flightDate`, `check-in`, and `passengerGender` dimensions. However, users can sometimes request the top granularity level defined by the k identifier. If this is the case, you could perform analyses at the individual ticket level in the ticketing example. This request mostly conceals that users may (improperly) wish to use their data marts for operational queries linked to everyday life operations, which would be far better addressed by an operational database. However, we still find it useful to show designers how they can proceed if they are asked to retain maximum granularity:

1. *Duplicate the root node of your attribute tree.* This means that you have to add a new node that becomes the new root. This new root is also labeled with the name of the identifying fact. To connect it to the previous root, you can use an arc showing a one-to-one association. No additional arc exits that new root.

2. *Now you can go on to selecting dimensions.* You may decide to mark as a dimension the only direct child of the root. This will result in the creation of a one-dimensional fact schema. Alternatively, you may decide to delete some functional dependencies so as to change parents of some of the tree attributes in order to transform them into direct root children. Moreover, you can choose these direct root children as further dimensions. If this is the case, it will result in a fact schema with functional dependencies between dimensions.

Figure 6-21 shows an example of the air ticketing case. We modified the attribute tree in Figure 6-14 to duplicate its root (top). If you choose `ticketNumber` (`TICKET`) as a dimension, you can create a one-dimensional fact schema. Or you can decide to turn `flightDate` and `flightNumber` into root children to create a fact schema with the `flightNumber`, `flightDate`, and the `ticketNumber` dimensions.

FIGURE 6-21
Duplicating the
root and deleting
functional
dependencies from
the attribute tree
in the air ticketing
example

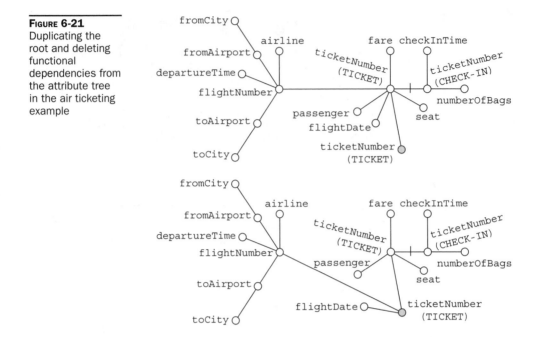

6.1.6 Time Dimensions

A fact schema should always contain at least one time dimension, as we previously mentioned. To learn how to insert time dimensions, you should remember that source operational databases can be classified into *transient* and *temporal* databases, depending on the way they are related to time.

A transient database defines the current status of a specific application domain. Older versions of data that vary over time are constantly being replaced by the new versions. Transient databases do not always represent time explicitly because they imply that a schema should display real-time data. If this is the case, you should add time (as a dimension) to fact schemata manually and you should properly evaluate it for every event when you carry out data population processes. For example, Figure 6-22 shows a simple transient database schema tracing bids in online auctions. This schema stores only the latest offer each user makes in each auction. We manually added the date attribute, which we can choose as a dimension at a later stage, to the attribute tree. Each bid event loaded into that data mart will be associated with the data population date.

On the contrary, a temporal database shows the evolution of an application domain over an interval of time. Old data versions are explicitly represented and stored. When you design a fact schema based on a temporal database, time is explicitly represented as an attribute. For this reason, it becomes an obvious candidate to be classified as a dimension. Figure 6-23 shows the temporal database schema corresponding to the transient database schema of Figure 6-22. This schema records multiple bids made on different days for an individual user-auction pair. The resulting attribute tree is identical to the one of Figure 6-22.

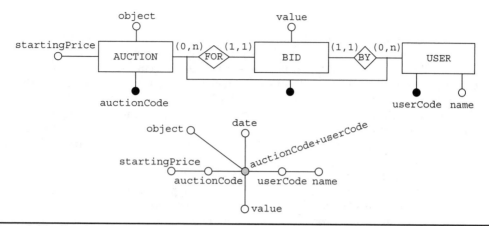

Figure 6-22 Transient database schema for online auctions and its attribute tree

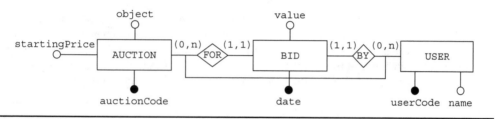

Figure 6-23 Temporal database schema for online auctions

Sometimes it is useful to graft or delete a functional dependency in order to make time become a direct root child and, consequently, a dimension if time is in an attribute tree as a child of a node, other than a root node. For example, look at Figure 6-10, which shows the order line Entity-Relationship schema. Figure 6-24 shows the original attribute tree (left) and the tree obtained by deleting the functional dependency between `orderCode` and `date` (right) where `date` is a candidate for becoming a dimension.

See sections 5.4.1. and 5.4.2. for more details on the choice between a representation based on a transactional or a snapshot fact schema, and for issues raised if updates are delayed.

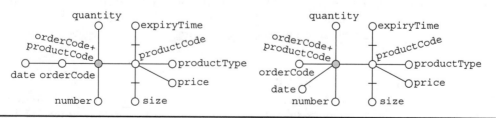

Figure 6-24 Attribute tree for order lines with/without the functional dependency between `orderCode` and `date`

6.1.7   Defining Measures

If all the attributes making up the identifier of the entity chosen as a fact are displayed among dimensions (in other words, if you are creating a lossless-grained schema), then measures will correspond to numeric attributes which are root children. If this is not the case (that is, if you are creating a lossy-grained schema), to define your measures you should apply aggregation operators, which operate on all the instances of F corresponding to each primary event, to the numeric attributes of your tree. Generally, this is a sum/average/maximum/minimum of an attribute expression, or a count of F instances. Remember that a fact schema may be without measures (*empty fact schemata*), if the only relevant information is a fact occurrence.

It is not absolutely essential to select measures from direct children of roots. However, designers must be aware that they sacrifice a functional dependency when they select an attribute that is not a direct child of a root as a measure. For example, assume that the unitPrice attribute is placed on the PRODUCT entity, rather than on SALE in the sales source schema. In order to be able to select this as a fact measure, you should first delete the product→unitPrice functional dependency. In practice, this means that you turn unitPrice into a child of the root.

Now we need to create a *measure glossary* that associates each measure with an expression defining how to obtain that measure from the attributes in the source schema. Figure 6-25 shows the measure glossary of the sales example. Aggregation operators of this glossary are applied to every instance of the SALE entity relating to an individual three-element group (date, store, product). See section 13.3.2. for further details on measure glossaries.

FIGURE 6-25   Measure glossary of the sales schema

```
quantity = SUM(SALE.quantity)
receipts = SUM(SALE.quantity*SALE.unitPrice)
unitPrice = AVG(SALE.unitPrice)
numOfCustomers = COUNT(*)
```

If the fact granularity is different from that of the source schemata, you may find it useful to define a number of measures that use different operators to aggregate the same attribute. For example, suppose that each event corresponds to a set of airline tickets sold for a specific flight on a specific date, and that the fare attribute belongs to the TICKET entity in the source schema. As a result, you can define one or more of the following measures in the fact schema: averageFare calculated by using the AVG operator; maximumFare calculated by using the MAX operator; minimumFare calculated by using the MIN operator; and receipts calculated by adding the fares for individual tickets together. Of course, the only additive measure will be receipts. To aggregate the other measures you should use the same operator that defines them.

6.1.8   Generating Fact Schemata

Now you can translate the attribute tree into a proper fact schema including the dimensions and measures specified in the preceding phases. Hierarchies correspond to sub-trees of the attribute trees with their roots in dimensions. Fact names typically correspond to the names of entities chosen as facts.

In this phase, you can prune and graft to eliminate any irrelevant details, but you can also add new aggregation levels (typically, to the time dimensions) and define appropriate ranges of numeric attributes.

You can mark attributes as descriptive if they are not used for aggregation but only for information. These attributes also generally include attributes determined by one-to-one associations with no descendants. As far as the attributes, which are root children but are not chosen as dimensions or measures, are concerned, the following points apply:

- If a fact schema is lossless-grained—that is, the granularity of the primary events is the same as the one of the *F* entity—those attributes can be represented as descriptive attributes directly linked to the fact. A descriptive attribute linked to a fact takes a value for each single primary event.

- If a fact schema is lossy-grained—that is, both granularity values are different— those attributes absolutely need pruning; otherwise multiple values of these attributes would be associated with each primary event.

Figure 6-26 shows the lossless-grained fact schema for the order line example. The attribute tree is the one on the right of Figure 6-10. The granularity value is the same as the one of the source schema because all the attributes (orderCode and productCode) that identify the fact entity were maintained as dimensions. For this reason, we can represent the line number as a descriptive attribute number linked to the fact. In addition to the price measure, which is non-additive because it shows the unit price of a product, we defined a derived measure called receipts, which shows the mathematical product of price and quantity for each order line. However, if we grafted the orderCode node and turned date into a dimension together with productCode to create a lossy-grained fact schema, we would need to prune the number attribute because it cannot be unequivocally defined in the order line set for an individual product issued on the same day.

If you find a shared hierarchy while you are building an attribute tree, you can choose to highlight it to simplify your fact schema.

In this phase, you can also highlight any cross-dimensional attributes and multiple arcs. It is very difficult to use source schemata as a starting point to identify these types of attributes because you would have to navigate to-many relationships, too. However, if to-many relationships could be navigated as well, this would extend navigation to entire source schemata, give rise to an extremely large number of possible paths, and make cycle management very difficult. Because you can neglect the frequency of cross-dimensional attributes and multiple arcs in normal fact schemata, we suggest that you define them on

---

FIGURE 6-26
Fact schema for
the order line
example

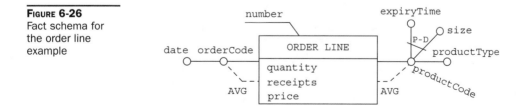

the basis of your user requirements. Then you should represent them in fact schemata at a later stage. For this purpose, remember the following:

- A cross-dimensional attribute generally corresponds to an attribute of a many-to-many relationship called R in the source Entity-Relationship schema. Cross-dimensional attribute parents in fact schemata then correspond to the identifiers of the entities involved in R. See Figure 6-27 for an example.

- A multiple arc corresponds to a to-many relationship called R from an entity called E to an entity called G. It will link the E identifier or your fact with an attribute of R or G in your fact schema. See Figure 6-28 for an example.

In this phase, you must identify any schema elements that are non-additive or cannot be aggregated. To do this, you need to analyze all the dimension-measure pairings. Given an n-dimension fact schema, the question about the d_i dimension and the m_j measure to ask is as follows:

If the $\{val_1 \ldots, val_k\}$ values are given to the m_j measure in the k primary events corresponding to k different values from the d_i domain, and from a preset value for each remaining $n - 1$ dimension, which aggregation operators does it make sense to use to mark all the k events with a single value for m_j?

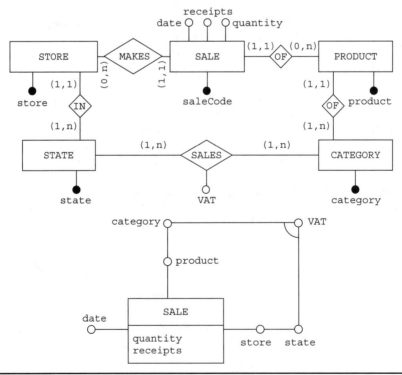

FIGURE 6-27   Entity-Relationship schema for sales and the corresponding fact schema

FIGURE **6-28**
Entity-Relationship
schema for
hospital
admissions and
the corresponding
fact schema

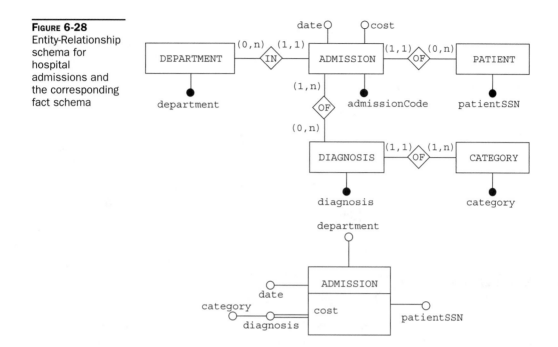

The sales schema, for example, supports the following remarks:

- Given a store and a product, if 10 items were sold yesterday and 3 items have been sold today, the total amount of items sold in both days would be 13. Then the quantity measure is additive along the date dimension.

- Given a day and a product, if 7 items were sold in the Columbus store and 5 items were sold in the Cleveland store, the total amount of items sold in Ohio stores would be 12. Then the quantity measure is also additive along the store dimension.

- Given a day and a store, if 4 boxes of Slurp milk and 3 boxes of Yum milk were sold, the total amount of boxes of milk sold would be 7. Then the quantity measure is also additive along the product dimension.

The INVENTORY schema with the product and date dimensions and the level measure supports the following remarks instead:

- Given an item, if there were 100 items in a warehouse yesterday and there were 95 items today, how many items would the warehouse total over both days? The answer 195 is obviously wrong, so level is non-additive along date. However, you can reasonably aggregate on the basis of AVG, MIN, or MAX.

- Given a day, if there were 40 boxes of Slurp milk and 30 boxes of Yum milk in a warehouse, the total amount of boxes of milk would be 70. Then the level measure is additive along the product dimension.

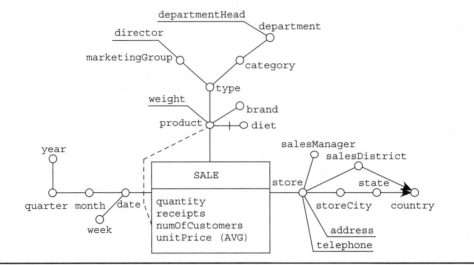

Figure 6-29 Fact schema for the sales example

Figure 6-29 shows a lossy-grained fact schema obtained from the source schema in Figure 6-1. We inserted the `month`, `quarter`, and so on, attributes and added them to the time dimension. As far as additivity is concerned, `unitPrice` is non-additive, but you can use the AVG operator to aggregate it. `numOfCustomers` cannot be aggregated.

Figure 6-30 shows two possible fact schemata that can be derived from the attribute tree of Figure 6-7. In the first schema, which is lossless-grained, we left the employee aggregation level unchanged and the fact is empty. In the second schema, we pruned the `empCode` node so that we turned this schema into a lossy-grained one. In this way, we managed to add the `number` measure, which counts the number of transfers made on each day between two departments. Note the shared hierarchy in `department`.

To conclude this section, we should comment that designers can sometimes "split" a single fact schema into two or more schemata to standardize their hierarchies. This is more properly referred to as fact schema *fragmentation*. From a logical viewpoint, the result obtained

Figure 6-30
Alternative fact
schemata for the
personnel transfer
example

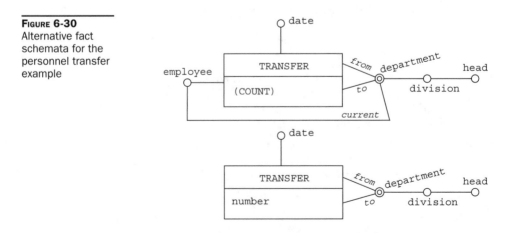

is very similar to the one obtained from horizontal fragmentation (section 9.3.2). To illustrate this, consider an example related to invoicing in a large retail chain. Assume that a company sells products in Italy and abroad. A hierarchy for foreign customers is less informative than the one for Italian customers. Moreover, the invoice line shows only the `currency` dimension for foreign customers. Figure 6-31 shows a comparison of two conceptual design alternatives. In the first conceptual design, the specific properties of the application domain cause the geographical hierarchy for customers to be incomplete, because information on the foreign customers' city and regions is missing. This also creates an optional dimension (`currency`). In the second conceptual design, the decision was made to create two separate fact schemata. The first fact schema models invoices issued to Italian customers. The second fact schema models invoices issued to foreign customers. The clear-cut advantage of this is that all the hierarchies are complete and compulsory, but every time you need the data summing up all the invoicing, you have to issue a drill-across query accessing the overlapped schema.

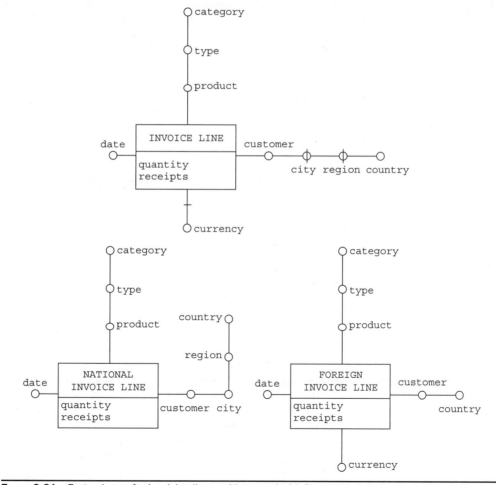

Figure 6-31 Fact schema for invoicing lines, without and with fragmentation

We recommend avoiding any abuse of fragmentation because it inevitably leads to a proliferation of fact schemata. For this reason, you should use fragmentation only after checking first with users that the percentage of analysis queries addressed only to one of the fact schemata is much higher than the one of analysis queries addressed to multiple fact schemata. Moreover, you should not confuse fact schema fragmentation with horizontal fact table fragmentation despite their obvious similarities. Fact schema fragmentation is conceptually relevant and can be deployed to improve fact schema simplicity and accuracy. On the contrary, horizontal fact table fragmentation is part of the logical design phase, which is strictly workload–dependent and aims at improving analytical query performance.

6.2 Relational Schema-based Design

The relational schema-driven approach to conceptual design is substantially the same as the approach mentioned in section 6.1. The main difference between both approaches is in the algorithm used to build attribute trees. Figure 6-32 shows a logical schema for the sales example that we will use in this section. This logical schema corresponds to the Entity-Relationship schema of Figure 6-1. Its primary keys are underlined. We specified the referencing relation of every foreign key. We put the attributes, which are part of composite foreign keys, in parentheses. We did not add any surrogate key in the interests of simplicity.

FIGURE 6-32   Relational schema for the sales operational database

```
PRODUCTS(product, weight, size, diet, brand:BRANDS, type:TYPES)
STORES(store, address, telephone, salesManager,
       (districtNum, country):SALES_DISTRICTS, inCity:CITIES)
SALE_RECEIPTS(saleReceiptNum, date, store:STORES)
SALES(product:PRODUCTS, saleReceiptNum:SALE_RECEIPTS, quantity, unitPrice)
WAREHOUSES(warehouse, address)
CITIES(city, state:STATES)
STATES(state, country:COUNTRIES)
COUNTRIES(country)
SALES_DISTRICTS(districtNum, country:COUNTRIES)
PROD_IN_WAREHOUSE(product:PRODUCTS, warehouse:WAREHOUSES)
BRANDS(codBrand, producedIn:CITIES)
TYPES(type, marketingGroup:MARK_GROUPS, category:CATEGORIES)
MARK_GROUPS(marketingGroup, director)
CATEGORIES(category, department:DEPARTMENTS)
DEPARTMENTS(department, departmentHead)
```

6.2.1   Defining Facts

In a relational schema, a fact corresponds to a relation. In the following sections, we will study a fact corresponding to the F relation. In the sales example, the most important fact, a product sale, is represented by the SALES relation.

Different relations can be candidates for expressing an individual fact as in Entity-Relationship sources. In section 6.2.2, we will show an example of how your selection can result in similar attribute trees showing different quantities of information.

6.2.2   Building Attribute Trees

If your design source is the relational schema for your operational database, your attribute tree will be built as follows:

- Each node corresponds to one or more[2] schema attributes.
- The root corresponds to the primary key of F.
- For each node v, the corresponding attribute functionally determines all the attributes that correspond to the descendants of v.

The tree-building procedure is based on the principle of following functional dependencies. In a relational schema, functional dependencies link the primary key of each R relation to all R attributes on the one hand, and each foreign key of R, which references S, to the primary key of S on the other hand. The first examined relation is the one that you choose as the F fact. Every time you examine a relation R, you create a new node v in your tree. The v node corresponds to the primary key of R, with a child node added for each attribute of R (including each single attribute that make up the primary key of R if this primary key is composite, but excluding the single attributes that are part of a composite foreign key, because those will be dealt with in the next recursion step). You should also add a child to v every time you find a foreign key c in R, and then recursively repeat the whole procedure for the relation S referenced by c:

```
R(k, c:S, a, b ...)
S(c, d, e ...)
```

A recursion is also triggered when a one-to-one association links R and S, and the primary key of S is foreign and references R:

```
R(k, a, b ...)
S(k:R, c, d ...)
```

In this case, you have to check that this procedure does not return to R after examining S, because this would result in an infinite loop.

Figure 6-33 shows pseudo-code that defines the basic operation of the algorithm building an attribute tree rooted in F. The comments on cycles and convergences that we previously made for Entity-Relationship schema–based design also apply to this case.

Figure 6-33   Pseudo-code for the attribute tree-building algorithm

---

```
root=newNode(pk(F));
// the root is labeled with the primary key
// of the relation chosen as a fact
translate(F, root);
```

---

[2]A node may correspond to multiple attributes only if a primary key or a foreign key of a relation consists of those attributes.

```
procedure translate(R, v):
// R is the current relation, v is the current node of the tree
{  for each attribute a∈R such that a≠pk(R) and ∃S: a∈fk(R, S)
   // pk(R) and fk(R, S) mark the sets of attributes of R that form,
   // respectively, the primary key of R
   // and a foreign key of R referencing S
      addChild(v, newNode(a));
      // add a child a to the node v
   for each set of attributes C⊂R such that
         ∃S s.t. (C=fk(R, S) or C=fk(S, R)=pk(S)) and (parent(v)≠S.C)
   // if the parent of v in the tree is C itself from S,
   // the infinite recursion is avoided
   {  next=newNode(C);
      // create a new node with the names of the attributes in C ...
      addChild(v, next);
      translate(S, next);
      // ... add it to v as a child and trigger the recursion
   }
}
```

Note that you cannot process optionality automatically. This is because no information in a relational schema clearly specifies whether you can give attributes null values.[3] Figure 6-6 shows the attribute tree corresponding to the sales schema, which is the same as the one obtained from the Entity-Relationship schema.

We will provide another example related to DVD rental and described in the transient database schema:

```
CARDS(cardNumber, expiry)
CUSTOMERS(cardNumber:CARDS, name, gender, address,
          telephone, personalDocument)
MOVIES(movieCode, title, category, director, length, mainActor)
COPIES(positionOnShelf, movieCode:MOVIES)
RENTALS(positionOnShelf:COPIES, cardNumber:CARD, date, time)
```

Here, RENTALS is the only relevant fact. Figure 6-34 shows the control flow for the translate procedure and explains how to build a branch of the attribute tree shown in Figure 6-35. Note that the association linking the card number to the customer number is one-to-one.

Figure 6-34   Operating flow of the translate procedure in the DVD rental example

```
root=newNode(positionOnShelf)

translate(R=RENTALS, v=positionOnShelf):
    addChild(positionOnShelf, date);
    addChild(positionOnShelf, time);
    for S=COPIES:
```

---

[3]SQL *Data Definition Language* allows for a NOT NULL standard clause. In principle, it could be used to extract optionality. As a matter of fact, this clause is normally used to express entity integrity constraints only. Entity integrity constraints specify that it is forbidden to give a null value to the attributes of which a key consists. For this reason, there is no point in inferring that all the attributes not specified as NOT NULL are actually optional.

```
        addChild(positionOnShelf, positionOnShelf);
        translate(COPIES, positionOnShelf);
    for S=CARDS:
        addChild(positionOnShelf, cardNumber);
        translate(CARDS, cardNumber);

translate(E=COPIES, v=positionOnShelf):
    for G=MOVIES:
        addChild(positionOnShelf, movieCode);
        translate(MOVIES, movieCode);

translate(E=MOVIES, v=movieCode):
    addChild(movieCode, title);
    addChild(movieCode, category);
    addChild(movieCode, director);
    addChild(movieCode, length);
    addChild(movieCode, mainActor);

translate(E=CARDS, v=cardNumber):
    addChild(number, expiry);
    for G=CUSTOMERS:
        addChild(cardNumber, cardNumber);
        translate(CUSTOMERS, cardNumber);

translate(E=CUSTOMERS, v=cardNumber):
    addChild(cardNumber, name);
    addChild(cardNumber, telephone);
    addChild(cardNumber, gender);
    addChild(cardNumber, address);
    addChild(cardNumber, personalDocument);
```

To conclude this section, the following example demonstrates how to select a fact in order to model as many concepts as possible. To this end, you should keep in mind how attribute trees are built. The operational database is shown next:

```
FLIGHTS(flightNumber, airline, fromAirport:AIRPORTS,
        toAirport:AIRPORTS, departureTime, arrivalTime, carrier)
FLIGHT_INSTANCES(flightNumber:FLIGHTS, date)
AIRPORTS(IATAcode, name, city, country)
TICKETS(ticketNumber, (flightNumber, date):FLIGHT_INSTANCES, seat, fare,
        passengerFirstName, passengerSurname, passengerGender)
CHECK-IN(ticketNumber:TICKETS, checkInTime, numberOfBags)
```

FIGURE 6-35
Attribute tree for the DVD rental example

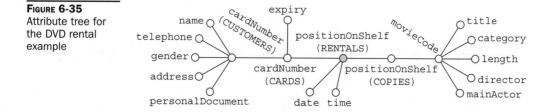

The relations that are candidates for expressing facts are FLIGHTS, FLIGHT_INSTANCES, TICKETS, and CHECK-IN in this example. Figure 6-36 clearly shows that the last two options are the best, because the existing functional dependencies make it possible to include the maximum number of attributes in the tree. However, note that the selection of TICKETS means that you opt for modeling the TICKET ISSUE fact. But if you select CHECK-IN, this

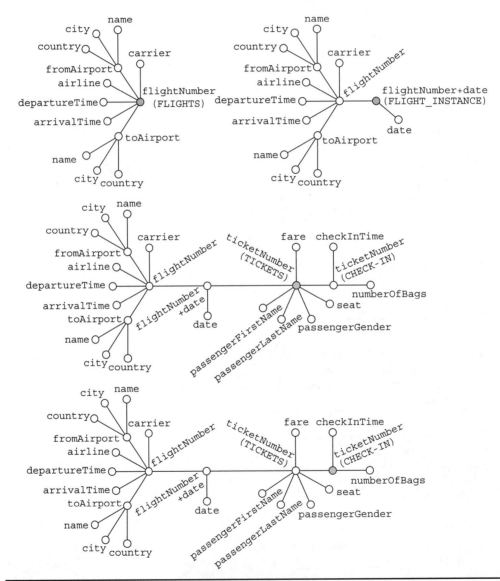

FIGURE 6-36   Attribute trees for the flights example, obtained by choosing different relations as facts, corresponding to the nodes in gray

results in the CHECK-IN fact. The difference between both solutions is not merely the name, because not all the tickets are necessarily checked in. As a result, the CHECK-IN fact primary events will presumably be a subset of the TICKET ISSUE fact primary events.

6.2.3   Other Phases

The other phases in the methodology are substantially identical to those mentioned in section 6.1 for the Entity-Relationship schema design.

You can choose to retain or graft any nodes corresponding to composite keys. You may also find it useful to modify, add, or delete a functional dependency, as in the case of the Entity-Relationship source. You need to add one or more functional dependencies if a non-normalized relation exists in your source schema. It would be useful, for example, to make country the child of city in the flights example. Figure 6-37 shows the tree built after grafting repeatedly and the final lossy-grained ticket issue fact schema. The check-in attribute is Boolean and we added it to the tree when we grafted the number node. Its value is TRUE only for those tickets whose passengers have checked in.

Figure 6-38 shows the transformed attribute tree in the DVD rental example of Figure 6-35. In Figure 6-38, we inverted movieCode and title, and cardNumber(CUSTOMERS) and name (renamed customer); we grafted positionOnShelf(COPIES) and cardNumber(CARDS); and we pruned time, expiry, telephone, address, personalDocument, movieCode, and cardNumber(CUSTOMERS).

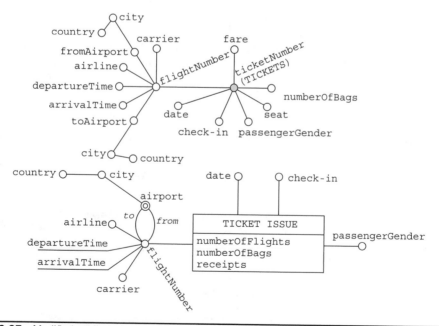

FIGURE 6-37   Modified attribute tree and fact schema for the flights example

FIGURE 6-38
Modified attribute
tree and fact
schema for
DVD rentals

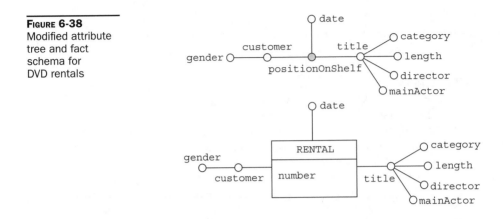

In case of relational sources, measure glossaries are typically written in SQL. If schemata
are lossy-grained, SQL queries defining measures will necessarily use the GROUP-BY
clause. Figure 6-39 shows the glossaries of the sales, flights, and DVD rentals examples.

FIGURE 6-39 SQL measure glossaries for sales, flights, and DVD rentals. The `check-in` dimension
was left out of the flights example to avoid making the query too complex.

```
quantity = SELECT SUM(S.quantity)
             FROM SALES S INNER JOIN SALE_RECEIPTS R
                ON R.saleReceiptNum = S.saleReceiptNum
             GROUP BY S.product, R.date, R.store
receipts = SELECT SUM(S.quantity*S.unitPrice)
             FROM SALES S INNER JOIN SALE_RECEIPTS R
                ON R.saleReceiptNum = S.saleReceiptNum
             GROUP BY S.product, R.date, R.store
unitPrice = SELECT AVG(S.unitPrice)
             FROM SALES S INNER JOIN SALE_RECEIPTS R
                ON R.saleReceiptNum = S.saleReceiptNum
             GROUP BY S.product, R.date, R.store
numOfCustomers = SELECT COUNT(*)
               FROM SALES S INNER JOIN SALE_RECEIPTS R
                  ON R.saleReceiptNum = R.saleReceiptNum
               GROUP BY S.product, R.date, R.store


numberOfFlights = SELECT COUNT(*)
                FROM TICKETS T INNER JOIN FLIGHT_INSTANCES I
                   ON T.flightNumber = I.flightNumber AND T.date = I.date
                GROUP BY T.passengerGender, I.date, T.flightNumber
numberOfBags = SELECT SUM(C.numberOfBags)
             FROM TICKETS T INNER JOIN FLIGHT_INSTANCES I
                ON T.flightNumber = I.flightNumber AND T.date = I.date,
                TICKETS T INNER JOIN CHECK-IN C
                ON T.ticketNumber = C.ticketNumber
             GROUP BY T.passengerGender, I.date, T.flightNumber
  receipts = SELECT SUM(T.fare)
             FROM TICKETS T INNER JOIN FLIGHT_INSTANCES I
                ON T.flightNumber = I.flightNumber AND T.date = I.date
             GROUP BY T.passengerGender, I.date, T.flightNumber
```

```
number = SELECT COUNT(*)
         FROM RENTALS R INNER JOIN COPIES C
             ON R.positionOnShelf = C.positionOnShelf,
             COPIES C INNER JOIN MOVIES F
             ON C.movieCode = F.movieCode,
             RENTALS R INNER JOIN CUSTOMERS C
             ON R.cardNumber = C.cardNumber
         GROUP BY F.title, R.date, C.name
```

6.3 XML Schema-based Design

Part of the data used in decision-making processes may be stored in XML form. The structure of XML consists of nested tags, defined by users. These tags can define the *meaning* of the data represented. This makes XML suitable for exchanging data on the Web without losing semantics. The Internet is evolving into a global platform for e-commerce and information exchange. Interest in XML is growing in step with this evolution. Now huge amounts of XML data are available online.

XML can be considered as a special syntax for the exchange of semi-structured data (Abiteboul et al., 2000). A feature common to all models of semi-structured data is the lack of a schema, which makes it possible for data to "self-describe." As a matter of fact, XML documents can be associated with a *Document Type Definition (DTD)* or an *XML Schema*. DTDs and XML schemata are both able to describe and constrain documents and contents. DTDs are defined as an integrating part of the XML 1.0 (World Wide Web Consortium [W3C], 2000) specification, and XML schemata have recently been recommended for W3C (W3C, 2002a). XML schemata are a major extension of DTD features, especially from the viewpoint of constraints and data standardization. If you use DTDs or XML schemata, data exchange applications can agree in the meaning of their tags. In this way, XML can release its full potential.

Now it is becoming vital to be able to integrate XML data into data warehouses because many companies look to the Web for communications and business support. This is also confirmed by some commercial tools that already support XML data extraction for data mart feeding. Nevertheless, they still require designers to define data mart schemata manually and to make sure of their mappings with source schemata.

Conceptual design of data marts from XML sources presents two basic problems. On the one hand, there are various approaches to representing associations in DTD and XML schemata, each with a different expressive power. On the other hand, you cannot be sure that you can derive all the information required for design because XML models semi-structured data. In the following sections, we will first discuss the issues involved in representing XML associations oriented to creating multidimensional schemata. Most topics are by Abiteboul et al. (2000). Then we will briefly describe a semi-automatic technique solving the problem of how to infer correct information by querying source XML documents and taking advantage of designers' skills.

6.3.1   Modeling XML Associations

An XML document consists of *element* structures nested on the basis of a root structure. Each element can contain *component* elements, or sub-elements, and attributes. Both elements and their attributes can have *values*. The structure of a document can be nested up to any level of complexity. Any number of additional elements and textual data may be placed between the opening and closing tags of an element. Attributes and attribute values are included in element opening statements. Figure 6-40 shows an XML document containing data on the traffic on a web site.

FIGURE 6-40   An XML document describing traffic on a web site

```
<webTraffic>
   <click>
      <host hostId="www.unibo.it">
         <country>italy</country>
      </host>
      <date>23-MAY-2008</date>
      <time>16:43:25</time>
      <url urlID="BL0023">
         <site siteID="www.csb.fr">
            <country>france</country>
         </site>
         <fileType>shtml</fileType>
         <urlCategory>catalogue</urlCategory>
      </url>
   </click>
   <click>
      ...
   </click>
   ...
</webTraffic>
```

An XML document is valid if it has an associated schema—that is, a DTD or an XML schema—and if it complies with the constraints expressed in that schema. The following discussion will focus on the ways you can display many-to-one associations in DTDs, because our conceptual design methodology is based on recognizing those associations. Similar considerations apply to XML schemata.

A DTD defines (i) the elements and attributes an XML document allows; (ii) element nesting modes; and (iii) element occurrences. The *element type* and the *attribute list* statements constrain document structures. The element type statements specify which sub-elements may be displayed as element children. The attribute list statements specify names, types, and default values (if necessary) of each attribute associated with a specific element type. Among the various attribute types, ID, IDREF, and IDREFS are of particular importance for our approach. ID type defines a unique element identifier. IDREF type shows that attribute values must correspond to the values of an ID attribute in the current document. IDREFS type shows that attribute values are lists of ID values.

There are two different ways to specify associations in a DTD: using sub-elements or IDREF(S).

In the first case, the association cardinality is described by an optional character that comes after the name of a nested element or a list of elements in the element-type statement. This defines whether elements may appear one or more ("+"), zero or more ("*"), or zero or one ("?") times. The default cardinality is precisely one. Figure 6-41 shows a DTD that validates the XML document of Figure 6-40. The webTraffic element is defined as a *document element*, and it becomes the root of XML documents. The `webTraffic` element may contain many `click` elements. But the `site` sub-element can be exactly displayed once in a `url` element; the `fileType` sub-element and many `urlCategory` elements can come after it. The `host` element may have either a `category` or a `country` element.

FIGURE 6-41   Sub-elements specifying associations in a DTD

```
<!DOCTYPE webTraffic [
   <!ELEMENT webTraffic (click*)>
   <!ELEMENT click (host, date, time, url)>
   <!ELEMENT host (category | country)>
   <!ATTLIST host
      hostId ID #REQUIRED>
   <!ELEMENT category (#PCDATE)>
   <!ELEMENT date (#PCDATE)>
   <!ELEMENT time (#PCDATE)>
   <!ELEMENT url (site, fileType, urlCategory+)>
   <!ATTLIST url
      urlId ID #REQUIRED>
   <!ELEMENT site (country)>
   <!ATTLIST site
      siteId ID #REQUIRED>
   <!ELEMENT country (#PCDATE)>
   <!ELEMENT fileType (#PCDATE)>
   <!ELEMENT urlCategory (#PCDATE)>
]>
```

If you need to represent a one-to-one or a one-to-many association in XML, you can use the sub-elements without any information loss. However, you can follow only one of both association directions in a DTD. For example, Figure 6-41 shows how a DTD expresses that a `url` element can have many `urlCategory` sub-elements. But there is no way to infer if a URL category can refer to many URLs. You can conclude that this is true if you already know the domain defined by the DTD.

The other way to specify element associations in DTDs uses ID and IDREF(S) attribute pairs. These attributes operate in the same way as primary and foreign keys in relational databases. The fundamental difference that prevents us from using IDREF(S) for our purposes is that their syntax does not allow for any IDREF(S) attribute to be constrained to contain identifiers of a specific element type.

6.3.2 Preliminary Phases

Before you can choose a fact and build its specific attribute tree, you need to simplify your source DTD and create a DTD graph. Sub-elements in DTDs may be stated in a complex and redundant way. If this is the case, they need simplifying (Shanmugasundaram et al., 1999). To simplify a DTD, transformations generally involve converting a nested definition into a "flat" representation. For example, `host (category|country)` is transformed into `host(category?, country?)` in the web traffic example. Moreover, the "+" operators are transformed into "*" operators.

After simplifying your DTD, you can create your *DTD graph*. This defines your DTD structure, as discussed by Lee and Chu (2000) and Shanmugasundaram et al. (1999).

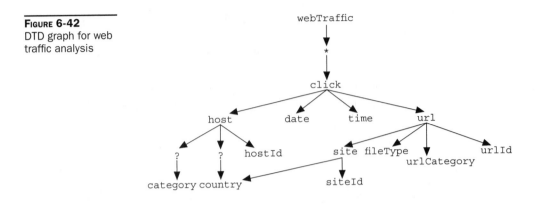

FIGURE 6-42
DTD graph for web
traffic analysis

Your graph nodes will correspond to your DTD elements, attributes, and operators. DTD graphs do not make any distinction between attributes and sub-elements because we can consider them as equivalent nesting elements for our purposes. Figure 6-42 shows the DTD graph of Figure 6-41.

6.3.3   Selecting Facts and Building Attribute Trees

Designers choose one or more DTD graph nodes as facts. Each chosen node becomes the root of an attribute tree. We will choose `click` as the only relevant fact in our example.

Figure 6-43 shows the algorithm that builds the tree in pseudo-code. The nodes in the attribute tree are a subset of the DTD graph nodes representing elements and attributes. We use the node of the F fact as a starting point for our tree. To grow our tree, we recursively navigate the functional dependencies between the DTD graph nodes. The following section shows how we insert each node called V to expand our tree (`translate` procedure):

1. *For each node called W that is a child of V in the graph:*
   When examining the associations in the same direction of the graph, the information on cardinality is expressed, either explicitly by the "?" and "*"nodes, or implicitly if they are not available. If W corresponds to an element or an attribute in the DTD graph, you can add it to the tree as a child of V. If W is the "?"operator, you can add its child to the tree as a child of V. If W is the "*"operator, you cannot add any node.

FIGURE 6-43   Pseudo-code for the attribute tree-building algorithm

```
root=newNode(F);
// the root is a node labeled with the name
// of the DTD graph node chosen as a fact
translate(F, root);

procedure translate(E, V):
// E is the current node of the DTD graph,
// V is the current node of the attribute tree
{  for each child W of E such that parent(V)≠W
 // the condition on the parent of V in the tree avoids the loop
       if W is an element or an attribute
```

```
       {  next=newNode(W);
          addChild(V, next);
          translate(W, next);
          // adds the child W to the node V and triggers the recursion
       }
    else
       if W="?"
          translate(W, V);
          // the nodes "?" are omitted
 for each parent Z of E s.t. parent(V)≠Z and Z is not a document element
 // the condition on the parent of V in the tree avoids the loop
    if Z="?" or Z="*"
       translate(Z, V);
       // the nodes "?" and "*" are omitted
    else
       if not to-many(E, Z)
          if askTo-one(E, Z)
          {  next=newNode(Z);
             addChild(V, next);
             translate(Z, next);
             // if the association is to-one,
             // Z is added as a child of V
          }
}
```

2. *For each node called Z that is a parent of V in the graph*:
   When examining the associations in this direction, you should skip the nodes corresponding to the "*" and the "?"operators because they express cardinality only in the opposite direction. You have to query your XML documents conformed to your DTD to examine your actual data because DTDs do not provide any further information on association cardinality. To do this, you need to use the to-many procedure, that counts the number of discrete Z values corresponding to every E value. If you find a to-many association, you cannot include Z in your tree. If this is not the case, you still cannot be sure that the cardinality of the E-to-Z association is to-one. In particular, only designers who are very familiar with their application domain can define whether cardinality is actually set to to-one or to-many (askTo-one procedure). You can add Z to the tree only if cardinality is set to to-one. You do not need to use any document elements because they have just one instance in XML documents; for this reason, they are not relevant to aggregation and you do not have to model them in your data mart.

When you pass a "?" node you should add an optional arc. Moreover, you should add controls to prevent your algorithm from looping back at one-to-one associations' end nodes. This is because you can navigate a DTD graph both bottom-up and top-down.

Uncertain associations are not navigated in our example. We did not add the urlCategory node to the attribute tree because it is a child of the "*" DTD graph node. Figure 6-44 shows the resulting tree. Before moving on to the fact schema, we need to apply some changes. We can apply the switching and grafting procedure mentioned in section 6.1.4 to the host, url, and site nodes. We can replace the time attribute with hour, whose granularity is coarser. The resulting schema is lossy-grained.

FIGURE 6-44
Attribute tree and
fact schema for
analyzing web
traffic

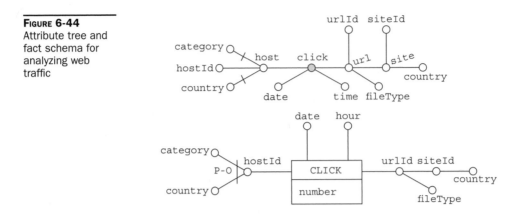

Here are some general remarks on the approach we adopted.

The problem of checking XML documents for cardinality is connected to the problem of determining functional dependencies in relational databases. This is dealt with at length in the literature on relational theory and on data mining (Mannila and Räihä, 1994; Savnik and Flach, 1993). In our case, the conditions are much simpler because no inference procedure is necessary. This means that we simply have to use an XML query language supporting aggregation to query our data properly. For example, W3C (W3C, 2002b) XQuery suggests using the *distinct* function for this purpose. On the contrary, Deutsch et al., (1999) recommend using the *group-by* function. The main issue concerns the number of XML documents to be examined to reasonably confirm the hypothesis of to-one cardinality.

Clearly, the semi-structured nature of the XML source data increases the level of uncertainty of the data structure in comparison with the Entity-Relationship sources. This requires designers' knowledge to be called upon more often. In our algorithm, we chose to ask designers questions interactively in the tree-building phase to avoid unnecessary document queries. Alternatively, we could create the tree first and specify uncertain associations. Then we should give the entire tree to designers so that they can examine it and, if necessary, delete those associations, together with their sub-trees. This solution allows designers to have a broader vision of their trees, but it is also a less efficient solution because a node deleted by the designers at this stage could have been expanded pointlessly in the previous XML document querying phase.

As matter of fact, you may also need to infer cardinality of associations when your design source is a relational schema. If a relation called *R* includes a *C* foreign key referencing the *K* primary key of an *S* relation, this implies that *C* functionally determines *K*, and then all the other attributes of *S*. But it does not provide any information about the number of distinct tuples in *R* linked to each tuple in *S*. In principle, it would be necessary to query a database to evaluate any uncertain cardinality, as in the case of an XML source. However, this issue for relational databases is somewhat less relevant than in the XML case. While XML document designers freely choose the direction in which they want to represent each link, the need to retain the first normal form forces relational schema designers to represent each association in a to-one direction. For this reason, the association from *S* to *R* is generally one-to-many and is not relevant to the purposes of multidimensional modeling. The only relevant case, managed by the algorithm mentioned in section 6.2.2, is when a designer used the *C* foreign key to model a one-to-one association.

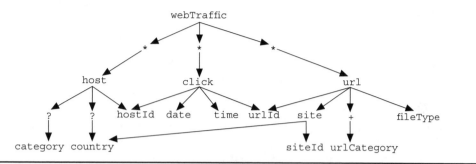

FIGURE 6-45 Another possible DTD graph for web traffic

FIGURE 6-46
Attribute tree for
the DTD graph of
Figure 6-45

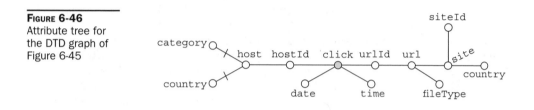

You can create many DTDs to represent an individual subject, and the algorithm can build a different attribute tree for each of those DTDs. For example, if your DTD graph was the one shown in Figure 6-45, Figure 6-46 shows how your attribute tree would look. If `click` is a fact, you have to analyze your data to check for any uncertain associations to navigate from `hostId` to `host` and from `urlId` to `url`. Figure 6-44 shows what the resulting attribute tree would look like after replacing `hostId` with `host` and `urlId` with `url`—this is allowed because these elements are linked to pairs by one-to one associations.

6.4 Mixed-approach Design

Our methodological framework for mixed-approach design uses the Tropos formalism to analyze requirements (section 4.3). To discuss conceptual design methods, we will assume that designers have already prepared the necessary diagrams—and, in particular, an extended rationale diagram for organization and one for decision-making processes for each of the actors involved. On the whole, organizational diagrams give a broad picture of source operational data, and decision-making diagrams show preliminary workload. Moreover, source data analyses and integration phases have resulted in an operational schema for the reconciled database, in either conceptual or logical form.

In the conceptual design phase, you can pair the requirements derived from organizational and decision-making modeling with your source operational schema to generate a conceptual schema for your data mart. You can break down this procedure into three phases:

1. *Requirement mapping phase.* The facts, dimensions and measures found in the decision-making modeling phase are associated with entities in the operational schema.

2. *Fact schema building phase.* After navigating the operational schema, you can create a draft conceptual schema.

3. *Refinement phase.* Draft conceptual schemata are fine-tuned to better meet users' expectations.

6.4.1   Mapping Requirements

The goal of the requirement mapping phase is to establish relationships between the facts, dimensions, and measures found in the decision-making modeling phase and the relations and attributes in operational schemata. This process is described in detail here:

Decision-making modeling facts are associated with entities or n-ary relationships (in case of Entity-Relationship schemata) or relations (in case of relational schemata) in source schemata. Now if you look at the banking example shown in section 4.3, the `transaction` fact is likely to correspond to a table called `TRANSACTIONS` in the source database.

As far as dimensions and measures are concerned, you can reach your goal if you use the attributes identified in the organizational modeling phase as a bridge. You can virtually set a double mapping between organizational modeling attributes and both the attributes in your operational schema and the dimensions and measures in your decision-making model. Look at the banking example. The `withdrawal card code` attribute, which is associated with the `enter withdrawal card code` goal of Figure 4-4, corresponds to the `card code` dimension, which is associated with the `analyze withdrawal amount` and `analyze withdrawal number` analysis goals of Figure 4-6. The same `withdrawal card code` attribute may correspond to a `numCard` attribute in the `WITHDRAWALS` operational schema table. Similarly, the `withdrawal amount` attribute of the `enter withdrawal amount` goal corresponds to the `total amount` measure of the `analyze withdrawal amount` analysis goal and to the `amount` attribute in the `WITHDRAWALS` table.

Note that you may partially automate this phase if the names used for operational schema and rationale diagrams are properly consistent.

6.4.2   Building Fact Schemata

This phase implements the data-driven part of a mixed approach. You should navigate the many-to-one associations expressed by your operational schema for every fact F identified in your decision-making model and successfully mapped onto your operational schema. This aims at building hierarchies and a draft fact schema for F.

You can use algorithms mentioned previously to carry out this navigation automatically (sections 6.1.2 and 6.2.2). The only difference is that navigation is "blind" in data-driven design—that is, all the source schema attributes linked to your fact by a many-to-one association are included in your hierarchies. On the contrary, user requirements actively guide navigation in the mixed approach. In more detail,

1. Each dimension d that was successfully mapped from an extended rationale diagram onto your operational schema is included in your fact schema. The navigation algorithm creates the whole hierarchy rooted in d.

2. Each measure m that was successfully mapped from an extended rationale diagram onto your operational schema is included in your fact schema. No hierarchy is created in this case.

3. Every time you find an organizational model attribute that is not included in your decision-making model, you have to decide if its main role is as a dimensional attribute or measure. You can add dimensional attributes to your fact schema and label them with "offers." The navigation algorithm specifies their positions in your hierarchies. Similarly, you can add measures to your fact schema and label them with "offers."

4. You can pick the dimensions and measures in your decision-making model rationale diagrams for which you have found no operational schema correspondence, still include them in your fact schema, and label them with "requests."

5. Fact schemata do not include those operational schema attributes that rationale diagrams cannot map and that you cannot reach when navigating.

As far as points 1 and 3 are concerned, note that sometimes you cannot reach a dimensional attribute to insert into your hierarchy from your fact if you exclusively navigate many-to-one associations. Then you may need to navigate many-to-many associations. This gives you the opportunity to add multiple arcs and cross-dimensional attributes automatically to your fact schema. On the contrary, you are supposed to carry out this operation manually in the data-driven approach.

Note that the names used for measures in a decision-making diagram may sometimes provide designers with valuable information for assessing which aggregation operators to use. For example, look at Figure 4-6: you can immediately realize that the decision-maker wishes to aggregate the amount measure both by SUM and by AVG.

Figure 6-47 shows the preliminary fact schema obtained for the banking example. The withdrawalFee measure is labeled with "request" because it is displayed as a measure paired with the analyze external withdrawals goal, but it is not in the organizational rationale diagram. The description dimension is labeled with "offer" because it is displayed as an attribute in the rationale diagram for organization, but decision-makers did not classify it as an analysis dimension in their rationale diagram for decision-making processes.

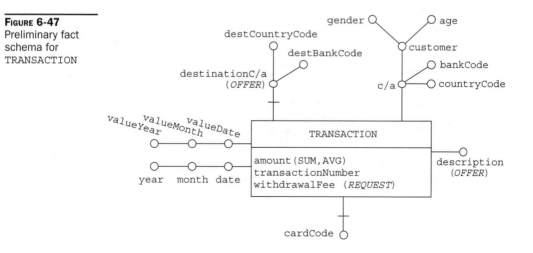

Figure 6-47
Preliminary fact schema for TRANSACTION

FIGURE 6-48
Fact schema for
TRANSACTION
after fine-tuning

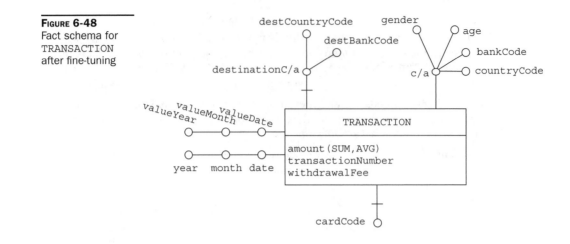

After a comparison with the data-driven approach, we can conclude that, in the mixed approach, (a) initial fact schemata may be considerably smaller and simpler; (b) diagrams for requirement analyses directly support the classification of facts, dimensions, and measures so that designers do not need to take any action; (c) modeling particular concepts, such as multiple arcs, cross-dimensional attributes, and additivity, becomes easier.

6.4.3 Refining

The aim of this final phase is to rearrange fact schemata to make them more suitable for users' needs. The main operations that you can carry out are those mentioned in section 6.1.3: pruning and grafting attributes, and adding and deleting functional dependencies.

Because dimensions and measures have been labeled in the previous phase, designers can now distinguish in fact schemata (i) all the necessary and available information (non-labeled dimensional attributes and measures); (ii) all the necessary information that is not currently available in operational schemata (dimensional attributes and measures labeled with "requests"); and (iii) the available information that is not clearly relevant for analyses (dimensional attributes and measures labeled with "offers"). The second category can make designers evaluate the option of adding on to operational schemata or using additional data sources. The third category may encourage decision-makers to try out different analysis directions.

Figure 6-48 shows a final fact schema for the TRANSACTION fact in the banking example mentioned in section 4.3. This schema assumes that (i) users have no interest in customer granularity; (ii) the data-staging phase calculates the withdrawalFee measure; and (iii) the description dimension is not considered as relevant to the analysis, but the destinationC/a dimension is relevant.

6.5 Requirement-driven Approach Design

In the mixed and data-driven approaches, operational schemata are the determining support factor in conceptual design, as we have previously mentioned. The functional dependencies expressed in those schemata are particularly useful to discover hierarchies quickly, in their early-stage forms. On the contrary, all the weight of hierarchy building falls squarely on designers' shoulders in the requirement-driven approach.

Consistently with the requirement-driven scenario outlined in section 2.4.2, we will assume that you have already drawn up the extended rationale diagrams required by the Tropos approach. The extended rationale diagrams you created during the decision-making modeling phase are those mainly used in the requirement-driven approach.

In both previous approaches, we can find a very precise set of design steps, some of which can be automated. However, the design process phases may show blurred outlines in the requirement-driven approach. The main guarantee of a successful outcome depends on designers' skills, experience, and ability to establish fruitful relationships with users and experts involved in the application domain. The starting point for requirement-driven conceptual design is a set of preliminary fact schemata obtained by associating each fact found in the decision-making rationale diagrams with its measures and dimensions. In the banking example of Figure 4-6, you can immediately design the preliminary schema of Figure 6-49. The main points you should take care of in close collaboration with users are listed next.

1. Identify any functional dependencies between the dimensions and code them in hierarchical form (for example, date→month→year).

2. Mark any optional dimensions (for example cardCode, that takes a value only in some types of transaction).

3. Merge those measures that differ only in the aggregation operator used (for example averageAmount and totalAmount).

4. If any dimensions or measures are related to specific primary event subsets, merge them or fragment your fact (for example, you can merge withdrawalNumber and transactionNumber into transactionNumber because all the withdrawals are a particular type of transaction).

Figure 6-50 shows the resulting fact schema after applying the previous criteria.

Now you can assume that your dimensions and measures are properly defined. You still have to extend and complete hierarchies. To do this, you must first decide which additional attributes are relevant to your analysis for aggregating and/or event-selection purposes.

FIGURE 6-49
Preliminary fact schema for TRANSACTION in the requirement-driven approach

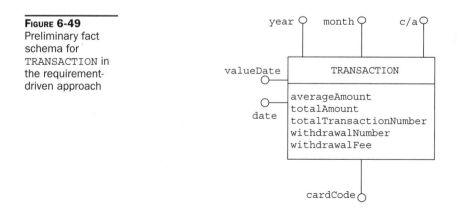

FIGURE 6-50
Fact schema for
TRANSACTION
after rearranging
dimensions and
measures

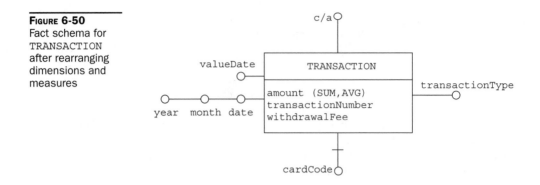

Then you can interview users in order to understand functional dependencies properly. We will make no secret of the fact that this is the most challenging stage in this approach, because the users often have only a rough idea of the actual dependencies that link attributes. If you are able to ask users all the right questions, you can achieve successful results.

When you have to design a conceptual schema even without Tropos diagrams on which to base your work, this is the most complicated condition. This means that you have to map the requirements expressed by users directly onto a fact schema. Section 4.2 showed that you must eventually briefly sum up those requirements in glossaries. Although these glossaries may help you better explain dimensions and measures, they can provide no information on hierarchy compositions and structures. Regarding hierarchy compositions, an in-depth analysis of the reports normally used by the company is required, so that you can edit a list of the main dimensional and descriptive attributes to include. Regarding hierarchy structures, the information exchange between designers and domain application experts is fundamental. If there are any doubts, you can find the necessary answers only if you carefully check the cardinality constraints on data. As a general rule, we recommend that you reuse as much as possible those hierarchies/parts of hierarchies that are frequently used in a particular application domain to reduce the complexity of design and maximize fact schema conformity. If you arrange them suitably in libraries, they become an invaluable and irreplaceable resource for designers because they or their semi-processed forms can be adjusted to users' real-worlds needs.

To conclude this chapter, we must not forget that one of the problems with the requirement-driven approach is rooted in finding mappings between fact schema attributes and source data. Those mappings are necessary to implement data-staging procedures. To do this, right from the start of the conceptual design phase it is vital that you make sure that fact schemata agree with source schemata, and that fact schemata fully seize the analysis potential of sources (Mazón et al., 2007a).

CHAPTER

Workload and Data Volume

I n this chapter, we discuss two different topics, *workload* and *data volume,* which have a point in common: they both describe how a data mart operates in a specific enterprise. Workload essentially consists of the set of queries issued by end users and processed by a data mart. Data volume consists of cardinality properties of the domains of attributes and cubes.

The data volume is essential for physically sizing data marts. It also has a fundamental significance in the logical and physical design phases because it allows designers to estimate the costs of queries and size of views and indexes (Vassiliadis, 2000; Gupta et al., 1997b).

The workload is a delicate matter. Online analytical processing (OLAP) queries of a data mart are extemporaneous by definition, so they cannot be predicted before they're needed. For this reason, a data mart workload is generally very dynamic. Nevertheless, we find it feasible and useful for designers to guess the workload beforehand to assess the comprehensiveness and correctness of conceptual schemata and to better tune the implementation process. On the one hand, designers should include the queries that end users expect to execute more frequently for statistical and decision-making purposes. On the other hand, designers should include the basic reports most frequently issued by end users in the near past.

The dynamic property of workloads causes any analysis of queries to be partially unreliable if it is conducted at design time. Many commercial tools offer a possible solution to this problem: They constantly monitor the actual workload when data marts are operating, and then logical and physical setups are regularly adjusted to fit the queries monitored. Even in this case, it is quite clear that workloads play an essential role in accurately defining a logical-physical schema that can effectively ensure top performance (Rizzi and Saltarelli, 2003a).

Note that data-loading queries (queries regularly loading data into data marts) are not generally included in workload estimates because data loading is typically carried out when data marts are offline and cannot be accessed by users. For this reason, loading data does not directly affect performance. However, you should make sure that this process is completed within a maximum time value.

7.1 Workload

In general, querying a transactional database means linking concepts by means of association paths to retrieve specific data. In particular, you should express a set of joins between relations to carry out this operation in relational databases. On the contrary, an essential part of data warehouse queries aims at retrieving information that sums up data to create reports that should be analyzed for statistical or decision-making purposes. As a matter of fact, the following paragraphs will show that *a standard OLAP query on fact schemata can be formulated by defining a set of events with a specific level of aggregation. In this way, users can analyze both event measures and coordinates.*

Workload

Given a set of fact schemata, the *workload* is a set of couples (q_i, η_i), where q_i denotes a query on one or more fact schemata, and η_i is the query frequency or relative importance for users.

7.1.1   Dimensional Expressions and Queries on Fact Schemata

This section explains how to select sets of events by writing *dimensional expressions*. We propose a language aimed at defining queries on a specific data mart. Those queries make up the expected workload that should be used for the logical and physical design. For this reason, it specifies only *which data* should be read and at *which level* data should be aggregated.

In the following grammars, nonterminal elements appear in angle brackets (< and >). Terminal elements appear in boldface. The parts followed by an asterisk (*) can be repeated one or more times. A vertical slash (|) marks an alternative. Self-explanatory nonterminal elements (such as *<attribute name>*) are not expanded for the sake of brevity.

Dimensional Expression

The following grammar regulates how to create dimensional expressions:

<expression> ::= <fact name> <aggregation clause>*
<aggregation clause> ::= [<group-by set>] | [<group-by set> ; <selection predicate>]
<group-by set> ::= <attribute name> | <group-by set> , <attribute name>

Group-by sets can be either primary or secondary. Selection predicates are Boolean expressions based on attributes and/or measures.

If an attribute included in an aggregation clause or in a selection predicate is not a dimension, you can place the hierarchy name to which the attribute belongs before the attribute name in order to make that expression easier to understand.

Dimensional Query

The following grammar regulates how to create dimensional queries:

<query> ::= <expression>.<measure name> | <expression>.<attribute name>

To understand the semantics of this language, consider a few examples based on the sales schema as shown in Figure 7-1. We will analyze only the *simple* expressions for which a single aggregation clause follows a fact name. In section 7.1.3, we will focus on *composite* expressions, where various aggregation clauses are nested.

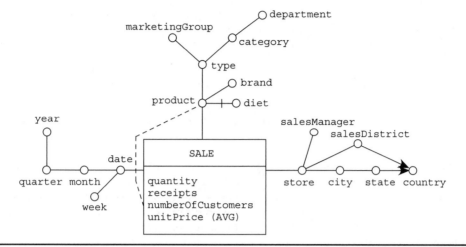

In the easiest case, the group-by set denoted is the primary one and conditions are expressed on attributes only. Then this expression denotes the set of primary events defined by those coordinates for which all the predicates are true. For example, consider the following dimensional expression:

```
SALE[date, product, store;
     date.month='12/2008' AND
     store.state='VIRGINIA' AND
     product='Shiny']
```

This expression denotes the sales of the Shiny product in every store in Virginia every single day in December 2008.

Given an expression denoting a set of events, formulating a query simply stands for specifying the measure or the attribute users are interested in. Then, this expression

```
SALE[date, product, store;
     month='12/2008' AND
     state='Virginia' AND
     product='Shiny'].receipts
```

denotes the receipts related to each sale of Shiny in every store in Virginia every single day in December 2008. But this expression

```
SALE[date, product, store;
     quantity>100 AND
     month='12/2008' AND
     state='Virginia' AND
     product='Shiny'].store
```

specifies Virginia's stores, where more than 100 Shiny packs were sold at least on one day in December 2008.

Generally, an expression denotes a G secondary group-by set. A selection predicate built on schema attributes can select a subset of secondary events or affect the aggregation defining them. For simplicity's sake, assume that a selection predicate is the AND logical conjunction of a set of simple predicates, such as this:

<p align="center"><em><attribute</em> or <em>measure> <comparison operator> <value></em></p>

NOTE *A simple predicate based on the* a *attribute is called* external *if* a *appears in G or it is functionally determined by an attribute in G. If this is not the case, it is defined as* internal.

An external predicate restricts the set of secondary events returned by an expression. For example, this applies to the predicates on the c and e attributes shown in Figure 7-2. Unlike external predicates, an internal predicate specifies which primary events are going to be part of each secondary event. An internal predicate is based on an attribute functionally determining an attribute in G (for example, d); an attribute placed onto a hierarchy branch that is different from the hierarchy branch onto which an attribute in G is placed (for example, a); or an attribute being part of a hierarchy not included in G (for example, b).

Consider the following queries based on the sales schema:

```
q₁ = SALE[month, type;
         month='10/2008' AND
         category='Food'].quantity
q₂ = SALE[month, type;
         month='10/2008' AND
         category='Food' AND
         brand='ACME'].quantity
```

These respectively denote the total amount of items sold per food category product type in October 2008, and the total amount of items sold per product type branded ACME in October 2008. The predicates based on month and category are external, and the predicate based on brand is internal. Now consider the sample data shown in Table 7-1 and the

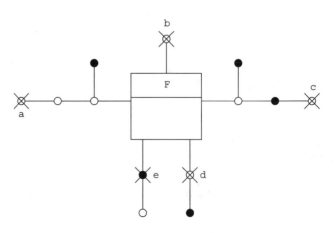

FIGURE 7-2
External predicates built on c and e, and internal predicates built on a, b, and d. The black dots show the attributes included in the G group-by set, and the crosses mark the attributes used to define simple predicates.

brand	category	type	product	month	10/2008	11/2008
ACME		Drinks	DrinkME		100	90
Best	Food		Coky		200	120
ACME		Cookies	Rolls		50	80
Best			Chocky		20	20
ACME	House	Cleaners	Shiny		80	50
Best	Cleaning		Bleachy		50	30

TABLE 7-1   Values of the `quantity` Measure for the Secondary Events with Group-by Set {product, month}

`quantity` measure that is additive along all the dimensions: Table 7-2 shows the results of both queries. It is easy to note that the predicate based on the `category` attribute specifies which secondary events are going to be returned to users, such as the secondary events related to October and both Drinks and Cookies types. Furthermore, the predicate based on the `brand` attribute changes the composition of secondary events, and it excludes a few primary events from the calculation of secondary events.

If a query grouping by G returns the a attribute instead of a measure, note that a has to be external to the G group-by set for this query to be correct. This means that a should be functionally determined by an attribute included in the G group-by set. For example, consider the following query:

```
SALE[date, product;
     date='10/1/2008' AND category='Food'].product
```

This returns all the products of category Food sold on 10/1/2008 in at least one store.

Things get slightly more difficult when you start working on selection predicates based on measures: now you have to specify *which group-by set should be used to evaluate predicates*.

NOTE *In a dimensional expression, you should always assume that the predicates built on measures are evaluated on the basis of the group-by set specified by the expression itself.*

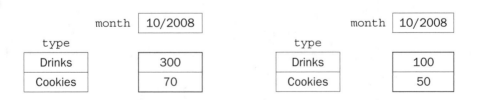

	month	10/2008			month	10/2008
type				type		
Drinks		300		Drinks		100
Cookies		70		Cookies		50

TABLE 7-2   Results of Both Queries Grouping by {type, month}: q_1 on the Left, q_2 on the Right

For this reason, consider the following queries:

```
SALE[date, product, store;
     date='12/24/2007' AND
     category='Food' AND
     quantity≥100].product
SALE[date, product;
     date='12/24/2007' AND
     category='Food' AND
     quantity≥100].product
```

They respectively denote the food products of which at least 100 items were sold on Christmas eve in at least one store—the Slurp Milk and the DrinkME items in the example of Table 7-3—and the food products of which at least 100 items were sold *in the aggregate* on Christmas eve in all the stores—the Slurp Milk, the DrinkME, and the Gnutella items in the example of Table 7-3.

On the contrary, consider the following query:

```
SALE[date, category, store;
     date='12/24/2007' AND
     category='Food' AND
     quantity<300].store
```

This returns the stores where the *total* amount of food items sold on Christmas eve is lower than 300—EverMore2 in Table 7-3.

Then consider the following query:

```
SALE[month, category;
     year='2008' AND
     category='Food' AND
     brand='ACME' AND
     quantity>160].month
```

This returns the months in 2008 when more than 160 food items branded ACME were sold in the aggregate—November 2008 in Table 7-1.

category	product	store	EverMore	SmartMart	EverMore2
Food	Slurp Milk		150	80	90
	Gnam Yogurt		50	30	–
	DrinkME		150	200	120
	Coky		–	–	20
	Gnutella		40	60	50
	Total:		390	370	280

TABLE 7-3   Primary Events Showing the `quantity` Measure for Food Items Sold on 12/24/2007

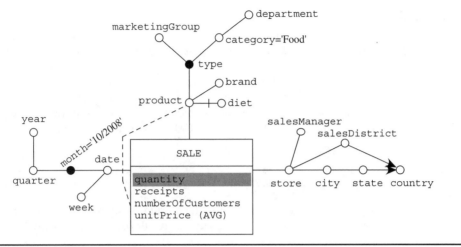

Figure 7-3   Graphically representing a simple query

You can also use the formalism of fact schemata to represent graphically a query denoted by a simple dimensional expression. Figure 7-3 shows an example of a graphical representation of the following query:

```
SALE[month, type;
     month='10/2008' AND
     category='Food'].quantity
```

To express this group-set by, its dimensional attributes are highlighted in black in the figure. The measure that should be returned is highlighted in gray, and text labels next to the attributes involved mark the selection conditions.

To conclude this section, we would like to make a remark on aggregations. The easy-to-understand language used for dimensional expressions does not specify which operator should be used to aggregate every measure when we process secondary events. In the preceding examples, we implicitly assumed that the aggregation operator used is the one specified in fact schemata. This means that the operator should be the SUM operator if measures are additive. However, remember that you can use various operators for an individual measure-dimension combination in a fact schema. As we mentioned in section 5.3.2, you should also be aware that there are complex aggregation conditions under which you have to aggregate measures along various dimensions using different operators. In this case, your result can depend on your aggregation order. Now we can easily realize that dimensional expressions do not generally define just one query (for example, expressed in SQL) on a cube. To overcome this stumbling-block, you need to use a language with more expressive power, such as the language used for nested Generalized Projection/Selection/ Join (GPSJ) expressions discussed in section 7.1.4. However, remember that our goal in this chapter is not to introduce a multidimensional query language, but to specify the workload that should be used for the logical-physical design of our data mart. The approaches to this design do not depend mainly on the aggregation operators used for individual queries.

7.1.2   Drill-Across Queries

A drill-across query needs to create relationships between two or more fact schemata. There are essentially two different types of drill-across queries in the scope of the Dimensional Fact Model (DFM).

The first type of drill-across queries needs a comparison between measures from comparable fact schemata. As a result, you can write this type of drill-across query if you write a dimensional expression based on an overlapped schema. For example, Figure 5-37 shows a schema overlapping SHIPMENT and INVENTORY. We can use this schema to issue the following query:

```
SHIPMENT+INVENTORY[month, category;
    year='2007'].(shippedQuantity-incomingQuantity)
```

This query calculates the difference between the total amount of items shipped and the total amount of items stored into warehouses, and groups its results by each month in 2007 and by each product category.

If we consider this type of drill-across query from the logical design point of view, we can break it down to a set of queries, each based on one of the fact schemata involved in the overlapping process. Consider the following expression:

$$q = F\ [G;\ \text{<selection predicate>}].\text{<measure expression>}$$

It is a query on the overlapped $F = F_1 + \cdots + F_m$ schema. This query can be broken down into m queries, such as $q_1 \ldots, q_m$ where

$$q_i = F_i\ [G;\ \text{<selection predicate>}].M_i$$

and M_i is the F_i measure subset included in <measure expression>. The preceding query can be broken down like so:

```
SHIPMENT[month, category;
    year='2007'].quantityShipped
INVENTORY[month, category;
    year='2007'].incomingQuantity
```

The second type of drill-across query is also called a *flow-across query*. These queries process a set of comparable fact schemata in a conceptually different way. They do not query overlapping schemata to define the values of a measure set, but they sequentially query across various fact schemata to determine one or more attribute values that should be used to make a selection from the following schemata. To construct those queries in our language, you must nest two expressions. One of those expressions uses the result achieved by the other in the selection predicate. For example, consider the following query:

```
INVENTORY[month, product;
    month='1/2008' AND
    product IN
    SHIPMENT[month, product;
        month='1/2008' AND
        shippedQuantity>1000].product].level
```

This query returns the average inventory level in January 2008 for each product totaling more than 1000 units shipped in that month. You can also issue this query across every warehouse, as shown in the following example:

```
INVENTORY[month, product, warehouse;
     month='1/2008' AND (product,  warehouse) IN
     SHIPMENT[month, product, warehouse;
          month='1/2008' AND
          shippedQuantity>1000].(product, warehouse)].level
```

Flow-across queries often occur when a regular fact schema is matched to a coverage schema. See section 5.3 for more details. For example, assume that you have both comparable schemata of Figure 7-4, and the second schema is a cover schema recording promotional products. You want to answer the question, Which products included in the April 2008 promotional sale by the EverMore store were not sold in April 2008? This is undoubtedly a flow-across query because it involves two separate schemata and you can formulate it as shown here:

```
PROMOTION[date, product, store;
     month='4/2008' AND
     store='EverMore' AND (date, product, store) NOT IN
     SALE[date, product, store].(date, product, store)].product
```

A special case for flow-across queries involves a given fact schema twice. For example, consider the following query:

```
SALE[month, store; year='2008' AND store IN
     SALE[year, store;
          year='2008' AND
          category='Clothes' AND
          receipts<10000].store].receipts
```

This query returns the monthly receipts made in 2008 by the stores that sold clothes totaling less than $10,000 during 2008.

7.1.3   Composite Queries

Even if the query formulations mentioned in the preceding sections are by far the most widespread, they do not cover all the wide range of possible queries in which users might be interested for data warehousing applications. For example, assume that you want to calculate the total amount of receipts in 2007 per state and product type, including in the total only the sales of 50 units or more. Obviously, you cannot formulate this query on the basis of the instructions given in section 7.1.1. If you issued the following query,

```
SALE[state, type; year='2007' AND quantity≥50].receipts
```

it would return the total amount of the receipts in 2007 grouped by state and product type, provided that the amount of items sold is greater than or equal to 50 units. For this reason, you have to express that the quantity measure predicate should be evaluated on the basis

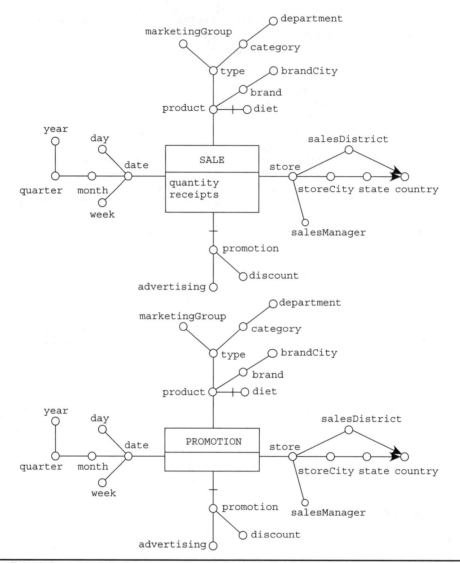

Figure 7-4 Sales schema (top) and coverage schema for promotions (bottom)

of a group-by set different from {state, type}. To do this, you should place two aggregation clauses in sequence after the fact name:

```
SALE[date, store, product; quantity≥50]
     [state, type; year='2007'].receipts
```

In this way, primary events are used instead of secondary ones to make a selection based on quantity.

Composite expressions generally show the following syntax:

$$F [G_1; <predM_1>] [G_2; <predM_2>] \ldots [G_p; <predM_p> \text{ AND } <predA>]$$

Where $G_{i+1} = G_i$ for every $i = 1 \ldots, p - 1$, and $<predM_i>$ is evaluated on the events with group-by set G_i. $<predA>$ is the predicate based on the attributes: you can place it into any aggregation clause because it does not depend on any aggregation.

Consider the following example of a query consisting of three aggregation levels based on the sales schema shown in Figure 7-1. This query calculates the yearly total amount of receipts due to those products totaling more than 1000 units sold per month, even if just one customer bought them in one day.

```
SALE[date, product; numberOfCustomers=1]
    [month, product; quantity>1000]
    [year].receipts
```

7.1.4 Nested GPSJ Queries

A category of queries that has even more expressive power is the one of nested *Generalized Projection/Selection/Join* (GPSJ) queries. These queries involve relational algebraic operators that apply to the relational schema resulting from the logical design of a fact schema. Because of the complexity involved, we will not analyze this type of expression here, but simply give a brief description of the basic points. See Golfarelli and Rizzi, 2000b and 2000c, for more details.

Nested GPSJ queries are not very different from composite dimensional expressions, except for the opportunity to explicitly define the aggregation operator that should be used for every measure at every aggregation step. In dimensional expressions, you should always use the same aggregation operator for a given measure—main operators are defined by fact schemata. By contrast, you can apply a sequence of different operators to a given measure in nested GPSJ expressions. Consider the following examples of nested GPSJ queries of the sales schema:

- *For each product, what is the total amount of units sold in the stores that sold more than 1000 units of that product?*
- *What is the total amount of drinks sold and the average of monthly total receipts per drink and year?*

The first query requires that primary events be grouped by {store, product}, that the total amount of units sold tq be calculated, that the stores where tq is greater than 1000 be selected, and then that they be grouped by {product} to calculate the total value of tq. On the contrary, the second query requires that the events be grouped by {month, product} to calculate the total amount of the units sold per month tq and the total amounts of the receipts per month tr, and then grouped by {year, product} to sum tq and calculate the average values of tr.

7.1.5 Validating a Workload in a Conceptual Schema

At the beginning of this chapter, we stated that workloads play a fundamental role for logical and physical design of data marts because they streamline an accurate tuning of the implementation process. The specification of a workload also plays another important role:

it allows designers to check for conceptual schemata to be comprehensive and correct. Its role is very similar to that of *navigation schemata* of queries in the design phase of relational databases by means of the Entity-Relationship model (ERM).

If the resulting fact schemata are comprehensive and correct, they can be used to formulate all the queries that end users want to issue. If this is not the case, formulating some queries may be impossible. Following are the main problems that can occur:

- *You cannot aggregate data at the required level because of lacking dimensional attributes.* Those dimensional attributes might have been defined as descriptive attributes, wrongly deleted in the conceptual design phase, or even neglected because they were not in source schemata. In a few cases, the minimum granularity level specified by designers may be inappropriate, so designers have to refine the primary group-by set.

- *Designers cannot define the aggregation level required as a group-by set even if all the attributes involved are available because the fact schema includes a false functional dependency between the attributes.* Designers will have to work with users to find and remove this dependency.

- *Users cannot select events the way they want to.* The problem with this condition is a lacking dimensional attribute.

- *There is no measure corresponding to the expected results.* It is likely that the necessary measure can be derived from the available ones after calculating an algebraic expression. If this is the case, designers should assess whether it is worthwhile to add it to the fact schema as a derived measure. It is also likely that the measure required can be calculated from a source schemata attribute that was deleted or turned into a descriptive attribute in the conceptual design phase. Lastly, a simple SQL query on the operational schema might be insufficient to calculate the required measure; in which case a complex query or processing procedure is probably necessary.

- *Designers are trying to formulate a drill-across query, but the overlapped schema involved lacks one or more attributes that are essential for aggregations and/or selections.* Perhaps the corresponding hierarchies in the overlapping schemata are too different from each other and designers should first make them compliant with each other. See section 5.5 for more details.

- *The aggregation operator required is not included in those shown by the additivity table for a specific measure-dimension combination.* Then, designers along with users must check for aggregation semantics and add the required operator to the additivity table.

The preceding examples show that problems can usually be solved if designers go back to the conceptual design phase to review the decisions made and restore wrongly deleted attributes. However, designers will sometimes be unable to find any solution in source schemata, because the data searched for is not available. As a result, designers should evaluate whether source schemata can be changed in order to add new attributes at reasonable costs. Because this scenario is not generally feasible, designers should evaluate whether they can manually enter unavailable operational data or import data from external sources.

7.1.6 Workload and Users

Designing a data mart also means defining the options to access data and providing *specific users* with the rights to access *specific data* in *specific modes*. To do this, you must classify end users and the types of queries that end users want to submit to a data mart. In this way, you can create a list of rights used by front-end interface designers to set up the system properly. In data warehousing projects, this issue is often addressed at a very late stage and system administrators have to solve it directly. On the contrary, we suggest that this issue should be reasonably included in the design phase when designers have to refine and validate workloads.

First of all, you should classify users into homogeneous groups aimed at defining *user profiles*. The main criterion for this classification is based on enterprise-specific roles played by users. These roles usually specify the set of information to which a specific user group can have access. For example, a few user profiles in the business domain are *store manager*, *sales district manager*, *marketing manager*, and *senior manager*. You can also specify specialization relationships among the previous user profiles so as to create a hierarchy structure in which the most specialized users inherit their rights from the generic ones. The formalism of use cases in Unified Modeling Language (UML) (Arlow and Neustadt, 2005) is particularly suitable for this purpose because it can model the hierarchies of actors interacting with a system and the analyses that those actors might conduct. Figure 7-5 shows an easy-to-understand example in the commercial domain.

TIP *This classification needs refining until you can create user profiles that have access to the same set of information, except for the selection criteria that can be parameterized on front-end tools. For example, all the store managers can have access to all their sales data. But each manager is granted access restricted to the items sold in their stores only. To avoid overloading your classifications, you can manage any exceptions to this right-management system separately.*

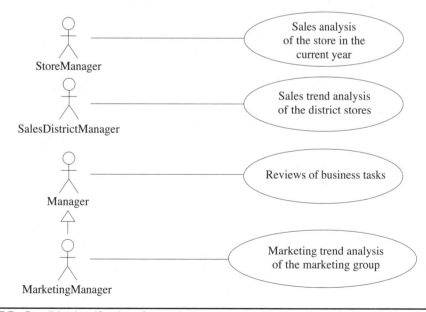

FIGURE 7-5   Possible classification of users in a commercial data mart

In this way, your classification normally shows a structure that also highlights the ways used by user profiles to access data, such as OLAP, dashboards, static reports, and semi-static reports. If a user profile cannot have homogenous access to information, you should further refine your classification because front-end tools also use this classification to enforce data protection policies.

NOTE *Classifying users into profiles based on how they access information is useful to evaluate the necessary front-end license number and type. Most software vendors diversify their products on the basis of the access rights granted so that costs may vary accordingly.*

After specifying the different types of user profiles, you need to specify users' access rights to fact schemata, including overlapped schemata. For each user profile and fact schema, you must specify the following:

- Which measures and which descriptive attributes can be viewed
- Which hierarchies and which dimensional attributes can be navigated
- Which restrictions must be applied to data

The first two specifications deal with the part of a schema that can be viewed and/or navigated. The third specification deals with the instances of a schema. All the preceding specifications are used to define access restrictions, such as *Sales district managers can access all the sales fact measures to the extent of their districts, but they cannot aggregate those measures by city, state, and country.* You can use a table, such as Table 7-4, or fact schemata, such as the one shown in Figure 7-6, to formalize the restrictions on information access. This approach is similar to the one adopted in section 7.1 to formalize a workload, but it represents the set of attributes that a specific user profile cannot navigate instead of representing group-by sets.

To check that the restrictions sets are correct, each user profile can be matched to the set of static and semi-static reports belonging to the workload. Reports are exactly created to provide each user profile with quick and easy-to-use access to information that is vital for user profile tasks to be performed. For this reason, you should be able to calculate user reports from the data to which users can have access.

	Store Manager	Sales District Manager	Marketing Manager	Senior Manager
SALE	– city – state – country – salesDistrict	– city – state – country		– store – date
	store = *<input par1>* year = *<input par2>*	salesDistrict = *<input par3>*	marketingGroup = *<input par4>*	
...	...	...	...	...

TABLE 7-4   Access Right Table for a Commercial Data Mart; the Attributes Listed are EXCLUDED from Navigation. If No Restriction Exists, Users Should Have Full Access to All Information.

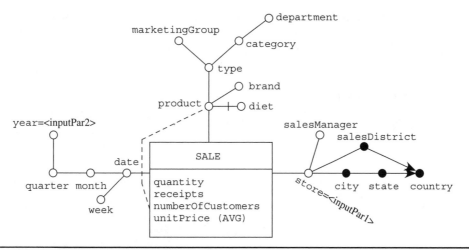

FIGURE 7-6 Graphical representation of navigation restrictions on the SALE fact for the store manager user profile. Black dots show that navigation is not allowed.

7.2 Data Volumes

To begin our discussion of data volumes, we should move from the intensional level of fact schemata to the extensional level of events. According to the terminology of the multidimensional model, we should move from the analysis of cube schemata to the analysis of specific cube instances.

> ### Cardinality of a Group-by Set
> Given a G (primary or secondary) group-by set of a fact schema, we will define as *cardinality* of G the expected number of (primary or secondary) events with group-by set G and we will mark it with *card* (G).

Expressing data volumes for data marts means evaluating the domain cardinality of all the dimensional attributes, indicating the cardinality of primary group-by sets, and specifying a way to evaluate the cardinality of every secondary group-by set.

Domain cardinality of dimensional attributes is generally quite easy to calculate. You simply need to query your data sources properly (for example, with a SELECT COUNT(DISTINCT) query) to measure the desired domain cardinality. If you don't have access to any operational data, you can turn to your application domain expert, who can easily indicate, for example, the number of stores or the number of products available.

As far as group-by set cardinality is concerned, you can easily estimate it if your data mart has already been populated. If this is the case, you can use statistical evaluation techniques that are generally based on histograms (Muralikrishna and DeWitt, 1988) or sampling (Hou and Özsoyoglu, 1991; Haas et al., 1995). Unfortunately, you cannot apply those techniques if your data mart design is still in progress.

Application domain experts are generally quite familiar with primary group-by set cardinality ($card(G_0)$) with regard to a specific time unit. Therefore, to calculate the total number of primary events expected for every fact schema, it just takes a little effort to agree with end users on the history interval that your data mart must cover. This interval generally ranges from one to five years. For example, you can be notified that every store sells approximately 1000 different products per day. If 10 stores exist and the time frame set covers three years, the group-by set cardinality will be approximately 10^7.

Sparsity of a Fact Schema

Given a fact schema whose primary group-by set is G_0, its *sparsity* is defined by the following ratio:

$$\frac{card(G_0)}{card_{max}(G_0)}$$

Where $card_{max}(G_0)$ stands for the highest cardinality value possible in the primary group-by set as the product of the domain cardinality of all the dimensions:

$$card_{max}(G_0) = \prod_{a_i \in G_0} card(Dom(a_i))$$

Things get more difficult when it comes to the number of secondary events, because you should evaluate how sparsity at the primary group-by set level impacts on the following aggregation levels. The exponential growth of possible secondary group-by sets makes it impossible to list the secondary group-by set cardinalities. However, this is essential in the logical design phase in order to represent the size of candidate views to materialization. See section 9.2.3 for more details on this point. For this reason, you will have to create a formula or an algorithm that is able to evaluate the cardinality of every secondary group-by set.

The approach based on probabilities is most widespread (Ross and Srivastava, 1997; Shukla et al., 1996; Golfarelli and Rizzi, 1999). It takes advantage of the so-called *Cardenas formula* (Cardenas, 1975) explained in the following paragraphs. If $G = \{a_1 \ldots, a_m\}$ is a secondary group-by set, and G_0 is the primary group-by set, the maximum cardinality of G (total number of coordinates) is the result of:

$$card_{max}(G) = \prod_{a_i \in G} card(Dom(a_i))$$

where $card(Dom(a_i))$ denotes the domain cardinality of the a_i attribute. If G is fine enough, you cannot achieve that maximum cardinality because of the sparsity of G_0. Recall that the secondary event corresponding to a coordinate exists when at least one primary event corresponds to that secondary event, if you apply the roll-up function. See section 5.6.3 for more details on this point.

Figure 7-7 shows that you can obtain the Cardenas formula if you take the following into account:

- The probability that a specific coordinate of G matches a specific primary event equates to $1/card(G)$.

- The probability that a specific coordinate of G does not match a specific primary event equates to $1 - 1/card(G)$.

FIGURE 7-7
Framework for the
Cardenas formula

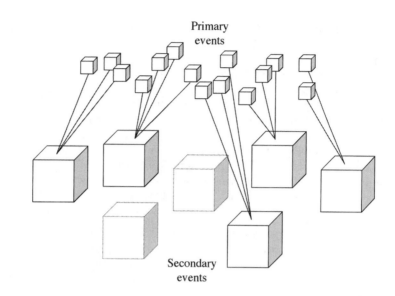

Primary events

Secondary events

- The probability that a specific coordinate of G matches no specific primary event equates to $(1-1/card(G))^{card(G_0)}$.

- The probability that a specific coordinate of G matches at least a specific primary event equates to $1-(1-1/card(G))^{card(G_0)}$.

If you multiply the last result by the total number of coordinates of G, you will achieve the following result:

$$card(G) \cong card_{max}(G) \times \left(1-\left(1-\frac{1}{card_{max}(G)}\right)^{card(G_0)}\right) \leq min\{card_{max}(G), card(G_0)\}$$

The problem in abstract terms justifying this formula can be explained as follows: *Given a box with an infinite number of balls of* n *colors and each color repeating for an infinite number of times, how many different colors are there when you draw* m *balls?*

As a matter of fact, we are aware that the Cardenas formula tends to overestimate. For this reason, it can happen that the space actually used by views is by far smaller than the space allocated in the view materialization phase. To solve this problem, Ciaccia and others (2003) introduced an approach using cardinality constraints from application domains to define *upper* and *lower bounds* of every group-by set cardinality. On the basis of those bounds, you use probability formulas to calculate the expected cardinality. Domain experts define cardinality constraints as the cardinality of one or more group-by sets or *k-dependencies* limiting the value of the relationship between the cardinalities of two group-by sets. To realize how those bounds can improve a cardinality estimate, consider the following example. An enterprise wants to monitor its employees transferred from one department to another. See Figure 6-30, which shows the reference fact schema. The primary group-by set is G_0 = {date, fromDepartment, toDepartment, employee}. The designer wants to evaluate the cardinality of G = {date, fromDepartment, toDepartment}. The value 10^4 represents the number of employees transferred from a department to another one at least once in a 10^3-day-long monitoring period, and 10^3 is the number of departments in place.

If there is no additional data, you can only state that the cardinality value of G has to be greater than 10^3 and lower than $10^3 \times 10^3 \times 10^3 = 10^9$ at the same time, because, at the utmost, each department can be involved in a personnel transfer to all the other departments every day. If your domain expert lets you know that an employee can be transferred to other departments twice in a year at the utmost, and your monitoring period consists of approximately three years, then you can calculate that the cardinality value of G_0 cannot be greater than 6 times the total number of employees or 6×10^4. For this reason, it is clear that the maximum estimate of G can be adjusted, because the cardinality value of a secondary group-by set cannot be greater than the cardinality value of a primary group-by set—secondary events are an aggregation of primary ones. To conclude, the result will be $10^4 \le card(G) \le 6 \times 10^4$. On the basis of the bounds created, you can adopt probability-driven approaches, such as the Cardenas formula, to estimate the cardinality value of G reliably.

NOTE *On very coarse-grained secondary group-by sets, there is a small probability that coordinates may exist that no primary event matches. Therefore, the coarser the granularity of group-by sets, the smaller their sparsity gets. The probability to generate errors consequently decreases, as well. If there is no sparsity, all the cube cells are full; then you can calculate the cardinality value of G as $card_{max}(G)$.*

CHAPTER

Logical Modeling

Conceptual modeling does not depend on the logical model the designer has selected in the architecture design phase, but the topics related to logical modeling clearly do. Three different logical models can be used to represent a multidimensional data structure: the relational model, used in the so-called Relational OLAP (ROLAP) systems; the multidimensional model, used in Multidimensional OLAP (MOLAP) systems; and the hybrid model called Hybrid OLAP (HOLAP). In the following sections, we will first provide a short description of MOLAP and HOLAP systems. Then we will focus on ROLAP systems, on which most commercial solutions are currently based.

8.1 MOLAP and HOLAP Systems

Before dealing with logical modeling, we would like to remind the reader of the essential concept of the *data cube* introduced by Gray et al., (1997). The definition of this concept is a generalization of the SQL group-by set operator specifying the space of basic and aggregate events that can be calculated and stored. Given a primary cube including all the primary events, its data cube consists of the primary cube surrounded by a collection of secondary, coarse-grained cubes, which aggregate the primary cube along one or more dimensions and include secondary events. If there is no hierarchy, the data cube for a d-dimensional base cube consists of 2^d cubes, each representing a unique data view at a specific granularity level. All the secondary cubes do not need to be physically available because you can calculate them by aggregating their primary cube along one or more dimensions. Nevertheless, you may need to store some or all the secondary cubes to improve the query response time.

Figure 8-1 shows a data cube for a simple sales fact that includes three dimensions without any hierarchy. In the aggregate, this data cube consists of eight cubes. Along with the primary cube (in gray), this figure shows three two-dimensional secondary cubes (by store, product; by store, time; by time, product) and three one-dimensional secondary cubes (by store; by time; by product) resulting from information increasingly aggregated. This figure does not show the 0-dimensional secondary cube, which consists of one single cell aggregating all the information of primary cubes.

Although data cubes should be viewed as an abstraction, they also play the role of logical models for MOLAP and HOLAP systems. MOLAP and HOLAP systems store all their data cube data or a part of it, respectively. To do this, they use multidimensional

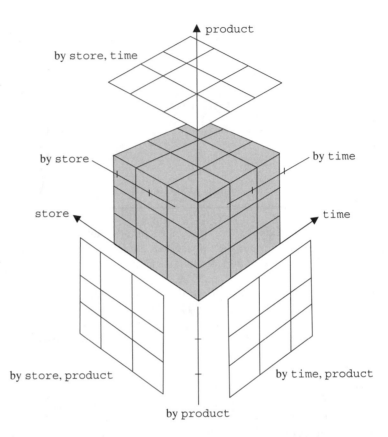

FIGURE 8-1
The data cube for a simple SALE fact containing three degenerate hierarchies (store, time, and product). In gray is the primary cube; in white are the secondary cubes.

structures, such as multidimensional vectors; each vector element is associated with a set of coordinates on a value space. This type of structure is the simplest representation of data warehouse data. It can also deliver top performance because it is perfectly suitable for OLAP tasks that can be directly based on data structures and do not have to be simulated via complex SQL queries. The main problem with MOLAP systems is data sparsity. On the average, less than 20 percent of data cube cells actually include any information (Colliat, 1996). The remaining cells are associated with events that do not take place. A multidimensional DBMS has to store all its cells. As a result, this system wastes some free hard disk space because it stores noninformative cells. Section 8.1.1 describes some ground-breaking techniques that have been developed to avoid the storage of noninformative cells. However, the use of those innovative storage systems takes a toll on system performance.

The lack of standards for logical models puts additional brakes on the spread of MOLAP systems. All the systems have common basics, such as multidimensional data structures and sparsity management. However, the implementation of those systems is often based on poorly documented proprietary data structures that make the systems hard to be replaced and accessed by third-party tools. Furthermore, those tools have no query standard playing the same role as the SQL language in relational systems, though

Microsoft has recently introduced the *Multidimensional Expression (MDX)* language that is supported by many vendors and progressively turning into a widely accepted de facto standard language.

Furthermore, designers and system administrators do not trust MOLAP technology. This skeptical attitude prevented MOLAP systems from becoming popular for many years. Now skepticism is fading away thanks to the investments made by renowned vendors and the new technological solutions being progressively discovered. At the time of writing this book, it is hard to estimate the extent to which new MOLAP solutions will be able to replace ROLAP systems. We cannot even forecast what kind of balance between both technologies will take place.

8.1.1 The Problem of Sparsity

The term *data sparsity* indicates that just a small part of the cells in a multidimensional cube actually include information. The remaining cells are associated with events that do not take place. Section 8.2 shows that sparsity has no effect on ROLAP systems because they can store only useful cells. On the contrary, the basic versions of MOLAP systems represent all the cells of a cube, making for a waste of disk space and time for information to be retrieved.

Even if sparsity management solutions in MOLAP systems have different implementations, they share some basic techniques (Zhao et al., 1997; Colliat, 1996):

- *Select the part of data cube to materialize.* As mentioned, there is no guarantee that all the secondary cubes of a data cube are actually materialized because they can be calculated from the primary cube. When you set the percentage of data cube materialization, this automatically balances the space allocated to storage and the time for query answering. This setting should depend on the sparsity degree of the data. However, this setting does not normally provide the opportunity to store more than 70 percent of all the data cube cells.

- *Partition cubes.* This process splits an *n*-dimensional cube into various sub-cubes called *chunks*. This strategy leads to small-sized blocks of data that can be quickly loaded into memory. Cube partitioning can also manage sparse chunks and dense chunks in different ways. A chunk is *dense* if most of its cells include data. If this is not the case, a chunk is *sparse*. At this stage, you can influence the efficiency of your system because partitioning into chunks impacts the resulting grade of sparsity (Kaser and Lemire, 2003).

- *Compress chunks.* Storing sparse chunks directly to memory implies a waste of free space because of the representation of the cells with no information. For this reason, an index that lists only the chunk cells containing information is normally used to create a compressed representation of sparse chunks.

- *Order chunks.* You should specify the order used to store every chunk to disk so as to streamline OLAP query processes (Otoo et al., 2007). You can use mapping functions, such as the Morton sequence or Z-order, to arrange chunks on a disk. Indexed structures can quickly find the chunks where specific data is located. You can use those quick-access structures to retrieve data for which a specific query searches to streamline the whole process (Lim and Kim, 2004). In particular, spatial indexes can be used for this purpose. Section 11.5 contains more details on this point.

Figure 8-2 shows a data cube on the left where some cells do not contain any data (transparent cells). On the basis of the percentage of unused cells, the data chunks on the right side of the figure are highlighted in white (sparse chunks) or in gray (dense chunks).

One of the problems affecting the data structures and the techniques described so far is the inability to maintain the existing roll-up and drill-down relationships between cells. This dramatically reduces the performance of the queries issued by main OLAP operators. In particular, the *hierarchical dwarf* (Sismanis et al., 2003) and the *QC-tree* (Lakshmanan et al., 2003) stand out for their importance among the data structures able to overcome that limit. These data structures are basically an attempt to remove any redundancy— *prefix redundancy* and *suffix redundancy* according to the dwarf approach terminology— from cube cells. For example, if you had a primary cube with three dimensions (*A*, *B*, and *C*), each *A* dimension value would be available in four cubes (*A*, *AB*, *AC*, and *ABC*) and many times in each cube except cube *A*. This kind of redundancy is the so-called prefix redundancy. Suffix redundancy occurs when you actually aggregate cells that belong to different cubes, from the same set of primary cube cells. Roll-up and drill-down relationships between cells are detected and preserved while searching for common prefixes and suffixes.

In HOLAP systems, two crucial design factors are the choice of the percentage of the data cube to materialize, and the definition of the policies to apply to select which data should be stored in ROLAP mode and which data should be stored in MOLAP mode. You can adopt different strategies:

- Store dense chunks in MOLAP mode and sparse chunks in ROLAP mode.
- Store primary cubes in ROLAP mode and secondary cubes in MOLAP mode.
- Store frequently accessed data in MOLAP mode and the remaining data in ROLAP mode.

Of course, the physical representation generated by the first two strategies is quite similar because data aggregation level and secondary cube density are closely connected variables.

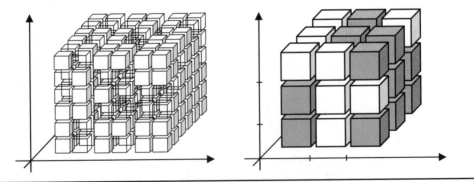

FIGURE 8-2   On the left side, the cells of a data cube. On the right side, splitting the cube into chunks.

8.2 ROLAP Systems

ROLAP systems adopt the well-known relational model to represent multidimensional data. The usage of a model based on a bidimensional element (relations have rows and columns) for multidimensional modeling seems to be strained. As a matter of fact, this choice is justified by many good reasons. First of all, the relational model is the database industry standard and every professional database designer is familiar with it. Additionally, relational DBMSs have been evolving for 30 years since they were originally marketed, making for highly sophisticated and optimized tools. By contrast, MOLAP systems were introduced in the mid-1990s and have been given much less research and industry attention. Lastly, there is no sparsity in relational systems when storing multidimensional data. This ensures that ROLAP systems are more scalable than MOLAP systems. Scalability is vital for ever-evolving databases, such as data warehouses.

Refer to the large number of available texts, such as Elmasri and Navate (2006) and Atzeni et al. (1999), for more details on the relational model. Familiarity with the relational model is important in your understanding of the following sections that describe the different types of relational schemata used to store multidimensional data.

8.2.1 Star Schema

Multidimensional modeling in relational systems is based on the so-called *star schema* and star schema variants.

Star Schema

A star schema consists of the following:

- A set of relations $(DT_1 \dots, DT_n)$ called *dimension tables*. Each of them corresponds to a dimension. Every DT_i features a primary (typically surrogate) key (k_i) and a set of attributes describing its dimension at different aggregation levels.

- A *fact table* (FT) referencing all the dimension tables. An FT primary key is the composition of the set of foreign keys (k_1 through k_n) referencing dimension tables. An FT also includes an attribute for every measure.

Figure 8-3 shows an example of a star schema for the sales fact, whose fact schema is shown in Figure 5-6. The SALES fact table key consists of the composition of the foreign keys referencing the three dimension tables.

Note some interesting properties:

- A multidimensional view of data is obtained when you join the fact table to its dimension tables. The SQL query that matches measure values to related attribute values in hierarchies so as to reconstruct the sales cube is

```
SELECT *
FROM   SALES AS FT, PRODUCT AS DT1,
       STORE AS DT2, DATA AS DT3
WHERE FT.keyP = DT1.keyP
AND    FT.keyS = DT2.keyS
AND    FT.keyD = DT3.keyD
```

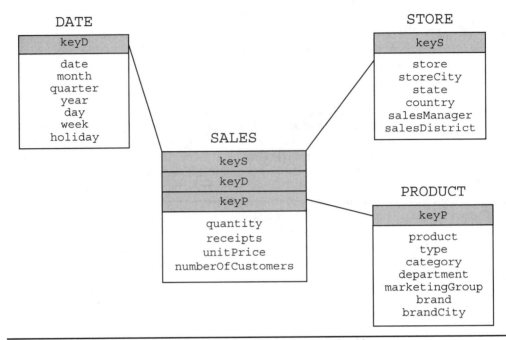

FIGURE 8-3 Star schema for sales; primary keys of tables are highlighted in gray.

- We can relate many fact tables to one dimension table key if hierarchies are conformed.
- Dimension tables are not in third normal form[1] because transitive functional dependencies exist due to the presence of all the attributes of a hierarchy in the same relation. This causes redundancy. For example, the category of a type of product is repeated for every product of that type. Redundancies require more disk space to store data, but they also reduce the number of joins needed to retrieve information. Recall that typical problems with normalization (the so-called insertion, deletion, and update anomalies) should not be viewed as problematic because hierarchies are mostly static.
- Sparsity is no issue because fact tables just store the combinations of key values that actually include a piece of information—that is, an event that has taken place.

Figure 8-4 shows a representation of a feasible instance of the sales star schema. Key attributes are underlined. The first fact table tuple is related to the Slurp Milk sold on 9/2/2008 in the COOP1 store in Columbus. The third tuple is related to the Slurp Yogurt sold on 10/3/2008 in the COOP3 store. The most noticeable property of this approach is the denormalization of the dimension tables. This process reduces the costs to retrieve data, but it results in the duplication of many values. For example, you have to repeat the Food category for every Dairy product type. However, consider that the cardinality of

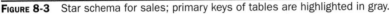

[1]A relation is in *third normal form* when no *nonprime attribute* of the relation (attributes that do not belong to any candidate keys) transitively depends on the key. The form of a *transitive dependency* is a→b, b→c.

SALES

keyS	keyD	keyP	quantity	receipts	.....
1	1	1	170	85	.....
2	1	2	320	160	.....
3	2	3	412	412	.....
.....	.....	.....	.....	.....	.....

STORE

keyS	store	storeCity	state	.....
1	COOP1	Columbus	Ohio	.....
2	COOP2	Austin	Texas	.....
3	COOP3	Austin	Texas	.....
.....	.....	.....	.....	.....

PRODUCT

keyP	product	type	category	brand	.....
1	Slurp Milk	Dairy product	Food	Slurp	.....
2	Fresh Milk	Dairy product	Food	Fresh	.....
3	Slurp Yogurt	Dairy product	Food	Slurp	.....
.....	.....	.....	.....	.....	.....

DATE

keyD	date	month	year	.....
1	9/2/2008	9/2008	2008	.....
2	10/3/2008	10/2008	2008	.....
3	10/5/2008	10/2008	2008	.....
.....	.....	.....	.....	.....

FIGURE 8-4   An instance of the star schema shown in Figure 8-3

dimension tables is usually far lower than that of fact tables. For this reason, the increase in size due to denormalization is negligible.

To conclude this section, we would like to make a few remarks on the use of surrogate keys, that often baffles beginners. Even if the use of surrogate keys is standardized for data warehouses, adding surrogate keys has advantages and disadvantages that should be understood. The advantages are listed here:

- Surrogate keys require less space in fact tables for referencing dimension tables.

- They provide quicker access to data because query execution plans can use simple indexes based on a single numeric attribute.

- They offer independence of any changes of identifier values applied to operational sources.

- They are able to represent many versions of an individual hierarchy instance in the case of dynamic hierarchies. See section 8.5 for more details on this point.

Their disadvantages are as follows:

- Surrogate keys cause an increase in size of dimension tables if natural keys are also included in dimension tables.

- They force you to use techniques other than an entity integrity test to check for dimension tables to be free from duplicates. For example, it may be necessary to create an additional UNIQUE index based on a natural key.

- In the population phase, they force you to transcode the natural keys included in source schemata. See Chapter 10 for more details on this point.

8.2.2 Snowflake Schema

Transitive functional dependencies are one of the main features of star schemata. For this reason, dimension tables are not in third normal form. For example, Figure 8-3 shows the STORE dimension table including the store→storeCity, storeCity→state transitive functional dependency. Even if this type of dependency offers the opportunity to process queries faster, decreasing the denormalization level can be useful to obtain a logical schema that better complies with relational theory requirements. *Snowflake schemata* are based on this last point. They feature a (typically partial) normalization of their dimension tables.

Snowflake Schema

A snowflake schema is obtained from a star schema by breaking down one or more dimension tables (DT_i) into various smaller tables ($DT_{i,1}$ through $DT_{i,m}$) to remove some or all transitive functional dependencies from dimension tables. Every dimension table consists of the following:

- one primary key (typically surrogate) $d_{i,j}$;
- a subset of DT_i attributes functionally depending on $d_{i,j}$;
- some foreign keys, each referencing another $DT_{i,k}$ table, necessary for any DT_i information to be properly reconstructed.

Dimension tables whose keys are referenced in the fact tables are called *primary* dimension tables. The remaining tables are called *secondary* dimension tables.

To create a snowflake schema, you should progressively delete some transitive functional dependencies existing in dimension tables. Each normalization step is related to an arc of a fact schema and marks a sub-hierarchy that should be stored separately. Figure 8-5 shows an example of a snowflake schema.

When you add the CITY, TYPE, and the CATEGORY tables, this causes the schema to be partially normalized. To be more precise, you break transitive dependencies between store and state, product and category, and type and department. This leads to the following result:

- The disk space required for data storage decreases, because, for example, the relationships between the storeCity and state attribute values are stored just once. If the number of stores per city is large, you can further save space because each store is matched to the (typically 4-byte) surrogate keyC instead of the storeCity attribute of at least 20 bytes.

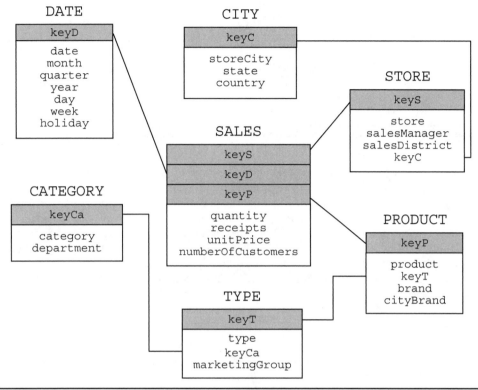

Figure 8-5 A snowflake schema for the star schema shown in Figure 8-3

- Snowflake schemata need new surrogate keys to be added in order to express the relationships between primary and secondary dimension tables. For example, referencing keyT in the PRODUCT table allows for associating each product with its own product type.

- Processing the queries that involve only fact table attributes and primary dimension table attributes is streamlined because their joins involve small tables.

- The time needed for queries of secondary dimension table attributes is longer because of a larger number of necessary joins. The following query explains this point. The query has three join conditions (in italics) resulting from the normalization process:

```
SELECT  *
FROM    DATA AS DT1, STORE AS DT21, CITY AS DT22,
        PRODUCT AS DT31, TYPE AS DT32,
        CATEGORY AS DT33, SALES AS FT
WHERE   FT.keyD = DT1.keyD
AND     FT.keyS = DT21.keyS
AND     DT21.keyC = DT22.keyC
AND     FT.keyP = DT31.keyP
AND     DT31.keyT = DT32.keyT
AND     DT32.keyCa = DT33.keyCa
```

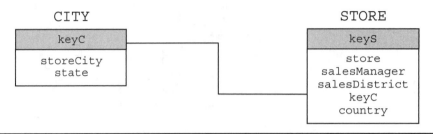

FIGURE 8-6   An incorrect snowflake schema for the star schema shown in Figure 8-3

When you decompose a dimension table to design a snowflake schema, you should check for an appropriate set of attributes to be inserted into the new relation. Star schemata normally include various transitive functional dependencies. For example, keyS→store, store→storeCity, storeCity→state, state→country. To break down a schema effectively, you need for all those attributes that—directly or transitively—depend on the snowflaking attribute (that is, on the natural key of the new relation) to be part of the new relation. If this is not the case, other transitive dependencies will still be present and they will make normalization invalid. For example, Figure 8-6 shows an invalid normalization of the STORE relation of Figure 8-3. Even if the keyS→store→storeCity transitive dependency is solved, the country attribute in the STORE relation dramatically impacts redundancy.

CAUTION *All the attributes functionally depending on the specific attribute from which a normalization process stems must be added into a new relation for snowflaking to be effective.*

8.3 Views

The huge amount of data stored in data warehouses makes users' analyses difficult. For this reason, users tend to apply selection and aggregation to decrease the parts of data they examine. Selection allows you to find data that is actually relevant to specific analyses. Aggregation collapses various non-aggregate elements into one single aggregate element to summarize relevant information. For example, when you sum the amounts of items sold on a given day, you can analyze just one piece of data, instead of as much data as many daily sales. Furthermore, aggregation can be used to extract general trends from specific cases and highlight them.

TIP *If you calculate in advance the most frequently used aggregate data, this can result in a significant increase in performance.*

The fact tables that include aggregate data are generally called *views*. In the fact schema terminology, a view can be identified by its group-by set. In the following sections, we use the term *views* to denote *all* the fact tables, including those that store elemental data. We will make a distinction between *primary* and *secondary* views. A primary view corresponds to the finest, primary group-by set—the one defined by the fact schema dimensions.

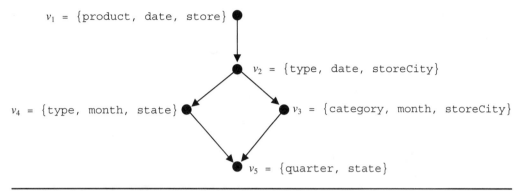

$v_1 = \{\text{product, date, store}\}$

$v_2 = \{\text{type, date, storeCity}\}$

$v_4 = \{\text{type, month, state}\}$

$v_3 = \{\text{category, month, storeCity}\}$

$v_5 = \{\text{quarter, state}\}$

FIGURE 8-7 A few sales schema views that can be materialized

Secondary views correspond to aggregate, secondary group-by sets. You can also distinguish secondary views from primary views after checking whether they can be populated by other views in our data warehouse or by operational data, instead. Figure 8-7 shows a few views that can be created for the star schema of Figure 8-3. v_1 is the primary view. An arrow from v_i to v_j shows that $G_j \le G_{i}$, where G_i and G_j are v_i and v_j group-by sets, respectively. As a result, the data included in v_j can be calculated by aggregating v_i data.

Let's assume that we adopt the materialization schema shown in Figure 8-7. A query, which needs sales data aggregated by product type, sales date, and store city where items were sold, will lead to reduced costs if we use the v_2 view rather than the v_1 view to answer this query. In this way, the query involves a fact table with a small number of tuples and does not need further aggregation. On the contrary, if a query aggregates the sales by product, sales date, and store city, it will have to access the v_1 view because this is the only view with a suitably fine-grained group-by set.

When you work on aggregate data, you should pay close attention to the proper use of aggregation operators. The following examples show two potential mistakes. To understand the first example, look at Figure 8-8, which shows two tables. The first table lists all the items sold (quantity and unit price). The second table shows that those data are aggregated by product types. The SUM operator was used to aggregate quantities and the AVG operator was used to aggregate product prices. Note that you can achieve a result that is different from the one obtained from the non-aggregate table if you want to calculate the total amount of items sold on the basis of the aggregate table. As we mentioned in section 5.3.2 regarding derived measures, the reason for this difference is that the information related to single prices is lost when you apply the AVG operator. Storing receipts values into the aggregate table is the only way to run queries using the aggregate table as a starting point.

To understand the second example, look at Figure 8-9. This figure shows a table recording the amount of a specific product in stock every day of the year and an aggregate table recording the average value of the amount of this product in a four-month-period. In this case, you cannot calculate any proper average value of the whole period of time from aggregate data. To solve this problem, you should also store a count attribute into your aggregate table. This attribute counts the number of primary events that take part in defining every secondary event in your aggregate table.

type	product	quantity	unitPrice	receipts
Dairy product	Slurp Milk	5	1.0	5.0
Dairy product	Fresh Milk	7	1.5	10.5
Drinks	Coky	9	0.8	7.2

Total: 22.7

SUM   AVG

type	quantity	unitPrice	quantity × unitPrice
Dairy product	12	1.25	15.0
Drinks	9	0.8	7.2

Total: 22.2

FIGURE 8-8   Calculating aggregate values can result in errors if you do not carefully take operator features into account.

The causes of the problems shown by these examples come from the aggregation operators used. As we mentioned in section 5.3.2, Gray et al. suggested (1997) that operators can be classified as follows:

- **Distributive**   They allow you to calculate aggregate data from data that is partially aggregated. The SUM, MIN, and MAX operators belong to this category.

4-MonthPeriod	date	stockLevel
I'09	1/1/2009	100
I'09	2/10/2009	200
I'09	4/31/2009	60
II'09	6/5/2009	85
II'09	7/18/2009	125
III'09	12/31/2009	110

Average: 113.33

AVG

4-MonthPeriod	stockLevel	count	stockLevel × count
I'09	120	3	360
II'09	105	2	210
III'09	110	1	110

Average: 111.66   *Weighted Avg*: 113.33

FIGURE 8-9   Calculating aggregate values can result in errors if you do not carefully take operator features into account.

- **Algebraic**   A finite number of additional information (*support measures*) is required to calculate aggregate data from data that are partially aggregated. The AVG operator belongs to this category, because it is necessary that counts (results of a counting activity) are stored in order to process aggregate data properly.

- **Holistic**   They do not allow you to calculate any aggregate data from data that is partially aggregated by using a finite number of additional information. For example, the MEDIAN and the MODE operators belong to this category.

This classification clearly shows that in order to be able to use pre-aggregate data for the calculation of data that are further aggregated—for example, if you want to calculate data aggregated by year from data aggregated by four-month-periods—it might be necessary to store additional information. Additional information can be support measures or derived measures that you want to calculate. If you use holistic operators, you cannot calculate any aggregate value from data that is partially aggregated. Adding the appropriate support and derived measures depending on the operators used to aggregate every measure is part of the logical design phase.

Aggregate navigators of most commercial systems—modules designed for processing OLAP queries using the "best" view available—currently manage aggregation through distributive operators only. For this reason, designers should be very careful when working with non-distributive operators.

8.3.1   Relational Schemata with Aggregate Data

If materialized views are present, you can use different variants of the standard star schema. Storing both primary view data and secondary view data in the same fact table is the easiest solution. The aggregation level of individual tuples in fact tables can be specified by the corresponding tuples in dimension tables. The dimension table tuples related to aggregate data will have NULL values in all the attributes whose aggregation level is finer than the current one. Figure 8-10 shows a part of the sales schema for this solution. While the first tuple of the fact table is related to just one sale, the second tuple stores aggregate data for every sale in Austin and the third tuple sums up all the sales in Texas.

SALES

keyS	keyD	keyP	quantity	receipts	.....
1	1	1	170	85	.....
2	1	1	300	150	.....
3	1	1	1700	850	.....
.....	.....	.....	.....	.....	.....

STORE

keyS	store	storeCity	state	.....
1	COOP1	Columbus	Ohio	.....
2	–	Austin	Texas	.....
3	–	–	Texas	.....
.....	.....	.....	.....	.....

Figure 8-10   Use of a single fact table to store aggregate data

If you apply this solution, you can use the same fact table to solve all the queries. This is detrimental to performance, which becomes poorer because of the huge size of the one and only fact table. This particularly affects the queries processing aggregate data because the percentage of data relevant to them is minimal.

Storing data related to different group-by sets into separate fact tables is another, more common solution. The fact tables that correspond to the group-by sets where one or more dimensions are completely aggregated do not have foreign keys referencing these dimensions. Having multiple fact tables available requires an additional decision on dimension tables. You can keep dimension tables merged, as shown in the previous solution, which leads to the so-called *constellation schema* (Figure 8-11), or you can replicate them for every aggregate view. A constellation schema optimizes the access to fact tables because each of them includes only data at a specific aggregation level. However, dimension tables keep on including attributes at different hierarchy levels. The size of those dimension tables continues to be large, and NULL values still need to be inserted into invalid attributes for a specific aggregation level. This design solution can be justified if you keep in mind that the size of fact tables is far larger than the size of dimension tables, so the cost reduction in query execution largely depends on fact table optimization.

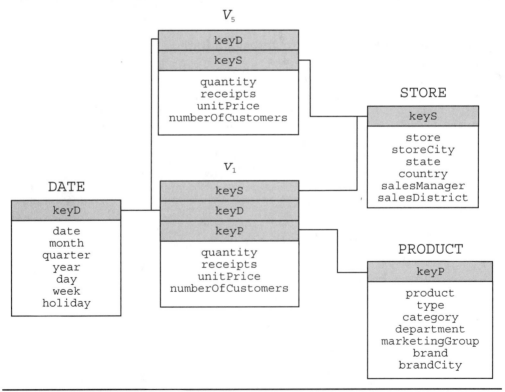

Figure 8-11   Use of a constellation schema for the sales schema to store aggregate data

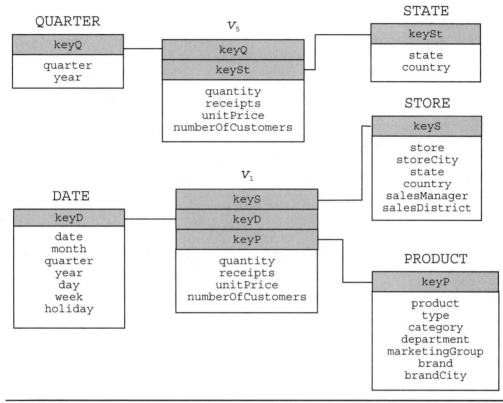

FIGURE 8-12 Use of multiple star schemata for the sales schema to store aggregate data

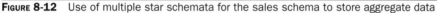

If dimension tables are replicated for every view, each of them will include only the set of attributes that are valid for the aggregation level at which that dimension table is created. Figure 8-12 shows two different views with their specific dimension tables. Note that the key of the fact table for the secondary view has no attribute related to the `store` hierarchy, which is completely aggregated. In general, this is the solution that is expected to deliver the best performance. The access to fact tables and dimension tables has been completely optimized. However, maximizing performance is detrimental to the disk space required for data storage, because more and more free space is needed not only to consolidate aggregate data, but also for redundant dimension tables.

A compromise between the solutions mentioned so far applies snowflaking at the aggregation levels where aggregate views are materialized. This solution takes advantage of the optimization achieved when you sort out aggregate data by aggregation level without replicating dimension tables, which are already very redundant. Figure 8-13 shows that the sales fact is modeled by a snowflake schema, whose normalization points are the same as the group-by set attributes of the aggregate view.

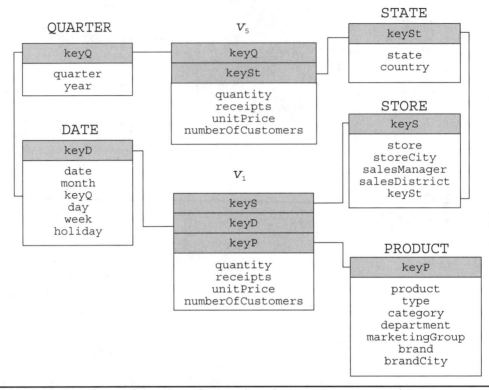

FIGURE 8-13 Use of a snowflake schema for the sales schema to store aggregate data

8.4 Temporal Scenarios

The multidimensional model assumes that the events instantiating facts are dynamic, and that the attribute values populating hierarchies are static. As we mentioned in section 5.4.3, though this is a representative view of this multidimensional model, it is not generally realistic because changes are progressively applied to hierarchies in real-world cases. In 1996, Kimball mentioned *slowly-changing dimensions*. In this book, we will call them *dynamic hierarchies* to be consistent with the terminology used so far. Employee advancement, classifying a product into a new category, and changing the address of a store are possible events that should be modeled in logical schemata of data marts. The opportunity to create different temporal scenarios according to varying dimension attribute values is a very important feature. However, this feature needs a few modeling tricks to be properly used.

As we mentioned in section 5.4.3, you should highlight temporal scenarios that are relevant for various nodes and arcs, such as *yesterday-for-today, today-for-yesterday, today-or-yesterday, and today-and-yesterday*, in the conceptual design phase. In the logical design phase, you should select the approach able to model the required scenarios. In the following sections, we will discuss four design solutions that meet the requirements of the preceding scenarios. Our design solutions are inspired by those described in Kimball (1996), but they make the range of feasible temporal scenarios wider. We believe that the increasing complexity of data warehouse applications should lead us to pay more attention to dynamic features of hierarchies, because they allow us to achieve very interesting results above all in the scope of what-if analysis. A limit on the complexity of the temporal scenarios that can be tracked is always set by extra costs they incur in terms of dimension table size and query response time. SAP Business Warehouse is a commercial software solution that can manage dynamic hierarchies with more advanced features than those mentioned in the following sections. However, those software solutions can be used in a small number of cases; for this reason, we'd rather not introduce them to our readers.

CAUTION *Using dynamic hierarchies implies extra costs in terms of disk space and may dramatically affect performance. For this reason, you should carefully assess the opportunity to use them.*

Figure 8-14 shows a few events related to the sales fact of Figure 8-3. We will use those events as an example in the following sections. Note that the hierarchy related to the stores on 1/1/2009 includes AllEvenMore, a new store, and Mr. Johnson, new sales manager of the EverMore store, in comparison with 1/1/2008. The right side of the figure shows the amount of items sold over a specific time frame.

8.4.1 Dynamic Hierarchies: Type 1

The Type 1 dynamic hierarchies support only the *today-for-yesterday* scenario. All the events including past ones are always interpreted from the viewpoint of the current hierarchy instance, without tracking previous instances.

To manage this type of scenario, we need a regular star schema. As soon as a change is applied to a tuple value of the dimension table, a new value simply overwrites the old one, so all the fact table data are associated with the new dimension table value. If we adopt this approach, the STORE dimension table on 1/1/2008 and on 1/1/2009 will include the values

Status on 1/1/2008

store	salesManager
EverMore	Smith
ProFitsOnly	Johnson
SmartMart	Johnson

Status on 1/1/2009

store	salesManager
EverMore	Johnson
AllEvenMore	Smith
ProFitsOnly	Johnson
SmartMar	Johnson

Sales Events

store	date	quantity
EverMore	2/8/2008	100
ProFitsOnly	10/18/2008	100
SmartMart	12/25/2008	100
EverMore	2/8/2009	100
AllEvenMore	7/5/2009	100
ProFitsOnly	10/18/2009	100
SmartMart	12/25/2009	100

FIGURE 8-14 Evolution of the store hierarchy and sales events from 2008 to 2009

STORE	keyS	store	salesManager	.....
Status on 1/1/2008	1	EverMore	Smith	.....
	2	ProFitsOnly	Johnson	.....
	3	SmartMart	Johnson	.....
	.....	.....	.....	.....

STORE	keyS	store	salesManager	.....
Status on 1/1/2009	1	EverMore	Johnson	.....
	2	ProFitsOnly	Johnson	.....
	3	SmartMart	Johnson	.....
	4	AllEvenMore	Smith	.....
	.....	.....	.....	.....

FIGURE 8-15   Evolution of the STORE dimension table using Type 1 dynamic hierarchies.

shown in the upper and lower parts of Figure 8-15, respectively. Table 8-1 shows the total amounts of items sold by Mr. Johnson and Mr. Smith every year on the basis of the *today-for-yesterday* analysis scenario, and compares the results achieved after conducting the analysis at two different times. We can immediately note that the amount of items sold by Mr. Smith on 2/8/2008 is assigned to Mr. Johnson if we conduct an analysis on 12/31/2008.

8.4.2   Dynamic Hierarchies: Type 2

This design solution supports the *yesterday-or-today* scenario, and it can record what really happened in the past. An event stored into a fact table has to be associated with the hierarchy instance that was valid when that event took place. To manage this type of scenario, you can use a regular star schema. Wherever a change is applied to a hierarchy, a new tuple should be added to store new values into the appropriate dimension table. New events can no longer be associated with old dimension table tuples. This solution helps you understand how useful surrogate keys are—they allow you to have two or more separate physical tuples related to an individual logical tuple.

NOTE   *Type 2 dynamic hierarchies allow you to sort out events by time without adding any constraint or timestamp.*

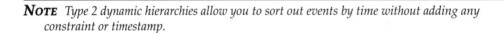

	year	2008			year	2008	2009
salesManager				salesManager			
Johnson		200		Johnson		300	300
Smith		100		Smith		–	100

TABLE 8-1   Amount of Items Sold by Various Sales Managers According to the *Today-for-Yesterday* Scenario. At Left, the Status on 12/31/2008; at Right, the Status on 12/31/2009.

	year	2008
salesManager		
Johnson		200
Smith		100

	year	2008	2009
salesManager			
Johnson		200	300
Smith		100	100

TABLE 8-2   Amount of Items Sold by Various Sales Managers According to the *Yesterday-or-Today* Scenario. At Left, the Status on 12/31/2008; at Right, the Status on 12/31/2009.

If you adopt this approach, the STORE dimension table on 1/1/2008 and on 1/1/2009 will include the values shown in the upper and lower parts of Figure 8-16, respectively. Table 8-2 shows the total amounts of items sold by Mr. Johnson and Mr. Smith every year on the basis of the *yesterday-or-today* scenario. Unlike Table 8-1, note that the items sold on 2/8/2008 are still associated with Mr. Smith even if the analysis is conducted on 12/31/2009.

NOTE *If you opt for the Type 2-based solution for a specific attribute, the* today-for-yesterday *scenario will not be supported. However, you can adopt different strategies for the attributes belonging to an individual hierarchy.*

Note that each event in a fact table is associated with a tuple of each dimension table exactly storing what really happened when that specific event occurred. If a query selects one value from an attribute that was changed, this approach can accurately determine the events related to that specific value. On the contrary, all the events are selected without any distinction if a query constrains only the attributes whose values show no previous change.

STORE
Status on
1/1/2008

keyS	store	salesManager	·····
1	EverMore	Smith	·····
2	ProFitsOnly	Johnson	·····
3	SmartMart	Johnson	·····
·····	·····	·····	·····

STORE
Status on
1/1/2009

keyS	store	salesManager	·····
1	EverMore	Smith	·····
2	ProFitsOnly	Johnson	·····
3	SmartMart	Johnson	·····
4	AllEvenMore	Smith	·····
5	EverMore	Johnson	·····
·····	·····	·····	·····

FIGURE 8-16   Evolution of the STORE dimension table using Type 2 dynamic hierarchies

This feature is obviously favorable because it provides many details on data without making this approach too difficult. For example, consider the product hierarchy that includes an attribute that stores a product version code. Even if this product version changes as time goes by, there is essentially no impact on product properties. If you use a Type 2 dynamic hierarchy, you can exactly calculate the amount of items sold for every single product version. However, it is also very easy to calculate the total amount of items sold for all the versions of an individual product.

If the values of dimension tables change very quickly, this approach can result in very large tables. If this is the case, you can snowflake dimension tables to prevent tuples from proliferating.

8.4.3 Dynamic Hierarchies: Type 3

This design solution expects data to be partially logged. To do this, dimension tables should include one or more attributes that track previous versions of attributes being changed and attribute modification date. It is clear that the time until version history is stored depends on how often changes take place and on how many attributes are added. In the example of Figure 8-17, we opted to store just one previous version of data. For this reason, the sales manager name of the EverMore store on 1/1/2008 can no longer be retrieved as soon as one more change is applied.

If you compare this approach with the Type 2-based one, you can note that it supports the *yesterday-for-today* and *today-for-yesterday* scenarios to a limited extent. Until data is available, you can aggregate along hierarchies that are currently valid and those that were valid before a given date. Furthermore, this approach is not prone to the uncontrolled growth of dimension tables because you insert neither new tuples nor new surrogate keys after applying changes.

TIP *We suggest the use of this approach when there are minor changes to be tracked, when changes do not have any deep impact on fact history, and when there is no need for a long-term fact history to be stored.*

STORE
Status on 1/1/2008

keyS	store	salesManager	prevManager	modificationDate	.....
1	EverMore	Smith	–	–	.....
2	ProFitsOnly	Johnson	–	–	.....
3	SmartMart	Johnson	–	–	.....
.....	.....	.....	.....	.....	.....

STORE
Status on 1/1/2009

keyS	store	salesManager	prevManager	modificationDate	.....
1	EverMore	Johnson	Smith	12/31/2008	.....
2	ProFitsOnly	Johnson	–	–	.....
3	SmartMart	Johnson	–	–	.....
4	AllEvenMore	Smith	–	–	.....
.....	.....	.....	.....	.....	.....

FIGURE 8-17 Evolution of the STORE dimension table using Type 3 dynamic hierarchies

8.4.4   Dynamic Hierarchies: Full Data Logging

Scientific literature has suggested many different approaches in addition to those discussed so far. Sometimes they are called Type 4 or Type 6, but they are all based on full data logging of dimension tables to support every temporal analysis scenario. The following shows the features required to manage a hierarchy:

- A specification of the validity time of tuples
- A process to discover all the tuples involved in a sequence of changes

Many solutions can be devised to achieve this goal; the one we propose delivers good querying performance. To each dimension table, the following should be added:

- A couple of `from-to` timestamps specifying the validity interval of tuples.
- A `master` attribute that specifies the key value of the tuple from which each tuple stems. If multiple changes are applied to a tuple, the reference tuple is the original one, not the tuple resulting from the latest change. You can easily determine original tuples because their `master` attribute references their own key values.

If you adopt this solution, you should add a new tuple to the dimension table whenever an attribute changes, as Type 2 dynamic hierarchies do. The values of timestamps and `master` attributes should then be updated accordingly. If we consider the events of Figure 8-14 and we assume that the SmartMart store name was changed twice in 2008, Figure 8-18 shows the values of the dimension table after 1/1/2009.

STORE	keyS	store	salesManager	.....	from	to	master
Status on 1/1/2008	1	EverMore	Smith	.....	1/1/2008	–	1
	2	ProFitsOnly	Johnson	.....	1/1/2008	–	2
	3	SmartMart	Johnson	.....	1/1/2008	–	3
	.....	.....	.....	.....	.....	.....	.....

STORE	keyS	store	salesManager	.....	from	to	master
Status on 1/1/2009	1	EverMore	Smith	.....	1/1/2008	12/31/2008	1
	2	ProFitsOnly	Johnson	.....	1/1/2008	–	2
	3	SmartMart	Johnson	.....	1/1/2008	6/30/2008	3
	4	BigMart	Johnson	.....	7/1/2008	10/31/2008	3
	5	HyperMart	Johnson	.....	11/1/2008	–	3
	6	AllEvenMore	Smith	.....	1/1/2009	–	6
	7	EverMore	Johnson	.....	1/1/2009	–	1
	.....	.....	.....	.....	.....	.....	.....

FIGURE 8-18   Evolution of the STORE dimension table using fully-logged dynamic hierarchies

Note that this dimension table also specifies the time until each tuple is valid (the `from` attribute). This table also gives the opportunity to determine which tuple each tuple comes from. For example, the tuples whose keys are 4 and 5 are both new versions of the tuple whose key is 3; the tuple whose key is 7 is a new version of the tuple whose key is 1; and the tuples whose keys are 2 and 6 have not yet been changed.

This approach gives the opportunity to manage dynamic features completely, because if you sort tuples out by the `master` attribute, you can determine all the tuples that were changed into a specific tuple, and all the tuples a specific tuple was changed into. For example, if you want to know the amount of items sold in every store with no regard to changes in the store name and sales manager, you can use the following SQL query:

```
SELECT    DT.master, SUM(FT.quantity)
FROM      SALES AS FT, STORE AS DT,
WHERE     FT.keyS = DT.keyS
GROUP BY DT.master
```

However, you can use the following query to find the original store names that should be linked to the amounts calculated:

```
SELECT store
FROM    STORE
WHERE   keyS = master
```

If you use the schema previously described, the following temporal scenarios can easily be supported:

- **Today-for-yesterday**   The dimension table tuples that are currently valid—that is, the tuples with a NULL value in the `to` attribute—are retrieved. Then the `master` attribute is used to retrieve all the other tuples from which each tuple is derived. Finally, the fact table is accessed for each tuple retrieved.

- **Yesterday-for-today**   After the user has set a specific date, the dimension table tuples that were valid at that time—that is, with a validity period to which the selected date belongs—are found. Then the same steps as the preceding scenario are followed. For example, consider the SQL code of the query that returns the total amount of items sold by every sales manager if you take into account their appointment on 10/1/2008:

  ```
  SELECT    S1.salesManager, SUM(quantity)
  FROM      STORE S1, STORE S2, SALES V
  WHERE     S1.from <= 1/10/2008
  AND       (S1.to > 1/10/2008 OR S1.to IS NULL)
  AND       S1.master = S2.master
  AND       S2.keyS = V.keyS
  GROUP BY S1.salesManager
  ```

- **Today-or-yesterday**   This scenario is feasible without using timestamps because dimension table tuples are updated in the same way as Type 2 dynamic hierarchies.

- **Today-and-yesterday**   Using timestamps, you can find the dimension table tuples that show no change over a specific period. After selecting those tuples, you can follow the same procedure as for the *today-or-yesterday* scenario.

TABLE 8-3 Amount of Items Sold by Sales Managers According to the *Yesterday-for-Today* Scenario. At Left, the Status on 12/31/2008; at Right, the Status on 12/31/2009. Valid Hierarchy Instances on 1/1/2008 Are Used as Reference.

Note that an event of a fact table might not be associated with any dimension table tuple in the *yesterday-for-today* scenario if there is still no hierarchy instance that the event refers to at the time set for analysis. Then, that event is not included in the result. This is the case when you analyze the items sold in the AllEvenMore store and you use 1/1/2008 as a reference date. If you want to know the amount of items sold by both sales managers from 2008 to 2009 and aggregate it according to the hierarchy instance that was valid in that period, Table 8-3 shows the results you can achieve. You can easily check that the event storing the sales made on 7/5/2009 in the AllEvenMore is left out from aggregation.

The same applies to the *today-and-yesterday* scenario. Table 8-4 shows the results of the today-and-yesterday scenario–based analysis.

8.4.5 Deleting Tuples

Deleting takes place very rarely in data warehouses because fact table tuples are normally added to track the evolution of relevant facts, but they are not deleted. However, you should define a period of time as relevant to an enterprise to avoid the uncontrolled growth of databases. This period of time generally ranges from three to five years. When a fact table tuple is related to an event that does not belong to the relevant period of time, it can be deleted.

As far as dimension tables are concerned, deleting a tuple aims at preventing attribute values that are no longer in use from using memory space in a data mart. Before deleting a tuple, you should check that no correlated tuples are present in a fact table to comply with referential integrity constraints. For example, if the star schema of Figure 8-3 stored the amount of items sold over the last five years and the store stopped selling a specific product today, the dimension table tuple related to the product could be deleted in five years only. Deleting is a process that is carried out regularly and is not relevant for the purposes of the dynamic features of hierarchies.

TABLE 8-4 Amount of Items Sold by Various Sales Managers According to the *Yesterday-and-Today* Scenario. At Left, the Status on 12/31/2008; at Right, the Status on 12/31/2009.

Logical Design

The logical design phase includes a set of steps that, starting from the conceptual schema, make it possible to define the logical schema of a data mart. On the one hand, the conceptual design phase marks out a part of an application domain that must be included in each data mart and helps designers make decisions on how users will perceive and exploit data marts. On the other hand, the logical design phase defines the data structures that represent data marts according to the preselected logical model and optimizes performance by fine-tuning these structures.

It is essential to emphasize that data mart logical design according to the relational model requires radically different techniques from those used for operational databases. These can often be in complete opposition, because the goals to be achieved are so different. On the one side, operational database design focuses on minimizing the quantity of information to be stored and solving the problems caused by concurrent transactions. On the other side, the primary goal of data warehouse design is to maximize the speed at which data is retrieved. Achieving this goal lets you repeatedly use redundant and denormalized data—traditionally seen as a sign of poor design in operational databases, as mentioned in the previous chapter. For this reason, to create a good logical design for a data mart, it is essential that designers rid themselves of the legacy generated by their own experience in operational databases.

Although statistics produced by market analysis have demonstrated that one of the main causes of the failure of data warehouse projects is the lack of an adequate conceptual design (Vassiliadis, 2000), most of the research on data warehousing has concentrated on the problems associated with logical and physical design. This phenomenon can be explained by the fact that good design solutions at the logical and physical levels are broadly responsible for system performance. The numerous results obtained from such fevered academic activity, together with the advances in computer technology, led to an improvement in query processing time nobody could have realized until a few years ago.

In the following sections we describe the phases that, starting from the conceptual schema of a data mart, make it possible to obtain a logical schema that can be directly implemented in a relational DBMS. The main steps in this process are

- Translating fact schemata into logical schemata: *star*, *snowflake*, and *constellation* schemata

- Materializing views

- Fragmenting fact tables vertically and horizontally

9.1 From Fact Schemata to Star Schemata

Fact schemata lend themselves to direct translation into star schemata. As soon as you switch from a conceptual level to a logical one, this causes a reduction in expressive power. This switch cannot be fully automatic and will require many interventions of designers.

In general, a relational implementation of a fact schema consists of a star schema, whose fact table contains all the measures and descriptive attributes linked to the fact. A dimension table that contains all the hierarchy attributes is created for every hierarchy. In addition to this simple rule, accurate translation of a fact schema requires the advanced constructs of the Dimensional Fact Model (DFM) to be handled in more depth.

9.1.1   Descriptive Attributes

A descriptive attribute (section 5.2.1) contains information that cannot be used for aggregating, but that is considered useful to retain. A descriptive attribute linked to a dimensional attribute must be included in the dimension table for the hierarchy that contains it. On the contrary, if a descriptive attribute is directly linked to a fact (that is, it gives a description of each primary event, but you can view it neither as a measure nor as a dimension), you should include it in the fact table together with measures.

CAUTION   *A descriptive attribute makes sense only when the granularity level of the information that it expresses is compatible with the granularity level of fact table events. For this reason, a descriptive attribute linked to a dimensional attribute may be entered only in a dimension table that also contains the dimensional attribute, and a descriptive attribute linked directly to a fact cannot be in a secondary materialized view that aggregates primary events.*

9.1.2   Cross-dimensional Attributes

From the conceptual point of view, a cross-dimensional attribute b defines a many-to-many association between two or more dimensional attributes, $a_1 \ldots, a_m$ belonging to different hierarchies. To translate this at the logical level, you should insert a new table that includes the b cross-dimensional attribute and has the $a_1 \ldots, a_m$ attributes as the primary key. Figure 5-8 shows an example related to sales and the VAT cross-dimensional attribute. Figure 9-1 shows the part of the logical schema necessary to model this element.

Note that we have directly included the country and the category attributes into the VAT table without introducing surrogate keys. Using surrogate keys can be a valid solution when the cardinality and the length of the attributes involved in defining a cross-dimensional attribute are such that it compensates for the extra amount of space required to store surrogate keys to dimension tables. Now consider the VAT example. If you used surrogate 4-byte keys to manage 5000 products, 1000 stores, 20 countries, and 30 categories (attribute length 20 bytes), the space required to model the cross-dimensional attribute with surrogate keys would be at the most equal to this:

$$\text{surrogate key space } DT + \text{surrogate key space } CDT = 5000 \times 4 + 1000 \times 4$$
$$+ 20 \times 30 \times (4 + 4) = 28{,}800 \text{ bytes}$$

But if the attribute values involved are included directly, they use $20 \times 30 \times (20 + 20) = 24{,}000$ bytes.

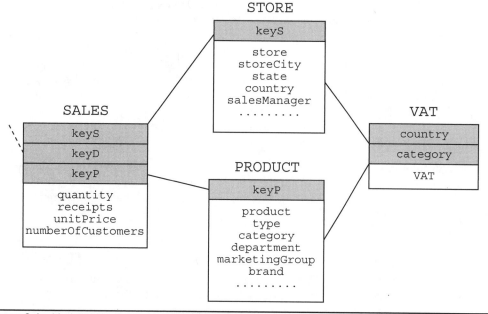

Figure 9-1   Modeling the VAT cross-dimensional attribute

9.1.3   Shared Hierarchies

It often happens that a fact schema contains repeating hierarchies, or parts of hierarchies, as we mentioned in section 5.2.4. If this is the case, we obviously do not suggest that you introduce multiple dimension tables, which contain all or part of the same data, at the logical level. Designers have two solutions open to them for two different situations:

- **Total sharing**   Two hierarchies contain exactly the same attributes used with different meanings. Figure 5-13 shows an example of this case: the CALL fact is related to a hierarchy for calling numbers, which is exactly the same as the called number hierarchy. Here, you just need to insert two foreign keys referencing the one dimension table that models the telephone numbers in the fact table, as shown in Figure 9-2. Then, by entering two (different) dimension table key values into a fact table tuple you will model a call between two numbers.

Figure 9-2
Modeling the telephone number shared hierarchy for the call fact

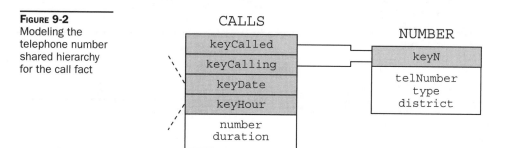

- **Partial sharing** Two hierarchies share some of their attributes. Figure 5-14 shows an example for this case: the SHIPMENT fact is related to the warehouse and the order hierarchies that share only the sequence of attributes coding the geographic information on warehouse sites and customer addresses. You now need to decide whether to introduce further redundancy into the logical schema and insert the common attributes in both dimension tables modeling these hierarchies, or whether to snowflake the first shared attribute and add a third shared table, as shown in Figure 9-3. If you opt for snowflaking, you can take advantage of an amount of space saved on the one hand, and have greater costs for queries due to the need to make a further join on the other hand.

The solution proposed also applies to *conformed* hierarchies—the same hierarchies in a number of facts. Here again, if part of the hierarchy instances are common to both hierarchies, there is no point in creating two separate dimension tables at the logical level. All the data should be included in an individual table, whose key can be used in all the fact tables involved.

9.1.4   Multiple Arcs

Hierarchies can also code many-to-many associations, although this is quite unusual (section 5.2.5). Different logical-level design solutions are used to model them.

The most obvious solution is probably to insert an additional table, known as a *bridge table*, to model multiple arcs. A bridge table key consists of a combination of the attributes linked by a multiple arc. Figure 9-4 shows an example that models the schema of Figure 5-15 at the logical level. As you can see, the BRIDGE_AUTHOR table makes it possible to identify correctly all the authors of each book. Moreover, the weight attribute also makes it possible to aggregate along individual authors correctly. Remember that the individual element weight values in a multiple arc must be normalized so that their sum is equal to 1.

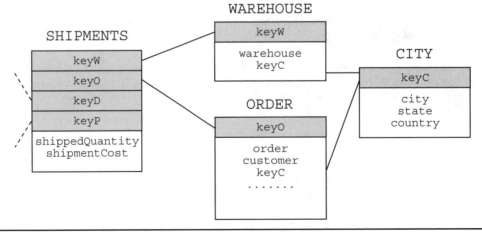

Figure 9-3   Modeling a partially shared hierarchy for the shipment example

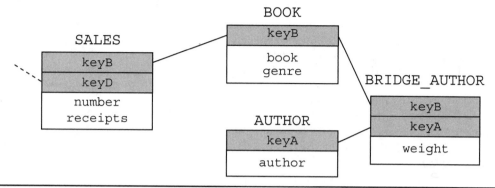

FIGURE 9-4   Modeling the `book-author` multiple arc using a bridge table

Figure 9-5 shows an instance of the proposed schema based on the data in Tables 5-16 and 5-18.

This bridge table, for example, makes it possible to code that the book with key 1 was written by the author with key 1 and by the one with key 2, and the author with key 2 was also a contributor to the books with keys 3 and 4. The following OLAP query calculates the total receipts for each author. As you can see, it requires three joins to retrieve the authors' names, while a standard star schema needs only one join to retrieve all the data in a hierarchy.

```
SELECT    AUTHOR.author, sum(SALES.receipts * BRIDGE_AUTHOR.weight)
FROM      AUTHOR, BRIDGE_AUTHOR, BOOK, SALES
WHERE     AUTHOR.keyA = BRIDGE_AUTHOR.keyA
AND       BRIDGE_AUTHOR.keyB = BOOK.keyB
AND       BOOK.keyB = SALES.keyB
GROUP BY AUTHOR.author
```

The sales aggregation does not necessarily have to be weighted. For example, if you want to calculate the number of books sold for each author, it is quite reasonable to formulate the query as follows:

```
SELECT    AUTHOR.author, sum(SALES.number)
FROM      AUTHOR, BRIDGE_AUTHOR, BOOK, SALES
WHERE     AUTHOR.keyA = BRIDGE_AUTHOR.keyA
AND       BRIDGE_AUTHOR.keyB = BOOK.keyB
AND       BOOK.keyB = SALES.keyB
GROUP BY AUTHOR.author
```

Therefore, bridge solution makes two types of query possible:

- **Weighted query**   The weight of a multiple arc is used to obtain a true total.
- **Impact query**   Resulting quantities are higher because the weight is not used.

If you want to stick to star schemata because your OLAP front-end does not support bridge tables properly, you should make your fact granularity finer to model the many-to-many association represented by your arc directly in your fact table. If you adopt this solution, you should add a new dimension in your fact table that corresponds to the end attribute, say a, of your multiple arc. From the conceptual point of view, this corresponds to pushing down a. See section 5.3.4 for more details. Any child attributes of a will form its hierarchy, and then they will be stored in the new dimension table. Figure 9-6 shows the logical schema obtained from the `author` push-down. The values used in this example correspond to those of Table 5-16. Note that you can reconstruct the primary events of Figure 9-5 if you aggregate by `keyB` and `keyD`.

Now let's look at the case in which the multiple arc links a fact to one of its dimensions. Figure 9-7 shows an example of the hospital admissions of Figure 5-27 referring to the data in Tables 5-20 and 5-21 and using the `BRIDGE_DIAGNOSIS` bridge table to model a many-to-many association between the `diagnosisGroup` and the `diagnosis` attributes.

BOOK

keyB	book	genre
1	Facts & Crimes	Technical
2	Sounds Logical	Technical
3	The Right Measure	Current affairs
4	Facts: How and Why	Current affairs
5	The 4th Dimension	Science fiction

AUTHOR

keyA	author
1	Matteo Golfarelli
2	Stefano Rizzi

BRIDGE_AUTHOR

keyB	keyA	weight
1	1	0.5
1	2	0.5
2	1	1.0
3	2	1.0
4	1	0.5
4	2	0.5
5	1	1.0

SALES

keyB	keyD	number	receipts
1	1	3	150
2	1	5	250
3	1	10	300
4	1	4	80
5	1	8	400

FIGURE 9-5   A possible instance for the Figure 9-4 schema

FIGURE 9-6
An instance for the
book sales fact
table with `author`
push-down

SALES

keyB	keyA	keyD	number	receipts
1	1	1	1.5	75
1	2	1	1.5	75
2	1	1	5	250
3	2	1	10	300
4	1	1	2	40
4	2	1	2	40
5	1	1	8	400

Figure 9-8 shows the corresponding solution with `diagnosis` push-down. The `keyGroup` attribute is no longer necessary because the date, department, and patient values define a unique admission and a specific diagnosis group, so the original primary events can be reconstructed by aggregating by date, department, and patient.

Now we can evaluate the push-down solution and compare it with the bridge table-based solution:

- The information power of both solutions is identical: to translate primary events from one solution into the other, you can aggregate them in the first case or weight them in the second case.

- The push-down solution introduces much redundancy into the fact tables, whose lines must be repeated as many times as there are corresponding items in multiple arcs. For example, the admissions fact table goes from two lines in Figure 9-7 to five lines in Figure 9-8.

DIAGNOSIS

keyDiag	diagnosis	category
1	Cardiopathy	C1
2	Hypertension	C2
3	Asthma	C2
4	Fracture	C3

ADMISSION

keyGroup	keyDate	keyDept	keyP	cost
1	1	1	1	1,000
2	1	1	2	2,000

BRIDGE_DIAGNOSIS

keyGroup	keyDiag	weight
1	1	0.5
1	2	0.3
1	3	0.2
2	3	0.3
2	4	0.7

FIGURE 9-7   An instance for the admission schema using a bridge table

ADMISSION

keyDiag	keyDate	keyDept	kP	cost
1	1	1	1	500
2	1	1	1	300
3	1	1	1	200
3	1	1	2	600
4	1	1	2	1,400

Figure 9-8   An instance for the admissions fact table with `diagnosis` push-down

- In the push-down solution, the weight with which each individual tuple contributes to a group is permanently coded in fact tables and cannot be modified without triggering costly updating operations. On the contrary, the bridge table-based solution explicitly stores weights in a nonredundant way, so they can be easily modified or ignored if necessary.

- While the bridge table-based solution can support weighted and impact queries equally, formulating impact queries is more complex with the push-down solution.

- Weighted primary event values are calculated at population time with the push-down solution and at querying time with the bridge table-based solution.

As a result, technically both proposed solutions can always be applied when there is a multiple arc. Compared to the bridge table solution, the push-down solution reduces the cost of executing queries because no extra joins are needed, but it increases the cardinality of fact tables. For this reason, you should evaluate the choice between both solutions for each single case.

In particular, the bridge table-based solution is practically compulsory when a multiple arc is not directly linked to a fact. If a multiple arc is directly linked to a fact, we also highly recommend this solution when the number of connections between both attributes involved is very high. In other words, you should adopt this solution when your arc models a many-to-many association in which most of the values of one attribute linked to most of the values of the other. Under those conditions, a push-down-based solution would dramatically increase your fact table cardinality.

Other solutions have been proposed in the scientific literature. They are quite justified in a few very limited cases. For example, they can be adopted if the maximum cardinality of the end attribute of the multiple arc is known and limited. We do not consider it worthwhile to cover these solutions in this book, but you can refer to the article by Song et al., (2001) for more details.

9.1.5   Optional Arcs

Some hierarchy arcs may be defined as optional, as we mentioned in section 5.2.6. To model an optional arc, you do not need to apply any changes to the schema of the dimension table. The end attribute of the optional arc is still included in that hierarchy dimension table, but you should specify how to give it a value for hierarchy instances when its value is missing. In relational schemata, the simplest solution is to enter the NULL value. However, we suggest that you use an additional fake value because the NULL value can also have many different meanings, such as an unknown value.

Note that due to entity integrity and referential integrity constraints[1], you cannot manage an entire optional hierarchy in a fact table by entering a NULL or fake value into the corresponding foreign key. Rather, you should add a whole fake tuple to your dimension table. This also applies to secondary dimension tables of snowflake schemata.

9.1.6 Incomplete Hierarchies

One or more aggregation levels are not available for some instances in incomplete hierarchies, as mentioned in section 5.2.7. As in the case of optional arcs, you can logically model incomplete hierarchies if you enter fake values into dimension tables. However, this is a more complicated operation, because the lack of a value at a certain aggregation level does not imply that no values at higher aggregation levels exist, so keeping roll-up consistent may become a problem. Look at the example of Figure 5-18 again. You cannot aggregate the measures related to the city of Norwich, such as the number of inhabitants, by state, because such a subdivision does not apply to the United Kingdom. However, if you want to count all the inhabitants of world states, you need to also include the UK's inhabitants; otherwise, your results would not be consistent with those aggregated by country. Three solutions are possible, as we mentioned in section 5.3.7; they differ in the values entered as a signpost for missing attribute values:

- **Balancing by exclusion**   Missing values are replaced by a single generic signpost, such as 'other', in all the dimension table tuples. We suggest that you opt for this solution if many instances have missing values to help you easily interpret final results. However, we would like to emphasize that this breaks regular roll-up semantics: if you further aggregate data, you will achieve results with a *greater* level of detail, as discussed in section 5.3.7. In the example, if you move from the state aggregation level to the country level, the single line that shows the total number of inhabitants in cities (in different countries, too) without any state-based classification will be replaced by more lines relating to individual countries (Figure 9-9).

- **Downward balancing**   Missing values are replaced by the value of the attribute that precedes it in its hierarchy in all the dimension table tuples. For example, the missing values of state are replaced by the corresponding values of county. This solution complicates the interpretation of the final results because some attribute values will also appear at the wrong aggregation level. Nevertheless, this solution provides more detailed information and does not break roll-up semantics. In the census example, when you aggregate the number of inhabitants by state, this will show the names of those counties that are not part of a state, too (Figure 9-10). This solution is preferable when there is only a very limited amount of missing data.

- **Upward balancing**   This procedure is the same as the preceding one, but you should insert a different signpost: the value of the following attribute in the hierarchy. For example, the missing state attribute values should be replaced by the corresponding country attribute values (Figure 9-11). If you use signposts with higher aggregation levels, the number of values returned will be smaller than those in the previous solutions and the output result will be more readable, even when much data is missing.

---

[1]The *entity integrity constraint* of the relational model prevents an attribute that is part of a primary key from having a null value. The *referential integrity constraint* asserts that, given a foreign key *a* referencing a primary key *k*, the permitted values for *a* are a subset of the *k* domain.

USA	Vatican City	UK	UK
California	Other	Other	Other
Orange	Other	Norfolk	Essex
Santa Ana	Other	Norwich	Epping

USA	Vatican City	UK	

Roll-up from
state to country

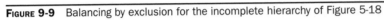

California	Other		

FIGURE 9-9   Balancing by exclusion for the incomplete hierarchy of Figure 5-18

USA	Vatican City	UK	UK
California	Vatican City	Norfolk	Essex
Orange	Vatican City	Norfolk	Essex
Santa Ana	Vatican City	Norwich	Epping

USA	Vatican City	UK	

Roll-up from
state to country

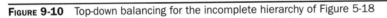

California	Vatican City	Norfolk	Essex

FIGURE 9-10   Top-down balancing for the incomplete hierarchy of Figure 5-18

USA	Vatican City	UK	UK
California	Vatican City	UK	UK
Orange	Vatican City	Norfolk	Essex
Santa Ana	Vatican City	Norwich	Epping

USA	Vatican City	UK	

Roll-up from
state to country

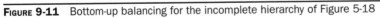

California	Vatican City	UK	

FIGURE 9-11   Bottom-up balancing for the incomplete hierarchy of Figure 5-18

Today many OLAP tools can explicitly support incomplete hierarchies, and they allow users to select one solution dynamically from those previously mentioned. To obtain this result, they associate a Boolean attribute to all the attributes for which missing data may be expected. This Boolean attribute is true for the instances that have a signpost value. In this way, when an individual query is processed, data can be aggregated by signpost values but it can also be aggregated by this Boolean attribute to group all missing values together.

9.1.7   Recursive Hierarchies

In recursive hierarchies, the number of aggregation levels cannot be coded in your fact schema and can also vary from instance to instance (section 5.2.8). This feature prevents you from using the basic star schema, because star schemata denormalize hierarchies in a single dimension table. Figure 9-12 shows a possible relational implementation for the employee hierarchy in figure 5-22, in which we used a self-referencing foreign key to model the recursion. This gives us the possibility to represent a variable, and potentially unlimited, number of levels.

The suggested solution conceals a number of problems caused by SQL limitations when it comes to managing recursive queries. Many commercially available DBMS products do not even support these. But even when they do (as does Oracle), their management imposes a number of limits.

Figure 9-13 shows an alternative and more powerful solution proposed by Kimball et al., (1998). The idea is to "flatten out" a hierarchy and set out all the links induced by it in a *navigation table* that models a many-to-many association between a fact table and a dimension table; in this way, the hours worked by an employee can also be associated with all the other employees that have a subordinate relationship with that employee. Figure 9-14 shows a possible hierarchy instance and a corresponding fragment of the NAV_E navigation table. Note that node 1 shows both direct and indirect descendants. Each descendant has a depth level related to its keyParent attribute. The leaf flag specifies whether the keyChild node has any further descendants. To properly associate each activity event with its corresponding employee, you have to add a 0-level reference, where the keyParent and keyChild attributes coincide.

Obviously, the deeper the hierarchy, the faster the exponential growth of the navigation table size. Figure 9-14 shows that you need 22 tuples to model a very small hierarchy. However, if the navigation table size can be managed, this solution makes it possible to navigate its levels effectively. In particular, given a specific employee, you could find out all the employee descendents, those within a specific level (level < *val*), or, alternatively, all the descendents at the lower level (leaf = TRUE). Moreover, you can go up that hierarchy and find out all the employee bosses if you use the following predicate to invert the join chain:

```
ACTIVITIES.keyE = NAV_E.keyParent AND NAV_E.keyChild = EMPLOYEE.keyE
```

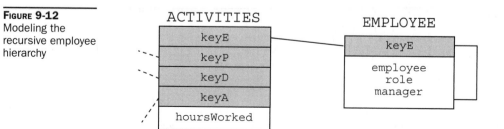

FIGURE 9-12
Modeling the recursive employee hierarchy

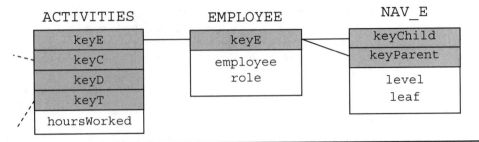

FIGURE 9-13   Using a navigation table to model recursive hierarchies

Finally, all the fact table events are also associated with a dimension table tuple, so you can always join both tables directly. In this way, you can exclude the navigation table if the hierarchy information is of no interest.

NOTE *Compared to the self referencing-based modeling, the navigation table-based solution ensures greater expressive power in the query phase. Moreover, every OLAP tool can support it because aggregation using navigation tables requires only the use of simple GROUP BY clauses. However, the exponential growth in the number of tuples prevents large size hierarchies from using navigation tables. The processing limits of a hierarchy depend on its structures and the DBMS in use.*

9.1.8   Degenerate Dimensions

The term *degenerate dimension* defines a hierarchy that includes only one attribute. You may find it helpful to dispense degenerate dimensions with the general translation rule; this should avoid reduced performance due to foreign keys proliferating in fact tables and an increasing number of joins needed to answer queries.

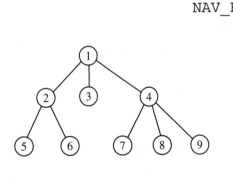

NAV_E

keyParent	keyChild	level	leaf
1	1	0	FALSE
1	2	1	FALSE
1	3	1	TRUE
1	4	1	FALSE
1	5	2	TRUE
....	....	....	....
2	2	0	FALSE
2	5	1	TRUE
2	6	1	TRUE
5	5	0	TRUE
....	....	....	....

FIGURE 9-14   A hierarchy instance and its navigation table

TIP *In practice, it is helpful to create a dimension table for a degenerate dimension only if its domain cardinality is small and the byte length of the single attribute available is greater than that of a surrogate key. If this is the case, each attribute value will be stored to the dimension table only once, while the surrogate key will be duplicated in the fact table. In all other situations, we suggest that you store your degenerate dimensions directly to the fact table and include them in the fact table composite primary key.*

Figure 9-15 shows a fact schema for the order lines and the corresponding star schema with three degenerate dimensions included directly in the fact table. This modeling causes the fact table size to increase, but no join will be necessary to retrieve any information on degenerate dimensions.

Junk dimensions (Kimball, 1996) are an alternative solution to the problem of degenerate dimensions. A junk dimension is a single dimension table that includes a set of degenerate dimensions and lets you reduce the number of foreign keys in a fact table. In contrast to regular dimension tables, a junk dimension does not contain any functional dependencies between attributes, so all the possible value combinations are valid. This results in a high number of tuples. For this reason, this solution is viable only when the number of valid combinations for the attributes involved is not very large, or when every domain has such low cardinality that their Cartesian product has a tractable size.

TIP *Those flags that mark primary event status are the main candidates to be grouped in a junk dimension.*

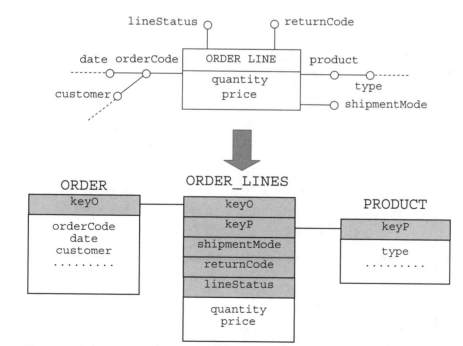

FIGURE 9-15 Modeling the `shipmentMode`, `lineStatus`, and `returnCode` degenerate dimensions in the `ORDER LINE` fact

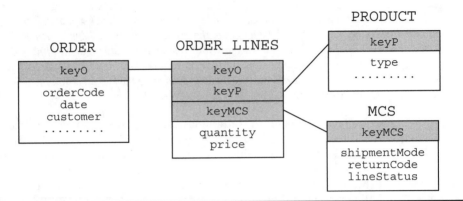

FIGURE 9-16 Modeling a junk dimension encapsulating the `shipmentMode`, `lineStatus`, and `returnCode` degenerate dimensions

Figure 9-16 shows the solution using the MCS junk dimension to model the degenerate dimensions for the fact in Figure 9-15. All the value combinations are possible since no functional dependency holds between the attributes involved. Figure 9-17 shows one possible instance of the MCS dimension table for the example in Figure 9-16. If the `shipmentMode` attribute can have three values (Post, Air, Courier), the `returnCode` attribute two (0, 1), and the `lineStatus` attribute three (Completed, In progress, Cancelled), the table will total $3 \times 2 \times 3 = 18$ tuples.

keyMCS	shipmentMode	returnCode	lineStatus
1	Post	0	Completed
2	Air	0	Completed
3	Courier	0	Completed
4	Post	1	Completed
5	Air	1	Completed
6	Courier	1	Completed
7	Post	0	In progress
8	Air	0	In progress
9	Courier	0	In progress
10	Post	1	In progress
11	Air	1	In progress
12	Courier	1	In progress
13	Post	0	Cancelled
......	......	......	......

FIGURE 9-17 An instance of the MCS junk dimension

9.1.9 Additivity Issues

You should evaluate the problems introduced by grouping operators when you define the structure of a materialized view starting from a fact schema. To be able to calculate grouped data from partially grouped data, you should assess whether your aggregation operator is distributive, algebraic, or holistic (section 8.3). After selecting an operator, you should include suitable support or derived measures into materialized views every time you want use aggregate data for further aggregation.

TIP *You should* always *insert the support measures required for grouping operators in materialized views, because you can hardly predict in the design phase which aggregation level will be requested for data.*

In addition to the previous conditions, a proliferation of attributes occurs in materialized views when a fact schema gives you the opportunity to use multiple operators for measure aggregation. Specifically, you should set a new measure for each aggregation operator because you cannot calculate aggregate data according to one operator from data aggregated with a different operator. Look at the example in Figure 9-18. It shows the star schema of the materialized view obtained by aggregating the inventory schema data by

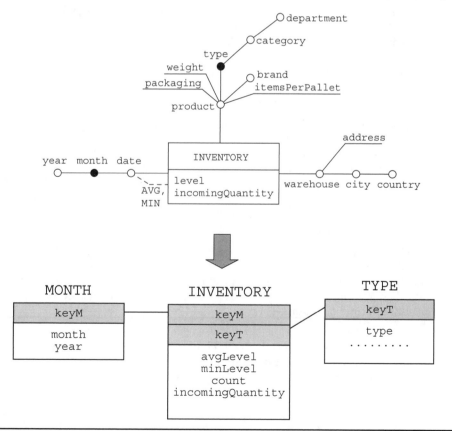

FIGURE 9-18 A materialized view for the inventory schema

month, product, and type. That materialized view has four measures rather than the two measures available in the fact: count is a support measure necessary to calculate the average warehouse level value, and minLevel is required to calculate the minimum inventory level for each month and for each product type. This is the only way to obtain that information from other measures.

The following section deals with additional points to consider when you model materialized views, such as avoiding replication of attributes common to dimension tables of multiple views.

9.1.10   Using Snowflake Schemata

Snowflaking—that is, partially normalizing a dimension table—has a profound influence on the resulting database structure, so this choice deserves careful attention. Conflicting considerations exist on the usefulness of snowflaking: Some authors consider it an "embellishment" that is in conflict with the founding philosophy of data warehousing. Others acknowledge that it can be useful, but only in particular contexts. The main considerations on that subject are listed here:

- *In principle, normalization could be applied to every attribute involved in a functional dependency.* However, it is difficult to justify this solution because it may lead to breaking the basic principles of star schemas. For this reason, snowflaking is often guided by materialized aggregate views. This means that secondary dimension tables are defined at the aggregation levels required for materialized views, so that secondary dimension tables of primary fact tables are primary dimension tables for aggregate fact tables. Figure 8-13 shows an example of this. The STATE and the QUARTER dimension tables are primary dimension tables for the v_5 view and secondary dimension tables for the v_1 view.

- *Snowflaking can be advantageous when part of a hierarchy is common to more than one dimension.* For example, the geographical sub-hierarchy can be part of the customer hierarchy and also part of the supplier hierarchy. In this case, you can actually use snowflaking to isolate this part and reuse the same secondary dimension twice. An example of this has already been suggested in Figure 9-3 as a possible design solution for a shared hierarchy. In fact, the splitting of the geographical sub-hierarchy belonging to the WAREHOUSE and the ORDER hierarchies can also be seen as a snowflake schema used for both hierarchies.

- *Snowflaking is particularly beneficial when the ratio between secondary dimension table cardinality and the primary dimension table one is very high.* For example, if there were many products of one type, but few product types, normalization would save a remarkable amount of space, and the extra cost of a join, which is necessary to retrieve information on product types, would be small.

- *When you dynamically manage a part of a hierarchy which updates frequently, snowflaking can also be useful.* Look at the schema in Figure 8-5. If sales managers changed frequently, if you used type 2 dynamic hierarchies to manage the salesManager attribute, and if the state and the country of stores never changed, then snowflaking would limit data proliferation caused by dynamic features. This is because the various STORE tuples relating to the same store with different sales managers correspond to a single tuple in the CITY table and just one value for the state and country attributes.

- *Finally, some authors believe that snowflaking is useful for readable schemata because it shows the functional dependencies between attributes.* On the contrary, we believe that it is much better to model and document the hierarchies on conceptual schemata, and that representing them explicitly at the logical schema level is not necessary.

9.2 View Materialization

> **View Materialization**
> The term *view materialization* refers to the selection process of a set of secondary views that aggregate primary view data (Gupta and Mumick, 1998). A set of design goals defines which views should be materialized.

This definition highlights two important parts of the process: setting materialization goals and choosing a selection technique. The materialization goals are partially linked to the architectural model used for your data warehouse (section 1.3). However, we will now proceed to present a classification regardless of the architecture adopted.

Theodoratos and Bouzeghoub (2000) stated that a goal may be either *minimizing a cost function* or *meeting a constraint*. Constraints can be divided into *system-oriented constraints* and *user-oriented constraints*. The following typical cost functions can be minimized:

- **Workload evaluation cost**   Many view selection techniques (including all those implemented in commercial tools) are based on the workload a data mart is expected to cope with (Baralis et al., 1997; Gupta and Mumick, 1999). To calculate the total workload cost, you should use a weighted sum of the cost of various queries—weight values are generally related to the frequency of each query and/or its relevance to users. Scientific literature proposes some query cost functions. Some of these are very simple and assume that the cost of a query is proportional to the size of the view it is executed on (Gupta et al., 1997b). Other, more sophisticated cost functions estimate, more or less precisely, the actual number of data pages to be accessed in order to answer a query (Golfarelli and Rizzi, 1999).

- **View maintenance cost**   Materialized views have to be regularly updated to replicate changes in operational sources (Griffin and Libkin, 1995; Quass, 1996; Gupta et al., 1996). The maintenance cost is the cost of the queries necessary to transmit those updates from operational sources to views. This cost calculation is quite complex because of the many different solutions that can be adopted. The simplest technique is to issue update queries directly accessing operational databases. Most techniques are based on incremental view updates from already updated views. Other techniques replicate operational data source tables *(auxiliary views)* in data marts to reduce the number of remote queries—that are usually slower because of data transfer costs.

System constraints are suggested by limitations on available resources and relate to the following:

- **Disk space**   The disk space made available to a data mart is not an infinite resource. This is normally the main constraint on view materialization (Gupta, 1997a; Harinarayan et al., 1996). To meet this constraint, you need a function to estimate view size. You should also remember that other ways are available to speed up the system performance, but they also require disk space. For example, normally indexes use up a very high percentage of the total free disk space available. For this reason, the choice of how to distribute your free disk space becomes a major design decision.

- **Update time**   A data mart is normally updated when the data warehouse system is offline, but this process causes a serious reduction in source operational database performance. Updating views is not the only regular operation to be performed on a data warehouse system (backup, synchronization, and so on), so the number of hours that can be set aside for updating views is necessarily limited. For example, if a weekly update occurs over the weekend with the system offline, the time windows for updating views should span no more than ten hours. The update time constraint means that the number of views to be materialized is limited to the number that can be updated within the available time (Gupta and Mumick, 1999).

User constraints are linked to specific system user requirements:

- **Query response time**   Users can set a maximum limit on time from the moment when a query is issued to the moment when the system returns an answer (Theodoratos and Bouzeghoub, 2001). Users may specify that time limit value for every query. That value also shows how urgently users want each query to be answered.

- **Data freshness**   Users can set a maximum limit on time since the last update of a view used to execute a query. Then they can define how "fresh" the data will be when they run a query.

These goals are clearly in conflict with one another. The optimum solution requires a compromise to be reached between their various requisites. If constraints are too restrictive, the problem of view materialization may not offer any solution.

Before tackling our study of view selection techniques, we need to specify a reference logical architecture. We will assume that materialized views are obtained by aggregating primary fact tables belonging to a data mart. For this reason, the information power of materialized views can never be greater than the one of primary fact tables. Conversely, other types of architecture consider a data mart as a collection of independent materialized views from which a group of basic views cannot be selected to answer any query; in those architectures, dealing with the queries to which data in materialized views cannot deliver any answer requires an access to operational data.

We will also assume that a *benchmark workload*, the set of users' most frequently executed queries, is available. This may seem in conflict with the basic idea of OLAP systems, that imply a workload which is not previously set and continuously changes. However, our practical experience has demonstrated that you can generally identify a core set of queries that are characteristic of and can represent the total workload because of their importance, or because they are included in standard reporting.

On the basis of the preceding assumptions, view materialization is normally considered a problem with minimizing workload response time and complying with the system constraints (disk space and update time). When you address this problem, you may find it simpler to transform view update time constraints into space constraints. This can be done if you know the writing speed of the DBMS hosting your data warehouse and if you are sure that views are completely rewritten when they are updated. In this way you can estimate the amount of data that can be updated within a specific amount of time.

View materialization is a complex problem because of the search space size, which grows exponentially in relation to the number of dimensional attributes in your fact schema. This happens because each combination of attributes defines a potential group-by set. For example, a fact with n degenerate dimensions defines 2^n possible views.

The problem-solving techniques mainly operate in two phases. In the first phase, they select the views that are actually useful for a specific workload from all the possible views that can be materialized. In the second phase, which is heuristic, and consequently sub-optimal, the view subset that minimizes a cost function and complies with system constraints is defined.

Remember that a materialized view is unequivocally determined by its group-by set, but its measures may change.[2] *Multidimensional lattice* (Baralis et al., 1997) is one of the most widely used data structures for coding valid group-by sets for a certain fact schema in both academic and commercial systems. A multidimensional lattice models partial roll-up orders between group-by sets. Figure 9-19 shows a simple fact schema with a and c dimensions and the associated multidimensional lattice. That lattice contains all the valid group-by sets that are in fact valid for that aggregation, namely all the sets of dimensional attributes that do not contain functional dependencies between their elements. For example, the {a, b, c} group-by set is not valid because of the a→b functional dependency. The arrows in the diagram show the partial ordering among the group-by sets. In particular, the arrow from G_i to G_j shows that $G_j \leq G_i$ (group-by set G_j is less fine-grained than G_i). As a result, the data contained in the view for G_j can be calculated by aggregating the data contained in the view for G_i.

A multidimensional lattice grows exponentially according to the number of dimensional attributes, as previously mentioned. For this reason, it is not suitable for real-life applications. To reduce the size of a lattice, you can use only the group-by sets corresponding to views that are actually useful for a decrease in the cost of dealing with a specific workload. Those views are known as *candidate views*. A candidate view gives a precise answer to one query—that is, view and query share the same group-by set—or it is the "best" one that answers more than one query—that is, the data required by two or more queries can be obtained by aggregating the data contained in that view. Figure 9-20 shows the candidate views for a workload consisting of three q_1, q_2, and q_3 queries based, respectively, on the G_6, G_7, and G_8 group-by sets. In addition to the group-by sets corresponding to the queries, the G_5 and G_3 group-by sets are also candidates because

- G_5 makes it possible to answer both q_2 and q_3, and there is no other G_x group-by set such that $G_x \leq G_5$ and that has the same property;

- G_3 makes it possible to answer all three queries and there is no other G_y group-by set such that $G_y \leq G_3$ and that has the same property.

---

[2] Aggregate views can have support and derived measures to facilitate aggregation from partially aggregated data. See sections 5.6 and 8.3 for more details on this point.

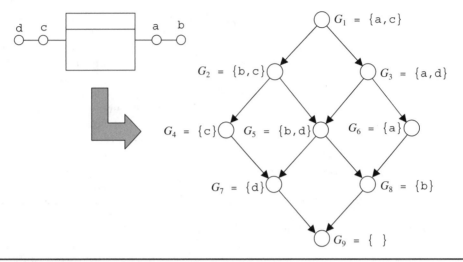

FIGURE 9-19   Multidimensional lattice for a simple fact schema

To achieve top optimization standards, you should materialize all those candidate views corresponding to the single queries. However, the system constraints, the available disk space constraint above all, make this solution unworkable in real-life situations. For this reason, you should define a subset of the candidate views ensuring good performance in compliance with the system constraints.

The example in Figure 9-21 shows three different possible solutions and their purely qualitative evaluation. The first solution materializes all the views corresponding to every query. Here the cost of executing the query is minimized, but the space and update time required do not meet the constraints imposed. The opposite is true of the second solution,

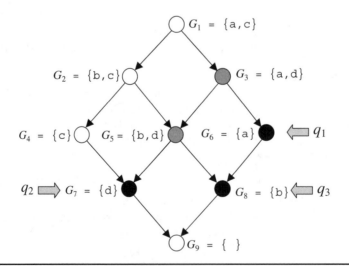

FIGURE 9-20   The candidate views for the workload q_1, q_2, and q_3 are highlighted in gray and black.

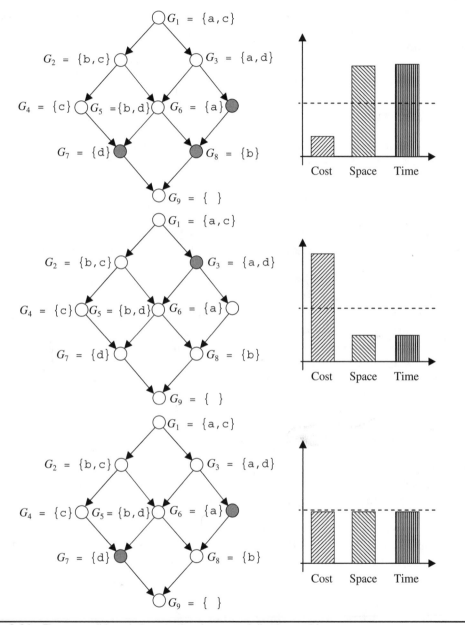

Figure 9-21 Three possible solutions to the view materialization problem

in which only one view is materialized to answer all the queries. In this case, the workload cost is high because the view is not optimal for any of the queries, but this view is well within the system constraints. The third solution is a good compromise between the two others as it makes possible a considerable reduction in the costs of execution and it is within the system constraints.

In section 9.2.2, our formalization of the view materialization problem is offered, and in section 9.2.3, an algorithm solving the view materialization problem and the related cost functions are proposed. However, if you do not have an available automatic view selection tool, you can stick to the following general rules, which are the result of practical experience and of analyzing experimental test results.

TIP *We suggest you should materialize a view when it directly answers a frequently issued query and/or allows several queries to be answered. We suggest you should not materialize a view when the view group-by set is very similar to that of a view already materialized, and/or the view group-by set is very fine-grained, and/or materialization does not significantly reduce the overall workload cost.*

In section 7.1.4 we discussed the difficulties found in capturing the expressive power of OLAP operators and proposed the nested Generalized Projection/Selection/Join (GPSJ) class of queries to fill any gaps. The lack of expressive power of query coding formalisms also affects materialization. If you adopt nested GPSJ expressions to express queries that define views, you can obtain much more complex aggregate data, which is often more useful for answering your queries. See the articles by Golfarelli and Rizzi (2000b and 2000c) for more details on this point.

9.2.1   Using Views to Answer Queries

When you choose the set of views to materialize, you should pay attention to the real possibility of answering a query with a specific view. See section 9.1.9 for a partial discussion of this point in relation to the problems caused by aggregation. This point can be summed up as follows: You can use a view v to answer a query q if, and only if, the $Gbs(v)$ view group-by set is more fine-grained than the $Gbs(q)$ query group-by set—that is, if $Gbs(q) \leq Gbs(v))$ —and the measures requested by q are derivable from those in v. The definition terms *query group-by set* and *derivable* need further clarification.

As shown in section 7.1.3, you can use dimensional expressions to formulate queries, which can include multiple group-by sets in sequence. So which of these group-by sets should be compared with view group-by sets?[3] The group-by set to be considered as $Gbs(q)$ will always be the most fine-grained (the first on the left of the dimensional expression denoting the query), because a group-by set in an expression explicitly shows that some data processing operation has to be performed at that aggregation level. If there are any internal predicates, that involve attributes at a more fine-grained aggregation level than the most fine-grained query group-by set, the attributes they consist of should be included in $Gbs(q)$, too. The following example shows a query accessing the sales fact:

```
SALES[state, type;
   year='2000' AND quantity≥50].unitPrice
```

Although the output data is requested at the {state, type} aggregation level, the data aggregated by {state, type, year} or other more fine-grained group-by sets can only be

---

[3]This problem does not arise for views, that are normally defined by a single group-by set.

used to answer your query, so you can use the `year` attribute for selection. This also applies to the following composite query:

```
SALES[date, store, product; quantity≥50]
   [state, type; year='2000'].receipts
```

You should use the {date, store, product} group-by set to evaluate whether you can answer the query using a materialized view, because the selection based on the `quantity` measure must operate on secondary events aggregated by date, store, and product. You cannot use a view aggregated by {state, type, year} instead.

As regards the availability of measures in a view, we emphasize that it is not strictly necessary for all the measures requested to be *physically* available, but they do have to be *derivable* from the available measures. However, you should take into account the problems caused by additivity of measures:

- **Derived measures**   In the preceding query, you can calculate the receipts value if the primary view includes unit prices and quantities sold. Unfortunately, this option is lost with aggregate views, because the result returned would be wrong if you multiply aggregate data. The sum of products is different from the product of sums! This is why you should explicitly store derived attributes to materialized views.

- **Non-additive measures**   If you want to calculate a non-additive measure value from partially aggregated data, it is essential for a view to contain the correlated support measures. For example, the view aggregated by {state, type, year} in the first query can be used only if it also has the `count` support measure in addition to the `unitPrice` measure so that it allows the contribution made by individual prices to be weighted on the basis of the quantities sold.

9.2.2   Problem Formalization

The view materialization problem has drawn the attention of many researchers because of its impact on performance and its complexity. These researchers have analyzed the problem from various points of view and proposed a number of different formulations, according to constraint types, goals set, and solution options. We will propose the version that we believe is the easiest to adjust to industrial contexts. This solution has also achieved broad consensus in academic circles. See the article by Theodoratos and Bouzeghoub (2000) for a detailed list of the formulations proposed in literature.

View Materialization Problem
Given a fact schema F, a workload Q for F, and a space constraint S, define a set V of the views of F that fulfills space constraint S and minimizes the cost of Q expressed by the $f(Q, V)$ cost function.

This problem can be solved with the following two-phase approach:

1. Identify the C set of candidate views that are potentially useful to reduce the Q cost.

2. Select the $V \subseteq C$ view subset minimizing the Q cost in compliance with the S constraint.

In the materialization process, a view is identified by its group-by set. This assumption is obviously limiting because it implies that you cannot use views that contain data to which selections and/or projections have been applied. However, we currently prefer to keep the connotation of our views as simple as possible because of the complexity of this problem, and to provide sufficiently general solutions.

Even if the views of *F* are characterized only by their group-by set, their number grows exponentially with the number of dimensional attributes of *F*. Figure 9-22 shows a simple example.

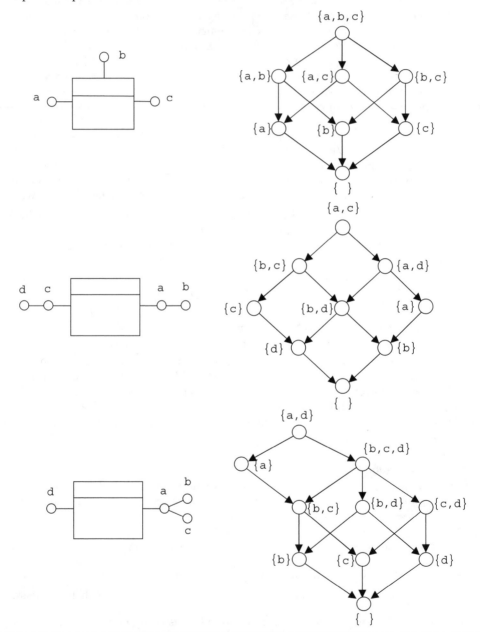

FIGURE 9-22   Three simple fact schemata and their multidimensional lattices

If the fact schema has n degenerate dimensions, the overall number of views is clearly 2^n (see Figure 9-22, top part).

In general, the number of views is below 2^N if hierarchies total N dimensional attributes, because existing functional dependencies mean that some subsets of attributes do not correspond to valid group-by sets. Now let's look at two limiting cases. If hierarchies are simple paths, as in the middle part of Figure 9-22, each node has at most one child and the number of views is

$$\prod_{i=1}^{n}(N_i+1)$$

where N_i is the number of dimensional attributes in the i-th hierarchy. When all functional dependencies in each hierarchy have a dimension on their left side (Figure 9-22, bottom part), the total number of views is as follows:

$$\prod_{i=1}^{n}\left(2^{N_i-1}+1\right)$$

Given the G_i and the G_j group-by sets, we denote with $G_i \oplus G_j$ the group-by set that is their upper limit in the multidimensional lattice induced by the partial roll-up ordering:

$$(G_i \leq G_i \oplus G_j) \wedge (G_j \leq G_i \oplus G_j) \wedge (\forall G{:}G_i \leq G \wedge G_j \leq G \Rightarrow G_i \oplus G_j \leq G)$$

For example, in the partial multidimensional lattice for the sales fact in Figure 9-23,

$$G_5 \oplus G_6 = \{\texttt{department, marketingGroup, storeCity, quarter}\}$$

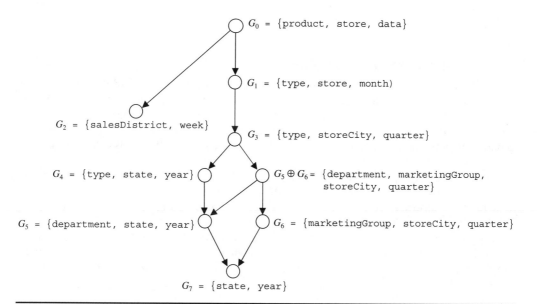

$G_0 = \{\texttt{product, store, data}\}$

$G_1 = \{\texttt{type, store, month)}$

$G_2 = \{\texttt{salesDistrict, week}\}$

$G_3 = \{\texttt{type, storeCity, quarter}\}$

$G_4 = \{\texttt{type, state, year}\}$

$G_5 \oplus G_6 = \{\texttt{department, marketingGroup, storeCity, quarter}\}$

$G_5 = \{\texttt{department, state, year}\}$

$G_6 = \{\texttt{marketingGroup, storeCity, quarter}\}$

$G_7 = \{\texttt{state, year}\}$

FIGURE 9-23 Part of the multidimensional lattice for the sales schema in Figure 5-6

You cannot use all the views in a multidimensional lattice to reduce the workload cost. Consider this example:

```
q₁ = SALE[department, state, year;
          quantity>100].receipts
q₂ = SALE[marketingGroup, storeCity, quarter;
          receipts<50].numberOfCustomers
```

Obviously, the view defined by the G_6 group-by set cannot be used to answer the q_1 query because $Gbs(q_1) = G_5 \nleq G_6$. Moreover, although the view defined by G_1 can be used to answer both q_1 and q_2, it would never be used for that purpose. This is because the view defined by G_3 is more cost-effective and it contains data that are more aggregate and, consequently, smaller. This principle gives rise to the definition of the term candidate view.

Candidate Views

Given an F fact schema and a Q workload, a v view built on F is defined as *candidate* if it meets one of the following conditions:

- a query $q \in Q$ exists, such that $Gbs(q) = Gbs(v)$, or
- a pair of candidate views v_i and v_j exist, such that $Gbs(v) = Gbs(v_i) \oplus Gbs(v_j)$.

In other words, a view is a candidate view if it precisely answers one query, or if it is the most aggregate view that can answer two or more queries. In the sales example, the group-by sets that define the candidate views for the $Q = \{q_1, q_2\}$ workload are G_5, G_6 and $G_5 \oplus G_6$.

NOTE *It can be proved that materializing a non-candidate view always results in a higher execution cost than that obtained from materializing a candidate view if you have a specific workload on a schema (Baralis et al., 1997).[4]*

9.2.3 A Materialization Algorithm

Partial roll-up ordering defines a lattice for the set of candidate views, called the *candidate view lattice*. Figure 9-24 shows the algorithm that can be used to create this lattice (Baralis et al., 1997). Initially it inserts the views corresponding to the group-by sets of the workload queries in a set C of candidate views. Then it applies the $\oplus$ operator to pairs of views in C to progressively generate the remaining candidate views. This process ends when all the possible pairings generate views that already belong to C.

After defining the C set of candidate views, you should select the V subset that minimizes the workload execution cost to comply with the S space constraint. As far as the cost function to be used is concerned, you cannot accurately define any execution plan of which your DBMS will take advantage in this design phase because the physical design of the database has not yet been completed. For this reason, we believe that there is no point in using a very detailed cost function at this time. You may reach a good compromise between precision and simplicity for estimates if you count the number of *logical accesses* necessary to retrieve tuples.

---

[4]As a matter of fact, this is true only if the cost function used grows monotonically with the size of views.

FIGURE 9-24   Pseudo-code for the algorithm used to create the candidate view lattice

```
// Insert those views that directly answer every single query
// to initialize the set of candidate views
C = {Gbs(q) : q∈Q};
Old = C;
// contains the candidate views identified in the previous cycle
New = Ø;
// contains the candidate views identified in the current cycle
while Old≠Ø
{   for each v∈Old
    // for each view inserted in the previous step...
        for each vₖ∈C, vₖ≠v
        // for each candidate view...
            if v⊕vₖ∉C
                // ... the new candidate view is determined
                New = New ∪ (v⊕vₖ)
    C = C ∪ New;
    Old = New;
    New = Ø;
}
```

The specific cost function you may adopt has no effect on the characteristics of the view selection algorithm, and it can be replaced as required. You can use the following expression to estimate the number of logical accesses needed to answer a query q on a view v:

$$f(q, v) = sel(q) \cdot card(v) + \sum_{i=1}^{n} sel(q, DT_i) \cdot card(DT_i)$$

where $card(v)$ and $card(DT_i)$, respectively, define the cardinalities of the v view and of the i-th dimension table; $sel(q)$ is the total selectivity of q; and $sel(q, DT_i)$ is the partial selectivity of q in relation to DT_i. Then the overall workload cost is this,

$$f(Q, V) = \sum_{q \in Q} min_{v \in V : Gbs(q) \leq Gbs(v)} \{f(q, v)\}$$

assuming that the minimum cost view is used to answer each query.

Given the candidate views and the space constraint, selecting a subset of views to be materialized can be formulated as a knapsack problem with constraints, which is proven to be NP-complete (Papadimitriou and Steiglitz, 1982). See the literature on numeric optimization for information on the precise solution techniques. In this section, we will describe a simple heuristic procedure that has been shown to achieve good results. Figure 9-25 shows a *greedy* algorithm[5] that first selects the views that most reduce the execution cost then improves the initial solution by evaluating whether it is cost-effective to replace one of the selected views with one of the views previously excluded.

---

[5]An optimization algorithm is called *greedy* if it selects the best local alternative at each step. Generally speaking, it is clear that this does not ensure that the final solution will be the best.

```
// The set of materialized views is initialized
V=∅;
while Size(V)<S
// Size(V) is the overall size of the views in V
// C is the set of candidate views
{   find v∈C: Size(V∪{v})<S AND f(Q,V∪{v}) is minimal;
    V = V ∪ {v};
    C = C - {v};
}
End = FALSE;
while not end
// while the set V is being modified
{   End = TRUE;
    for each v∈V
    {   // try to remove a view from V and add another from C
        v  = Best(Q,C);
         m
        if f(Q,V-{v}∪{v })<f(Q,V)
                        m
        {   V = V - {v} ∪ {v };
                            m
            end = FALSE;
            // V has been modified, you must continue
        }
    }
}
```

9.3 View Fragmentation

In the context of relational databases, the term *fragmentation* means the subdivision of a table into multiple tables, known as *fragments*, to improve system performance. Fragmentation is by no means a method of optimization specific to data warehousing; rather, it has been widely studied and used for both centralized and distributed databases (Chu and Oieong, 1993; Valduriez, 1987). However, specific data warehouse properties, such as major data redundancy and existing multiple multidimensional cubes correlated by drill-across queries, add new interest to fragmentation techniques and greatly increase their optimization capabilities. Advantages are particularly evident if your data warehouse is built on a parallel architecture. The use of disk arrays and an appropriate fragment allocation algorithm makes it possible to operate in parallel mode and retrieve data fragments from different disks to execute an individual query.

A table can be fragmented in two ways: The first is called *horizontal fragmentation*, which divides a relation into multiple parts, each of which has all the attributes but only one subset of tuples of the original relation. The second way is *vertical fragmentation*, which divides a relation into multiple parts, each of which contains all the tuples and a subset of the attributes of the original relation. In vertical fragmentation, key attributes from the original table must be replicated in every fragment to allow the original table to be reconstructed. In the following sections, we discuss how these two basic techniques can be extended to the data warehouse context and how they can be used, even simultaneously (Agrawal et al., 2004), to improve system performance.

9.3.1 Vertical View Fragmentation

Standard approaches to view materialization use "all or nothing" solutions to cope with the selection of data to pre-aggregate. This means that you will materialize all the measures that belong to a specific fact whenever you materialize an aggregate view of that fact. However, under real-word conditions, some measures may be useful at a few particular aggregation levels and rarely required at other aggregation levels. For example, it could be very useful to know the total VAT to be paid. To do this, you should aggregate VAT values on the basis of payment periods, such as months or quarters. But very rarely would users need to aggregate this value on the basis of other periods, such as weeks or four-month periods.

A different situation occurs in drill-across queries because they require measures at the same grouping level, but from different cubes. In this case, it could be useful to create a single fragment that merges all the required measures to be able to execute drill-across queries by accessing just one fact table. For example, look at the following query:

```
SHIPMENT+INVENTORY[month, category;
    year='2000'].(shippedQuantity-incomingQuantity)
```

This query accesses the schema obtained by overlapping the inventory and shipment fact schemata (Figure 5-37) and calculates the difference between the quantity dispatched and the quantity bought. The cost of executing this query would be minimized if you could access a single fact table containing both the required measures aggregated by month and product category.

We will use the general term *vertical fragmentation* because you can either partition or merge measures from one or more views.

Vertical Fragmentation

The term *vertical fragmentation*, or *multi-cubing*, stands for a set of views created to contain a subset of the measures defined in one or more fact schemata. The result of the vertical fragmentation process must show the following properties:

1. **Consistency** Fragment group-by sets must be chosen among candidate view group-by sets.

2. **Completeness** Each measure of each fact schema must be in a primary fragment—that is, a fragment defined at the primary group-by set level.

3. **Non-redundancy** An individual measure cannot be inserted in more than one fragment for the same group-by set.

The first constraint ensures that fragments are really useful for the current workload. The second constraint avoids loss of information. The third constraint avoids proliferation of redundant fragments.

Note that fragmentation results in a more specialized solution for workloads than the solution that you could obtain from mere materialization. This feature may turn out to be an advantage, or it may not. This depends on how closely your current workload represents the real workload. However, the second constraint ensures that queries not included in the workload can always be answered even if this is likely to take more time.

The reasons for vertical fragmentation are as follows:

- **Optimized workload cost**   If we compare fragmentation with standard view materialization, fragmentation can reach two goals at the same time. Firstly, partitioning may be useful whenever you need only a subset of the measures contained in a cube. Secondly, merging can be cost-effective if the number of drill-across queries is large.

- **Saved space**   Although all the measures in fact schemata have to be stored in primary fragments—the most fine-grained aggregation level—to avoid information loss, this does not apply to secondary fragments. Depending on workload features, you may not have to materialize all measures in secondary fragments. This can result in greater disk space savings than can be achieved in non-fragmented solutions. The disk space that you save can then be used to store additional, useful fragments.

- **Reduced key replication**   Partitioning a view into two or more fragments requires the replication of view keys. However, this redundancy does not lead to sky-rocketing extra costs in terms of disk space because surrogate keys normally use very few bytes. Moreover, materialized fragments are often very aggregated. The foreign keys relating to the completely aggregated dimensions are not included in those fragments.

- **Generalization**   Vertical fragmentation is a generalization of view materialization. The non-fragmented solution is still a potential solution, and it is more and more likely to be adopted as the number of measures required by workload queries increases.

The elements that make you select specific fragments are the measure sets requested by queries at different aggregation levels. When designers define those sets, they must evaluate the number of times two measures are required at the same time, and the number of times those measures are requested separately. See the articles by Golfarelli and Rizzi (2000a) and Maniezzo et al. (2001) for more details on vertical fragmentation, vertical fragmentation formalization, and a vertical fragmentation problem-solving algorithm.

A series of tests performed on the TPC-H benchmark[6] confirmed how useful this technique can be. Figure 9-26 shows a comparison between the cost of executing benchmark queries with and without fragmentation and with the same amount of disk space used by the data. The unit of measure for the cost is the number of disk pages read. Note that the fragmented solution is always better than the one obtained by the "all or nothing" approach—by 18 to 73 percent in the various tests.

Another interesting test result shows how robust views and fragments are in comparison with a changing workload. Although it is reasonable to assume that you are aware of the set of most frequently issued queries beforehand, you cannot know the *whole* workload in detail at design time. This is because the OLAP sessions are inherently interactive and they cannot be planned. To simulate this condition, we defined views and fragments to be materialized

---

[6]The TCP-H is a decision support benchmark issued by the Transaction Processing Performance Council (Poess and Floyd, 2000). It consists of a suite of business oriented ad-hoc queries and concurrent data modifications.

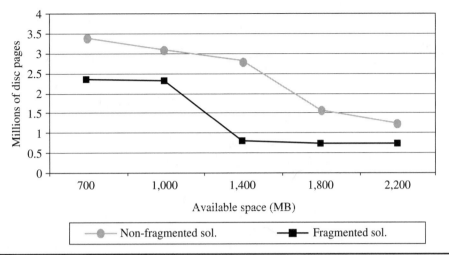

FIGURE 9-26   View fragmentation decreasing execution costs

on the basis of a reference workload that includes only 20 TPC-H queries (W_0); then we applied two different workloads to the resulting view fragments. Both workloads contain the TPC-H queries and an increasing percentage of other unplanned queries (W_1: 25 percent of unplanned queries; W_2: 50 percent of unplanned queries). Table 9-1 shows the results and compares the fragmented solutions with the non-fragmented ones. It also shows that executing unplanned workloads leads to a major increase in costs. It was easy to predict that the fall-off in performance would be greater, yet not dramatically, for the fragmented solution.

CAUTION   *The usefulness of the aggregate data dramatically falls off when workloads are not properly determined. In particular, vertical fragmentation cannot be used in a generalized way unless you know your exact data mart workload. This is because vertical fragmentation gets less and less robust as the amount of unplanned queries increases in your workload.*

Figure 9-27 shows a fragmentation for the views of Figure 8-12. After fragmenting, those queries that request measures belonging to one fragment will experience better performance.

Workload	W_1		W_2	
Reference workload	W_1	W_0	W_2	W_0
Non-fragmented solution	4,138	12,989	6,424	49,537
Fragmented solution	3,411	11,204	4,565	52,772

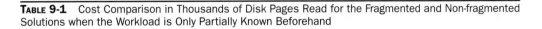

TABLE 9-1   Cost Comparison in Thousands of Disk Pages Read for the Fragmented and Non-fragmented Solutions when the Workload is Only Partially Known Beforehand

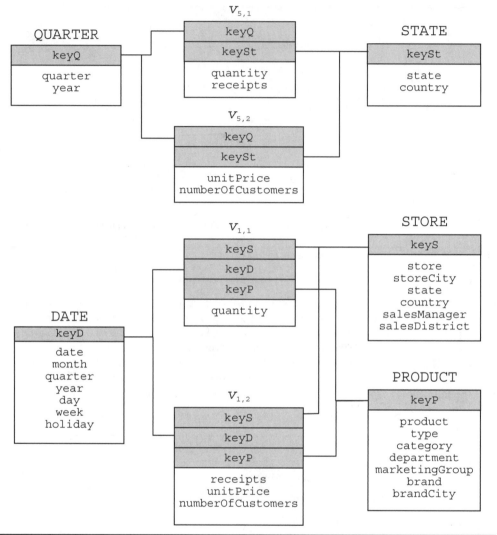

Figure 9-27   A vertical fragmentation of the views in Figure 8-12

For example, this applies to the quantity sold and the receipts grouped by quarters. The $v_{1,1}$ and $v_{1,2}$ fragments must absolutely be materialized in order to comply with the completeness constraint. However, you can delete the $v_{5,1}$ or the $v_{5,2}$ fragments if the measures they contain are not useful for workload queries.

9.3.2   Horizontal View Fragmentation

Many considerations on vertical fragmentation can also apply to horizontal fragmentation. Although specific properties of horizontal fragmentation applied to data warehouses have not been widely studied in academic circles (Ezeife, 2001; Gopalkrishnan et al., 2000), this type of optimization is now in common use in commercial systems.

Horizontal Fragmentation

The term *horizontal fragmentation* refers to a set of views created to contain all the measures of a specific fact schema, but only the subset of tuples that meets specific Boolean predicates. The result of the horizontal fragmentation process must show the following properties:

1. **Consistency** Fragment group-by sets must be chosen among candidate view group-by sets.

2. **Completeness** Each tuple in the primary view must be in a primary fragment.

3. **Non-redundancy** A tuple cannot be inserted in more than one fragment for the same group-by set.

Horizontal fragmentation deals with individual cubes. As a result, you cannot merge tuples from different cubes. Obviously, vertical fragmentation can be carried out first, and then the resulting fragments can be horizontally partitioned.

The reasons for using horizontal fragmentation are broadly similar to those for using vertical fragmentation. In particular, a reduction in query execution time is the result of the opportunity to access smaller fact tables that are free from those tuples that do not satisfy specific conditions. The key criteria for the tuples to be selected and inserted into fragments are a mix of data aggregation level and selection conditions (based either on measures or on dimensional attributes) in workload queries. The v fragment is useful to answer the q query if the fragment tuples satisfy the q selection conditions and if $Gbs(q) \le Gbs(v)$.

Time is an attribute often used for horizontal fragmentation because it is often used in queries. Moreover, time-based fragmentation follows insertion orders when fact table updates take place. Updated tuples do not have to be divided up between different fragments, but they can be appended to the most recent one. Horizontal fragmentation not only results in higher performance, but it also makes tables easier to manage during updates.

In contrast to vertical fragmentation, also note that horizontal fragmentation does not lead to any additional cost in terms of disk memory space used, because every tuple key is stored just once. Horizontal fragmentation can also be used as a starting point for the parallel execution of queries (Özsu and Valduriez, 1991). See section 12.3 for more details on this point.

Finally, we emphasize that the approach to fragmentation mentioned in this chapter is aimed at logical optimization. Conversely, fact schema fragmentation, as discussed in section 6.1.8, is conceptually relevant and aims at cleaning schemata and making them more accurate.

Data-staging Design

In the data-staging design phase, procedures are defined in order to load the data coming from operational sources into data marts. If a reconciled layer is available, the population process is divided into two phases:

- **From the operational sources to the reconciled database** This is the most complex phase because it entails the definition of the procedures that act on data and implement the transformations at the extensional level, as specified in the integration phase. Moreover, this phase also designs data cleansing procedures.

- **From the reconciled database to the data mart** This phase defines the procedures to adjust the reconciled data to the star schema used for multidimensional analyses. The procedures for the calculation of derived data—data that is not available at the operational level—are defined, as well as the procedures for denormalizing data and entering surrogate keys. Data updates need to be not only propagated to the star schemata related to primary views (elementary data), but also to those related to the secondary views (aggregate data).

As mentioned in Chapter 3, we suggest a three-layer architecture, because populating data marts directly is a very complex task and it often leads to poor results. The availability of an intermediate layer facilitates the designer's task, makes data-staging and cleansing easier, and prevents the integrated schema for sources from remaining encrypted in Extraction, Transformation, and Loading (ETL) procedures.

TIP *The reconciled data is intended as an integrated and normalized version of the operational database, and it maintains the same properties in terms of information granularity. The time span of the reconciled data should be equal to or longer than that of the operational data.*

Populating the reconciled database is the goal of the data integration and cleansing phases. Both reconciled schema and its data should be consistent and error-free. We find it very important that reconciled databases be created in two-layer architectures, too, even if they are not materialized. In fact, the existence of a reconciled database proves that data mart designers have definitively gained accurate knowledge of their operational data sources, which is essential for data marts to be properly populated. Obviously, if the reconciled database has not been materialized, the data mart will be populated with data directly extracted from data sources.

Before getting to the heart of the various phases, it is worth mentioning that the topics related to data-staging design have been raising more and more interest over the last ten years, even though the international research community ignored them for a long time. Please refer to works on ETL conceptual design (Vassiliadis et al., 2002), optimization (Simitsis et al., 2005), and implementation (Tziovara et al., 2007) for more details.

10.1 Populating Reconciled Databases

The schemata (conceptual and/or logical) of the reconciled database and of the sources were made available by the data analysis and reconciliation phase, which also defined a mapping between both layers. In this section, we discuss the design phase that implements the mapping on that data and defines the procedures aimed to perform the following tasks for each concept in the reconciled schema:

- **Extraction**   Tasks aimed at collecting data from sources
- **Transformation**   Tasks aimed at adjusting the format of data from source schemata to reconciled schemata
- **Loading**   Tasks aimed at entering the transformed data into the reconciled database and updating the already existing data

These three tasks should be associated with the data cleansing procedures, which help eliminate the inconsistencies due to errors and failures. Figure 10-1 shows that the population

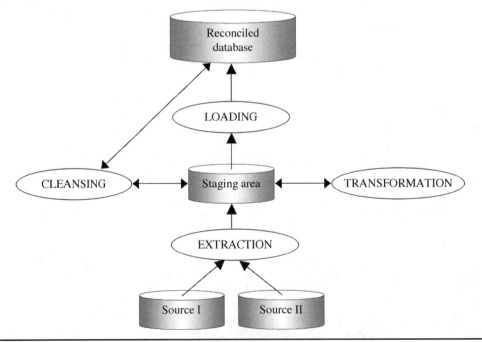

FIGURE 10-1   The population process of the reconciled database

of the reconciled database generally uses a *staging area* containing the "raw" data to which the transformation and cleansing procedures are to be applied. The staging area can require a lot of space, and designers should not underestimate its sizing.

Although according to the Global-As-View (GAV) approach every single concept of the reconciled schema is defined as a view on the source schemata and can therefore be singularly populated (see section 3.4), several concepts are actually populated at the same time. To this end, the staging area is used as a temporary buffer to minimize the cost of the access to sources.

Finally, note that data cleansing techniques are sometimes applied after loading data into the reconciled database to compare as much data as possible. This opportunity is available only if the reconciled database has actually been materialized, and it can considerably enhance the quality standard of data.

10.1.1 Extracting Data

The extraction operations are first carried out during the initialization of the reconciled database. They are then repeated periodically, depending on the update frequency established by designers. This enables users to acquire up-to-date information on the events occurring in the enterprise.

To define extraction procedures, you should first classify the types of data in your sources. This data is called *transient* data if your source database keeps only a snapshot of the current data and overwrites data that is no longer valid. It is called *semi-periodic* data if your database keeps a limited number of previous data versions but you do not know how long each piece of information will be available. Finally, it is called *temporal* (or *periodic*) data when your database keeps track of all data changes for a clearly defined interval. Of course, problems arise in cases of transient or semi-periodic sources, because they require the definition of a mechanism able to extract data independently of their short life span.

Inventory data, such as stock-in-trade levels, is usually transient—it is usually overwritten as soon as new goods arrive. On the contrary, semi-periodic databases store the last n versions of data. The exact time when the oldest version is deleted depends on when the $(n + 1)$-th change takes place, which cannot be determined beforehand. Insurance and banking industries usually have temporal data. In those industries, information on current accounts and insurance policies must be kept for a period of time specified by laws and regulations.

The simplest approach to data extraction is the so-called *static extraction,* which completely scans all the data in operational sources. Static extraction is mandatory when you start up your system, but you can also use it each time the reduced size of data allows for it to be carried out within an acceptable time frame. However, the volume of data involved limits the usage of static extraction in most real-world cases when updates need to be performed in a short period of time, such as overnight or over a weekend.

The techniques that help you detect changes to limit the amount of data to read are more effective than static extraction because the amount of modified data in one specific period of time is far smaller than that of the entire database. The techniques based on this approach are called *incremental extraction* and can be classified as *immediate* and *delayed*.

Immediate techniques record the changes to data as soon as the operational database is updated. Delayed techniques postpone this operation. Devlin (1997) defined five different techniques:

- **Application-assisted extraction**   This is an immediate-extraction technique that creates a set of functions in the operational applications to store data changes to the staging area without modifying the external behavior of applications. Application-assisted extraction provides a very powerful solution, although it can be difficult to implement because it requires the modification of existing applications, which often show poor design and documentation. However, it could be the only incremental technique that can be used, especially for legacy systems that do not support triggers, logs, and timestamps. Application-assisted extraction can also be used for new-generation operational systems for which a layer of primitives (APIs, or application programming interfaces) are uniformly used by all the applications to access data and to be DBMS-independent. In case of an API level, data extraction can be centralized with respect to applications, and transparent both to designers of applications and to DBMS administrators. In this way, applications can be modified and DBMSs can be replaced. Figure 10-2 shows both architectural solutions.

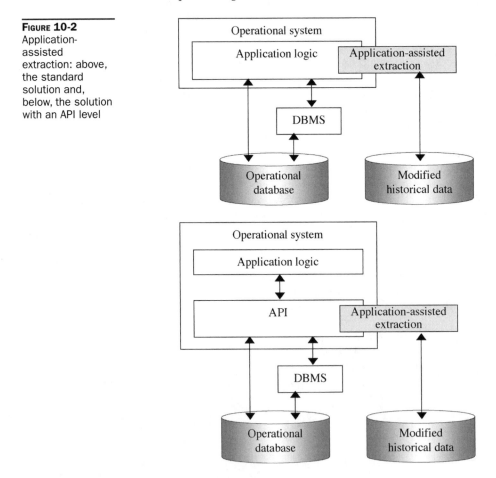

FIGURE 10-2
Application-assisted extraction: above, the standard solution and, below, the solution with an API level

- **Trigger-based extraction**   This is an immediate extraction technique in which data is extracted by a DBMS instead of applications. A trigger is a procedure directly started by a DBMS when specific events occur. To extract data, a trigger is associated with each event applying changes to the data to be monitored. Triggers store modified data to a special file or table in the staging area, from which they are retrievable for proper processing. Figure 10-3 shows the architectural solution resulting from this technique.

CAUTION   *This technique cannot be broadly used due to performance reasons: it forces the DBMS to constantly monitor the transactions that could invoke triggers.*

- **Log-based extraction**   This is an immediate-extraction technique in which the operations for extracting changes are based on DBMS log files. Log files are generated by every modern DBMS, and they are the main tool for backing up and restoring data. The main limit of log-based extraction is the correct interpretation of the log file, whose format is usually proprietary to the specific DBMS. Figure 10-3 shows the architectural solution required for this technique.

TIP   *After considering the complexity of interpreting log files, we suggest that a log-based extraction be used only when extraction modules are developed directly by DBMS producers.*

- **Timestamp-based extraction**   According to this delayed-extraction technique, source schemata should have one or more timestamp attributes used to mark the tuples modified with respect to the latest execution of the data extraction process. Figure 10-4 shows that operational systems are in charge of timestamp updates and data extraction modules directly process source data at a later stage to generate the set—even if incomplete—of changes applied to data.

FIGURE 10-3
Extractions based
on triggers and
log files

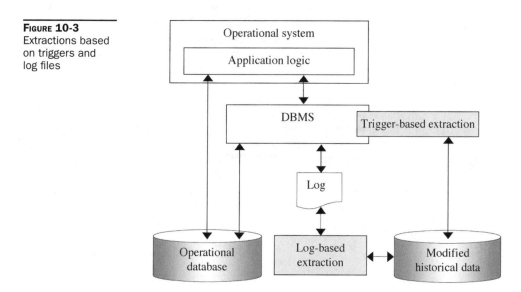

Figure 10-4
Timestamp-based
extraction

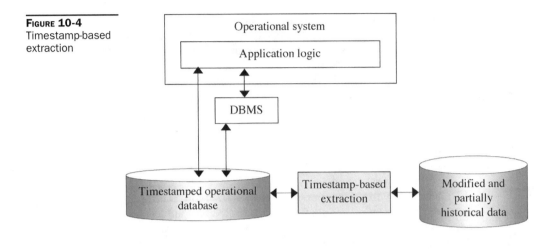

CAUTION *In comparison with the other techniques proposed, the effectiveness of the timestamp-based technique depends on the operational database. If operational data is transient or semi-periodic, timestamp-based extraction cannot identify any intermediate version of those tuples modified more than once since the last extraction.*

Figure 10-5 shows three snapshots taken at different times of a relation storing purchase orders in a transient operational database. Note that the presence of the lcDate timestamp in the ORDERS relation to show the date of the latest change to orders does not mean that ORDERS is temporal—in a temporal relation, you would never overwrite the modified tuples. Mr. Brown's purchase order (100 units) is extracted overnight to be subsequently entered in the data mart. The following day, the purchaser increases the order to 200 units. The operational database records this fact and overwrites the previous value. The following day, the purchase order is again amended to the final value of 150 units due to the lack of product. When the extraction module is activated the following week (4/8/2008), it identifies the modified tuple on the basis of the lcDate timestamp. However, the version on 4/2/2008 is lost because it is overwritten by the latest change. Obviously, a loss of information occurred; its importance is to be assessed together with users. If they believe that this loss affects the significance of the information in your data mart, the timestamp-based technique should be ruled out. A further problem connected to the timestamp-based technique arises if tuples are deleted. Look again at the example of Figure 10-5. Assume that Mr. Brown's order was filled on 4/4/2008 and as a result the tuple is deleted as usually happens in a non-temporal database. Obviously, the timestamp-based system cannot detect a tuple that no longer exists. The correct sequence of the events can be reconstructed only if the operational system does not physically delete the tuple, but instead flags it as invalid until the next execution of the extraction procedure.

Version on 4/1/2008

code	orderDate	product	customer	quantity	lcDate
1	3/20/2008	Cabernet	Smith	50	3/20/2008
2	4/1/2008	Chianti	Brown	100	4/1/2008
......	......	......	......	......	......

Extracted on 4/1/2008

Version on4/2/2008

code	orderDate	product	customer	quantity	lcDate
1	3/20/2008	Cabernet	Smith	50	3/20/2008
2	4/1/2008	Chianti	Brown	200	4/2/2008
......	......	......	......	......	......

Version on4/3/2008

code	orderDate	product	customer	quantity	lcDate
1	3/20/2008	Cabernet	Smith	50	3/20/2008
2	4/1/2008	Chianti	Brown	150	4/3/2008
......	......	......	......	......	......

Extracted on 4/8/2008

FIGURE 10-5   Timestamp-based extraction for a non-temporal operational database

- **File comparison**   This is a delayed extraction technique that compares two subsequent versions of data in order to highlight their differences. This requires that, after each extraction, the data extracted be kept in the staging area until the next extraction, to enable its comparison to the new data extracted. The effectiveness of this technique depends on the types of data, as in timestamp-based extractions. In case of transient or semi-periodic data, some changes that occurred during subsequent extractions may be lost. This technique should be considered only when none of the previous techniques can be applied, because it maintains two full data versions and has high execution costs. The technique is normally used when operational data storage is file-based or when the DBMS in use does not support triggers or logs. Moreover, this technique is particularly suitable for legacy systems because it does not require any changes to operational applications.

CAUTION *Delayed-extraction techniques are useful for transient or semi-periodic operational databases only if users do not need to record each change to data versions.*

Table 10-1 shows a comparison between the different techniques proposed on the basis of the features discussed.

Regardless of the incremental technique in use, the result of the extraction phase consists of the set of source tuples that have been modified, added, or deleted since the previous extraction. They can be temporarily stored in the staging area. To simplify the following phase aimed at loading data into your data mart, you should associate the type of operation (Insert, Update, or Delete) that caused the change with each tuple previously extracted. In this way, the data loading process can determine how each tuple should be managed.

	Static	Timestamps	File Comparison	Application-assisted	Trigger	Log
Management of transient or semi-periodic data	No	Incomplete	Incomplete	Complete	Complete	Complete
Support to file-based systems	Yes	Yes	Yes	Yes	No	Rare
Implementation technique	Tools	Tools or internal development	Tools	Internal development	Tools	Tools
Costs of enterprise-specific development	None	Medium	None	High	None	None
Use with legacy systems	Yes	Difficult	Yes	Difficult	Difficult	Yes
Changes to applications	None	Likely	None	Likely	None	None
DBMS-dependent procedures	Limited	Limited	Limited	Variable	High	Limited
Impact on operational system performance	None	None	None	Medium	Medium	None
Complexity of extraction procedures	Low	Low	Low	High	Medium	Low

TABLE 10-1   Feature Comparison of Different Incremental Extraction Techniques (Devlin, 1997)

Figure 10-6 shows two instances of the ORDERS relation at different times, and the tuples resulting from the application of an incremental extraction technique. The oper attribute gives the opportunity to identify the operation that caused the extraction.

10.1.2 Transforming Data

In this phase, data from sources is properly transformed to adjust its format to the reconciled schema. We mention only the most common categories of operations without going into too much detail.

- **Conversion**   This is applied to individual attributes whose format in source schemata is different from the one of reconciled schemata. Conversions usually include type conversions, such as from integer to decimal, from Extended Binary Coded Decimal Interchange Code (EBCDIC) to ASCII; measure conversions, such as from the American system to metric system; and format conversions, such as from lowercase to uppercase. In particular, format conversions occur any time the information stored in an attribute is not strictly structured. For example, you can specify a country in an address with or without a short form, such as I, IT, or Italy, or you can write the name of a company in different ways, such as 'The Coca-Cola Company', 'Coca Cola', 'Coca-Cola Co.' and so on.

- **Enrichment**   This allows you to combine information from one or more attributes to create new information or to improve the usability of the existing one. A typical example of this type of transformation is the calculation of derived data.

Version on 4/15/2008

code	orderDate	product	customer	quantity	lcDate
1	3/20/2008	Cabernet	Smith	50	3/20/2008
2	4/1/2008	Chianti	Brown	150	4/3/2008
3	4/9/2008	Barbera	Wang	75	4/9/2008
4	4/11/2008	Merlot	Fernandez	45	4/11/2008

Version on 4/22/2008

code	orderDate	product	customer	quantity	lcDate
1	3/20/2008	Cabernet	Smith	50	3/20/2008
2	4/1/2008	Chianti	Brown	150	4/3/2008
4	4/11/2008	Merlot	Fernandez	145	4/18/2008
5	4/19/2008	Pinot	Bean	25	4/19/2008
6	4/20/2008	Chianti	Bean	150	4/20/2008

Incremental difference

code	orderDate	product	customer	quantity	lcDate	oper
3	4/9/2008	Barbera	Wang	75	4/22/2008	D
4	4/11/2008	Merlot	Fernandez	145	4/18/2008	U
5	4/19/2008	Pinot	Bean	25	4/19/2008	I
6	4/20/2008	Chianti	Bean	150	4/20/2008	I

FIGURE 10-6   Incremental extraction for the ORDERS table

- **Separation/concatenation**   This separates the data that is stored together in source schemata but must be kept separate in the reconciled schema, and vice versa. Data normalization and denormalization are the most common cases of this type of transformation.

CAUTION *The most complex operation is data concatenation. Data concatenation usually means extracting data from multiple sources to recombine it on the basis of the reconciled schema. This implies the use of temporary tables, which could even have considerable dimensions. When designers specify the data population process, they should take care to allocate a proper amount of resources in the staging area for this purpose.*

10.1.3   Loading Data

In this last phase, data extracted from operational sources and properly transformed is loaded from the staging area to the reconciled database. The type of loading process depends on the technique used in the extraction phase and may vary according to temporal or non-temporal portions of the reconciled database to be populated.

If you use a static extraction technique, the data in your reconciled database will be completely eliminated and replaced with new data. On the contrary, if you use an incremental technique, the update policy will depend on the time span covered by your reconciled database. Entering new tuples is no issue, but updates to tuples need to be carefully assessed:

- If reconciled data is transient, you should identify the tuples to which any changes were applied and replace them. This operation is not generally complex, because it is generally easy to identify those tuples in your reconciled database which correspond to the tuples of your operational sources. However, the process can become complex if the extraction and transformation phases have deeply impacted tuple structures—for example, if tuple keys were modified. To enable incremental population of your data mart, you should specify which reconciled database tuples have been changed by the loading phase; to do this, add a flag to each relation to track which operation caused a change. Figure 10-7 shows an example similar to the one shown in Figure 10-6. The oper attribute classifies tuples on the basis of the type of changes applied by the extraction phase. The tuples with key values 1 and 2 show no change; the value of their oper attribute is set to NULL and they are not going to be involved in the following data mart population phase. Note that the values of the oper attribute may be different for the same tuple every time the extraction procedure is executed. To better understand the example, note that the tuple whose key value is 3 will be eliminated from the reconciled database after the extraction on 4/22/2008. It is no longer useful as soon as the information related to the deletion of that tuple is propagated to the data mart.

Version on 4/15/2008

code	orderDate	product	customer	quantity	lcDate	oper
1	3/20/2008	Cabernet	Smith	50	3/20/2008	–
2	4/1/2008	Chianti	Brown	150	4/3/2008	–
3	4/9/2008	Barbera	Wang	75	4/9/2008	I
4	4/11/2008	Merlot	Fernandez	45	4/11/2008	I

Version on 4/22/2008

code	orderDate	product	customer	quantity	lcDate	oper
1	3/20/2008	Cabernet	Smith	50	3/20/2008	–
2	4/1/2008	Chianti	Brown	150	4/3/2008	–
3	4/9/2008	Barbera	Wang	75	4/22/2008	D
4	4/11/2008	Merlot	Fernandez	145	4/18/2008	U
5	4/19/2008	Pinot	Bean	25	4/19/2008	I
6	4/20/2008	Chianti	Bean	150	4/20/2008	I

FIGURE 10-7 Two versions of the transient ORDERS relation in a reconciled database

Version on 4/15/2008

code	orderDate	product	customer	quantity	startDate	endDate	oper
1	3/20/2008	Cabernet	Smith	50	3/20/2008	–	–
2	4/1/2008	Chianti	Brown	100	4/1/2008	4/2/2008	–
2	4/1/2008	Chianti	Brown	150	4/3/2008	–	–
3	4/9/2008	Barbera	Wang	75	4/9/2008	–	I
4	4/11/2008	Merlot	Fernandez	45	4/11/2008	–	I

Version on 4/22/2008

code	orderDate	product	customer	quantity	startDate	endDate	oper
1	3/20/2008	Cabernet	Smith	50	3/20/2008	–	–
2	4/1/2008	Chianti	Brown	100	4/1/2008	4/2/2008	–
2	4/1/2008	Chianti	Brown	150	4/3/2008	–	–
3	4/9/2008	Barbera	Wang	75	4/9/2008	4/22/2008	D
4	4/11/2008	Merlot	Fernandez	45	4/11/2008	4/17/2008	–
4	4/11/2008	Merlot	Fernandez	145	4/18/2008	–	U
5	4/19/2008	Pinot	Bean	25	4/19/2008	–	I
6	4/20/2008	Chianti	Bean	150	4/20/2008	–	I

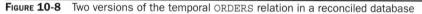

FIGURE 10-8 Two versions of the temporal ORDERS relation in a reconciled database

- If you chose to log the reconciled data, you need to manage the timestamps that define the validity period of tuples. Figure 10-8 shows the temporal version of the example in Figure 10-7. The startDate and endDate timestamps determine the validity period of each tuple. The key of this relation includes the startDate attribute to single out more versions of the same tuple. In this solution, the tuple 3 is not physically deleted, but a non-NULL value in its endDate attribute denotes that the tuple is no longer valid. The tuples involved in the subsequent phase aimed at populating star schemata can be extracted after checking their startDate and endDate timestamps. However, you could also simply extract the tuples whose oper attribute is not NULL, as in the case of transient reconciled databases.

NOTE *Remember that the three-layer architecture with its reconciled layer implies that the reconciled database should cover a time span at least equal to that of the operational source database.*

10.2 Cleansing Data

The terms *data cleansing*, *data cleaning*, and *data scrubbing* refer to the set of operations aimed at guaranteeing the consistency and correctness of the data in the reconciled database. Although this phase can be seen as an integral part of data transformation, we prefer to deal with it separately because of its importance.

The main causes of data inconsistency are the following:

- **Typing mistakes**   You can always make typing mistakes if no procedures are in place for checking the data when you enter it, such as the correctness check of taxpayer codes.

- **Inconsistency between attribute value and description**   This problem can arise because of the evolution of corporate operating modes or changes in everyday life that require the recording of new information not planned for in the original design. To fill this gap, users might enter data into a correlated attribute; for instance, they might enter the mobile phone number together with the landline telephone number into a single `phoneNumber` attribute. Or they might enter data into an attribute of minor importance, such as the e-mail address into a generic `notes` attribute. An additional reason for this problem could be the negligence of a corporate sector that adopts conventions different from those established by its information system because of its own convenience or habit, such as an internal special code for products instead of the standard product code.

- **Inconsistency between the values of correlated attributes**   This problem arises when the values in two or more attributes are individually correct, but they are inconsistent with each other. For example, a tuple storing `city= 'Miami'`, `state='California'` is certainly inconsistent in a table with personal details. These conditions usually occur when users make mistakes in the data entry phase. You can run more serious risks when the information coming from two different sources shows contrasting details on the same subject. Master data managed separately by every department because of the lack of an integrated information system is a typical example of such inconsistency.

- **Missing information**   When operational applications give users the opportunity to leave some attributes blank, lack of time or interest in specific data often causes users to fail to enter that data. For example, consider the form filled out at a bank counter when opening a new account. The customer's date of birth is a piece of information of little interest for the employee drawing up a contract, and this information will be probably left out. However, this information would be very useful to a marketing department that seeks to classify customers.

- **Duplicating information**   This problem typically occurs when two sources provide the same information, but their tuples use different keys. Identifying correspondences between tuples when merging information becomes a very difficult task.

NOTE *You can avoid most inconsistencies if you enforce stricter rules for entering data into operational applications. Designers are in charge of notifying managers and operational system administrators of those problems. However, the update time for applications is usually incompatible with data warehouse implementation time, so data warehouse data consistency will be based on the quality of data-cleansing procedures. Even if designers work accurately, it is difficult to reach 100 percent data quality. Some errors will still exist in the data warehouse and will be displayed to users. This is a fact that designers need to accept.*

Each type of problem requires different techniques for its solution. The main techniques used are described in the following sections. Although most commercial ETL tools propose some modules able to handle the most frequent cleansing problems, the huge variety of real-world cases often requires the implementation of ad-hoc procedures.

10.2.1   Dictionary-based Techniques

These techniques are used for checking the correctness of the attribute values based on *lookup tables* and dictionaries to search for abbreviations and synonyms. They can be applied only when the attribute domain is known and limited, such as names of medicines or municipalities of a certain country. The basic idea is to scan all values of a specific attribute and check to determine whether they belong to the specified domain or are synonyms or abbreviations of a domain value. In the first case, no operation is undertaken. In the second case, the value is replaced by the corresponding domain value. Finally, the data is either discarded or reported to the data mart administrator if no correspondence is found.

Dictionary-based techniques are suitable for solving problems such as typing mistakes and format discrepancies. They normally offer good results when they operate in restricted application domains. They can also be applied to more attributes at the same time to check for any inconsistencies between two correlated attributes. For example, you can check that the `city` and the `state` attributes of an address are consistent with each other if a reference table containing the American states and a complete list of the cities per state are available.

10.2.2   Approximate Merging

Any time you need to merge data coming from different sources without any common key, you should identify matching tuples. In the following sections, we describe two typical conditions when this problem arises.

In Figure 10-9 an implicit association was found between the CUSTOMER entity in the marketing department database and the ORDER entity in the administration database after the integration phase. To make this association explicit, you need to identify which customer placed a particular order. Unfortunately, the two databases identify customers in different ways. The join will therefore be performed on the basis of the common attributes (`customerAddress`, `customerSurname`). These attributes, however, are not an identifier for the customer, and, being descriptive by nature, they are not subject to control procedures that could ensure the respect for the referential integrity constraints and the absence of entry errors. Under those conditions, we talk about *approximate join* because there is no certainty in the detection of matching tuples.

Figure 10-10 shows a slightly different situation. In this case, two different instances of the same schema need to be merged together (*purge/merge problem*). Both instances are not disjoint because a customer can make a purchase both in Austin and in Raleigh. Moreover, a customer could be entered more times into an individual database because of typing mistakes that make it impossible to trace previous tuples.

The problem of similarity between tuples was studied by Monge and Elkan (1996; 1997), who proposed a few algorithms to calculate the level of similarity between two alphanumeric

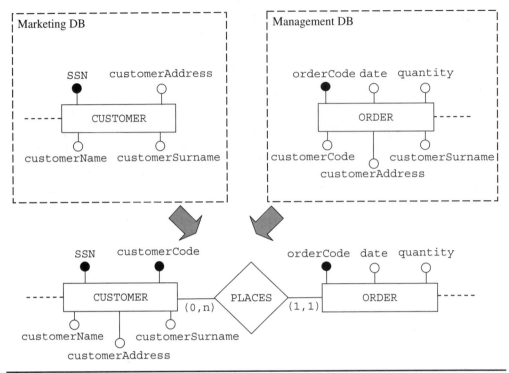

Figure 10-9 Merging data from two local schemata requires an approximate join due to the lack of a common identifier for the customer concept.

attributes (A and B). The similarity function compares the word pairs $A_i \in A$ and $B_i \in B$ and calculates the similarity according to this formula:

$$affinity(A, B) = \frac{1}{|A|} \sum_{i=1}^{|A|} \max_{j=1}^{|B|} affinity(A_i, B_j)$$

The similarity between two words is calculated as their *edit distance* (Bunke, 1993) and by checking for abbreviations according to well-defined schemata:

- An abbreviation could be a prefix of a substring, for instance 'Univ.' is a prefix for 'University'.

- An abbreviation can combine a prefix and a suffix of a substring, such as 'Dr' that abbreviates 'Doctor'.

- An abbreviation could be an acronym of a string—for example, 'DESA' is an acronym for 'Department of Electronics and Systems Analysis'.

- An abbreviation can be the concatenation of more prefixes contained in a string— for example, 'UNIBO' abbreviates 'University of Bologna'.

An additional set of techniques for tuple matching is based on groups of rules assessing the similarity between the corresponding attributes of two tuples (Hernandez and Stolfo, 1995). These techniques usually measure properties such as the edit distance between two strings or the difference in value between two numeric attributes. By way of example,

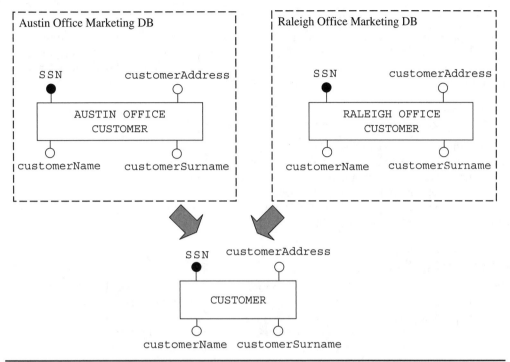

Figure 10-10   Merging data from two local schemata needs to check for duplicate tuples.

Figure 10-11 shows the pseudo-code of some rules proposed by Hernandez and Stolfo (1998) for the solution of the purge/merge problem applied to tuples containing people's information. The basic idea is to calculate the similarity between tuple pairs; all those tuples whose similarity exceeds a certain threshold are then merged in one single tuple.

Figure 10-11   Pseudo-code of a rule-based algorithm for cleansing people's personal data

```
// In input: two tuples P1, P2 including the attributes
// code, name, address, city, zip, country
// In output: TRUE if P1 and P2 are the same tuple,
//            FALSE if P1 and P2 are not the same tuple
similarCode = CompareCodes(P1.code,P2.code);
similarName = CompareNames(P1.name,P2.name);
similarAddress = CompareAddresses(P1.address,P2.address);
similarCity = CompareCities(P1.city,P2.city);
similarZIP = CompareZips(P1.zip,P2.zip);
similarCountry = CompareCountries(P1.country,P2.country);
if (similarCode and similarName)
    return TRUE;
verySimilarAddress = (similarAddress and similarCity and
                      (similarZIP or similarCountry));
if ((similarCode or similarName) and verySimilarAddress)
    return TRUE;
.........
```

10.2.3 Ad-hoc Techniques

Every application domain has its own features and business rules, and they can be so specific that standard tools cannot be used to check them. Under those conditions, designers must write ad hoc queries or scripts to ensure that data complies with those rules. For example, the following equations must always be checked in a database with financial data:

$$profit = receipts - expenses$$
$$capital = assets + credits - debts$$

In other cases, you can discover errors if you search for nonstandard values (*outliers*). For example, a change in a sales price higher than 20 percent is probably caused by an error.

A final check for functional dependencies—very common in dimension tables—is performed very often. If you want to check a many-to-one relationship between two attributes a and b, simply sort the tuples out by a, and then check for each value of a to be associated with only one value in b.

10.3 Populating Dimension Tables

Dimension tables are the first tables to be populated in data marts. This obligation stems from the star schemata structure, which implies a referential integrity constraint between the primary key of each dimension table and the corresponding foreign key of the fact table.

The technique used for the loading process depends on the way information is managed in both layers involved: the reconciled layer and the data mart layer. If updates are performed incrementally in the reconciled database, data marts can also be incrementally populated. Otherwise, it may be more efficient to re-create the entire dimension table. The latter solution is obviously simpler than the former from the design point of view, but it can yield a longer execution time. However, you always need to plan a static loading (or *refresh*) procedure because it is necessary when you initialize data marts.

In the following sections we focus on incremental population (or *update*). Even if this is the most complex technique, it can be considered as a generalization of the static population. Two main operations must be carried out in this phase:

- Identify the set of data to load.
- Replace the table keys of the reconciled database with the surrogate keys used in the star schemata.

10.3.1 Identifying the Data to Load

The correspondence between attributes of the reconciled schema and attributes of the dimension tables was defined in the design phase of the star schemata. To identify which relations and which attributes are involved in the population of a dimension table, you can read the project documentation written in the logical design phase.

It is more complex to establish whether the tuples of a dimension table have actually been modified. Tuples contain attributes from various reconciled schema relations because of the denormalization process, but they do not necessarily include *all* the attributes of those relations. Unfortunately, though the ETL procedures populating reconciled databases mark the updated tuples, they do not record which single attribute in a tuple has been changed.

This implies that a tuple is sometimes viewed as modified even if its relevant attributes were not actually updated. This condition might cause problems in case of dynamic dimensions as it leads to a proliferation of dimension table tuples containing the same values.

TIP *There is no solution to this problem except for a comparison between the reconciled database tuples that appear to have been modified and their corresponding dimension table tuples. To do this in the most efficient way, you should temporarily duplicate your dimension table in the staging area and perform your comparison on the duplicate table. As an alternative, if your reconciled schema is not materialized, you can compare dimension table tuples with their corresponding source database tuples.*

10.3.2   Replacing Keys

Inserting surrogate keys is the second important operation to perform. Creating surrogate keys for the new tuples is an easy process because you simply need to choose a numeric value not already used in dimension tables. Your DBMS will normally take care of this. On the contrary, you should keep a connection between dimension table tuples and reconciled database tuples to apply changes to the existing tuples. To do this, you should permanently store in the staging area a lookup table that includes the dimension table surrogate key and the primary key of the reconciled schema relation that originated the dimension table. In this way, it just takes a search to identify the dimension table tuple corresponding to each reconciled database tuple.

After determining the content of the tuples involved in the population process, proceed with the loading process. While it takes the addition of a tuple to the dimension table to enter a new instance for one dimension, such as a new product, a change to an attribute value of a pre-existing instance, such as the replacement of a sales manager, is a different process that depends on the dynamic properties previously specified for the corresponding hierarchy:

- **Static hierarchies**   Adding new tuples is the only operation allowed, because the existing tuples cannot be modified. For this reason, it is not strictly necessary to store the key lookup table.

- **Type 1 hierarchies**   These involve the replacement of modified data without keeping track of previous values. In this case, simply overwrite the dimension table tuple corresponding to the operational database tuple modified. Use the key lookup table to identify it.

- **Type 2 hierarchies**   These involve keeping both the old and the new values of updated dimension table tuples. In this case, a change leads to entering a new tuple with a new surrogate key value and updating the key lookup table.

- **Type 3 hierarchies**   These use a single tuple to store a finite number of versions for each hierarchy instance. As with Type 1 hierarchies, a change leads to overwriting the dimension table tuple corresponding to the operational database tuple modified.

- **Fully-logged hierarchies**   These involve complete dimension table data logging. If you use the solution proposed in section 8.4.4, an old dimension table tuple needs to be modified after applying a change by entering a timestamp that specifies that the tuple is no longer valid. Then, add a new tuple with the updated data and update your key lookup table.

> **NOTE** *The timestamps to be entered into the Type 3 and fully-logged hierarchies are the ones extracted from the reconciled database if the reconciled database is temporal. If it is not, you should use the population date.*

Figure 10-12 shows a graphical representation of the sequence of operations described so far. We assume that the hierarchy modeled by the DT dimension table includes the attr1, attr3, attr5, and attr6 attributes, and that it is the result of the join between three reconciled schema tables.

Sometimes dimension tables have attributes not included in your reconciled schema, and those values need to be entered manually. We recommend that you enter dummy values for those attributes, such as 'to be completed,' when populating dimension tables. But you should also set up small dedicated applications allowing the personnel in charge to fill them in directly.

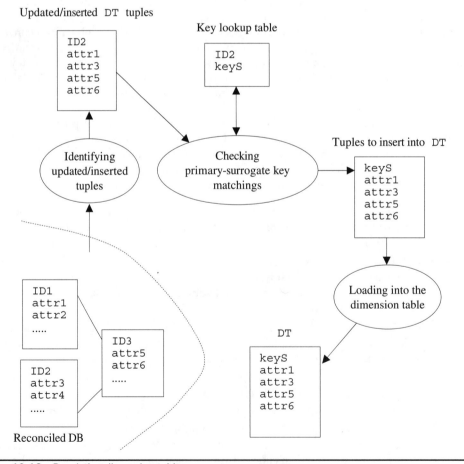

FIGURE 10-12 Populating dimension tables

Finally we would like to remark on dimension table indexes, which should be updated after applying your changes. The most efficient technique depends on the type of index and on the percentage of modified data. In a heuristic way, we recommend that you re-create an index from scratch when the percentage of modified data is greater than 15 percent of the total (Kimball et al., 1998).

10.4 Populating Fact Tables

The procedure for populating fact tables is very similar to the one for populating dimension tables. This procedure is always incremental except for the first time you perform it—that is, when you initialize your star schema.

CAUTION *You should always update fact tables after updating the dimension tables connected to them. In this way, you can fulfill referential integrity constraints between dimension table keys and the corresponding foreign keys of fact tables.*

As for dimension tables, you should refer to your logical design documentation to identify the correspondence between reconciled schema attributes and fact table measures. Use the key lookup tables created in the dimension table population phase to determine the surrogate key values that should be entered into fact table tuples. Figure 10-13 shows a graphical representation of the fact table population process. The meas1, meas3, meas5, and meas6 fact table measures are derived from the attr1, attr3, attr5, and attr6 reconciled schema attributes.

If you followed the steps described in section 10.1, the tuples stored in the reconciled database should have a flag indicating which operation generated their data (insert, update, delete) and how that data should be managed when loading the fact table. Though inserting new events is the most common operation on the fact table, the events already loaded can sometimes be modified or deleted due to late updates (section 5.4.2). For this purpose, it is necessary to distinguish between two scenarios. If you choose to model only the validity time in your star schema (monotemporal schema), more versions of an individual event recorded at different times must be recorded in the same tuple. Modifications and deletions of reconciled database tuples can then cause physical updates and deletions in the fact table. On the contrary, if you choose to model also the transaction time (bitemporal schema), the tuples previously inserted will not be updated because any change to the events that previously occurred creates new tuples with new transaction time values.

Finally, we want to highlight the semantics that should be associated with updates, which can be modeled as *consolidated events* or *delta events*. In the first case, if you apply a change to an old event, you record a new event that is given the up-to-date value. In the second case, you will give the new event a delta value of the up-to-date value and the previous one (for example, the additional number of bottles to order or other enrollments on a specific date). On the one hand, the use of consolidation semantics is obvious in the case of changes applied by a rectification of an error in operational data. On the other hand, delta semantics can be used when events inherently evolve over time.

Table 5-36 shows an example of consolidation semantics. In this case, delta semantics could have been adopted as well. Assessing advantages and disadvantages of different solutions is complex because the effects of semantics you adopt also depend on whether you are using a transactional or a snapshot fact schema (section 5.4.1). Please refer to specialized literature for an in-depth analysis of the possible cases (Golfarelli and Rizzi, 2007).

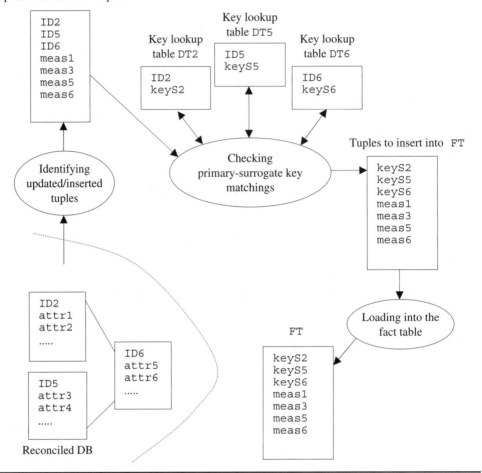

Figure 10-13   Populating fact tables

Tip *Regardless of the type of fact schema used (transactional or snapshot), if you adopt a bitemporal schema in case of late updates, the consolidation semantics streamlines loading and querying processes. Therefore, updates stored in fact tables should always show new, up-to-date values for the events modified.*

10.5 Populating Materialized Views

Primary fact table updates should be propagated to the related materialized views. Although many commercial DBMSs natively support materialized views and manage updates in an autonomous and transparent way, we should highlight the complexity caused by operations carried out efficiently. From the logical point of view, this process is very simple because you can use an aggregate query of a primary fact table to feed a materialized view. You can actually use this approach to updates when the amount of data to process gives you the opportunity to delete and re-create views from scratch. However, you frequently need to use more sophisticated techniques to keep the update time as quick as possible.

A way to reduce the costs of updating views requires an analysis of the roll-up order for group-by sets to populate a secondary view from other secondary views. As we mentioned in section 9.2.1, if the group-by set of the v view to be populated is less fine-grained than a v' view previously updated, and the v measures can be derived from the v' measures, then you can use a query of v' to populate v. If you populate views from tables that are more aggregate (with a lower cardinality) than fact tables, costs are obviously reduced. Figure 10-14 includes a portion of the multidimensional lattice showed in Figure 9-23 for the sales schema. If a materialized view corresponds to each group-by set and you can always derive view measures from finer group-by set view measures, this figure shows a correct update order of the views. To update the v view, you should query the v' view with a minimum cardinality value among those views directly connected to v. Many equivalent solutions are possible, because the update of some views does not depend on the update of some other views.

In some cases, the execution of an aggregate query involving an entire fact table might entail too high costs. Then you need to use incremental updates for views, too. In this case, the same information used for the incremental updates of primary fact tables can also be used for views. After analyzing hierarchies, you can identify which tuple of a view needs to be modified due to a primary event that took place. For example, Figure 10-15 shows an instance of the primary fact table of the sales fact with the {product, store, date} primary group-by set and the corresponding materialized view with the {type, state, date} group-by set. If a new sales event takes place, this also implies that the corresponding tuple of the materialized view changes, consequently.

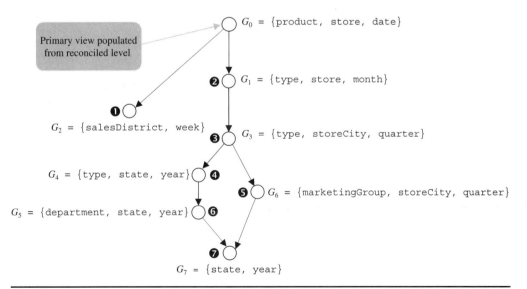

Figure 10-14   A correct update sequence of materialized views

SALES

keyS	keyD	keyP	quantity	receipts	.....
1	1	1	170	85	.....
2	2	2	320	160	.....
3	1	3	412	200	.....

New tuple ➡

STORE

keyS	store	city	state	.....
1	COOP1	Columbus	Ohio	.....
2	COOP2	Austin	Texas	.....
3	COOP3	Dayton	Ohio	.....
.....	.....	.....	.....	.....

PRODUCT

keyP	product	type	category	brand	.....
1	Slurp Milk	Dairy products	Food	Slurp	.....
2	ChokoLocko	Sweets	Food	Mutella	.....
3	Yum Yogurt	Dairy products	Food	Yum	.....

DATE

keyD	date	month	year	......
1	2/9/2009	9/2009	2009	.....
2	3/10/2009	10/2009	2009	.....

SALES1

Modified tuple ➡

keySt	keyD	keyT	quantity	receipts	.....
1	1	1	582	285	.....
2	2	2	320	160	.....

STATE

keySt	state	.....
1	Ohio	.....
2	Texas	.....

TYPE

keyT	type	category	.....
1	Dairy products	Food	.....
2	Sweets	Food	.....

Figure 10-15 If a tuple is added to the SALES primary fact table, one tuple of the SALES1 view changes accordingly. To identify this tuple, use hierarchy information.

As far as the views aggregated along a time hierarchy are concerned, you will be forced to update the tuples that model secondary events related to the current aggregated period. For instance, if we consider again the sales schema (populated daily), the view with the {type, state, month} group-by set will be updated 30 times per month. In this case, two approaches are possible:

- Do not enter the data of the current month into the aggregate view. You can avoid problems connected to changes if you set up a monthly process updating this view.

- Enter a tuple with the current month data into the aggregate view. In this case, you need to set up a daily process updating current month data.

Updating aggregate views is a particularly difficult problem if specific events that modify a large amount of the data take place, such as a new assignment of sales areas that implies a new allocation of turnovers. If this is the case, you should completely delete any views involved and process them from scratch.

CHAPTER

Indexes for the Data Warehouse

Defining and selecting indexes make up some of the main research topics in data warehousing because they, along with materialized views, are the most effective techniques for enhancing system performance. The specific data warehouse, properties allow for the use of index classes that are different from the well-known B⁺-Trees, which are most commonly used in the majority of commercial DBMSs. While some indexes have been developed to meet specific needs of data warehouses, other indexes, already known, are seldom used in transactional applications because of their features. For example, users only access data warehouses in read-only mode, and this allows for the use of structures with high update costs without affecting the system query response time.

In the relational database terminology, the term *key* means a set of attributes whose value allows them to unambiguously identify every relation tuple. In this chapter we will use this term with a different meaning, instead: the term *index key* will stand for the set of attributes upon which the index was built—that is, the set of attributes that you can use to access relation tuples quickly.

11.1 B⁺-Tree Indexes

B⁺-Tree indexes are by far the most used data structures to improve query processing time in operational databases.

> **B⁺-Tree**
>
> A *B⁺-Tree index* on an attribute c of a relation R is a balanced tree providing associative access to the tuples of R on the basis of the values of the c key. The leaves of this tree are linked to each other and store the pointers to the disk blocks containing tuples. Internal nodes create a sort of map to find key values quickly.

B⁺-Trees evolved from B-Trees (Bayer and McCreight, 1972). They were created to fill the gaps of B-Trees searching sequentially and for intervals. In a B⁺-Tree, the internal nodes have an alternate sequence of pointers to child nodes and *separators*—that is, the key values used to quickly find those B⁺-Tree leaves that make reference to the relation tuples including the value searched for. Sequential search and interval search are streamlined because leaves are linked to each other by pointers (Elmasri and Navate, 2006).

Figure 11-1 shows a portion of a B[+]-Tree built on a numeric key. The sub-tree to the left of every separator contains key values smaller than or equal to the separator. The sub-tree to the right contains greater values than the separator. The leaves contain all the key values together with the pointers to specific tuples (RIDs, *Row IDentifiers*).[1]

B[+]-Trees can be either primary or secondary. A *primary index* is built on the relation primary key, so each leaf points to a single tuple. A *secondary index* is built on any other relation attribute, so each leaf contains a RID list of the tuples with a specific key value. A B[+]-Tree built on a key *c* is called *clustered* tree if the underlying relation is physically ordered by *c*. If this is not the case, a B[+]-Tree is called *unclustered*. Note that key values are ordered in leaves even if their index is unclustered, and this is a direct result of the tree structure.

To search for a specific key value *v*, you should go down the tree following the pointer map. In this way, you can single out a leaf node containing a RID list of the tuples with the *v* value. To search for an interval of values [*a*, *b*], you can use *a* as key value to go down the tree. Then you should follow the leaf node sequence until you find a value that is greater than *b*.

Just as in B-Trees, in B[+]-Trees each node can store a number of separators ranging from *g* to 2*g*, where the *g* parameter is called *degree* or *order*. The size of a node normally matches the *D* size of a disk page in order to maximize the efficiency of this structure.

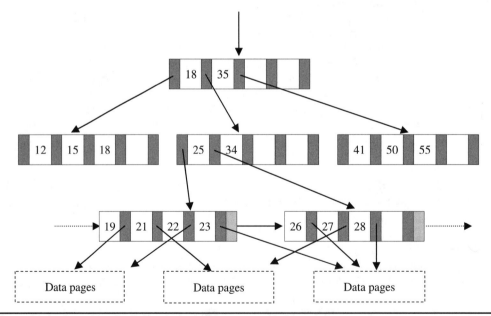

FIGURE 11-1 A portion of a B[+]-Tree index built on a numeric key

---

[1]In the following sections, we will use the term *RID* generically to identify the physical references to the tuples of relational tables. A RID stands for a disk page and location where a particular tuple is stored, regardless of how the RID is implemented.

If *len(p)* is the length of a pointer to a node and *len(s)* is the length of a separator, the following relation applies:

$$g = \left\lfloor \frac{D - len(p)}{2(len(s) + len(p))} \right\rfloor$$

If you select separators from key values, you will achieve this result: *len(s)* = *len(k)*, where *len(k)* is the length of a key value. Selecting separators is a particularly important task if you use alphanumeric keys because you can save space and reduce your tree height when you use separators of reduced length.

The overall size of a B⁺-Tree depends on multiple factors, such as separator length, RID length, and disk page size, and it can vary due to balancing. The number of tree leaves, *NL*, can help you make an approximate estimate for the tree size,

$$NL = \left\lceil \frac{NK \cdot len(k) + NR \cdot len(r)}{D \cdot u} \right\rceil$$

where *NK* is the number of distinct key values in this relation; *NR* is the number of tuples; *len(r)* is the length of a RID; and *u* is the *fill factor* of nodes. The use of balancing offers the opportunity to keep the fill factor of any node above 50 percent. Statistical evaluations actually show that the average value of the fill factor is approximately 70 percent.

You can calculate the number of logical disk pages that should be read to find a key value if you add the number of nodes that you should cross to reach a leaf node (tree height), the number of leaves containing your key value, and the number of data pages containing tuples (Elmasri and Navate, 2006). The height *h* of a B⁺-Tree is constant for all the paths thanks to the balancing procedures triggered when deleting (*catenation*, *underflow*) and inserting items (*split*). This height may vary according to the fill level of nodes if the number of leaves *NL* remains unchanged:

$$1 + \left\lceil \log_{2g+1} NL \right\rceil \leq h \leq 2 + \left\lfloor \log_{g+1} \frac{NL}{2} \right\rfloor$$

Table 11-1 shows the h_{max} maximum height and the *NL* number of leaves of a B⁺-Tree, where *D* = 1024 bytes, *len(r)* = 4 bytes and *NR* = 10^6, when the *NK* number of distinct key

$\log_{10}(NK)$	len(k) = 10 bytes		len(k) = 20 bytes	
	NL	h_{max}	NL	h_{max}
1	5,636	4	5,636	4
2	5,637	4	5,639	4
3	5,650	4	5,664	4
4	5,770	4	5,918	4
5	7,045	4	8,454	4
6	19,725	4	33,814	5

TABLE 11-1   The Number of Leaves and the Maximum Height of a B⁺-Tree Vary According to the Number of Distinct Key Values

values and the *len*(k) length of a key value vary. Note that the maximum height and the number of leaves only partly depend on the number of distinct key values if the *NR* number of tuples remains unchanged. See section 11.2.1 for more details on this point when comparing B⁺-Trees and bitmap indexes.

11.2 Bitmap Indexes

The bitmap indexes were developed from the Model 204 project (O'Neil, 1987). They are certainly among the most useful types of indexes for physical data warehouse design.

> **Bitmap Index**
> A *bitmap index* on an attribute c of a relation R consists of a bit matrix B with as many columns as the distinct values of c, and as many rows as the tuples of the R relation. The $B_{i,j}$ bit is set to 1 if the c attribute value of the i-th tuple is c_j.

Figure 11-2 shows the bitmap index on the `position` attribute of the table EMPLOYEES. The possible values are 'Administrative', 'Assistant', 'Consultant', 'Manager', 'Programmer', and 'Technician'. The RID column allows you to identify the relation tuple an index row corresponds to at the physical level. For example, tuple 1 will be related to a consultant, and tuple 3 will be related to a programmer.

To speed up spotting relevant columns, bitmap indexes have tree structures that are identical to those of the B⁺-Trees, except that bitmap index tree leaves contain bit vectors in the place of RID lists (Figure 11-3). The search for specific relation tuple values sticks to the following steps:

1. Descending trees
2. Loading a tree bit vector to memory
3. Singling out RIDs related to bits set to 1
4. Retrieving specific tuples

Figure 11-4 shows a simplified example of a research of the tuples related to managers. The matching tuples are RID 2 and 4 tuples.

If you organize bitmaps as sets of vectors, you can reduce the I/O cost required to retrieve the information on a particular key value. Instead of loading an entire bitmap, you can retrieve only the disk pages containing the vector related to the value being searched for. This will use approximately an *NK*-th of the space required by the whole index.

RID	Administrative	Assistant	Consultant	Manager	Programmer	Technician
1	0	0	1	0	0	0
2	0	0	0	0	0	1
3	0	0	0	0	1	0
4	0	0	0	1	0	0
5	0	0	0	0	0	1

FIGURE 11-2   Bitmap on the `position` attribute of the EMPLOYEES relation

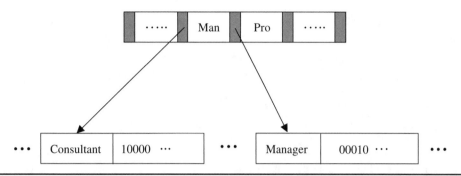

FIGURE 11-3   A bitmap index on the `position` attribute: the tree leaves contain attribute values and bit vectors.

A further strength of bitmap indexes consists of the opportunity to use Boolean operators very efficiently, such as AND, OR, and NOT. The usage of Boolean operators is very common in online analytical processing (OLAP) queries when you need to filter data on the basis of multiple criteria. If you use bitmap indexes, you can sometimes solve queries without even accessing data. For example, consider the question *How many people in Ohio are insured?* If you have three bitmap indexes on the `gender`, `insured`, and `state` attributes, the first two are associated with Boolean attributes and consist of two columns, and the third one will have as many columns as US states. Figure 11-5 shows that the query can be solved without accessing the data if Boolean operators are properly used. This means that you get the information you are looking for if you use the AND operator on the relevant column bits of the three indexes, and then you total the results.

FIGURE 11-4
Search for
managers in the
EMPLOYEE relation

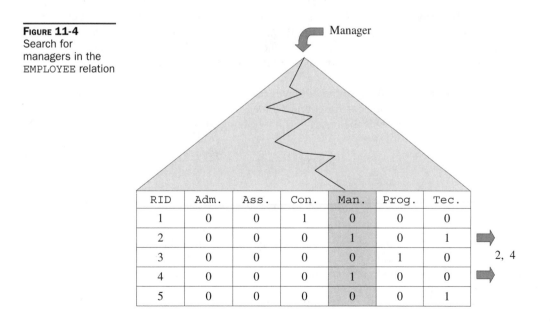

RID	gender	insured	state
1	M	N	Colorado
2	M	Y	Ohio
3	F	N	Texas
4	M	Y	Ohio

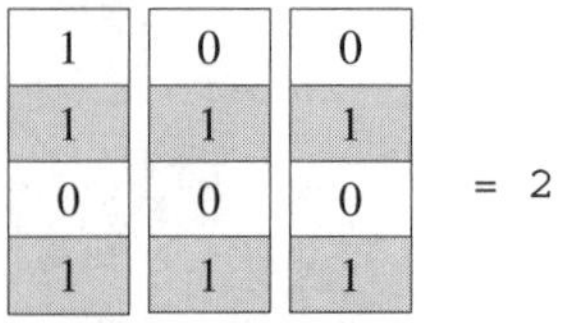

1	0	0
1	1	1
0	0	0
1	1	1

= 2

FIGURE 11-5   Calculating the number of insured people in Ohio by using bitmap indexes

Bitmap indexes have been extensively studied. In particular, important areas addressed have been:

- Compression of the bit matrixes (Chan and Ioannidis, 1998) to define how to efficiently index attributes associated with sparse matrixes, that are common when keys have a large number of distinct values.

- Specialization of the ways to select data on the basis of several types of queries, and in particular, interval queries, aggregation queries, and OLAP queries (O'Neil and Graefe, 1995; Wong et al., 1985; Chan and Ioannidis, 1999).

- Definition of algorithms for index selection (Labio et al., 1997).

11.2.1   Bitmap Indexes vs. B⁺-Trees

Both bitmaps and B⁺-Trees are designed to allow you to quickly find those tuples that have a specific key value. For this reason, they are suitable for speeding up selection operations common to OLAP queries. Even though they are used for the same function, their structural features make their performance vary according to the properties of indexed attributes, and their use varies consequently. The difference between the indexes lies in the way RID sets are stored to disk. B⁺-Trees explicitly store RIDs for every key value. Bitmap indexes give every key value a bit vector that is as long as the number of relation tuples—that is, as long as the total number of RIDs. Then, the size of bitmap indexes strongly depends on the number of distinct key values.

Figure 11-6 compares the number of leaves used by a bitmap index with the number of leaves used by a B⁺-Tree index as function of the NK number of distinct key values. The estimate (number of pages) is the result of the following formulas:

$$\text{B}^+\text{-Tree index:} \left\lceil \frac{NK \cdot len(k) + NR \cdot len(r)}{D \cdot u} \right\rceil$$

$$\text{Bitmap index:} \left\lceil \frac{NR}{D \cdot 8} \right\rceil \cdot NK$$

where $D = 4096$ bytes is the disk page size; $NR = 10^7$ is the number of relation tuples; $u = 1$ is the fill factor for leaves; and $len(k) = 4$ bytes and $len(r) = 4$ bytes are respectively the key length and the RID length. Note that the B⁺-Tree size virtually remains unchanged, while the bitmap size grows very quickly and exceeds the previous one approximately when the number of distinct key values becomes larger than the number of bits used to code a RID ($NK > 8 \, len(r) = 32$).

FIGURE 11-6
A comparison
between the
number of leaves
required to store
a bitmap and a
B$^+$-Tree depending
on the number of
distinct key values

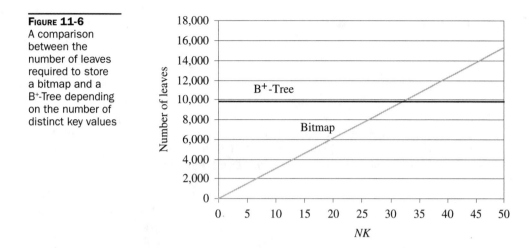

The strong growth in size makes the bitmap indexes more suitable for indexing attributes with a reduced number of distinct key values. Under those conditions, the suitability of bitmap indexes depends not only on the lower space requirements for storage, but on lower I/O cost for query execution as well. Figure 11-7 shows that the number of leaves with specific key value RIDs is inversely proportional to the number of distinct key values in a B$^+$-Tree if the number of relation tuples is the same. However, it remains constant in a bitmap index. The results of Figure 11-7 can seem contrary to those of Table 11-1. However, you should not be deceived because the strong change in the number of disk pages (leaves of the B$^+$-Tree) related to a *single* key value does not imply any equally strong change in the *total* number of leaves.

Several techniques have been studied to compress bit matrixes (Chan and Ioannidis, 1998; Wu et al., 2006) because bitmap indexes built on attributes with a large number of values have proven to be inefficient. Those techniques noticeably reduce the disk space used and make structures more efficient even if the sparsity level is very high.

FIGURE 11-7
Comparison
between the
space used by the
RIDs related to a
single key value in
bitmap indexes
and B$^+$-Trees

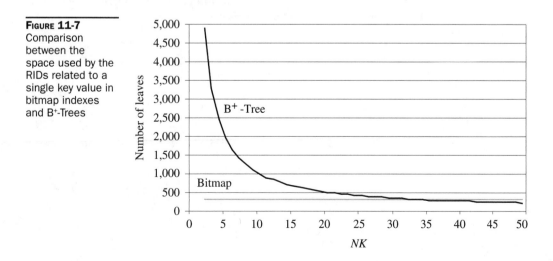

11.2.2   Advanced Bitmap Indexes

Starting from the basic idea of a bitmap index, other kinds of indexes have been defined which are useful in a number of contexts.

Bit-sliced Index

A *bit-sliced index* (O'Neil and Quass, 1997) for a numeric attribute c of a relation R consists of a bit matrix B with n columns $B_0 \dots, B_{n-1}$ (where n represents the bits needed by a binary coding of the values of c) and as many rows as the tuples of the R relation. The $B_{i,j}$ bit is set to 1 if coding the value of c in the i-th relation tuple has the j-th bit set to 1. You can add to this index a further bit vector B_n marking the tuples where the value of c is non-null.

As with bitmap indexes, each column of this index (*slice*) is stored separately. Bit-sliced indexes are used for numeric keys (integers or real) because they help efficiently calculate aggregate values. If the key has positive integer values, the number of bits required to store them is $\lceil \log_2(\textit{ValMax}) \rceil$, where *ValMax* is the maximum integer value belonging to the key domain. On the contrary, if the key domain type is real, you need to use a fixed point representation to make codings of bit slices comparable.[2]

Figure 11-8 shows a bit-sliced index on the quantity attribute in the SALES table. The possible key values range from 1 to 100. In this way, you will need $\lceil \log_2(100) \rceil = 7$ bits for every tuple.

The coding type used makes it possible to use this type of bitmap also for high-cardinality domains. In the previous example, a bitmap index could require 100 different columns, but the bit-sliced index needs just 7 columns. Standard bitmap indexes linearly get larger as the number of distinct key values increases, but bit-sliced indexes show a logarithmic growth. Nevertheless, it is still possible to apply Boolean operators to an index slice. For example, Figure 11-8 shows that you need to single out the RIDs where $B_6 = 1$ to retrieve the tuples where quantity>63. Bit-sliced indexes can be also used to calculate some aggregate values, such as sums and averages. For example, you can calculate a sum of values without accessing your data. To do this, you should use the information on the slice positions and sum the powers of 2 for the bits whose value is set to 1 in your index. Figure 11-9 shows the pseudo-code for this operation: the count B_i function counts the number of bits set to 1 in the i-th slice.

FIGURE 11-8

Bit-sliced index on the quantity attribute of the SALES relation

RID	B_6	B_5	B_4	B_3	B_2	B_1	B_0
1	0	1	0	1	1	1	1
2	0	1	0	0	0	0	0
3	1	0	1	1	0	0	1
4	0	1	1	0	1	1	0
5	0	0	1	0	0	0	0

SALES

...	quantity	...
...	47	...
...	32	...
...	89	...
...	54	...
...	16	...

---

[2]Domains of real numbers with a wide interval of variation entail a large number of slices. However, these domains are not very frequent in commercial applications.

Figure 11-9 Pseudo-code for the sum algorithm exploiting bit-sliced index properties

```
// Input: bit-sliced index B consisting of n slices
// built on the c integer key;
// Output: sum of values of c
Sum=0;
for i=0,...n
    Sum += 2^i × count(B_i);
return Sum;
```

The idea of storing binary coding of numeric values to be represented has been applied to non-numeric domains as well, giving life to so-called *bitmap-encoded* indexes (Chan and Ioannidis, 1999; Wu and Buchmann, 1998).

Bitmap-Encoded Index

A *bitmap-encoded index* on an attribute c (with k distinct values) of a relation R consists of a bit matrix B and a conversion table T. B contains $\lceil \log_2(k) \rceil$ columns and as many rows as the tuples of the R relation. T contains k rows; the i-th row shows the binary coding chosen for the c_i value. The $B_{m,n}$ bit is set to 1 if the coding via T of the value of c in the m-th tuple of R has the n-th bit set to 1.

In other words, the T table defines a bijective function (*coding function*) between the c attribute domain and the domain of $\lceil \log_2(k) \rceil$-bit–long binary numbers.

Figure 11-10 shows the bitmap-encoded index on the `position` attribute in the EMPLOYEES table. The possible values are: 'Administrative', 'Assistant', 'Consultant', 'Manager', 'Programmer', and 'Technician'. Note that you need to use the conversion table to translate the values coded in the index. However, this additional step allows you to considerably reduce your index size, which shows only logarithmical growth with the number of distinct key values.

EMPLOYEES

...	position	...
...	Adm.	...
...	Prog.	...
...	Adm.	...
...	Tec.	...
...	Prog.	...
...	Ass.	...
...	Cons.	...
...	Cons.	...

B

B_2	B_1	B_0
0	0	0
1	0	0
0	0	0
1	0	1
1	0	0
0	0	1
0	1	0
0	1	0

T

value	coding
Adm.	0 0 0
Ass.	0 0 1
Cons.	0 1 0
Man.	0 1 1
Prog.	1 0 0
Tec.	1 0 1

Figure 11-10 Bitmap-encoded index and coding table for the `position` attribute of the EMPLOYEES relation

---

NOTE *Bit-sliced indexes are a specific case of bitmap-encoded indexes. In particular, a coding table of a bitmap-encoded index models the standard coding function of binary numbers and it can be omitted for this reason.*

Boolean operators can be applied to this index class, too, to perform selections efficiently. Any selection predicate on key values can be represented by a Boolean expression (*retrieval function*), which selects intervals of valid binary values. It is fundamental that you choose the appropriate coding function to increase the performance of your operations. This is because the opportunity to simplify retrieval functions, and then to reduce the number of bit vectors to be read, depends on that appropriate choice.

NOTE *A bitmap-encoded index coding function is well defined for a set of selection predicates if it minimizes the number of bit vectors to be accessed to check for the selection predicates.*

Figure 11-11 shows the coding table for a bitmap-encoded index built on the key attribute with the {a, b, c, d, e, f, g, h} domain. If you know that the {a, b, c, d} and the {c, d, e, f} value intervals are the most frequently selected ones, the coding on the left side of Figure 11-11 is well defined. This is because you need to access only a single bit vector to select the tuples belonging to the intervals previously mentioned. This means that the key$\in$ {a, b, c, d} and key$\in${c, d, e, f} predicates can be expressed respectively as follows:[3]

$$\bar{B}_2\bar{B}_1\bar{B}_0 \text{ OR } B_2\bar{B}_1\bar{B}_0 \text{ OR } \bar{B}_2\bar{B}_1B_0 \text{ OR } B_2\bar{B}_1B_0$$
$$\bar{B}_2\bar{B}_1B_0 \text{ OR } B_2\bar{B}_1B_0 \text{ OR } \bar{B}_2B_1B_0 \text{ OR } B_2B_1B_0$$

If we use general rules of Boolean algebra, they can be simplified and turned into $\bar{B}_1$ and B_0, respectively. In other words, the relation tuples belong to the {a, b, c, d} interval if their B_1 vector bit is 0, and they belong to the {c, d, e, f} interval if their B_0 vector bit is 1. On the contrary, the code on the right side of Figure 11-11 is not well defined for the previous

---

FIGURE 11-11
Codings for the key attribute with the {a, b, c, d, e, f, g, h} domain

value	coding $(B_2B_1B_0)$	value	coding $(B_2B_1B_0)$
a	0 0 0	a	0 0 0
c	0 0 1	b	0 0 1
g	0 1 0	c	0 1 0
e	0 1 1	d	0 1 1
b	1 0 0	g	1 0 0
d	1 0 1	h	1 0 1
h	1 1 0	e	1 1 0
f	1 1 1	f	1 1 1

---

[3]Boolean expressions operate on variables that can assume the values 1 and 0. Where it will not create ambiguity, we will denote the generic $B_{i,j}$ position bit through the name of the vector B_j to which it belongs. The symbol $\bar{B}_j$ will indicate the negation of B_j.

FIGURE 11-12
product→
type→category
hierarchy values
and coding table
for the bitmap-
encoded index on
`product`
optimizing
`category`
selections

category	type	product	value	coding $(B_2 B_1 B_0)$
Food	Soft drink	Coca Mola	Button up	1 0 0
Food	Cookies	Chockly	Chockly	0 0 1
Food	Cookies	Dippy	Classic	1 0 1
Clothes	Shirt	Button up	Coca Mola	0 1 0
Clothes	Shirt	Classic	Dippy	0 0 0
Clothes	Necktie	Imperial	Imperial	1 1 0

selection predicates because it needs to access all bit vectors as the retrieval functions respectively are as follows,

$$\bar{B_2}\bar{B_1} \text{ OR } \bar{B_2}B_0 \text{ OR } \bar{B_1}B_0$$
$$\bar{B_1}B_0 \text{ OR } B_2\bar{B_1} \text{ OR } B_2B_0$$

and they cannot be further simplified.

One of the most interesting ways to define a coding function is the one based on attribute hierarchies, which is particularly effective in supporting OLAP processing because the main OLAP operators are based on the functional dependencies between dimensional attributes in hierarchies. Look at Figure 11-12, which shows the data related to the `product→type→category` hierarchy. It is easy to check that the coding table related to the bitmap-encoded index built on the `product` attribute allows you to find the products belonging to a specific category after accessing just the B_2 vector. Likewise, you can single out the products belonging to a specific type if you access only two bit vectors (B_2 and B_1).

NOTE *The coding functions allow you to code both many-to-one and many-to-many associations in hierarchies.*

11.3 Projection Indexes

Projection Index
A *projection index* (O'Neil and Quass, 1997) on an attribute *c* with fixed-length values of a relation *R* consists of a structure storing a sequence of the *c* attribute values in *R* (keeping duplicates). The value order is the same as the order of the tuples in *R*.

The simple formulas shown next define the correspondence between the index and the tuples, because the values stored to the index have the same order as the value in the relation:

$$Pag = RID \text{ div } Cap$$
$$Offset = RID \bmod Cap$$
$$RID = Pag \cdot Cap + Offset$$

where *Cap* is the number of values that can be stored onto an index page, and *Pag* and *Offset* are the index page number and index page position where the key value of the tuple identified by the *RID* is stored, respectively.

CAUTION *If the key length is not fixed, the preceding formulas are not valid because the value of Cap is no longer unambiguously defined. To use projection indexes built on variable-length keys, you need to set the maximum length that key values can have and use this length as the index slot dimension. Obviously, this may dramatically affect performance.*

Projection indexes are based on one simple concept: reading a set of values from a small data structure is quicker than reading a large structure. The index size is the number of disk pages used and depends on the number of tuples *NR*, the key length *len(k)*, and the disk page size *D*:

$$\left\lceil \frac{NR}{\frac{D}{len(k)}} \right\rceil$$

The projection indexes can be used for two different kinds of access:

- **Retrieving key values**   If you know the RID of a tuple (for example, obtained by accessing a B⁺-Tree), you can retrieve the corresponding key value without accessing your relation. This type of access is obviously more efficient than accessing your relation when you need to retrieve a large number of key values, because it is very likely that many key values are retrieved from the same index page. Figure 11-13 shows a chart with the estimate—applying the Cardenas formula—for the number of pages to be read to retrieve the key values. This number varies according to the amount of distinct values to be retrieved. To calculate the estimate values of Figure 11-13, the index was supposed to be built on a 4-byte attribute of a relation with 1 million, 200-byte–long tuples. If you use 4-Kbyte blocks, you can store 1024 values onto each index page while each disk page can contain just 20 relation tuples. Note that the smaller the amount of data to retrieve, the less useful an access via index gets.

- **Selecting relation tuples**   If you know the key values to select, you can reduce the cost of accessing tuples by scanning the index and finding the RIDs meeting your selection predicate. This is the regular way to access data via an index and is also used by B⁺-Tree and bitmaps. Projection indexes can become more efficient than B⁺-Tree and bitmaps only when the amount of values to be retrieved and the number of distinct values per attribute are both large. When both conditions are fulfilled at the same time, the bitmap index size will be large because of the large number of distinct values, and the access via B⁺-Tree will be hardly suitable because of the large number of internal pages read when you descend the tree every time you need to retrieve a value.

The basic idea of projection indexes is quite similar to vertical fragmentation of relational tables (Özsu and Valduriez, 1991). However, projection indexes are still accessory structures,

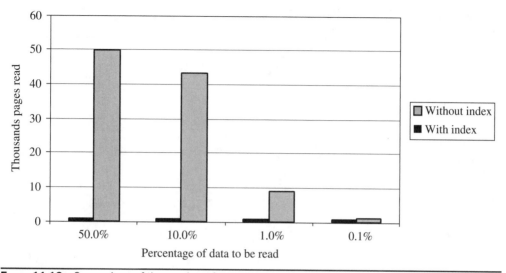

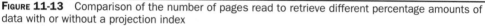

FIGURE 11-13   Comparison of the number of pages read to retrieve different percentage amounts of data with or without a projection index

so relational table data keeps on being stored separately. Furthermore, vertical fragmentation implies a replication of the relation primary key, which is not required in a projection index.

11.4 Join and Star Indexes

Even though star schemata explicitly aim at reducing the number of joins necessary to retrieve data, joins still mainly determine the cost of OLAP queries. Researchers have been working for a long time to reduce the join execution time. To do this, they have developed more efficient join algorithms, such as *hybrid hash join* (Graefe et al., 1994; Li and Ross, 1999), on the one hand, and they have studied ad hoc data structures on the other hand.

> **Join Index**
>
> A *join index* between two relations R_1 and R_2 stores couples of tuple RIDs that fulfill the c_1 *<operator>* c_2 join predicate between two attributes $c_1 \in R_1$ and $c_2 \in R_2$.

Join indexes (Valduriez, 1987) strongly improve performance because they preprocess and explicitly store RIDs of the matching tuples in two relations. To check for the tuples to fulfill your join predicate, you no longer need to check all the combinations, but you need to scan your index. Figure 11-14 shows the pseudo-code required to carry out a join between the R_1 and R_2 relations using the nested loop algorithm and a join index, respectively. Note that when the nested loop algorithm is used, (i) the R_1 tuples, which are not involved in the join, are also read, and (ii) the tuples of the R_2 internal relation are read as many times as the number of R_1 tuples. Normally, join indexes are used together with a B+-Tree to prevent the indexes from being completely scanned when there are extra selection predicates that reduce the number of RIDs to be accessed.

FIGURE 11-14   Pseudo-code joining the R_1 and R_2 relations via a nested loop algorithm (top) and a join index (bottom); OP is the join operator.

```
// Nested loop-based join
open R₁;
while not EndOfFile(R₁)
{   tuple₁=read(R₁);
    open R₂;
    while not EndOfFile(R₂)
    {   tuple₂=read(R₂);
        if (tuple₁.c₁ OP tuple₂.c₂) then
            return tuple₁+tuple₂;
        next R₂;
    }
    close R₂;
    next R₁;
}
close R₁.
//
// Join index-based join
open R₁;
open R₂;
open JI₁₂;
while not EndOfFile(JI₁₂)
{   couple=read(JI₁₂);
    tuple₁=read(R₁, couple[1]);
    tuple₂=read(R₂, couple[2]);
    return tuple₁+tuple₂;
    next JI₁₂;
}
close R₁;
close R₂;
close JI₁₂.
```

Figure 11-15 shows the SALES and STORE relation join index fulfilling the SALES.keyS=STORE.keyS join predicate. Each row of that index singles out a pair of joined tuples of both relations. For example, the first row shows that the tuple with RID 1 in the STORE table joins the tuple with RID 1 in the SALES table. To carry out a complete equi-join between both tables, you need to scan the index and retrieve the corresponding tuple pairs. If you have any additional selection predicates for dimension table attributes, such as store='EverMore', you can avoid scanning the entire index by first singling out the dimension table RIDs that fulfill your predicate, and then accessing the index via the B⁺-Tree.

Join indexes were created before data warehouses. However, their use has always been severely reduced due to the expansive update costs of this index type in the scope of operational databases. Every time you add a new tuple to one of the tables involved in a join, you have to update your join index by finding all the tuples that fulfill the join predicate. This may entail executing the join every time you enter new data. For this reason, you can hardly justify it in operational databases. However, it is very suitable for data warehouse systems, where data are periodically updated offline.

FIGURE 11-15
The join index based on the SALES.keyS= STORE.keyS predicate

SALES

RID	keyS	keyD	keyP	quantity	receipts	...
1	1	1	1	170	1,500	...
2	2	1	2	320	3,470	...
3	3	2	3	412	5,215	...
4	2	2	1	230	3,740	...
5	1	2	1	90	875	...
...	...	...	...	...	...	...

STORE

RID	keyS	store	city	state	...
1	1	EverMore	Columbus	Ohio	...
2	2	ProFit	Austin	Texas	...
3	3	EvenMore	Austin	Texas	...
...	...	...	...	...	...

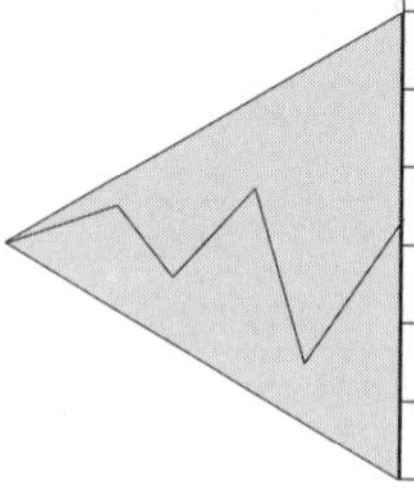

storeRID	salesRID
1	1
1	5
2	2
2	4
3	3
...	...

NOTE *A join index in a star schema normally connects a dimension table primary key to the corresponding foreign key in the fact table to speed up all queries involving the hierarchy modeled by that dimension table.*

11.4.1 Multi-join Indexes

OLAP queries normally involve more dimension tables and need more join operations linking each tuple in a fact table with the corresponding tuples in dimension tables (*star join query*). This resulted in the creation of *star join indexes*, which stretch join indexes to multi-table joins by connecting sets of RIDs belonging to different tables.

Star Join Index

A *star join index* between a fact table *FT* and *n* dimension tables $DT_1, \ldots DT_n$ stores a set of tuples consisting of $n + 1$ RIDs from the fact table and the *n* dimension tables. Those tuples store the RID combinations that fulfill the *n* join predicates $d_i = ft_i$, where d_i and ft_i are respectively the primary key of the *i*-th dimension table and the corresponding foreign key in the fact table.

Figure 11-16 shows a star join index on the star schema of Figure 8-3. For example, the third row of that index shows that the third tuple of the SALES fact table corresponds to the EvenMore store, the 10/3/2008 date, and the Slurp Yogurt product.

SALES

RID	keyS	keyD	keyP	quantity	receipts	...
1	1	1	1	170	1,500	...
2	2	1	2	320	3,470	...
3	3	2	3	412	5,215	...
4	2	2	1	230	3,740	...
5	1	2	1	90	875	...
...	...	...	...	...	...	...

STORE

RID	keyS	store	city	state	...
1	1	EverMore	Columbus	Ohio	...
2	2	ProFit	Austin	Texas	...
3	3	EvenMore	Austin	Texas	...
...	...	...	...	...	...

PRODUCT

RID	keyP	product	type	category	brand	...
1	1	Slurp Milk	Dairy products	Food	Slurp	...
2	2	Yum Milk	Dairy products	Food	Yum	...
3	3	Slurp Yogurt	Dairy products	Food	Slurp	...
...	...	...	...	...	...	...

DATE

RID	keyD	date	month	year	...
1	1	9/2/2008	9/2008	2008	...
2	2	10/3/2008	10/2008	2008	...
3	3	10/5/2008	10/2008	2008	...
...	...	...	...	...	...

salesRID	storeRID	productRID	dateRID
1	1	1	1
2	2	2	1
3	3	3	2
4	2	1	2
5	1	1	2
...	...	...	...

FIGURE 11-16 The star join index on the star schema of Figure 8.3.

Star join indexes explicitly show multidimensional features of data. They are very efficient when queries involve all index columns or only the first index columns. Otherwise, performance may be poor; in particular, index access time strongly depends on the order of columns. For that reason, the number of star join indexes required to answer queries involving an arbitrary set of dimensions in an efficient manner is a function of the number of permutations of the set of dimensions, which grows exponentially with the number of dimensions.

If you use O'Neil and Graefe's so-called *bitmapped join index*, which is currently the most advanced solution to carry out multi-table joins, you can bridge the gap of the reduced flexibility of star join indexes.

Bitmapped Join Index

A *bitmapped join index* built on the attributes c_R of a relation R and c_S of a relation S is a bit matrix B with as many rows as the tuples of R and as many columns as the tuples of S. The $B_{i,j}$ bit is set to 1 if the i-th tuple of the R relation and the j-th row of the S relation fulfill the join predicate.

In other words, the B matrix is a bitmap index built on the R relation based on the RIDs of S; the join predicate sets the correspondence between both relations. Figure 11-17 still makes reference to the SALES cube of Figure 8-3 and shows the bitmapped join index built on the SALES.keyS=STORE.keyS predicate. That index shows that tuple 4 in the fact table is joined to tuple 2 of the dimension table, or equally that tuple 2 in the dimension table is joined to tuples 2 and 4 in the fact table. To carry out the join between both tables, you need to read through the rows of your index and single out the columns whose value is 1. If any additional selection predicates reduce the number of RIDs to be used, you can narrow down your index search by loading only the bit vectors corresponding to the values that fulfill such predicates.

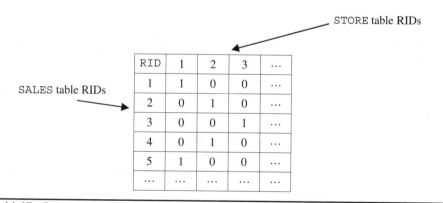

STORE table RIDs

SALES table RIDs

RID	1	2	3	...
1	1	0	0	...
2	0	1	0	...
3	0	0	1	...
4	0	1	0	...
5	1	0	0	...
...	...	...	...	...

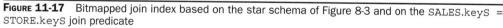

FIGURE 11-17 Bitmapped join index based on the star schema of Figure 8-3 and on the SALES.keyS = STORE.keyS join predicate

Even if a bitmapped join index joins two tables, you can also use it to execute queries with multiple joins. Figure 11-18 shows an example of this type of query, which joins the FT fact table and the $DT_1,...DT_n$ dimension tables. If you had a bitmapped join index for every join predicate ($FT.a_i=DT_i.a_i$) and a bitmap index for every dimensional attribute ($DT_i.b_i$) involved, the execution plan for this query could be as follows (see Figure 11-19):

1. Access the bitmap indexes to single out the RIDs that fulfill the predicates on dimensional attributes in every dimension table.

2. For every bitmapped join index, load only the bit vectors corresponding to the RIDs previously identified. If you perform a bitwise OR operation, you can obtain the RID_i vector which fulfills all the predicates on a dimension table.

3. Perform a bitwise AND operation between the n vectors previously created to select the fact table tuples fulfilling your query.

FIGURE 11-18 A star join query accessing the FT fact table and the $DT_1,...DT_n$ dimension tables; in addition to the join predicate is a set of additional predicates on dimension table attributes.

```
SELECT DISTINCT FT.m, DT₁.a₁, DT₂.a₂ ,... DTₙ.aₙ
WHERE FT.a₁=DT₁.a₁ AND
      FT.a₂=DT₂.a₂ AND ...
      FT.aₙ=DTₙ.aₙ AND
      DT₁.b₁='val₁' AND
      DT₂.b₂='val₂' AND ...
      DTₙ.bₙ='valₙ'
```

The preceding execution sequence is conceptually similar to the one to be followed for a star join index. However, the number of star joins necessary to solve queries efficiently grows exponentially with the number of dimension tables. On the contrary, the number of bitmapped join indexes grows linearly because the powerset of the predicates is obtained by applying the AND operator to the bit vectors.

The size of a bitmapped join index can be large because it depends on the number of tuples in both relations R and S involved. If you store a bit vector for each RID in relation S, you can calculate your index size in disk pages as follows:

$$\left\lceil \frac{NR_R}{D \cdot 8} \right\rceil \cdot NR_S$$

Bitmapped join indexes in star schemata are normally created between dimension table primary keys and the corresponding fact table foreign keys.

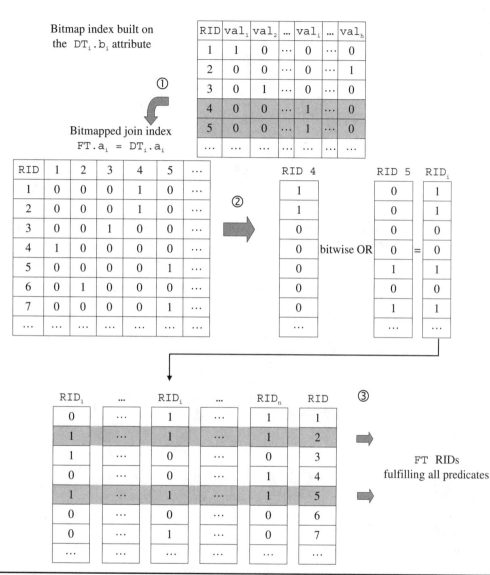

FIGURE 11-19   Execution plan of the star join query of Figure 11-18. Repeat steps 1 and 2 for each dimension table involved in the join. The `RID`$_i$ vector includes the `FT` RIDs fulfilling the predicate on the `DT`$_i$.`b`$_i$ attribute.

11.5 Spatial Indexes

Indexing techniques used in spatial databases are particularly suitable for multidimensional data to be indexed. Those techniques are optimized for queries based on selections operating on multidimensional intervals, that are also very common in OLAP applications. In particular, OLAP applications often analyze specific portions of data cubes, defined by specifying a set of selection intervals based on different analysis dimensions.

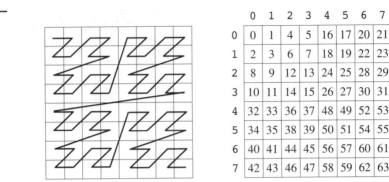

FIGURE 11-20
Z-curve and
Z-addresses of
a bidimensional
space

	0	1	2	3	4	5	6	7
0	0	1	4	5	16	17	20	21
1	2	3	6	7	18	19	22	23
2	8	9	12	13	24	25	28	29
3	10	11	14	15	26	27	30	31
4	32	33	36	37	48	49	52	53
5	34	35	38	39	50	51	54	55
6	40	41	44	45	56	57	60	61
7	42	43	46	47	58	59	62	63

Some authors have suggested the adoption of ad hoc indexing structures for this kind of query, such as the *R-Tree* (Guttman, 1984) or the *Quad-Tree* (Finkel and Bentley, 1974), which have never been completely integrated into commercial DBMSs. *UB-Trees* (*Universal B-Trees*) by Bayer, the same inventor of B-Trees, are one of the most innovative ideas. UB-Trees, integrated into the commercial DBMS Transbase (Markl et al., 2001), are based on the use of a space-filling curve (*Z-curve*) that allows us to partition multidimensional space in such a way as to partially preserve the spatial contiguity of elements. A space element has a *Z-address* that corresponds to its position along a Z-curve. To calculate it, *bit-interleaving* techniques can be used (Orenstein and Merret, 1984). The UB-Tree is just a B^+-Tree built on Z-addresses; RIDs are stored into leaf nodes. Figure 11-20 shows the Z-curve of a bidimensional space. As you can see, Z-addresses preserve spatial contiguity.

To take any sparsity of multidimensional data properly into account, the space is divided into *Z-regions* defined by a couple of Z addresses. Z-region sizes can vary so that the data they include can always be stored into a single disk page. Figure 11-21 shows a bidimensional

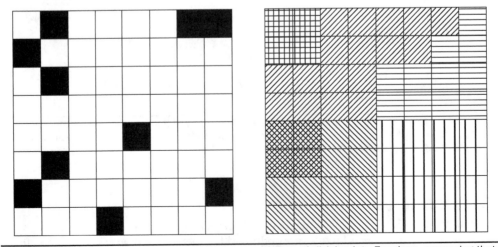

FIGURE 11-21   A bidimensional space and the corresponding subdivision into Z-regions, supposing that a page can host up to two RIDs

space where only black cells actually contain RIDs on the left side, and the subdivisions into Z-regions supposing that each disk page can contain two RIDs on the right side.

To take full advantage of UB-Trees in relational applications, a few implementation tricks to reduce the number of disk pages read are used. Specifically, the OLAP queries make selections from dimension tables and joins between dimension tables and fact tables. You can dramatically reduce these costs when

- the number of pages read is as close as possible to the actual number of pages including relevant data;
- the join operations take benefit from the page retrieval order. A good retrieval order exactly coincides with the order of tuples in a dimension table.

You can reach both of these goals if you use UB-Trees in combination with the so-called *Tetris* algorithm (Markl et al., 1999). The Tetris algorithm orderly retrieves the pages within a range of Z-addresses $[\alpha, \beta]$ according to one of the attributes A_i that defines the multidimensional space. That algorithm identifies all the Z-regions overlapping the range $[\alpha, \beta]$ and returns the Z-addresses ordered by the A_i values instead of the Z-curve. Figure 11-22 shows a range query accessing a bidimensional domain defined by the A_1, A_2 attributes. The set of data to retrieve is marked with the gray area overlapping four Z-regions (marked with different types of dashes). If your cache memory is large enough to support this process, the Tetris algorithm can follow the retrieval order defined by the A_1 attribute values (marked with arrows on the left side of the figure) even if it reads those regions in the order shown on the right side. Note that the Tetris algorithm could also be used in combination with other types of spatial indexes.

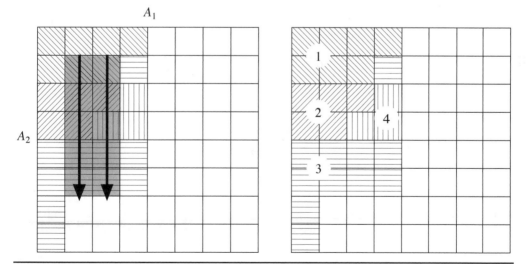

Figure 11-22   Output order (left side) and reading order (right side) of Z-regions

11.6 Join Algorithms

To conclude this chapter, we believe it is useful to introduce the most common join algorithms used by the commercial DBMSs (Elmasri and Navate, 2006; Atzeni et al., 1999) to give you a complete overview of those techniques designed to speed up query execution. Selecting the algorithm that best suits the properties of a query is deeply influenced by the available set of indexes, and plays a basic role in defining your system performance.

11.6.1   Nested Loop

Nested loop is the simplest join algorithm and directly stems from the definition of the join operator. Let R and S be two relations, F_R and F_S be local predicates respectively on R and S, and F_J be the join predicate. One of these relations is defined as *external*, say R, and the other as *internal*, say S. The nested loop algorithm finds all the S internal relation tuples fulfilling F_S and the join predicate for every R external relation tuple fulfilling F_R. The tuples in each resulting pair are then concatenated to form a tuple to be returned. Figure 11-23 shows the pseudo-code of this algorithm.

FIGURE 11-23   Pseudo-code of the nested loop algorithm

```
open R;
while not EndOfFile(R)
{  Rtuple=read(R);
   if (F_R(Rtuple)) then
   // Rtuple satisfies the local predicate
   {  open S;
      while not EndOfFile(S)
      {  Stuple=read(S);
         if (F_s(Stuple) and F_J(Rtuple, Stuple)) then
            return Rtuple + Stuple;
      }
      next S;
      close S;
   }
   next R;
}
close R;
```

The algorithm execution cost in number of disk pages read is equal to

$$cost(R) + ET_R \times cost(S)$$

where $cost(R)$ and $cost(S)$ measure the cost to access the relations and can vary if any index is built on the attributes. ET_R is the expected number of tuples in R that fulfill the F_R local predicate.

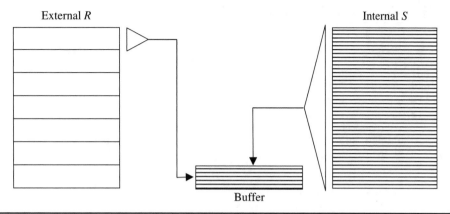

External *R*   Internal *S*

Buffer

FIGURE 11-24   Buffer management when executing a nested block algorithm

Under the easiest conditions, there is no local predicate and the relations can be accessed by sequential scan; the execution cost will then be as follows,

$$NP_R + NT_R \times NP_S$$

where NP_R and NP_S are the number of disk pages necessary to store *R* and *S*, respectively, and NT_R is the number of tuples in *R*.

The *nested block* is an advanced version of nested loop based on the same execution principle. This algorithm has a buffer of *B* pages stored to central memory to reduce the times the *S* internal relation is scanned. Figure 11-24 shows that *S* is scanned for every group of *B*–1 pages of the *R* external relation, which are loaded to memory. In this way, if there is no local predicate, the join execution cost in terms of disk pages read becomes

$$NP_R + \left\lceil \frac{NP_R}{B-1} \right\rceil \times NP_S$$

The cost of the nested block is lower than the cost of the nested loop (because $NP_R < NT_R$), and it is inversely proportional to the buffer size.

11.6.2   Sort-merge

Sort-merge exploits the tuple ordering by the join attribute to reduce the number of tuple comparisons. Both relations involved must be previously ordered by the join attribute so that they can be scanned in parallel to search for an individual value in tuple couples. Figure 11-25 shows the pseudo-code of the sort-merge algorithm in case of an equi-join on the *j* attribute and if the tables have no duplicate values.

FIGURE 11-25   Pseudo-code of the sort-merge algorithm

```
sort R by c_R;
sort S by c_S;
Rtuple=read(R);
Stuple=read(S);
while not EndOfFile(R) and not EndOfFile (S)
    if (Rtuple.j=Stuple.j) then
    {   return Rtuple+Stuple;
        Rtuple=read(R); next R;
        Stuple=read(S); next S;
    }
    else
        if (Rtuple.j>Stuple.j) then
        {  Stuple=read(S);  next S;  }
        else
        {  Rtuple=read(R);  next R;  }
next;
close R;
close S.
```

From the processing viewpoint, the advantage of using the sort-merge algorithm instead of nested loop is clear because sort-merge scans both relations involved only once. However, if relations are not ordered, you must also include the ordering cost.

CAUTION *If the join attributes are indexed, for example with a B+-Tree, sort-merge can be applied without ordering the relations, because B+-Tree leaf nodes always store RIDs in an ordered way, so that ordered access to tuples can be obtained by scanning all the leaf nodes. However, if both indexes are unclustered, the total cost can be high.*

11.6.3   Hash Join

If you take advantage of the properties of *hash* functions, you can reduce the number of comparisons to make to perform a join operation without first ordering your relations. If there are two relations, R and S, to be equi-joined on the c_R and c_S attributes, an h hash function can be applied to the key values of R (*build relation*) to partition the c_R domain values into B buckets. If the same h function is applied to the values of c_S, S (*probe relation*) will be similarly partitioned, and then the join operation will be performed by comparing only the tuples of corresponding partitions with each other. If key values show a uniform distribution across tuples, each partition will contain a B-th part of the relation tuples.

The correspondence between tuples and partitions is stored into an appropriate data structure (*hash table*). Hash tables store the tuple RIDs and the values of the join attribute for every bucket. Figure 11-26 shows an example: The hash table is initialized with the values of c_R, and then the probe relation tuples are compared with those of the buckets whose numbers are the result of the h function applied to the values of c_S.

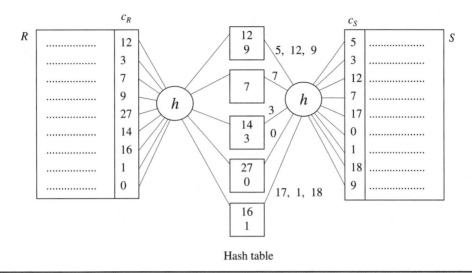

Hash table

FIGURE 11-26   Operating schema of the hash join algorithm

The hash table cannot be permanently stored to main memory because of its size. To solve this problem, some algorithms, in particular the *hybrid hash join* (Patel et al., 1994), use two different hash functions (h_1 and h_2): the first one partitions the relations into B_1 smaller fragments so that the hash tables created by the h_2 function can be stored to main memory. When this technique is used, the join process can be summed up as follows:

- *Step 1 (build)*   Read the R build relation and apply any local predicates to tuples. Apply the h_1 function to the selected tuples. If the value of c_R for the current tuple is associated with the first of the B_1 buckets, this tuple is kept in memory and the h_2 function is directly applied to c_R to create a hash table in main memory. Otherwise, the tuple is saved to one of the B_1-1 files in your disk on the basis of the h_1 function.

- *Step 1 (probe)*   Read the S probe relation and apply any local predicates to tuples. Apply the h_1 function to the selected tuples. If the value of c_S for the current tuple is associated with the first of the B_1 buckets, this tuple is kept in memory and the h_2 function is directly applied to c_S to identify a hash table bucket in main memory; then the current tuple of S is compared with all the tuples of R in that bucket. If the current value of c_S is not associated with the first bucket, the tuple is saved to one of the B_1-1 files in your disk on the basis of the h_1 function.

NOTE   *At the end of step 1, the result of joining the tuples inserted by the h_1 function into the first bucket is available, and the remaining tuples are partitioned into B_1-1 separate files.*

- *Step i = 2... B_1 (build)*   The *i*-th file of the *R* build relation is loaded to main memory and the h_2 function creates a hash table.

- *Step i = 2... B_1 (probe)*   The *i*-th file of the *S* probe relation is loaded to main memory and the h_2 hash function is applied to the values of c_S to find the bucket to be used to make comparisons.

Figure 11-27 shows step 1: Each tuple is either kept in main memory or temporarily stored to disk according to the bucket into which it falls.

TIP   *To reduce join execution costs, you should choose the relation with the lowest cardinality as the build relation.*

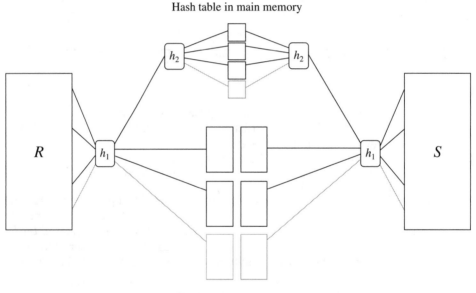

Hash table in main memory

Files in secondary memory

FIGURE 11-27   Operating schema of step 1 of the hybrid hash join algorithm

12 CHAPTER

Physical Design

Physical design implements the choices made in the previous design phases and gives data mart schemata their final shape. The term "final shape" is actually misleading because both the logical and physical structures of a data mart are constantly evolving to meet the needs that become obvious as soon as a system is up and running and the ever-changing needs of users.

In general, the best results are achieved when the logical design phase and the physical design phase are executed together, because they are closely interdependent. For example, materializing a view or creating a fact table index are two competing alternatives whose common goal is to improve system performance. However, we'd rather handle these tasks separately because of their complexity, bearing in mind that this results in less than optimum performance, something that must be compensated for by subsequent adjustments. Figure 12-1 shows a summary schema for the operations to be performed in both phases. In contrast to other authors, we prefer to include the horizontal and vertical fragmentation operations in logical design. This is because we maintain that the term "physical design" should include only those operations linked to specific features of the DBMSs, such as choices of indexes and adjustment of allocation strategies.

The strong correlation between the features of the DBMS used to implement a data mart and the choices linked to physical design makes it impossible to define a set of universally applicable design rules. In this chapter, we highlight only the critical points of this design phase and provide a set of generally valid guidelines. However, it must be emphasized that the experience of the designer and database administrator remains the crucial factor in achieving good results.

12.1 Optimizers

Physical design is built on knowledge of the particular features of the DBMS used for implementation. At the heart of this is the *optimizer*, the module set up to evaluate and compare query execution plans.

> **Query Execution Plan**
> The *execution plan* for a query is the sequence of operations performed by a DBMS to answer that query at the physical level. Each step in the execution plan sets out the tables, the accessory structures, and the algorithms to be used.

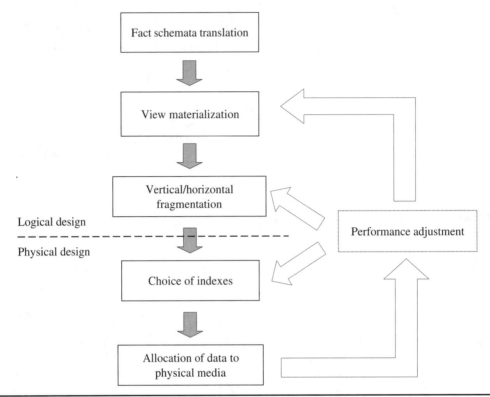

Figure 12-1 General functional schema for the logical and physical design phases. The dotted box marks a cyclic optimization process to be carried out once the system is online.

Just as in online transactional processing (OLTP) applications, query execution plans for data warehouse systems depend on three factors: the optimizer features, the types of indexes the DBMS makes available, and the logical data schema. In contrast to OLTP, the wide range of indexes used for data warehouses increases the number of possible plans on the one hand, but very strict logical schemata result in a reduction of possible plans on the other hand. With a few rare exceptions, the only logical schema used in relational online analytical processing (ROLAP) systems is the star schema—or one of its derivatives—consisting of a fact table, whose primary key consists of the foreign keys referencing one or more dimension tables. This type of organization produces remarkable constraints on the set of reasonable execution plans, and simplifies the designer's range of options. For example, an execution plan requiring a join between two dimension tables would be difficult to justify logically because it would entail a Cartesian product of the tuples of both relations.

Tip *Designers must know the answer to these questions: What type of indexes are available in your DBMS? What indexes can be used simultaneously? What rules govern the operation of your optimizer? If neither designers nor technical staff of a company are able to determine the strategies followed by the optimizer of the DBMS used for data mart implementation, time and resources must be directed to fill this gap.*

In-depth knowledge of DBMSs should be one of the company's internal assets, but if external consultants are used, it is essential that you check that they have all the specific knowledge and skills needed for data warehousing. Any consultants who have experience only in OLTP systems would find it difficult to identify critical points and optimum strategies for OLAP queries accessing denormalized schemata.

Optimization process features and the expected types of query execution plan have a strong influence on the usefulness of the indexes. Creating indexes that support plans not used by optimizers is clearly of no benefit. We will demonstrate this point with a simple example. Figure 12-2 shows a fact schema for purchase orders, together with the corresponding star schema, derived from the TPC-H benchmark—a standard for evaluating data warehouse performance (Poess and Floyd, 2000). Each tuple of the LINE_ITEMS fact table corresponds to a product order provided by a supplier and sent to the customer on a certain date. Let us assume that the following indexes have been created: an index on each of the primary keys in dimension tables, an index on the date attribute of the DATE dimension table, and an index on the primary key of the LINE_ITEMS fact table in which foreign keys are sequenced as (keyO, keyP, keyS, keyD, keyMSR). Now consider Figure 12-3, which shows the star schema SQL query formulated as a dimensional expression here:

```
LINE ITEM[product, state, date;
    date='1/1/2008'].quantity
```

FIGURE 12-2   Fact schema and star schema for line items

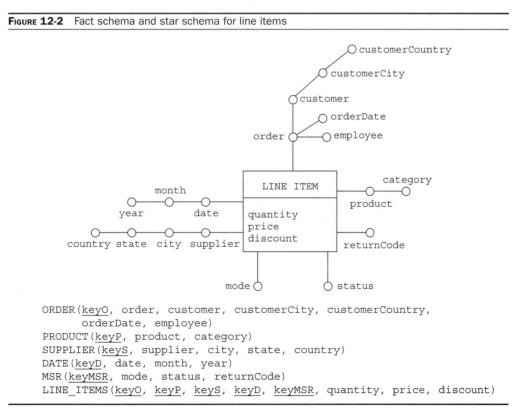

```
ORDER(keyO, order, customer, customerCity, customerCountry,
      orderDate, employee)
PRODUCT(keyP, product, category)
SUPPLIER(keyS, supplier, city, state, country)
DATE(keyD, date, month, year)
MSR(keyMSR, mode, status, returnCode)
LINE_ITEMS(keyO, keyP, keyS, keyD, keyMSR, quantity, price, discount)
```

FIGURE **12-3**   An OLAP query on the line item schema

```
SELECT    SUM(FT.quantity), DT1.product, DT2.state, DT3.date
FROM      LINE_ITEMS AS FT, PRODUCT AS DT1,
          SUPPLIER AS DT2, DATE AS DT3
WHERE     FT.keyP = DT1.keyP AND
          FT.keyS = DT2.keyS AND
          FT.keyD = DT3.keyD AND
          DT3.date = '1/1/2008,
GROUP BY DT1.product, DT2.state, DT3.date
```

Figure 12-4 shows an execution plan for this query. Each box contains an operation performed as the query is being executed. If the box shows the name of a table, this means it is scanned sequentially. IX($R.a$) marks an access to an index on the a attribute of the R table. This plan first accesses the index on the dimension table in which the condition is expressed. The single tuple selected is joined with the fact table tuples, and then with the other dimension tables in sequence. It is immediately clear that the index created for the primary key of the fact table cannot be used because the keyD attribute does not appear in the first position. For this reason, the fact table must be scanned sequentially at high costs.

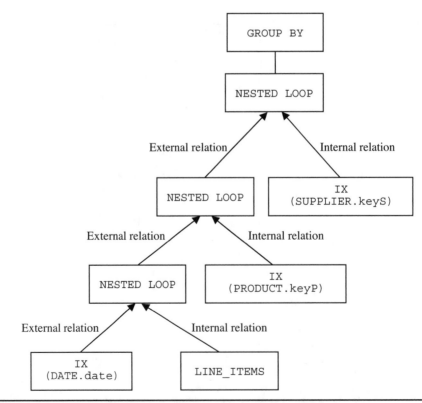

FIGURE **12-4**   A possible execution plan for the query shown in Figure 12-3

Now let's look at the alternative execution plan shown in Figure 12-5. To reduce the number of tuples involved in the joins, the GROUP BY operation is performed in a number of stages. First, the data is grouped by `keyP`, `keyS`, `keyD`, and then it is sorted by `state`. This operation is known as the GROUP BY *push-down* (Yan and Larson, 1995). This new plan may be more efficient than the preceding one if the additional cost for ordering the tuples— a necessary process to perform the GROUP BY operation—is compensated for by the lower cost of executing the joins with smaller tables. The push-down operation changes the cardinality of the tables involved in the second join and forces the optimizer to choose the hash join algorithm. This makes it impossible to use the index on the `PRODUCT` primary key, `keyP`. For this reason, if designers know whether or not the DBMS optimizer allows GROUP BY push-down, they are able to choose their indexes more effectively.

The examples shown demonstrate that it is necessary to have a full understanding of the optimization logic to select indexes effectively. Unfortunately, many DBMS producers provide very little information about this, and optimizer operations are frequently so

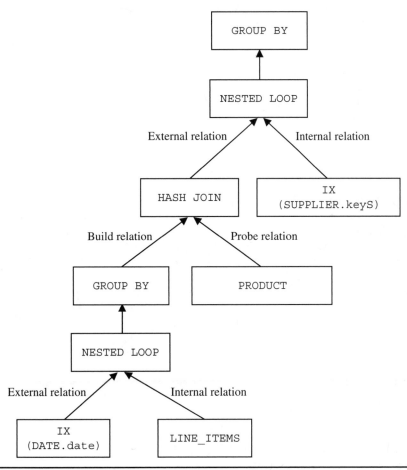

Figure 12-5   Alternative execution plan to the one shown in Figure 12-4

complex that even the most qualified database administrators do not completely understand them. The best advice we can give is to proceed step by step. First, examine DBMS user manuals carefully and any other documentation provided by manufacturers to understand basic optimizer operation. For example, carefully study whether more than one index can be used simultaneously in the same table. If the information provided is vague or imprecise, we suggest you use a *black-box analysis*. This type of analysis examines the execution plans generated in response to a precise set of test queries to define logical core processes for optimizer operation. Once your data mart is up and running, you can progressively fine-tune your system. To do this, analyze the execution plans generated by the actual workload and apply any required changes to the original index schema.

12.1.1   Rule-based Optimizers

> **Rule-based Optimizers**
>
> Query execution plans for *rule-based optimizers* are defined by sets of rules that take into account data structure, query structure, and indexes available *without* using any of the statistical profile information on data.

In other words, the optimization process is entirely based on logical-physical schemata of the database without regard to any instance-specific information. This means that the query execution plan generated will always be the same, regardless of, for example, table cardinality and attribute value distribution. This obviously is a limitation because considering instance-specific information could lead to a considerable reduction in execution costs. For example, consider the following query based on the line item schema of Figure 12-2:

```
LINE ITEM[city, date;
     city='Dayton' AND date='1/1/2008'].quantity
```

Figure 12-6 shows the SQL code for this query. The effectiveness of both execution plans shown in Figure 12-7 for this query depends on the cardinality of the dimension tables and on the selectivity of both predicates. If the number of tuples selected from the SUPPLIER table is lower than the number of tuples selected from the DATE table, the plan in the lower part of the figure will be more efficient. If this is not the case, the opposite will apply. This is because it is normally more efficient to anticipate the most restrictive selections because they reduce the number of tuples in the following joins. Rule-based optimizers do not take into account these factors. For a rule-based optimizer, both plans are equivalent.

FIGURE 12-6   An OLAP query on the line item schema

```
SELECT    SUM(FT.quantity), DT1.city, DT2.date
FROM      LINE_ITEMS AS FT, SUPPLIER AS DT1,
          DATE AS DT2
WHERE     FT.keyS = DT1.keyS AND
          FT.keyD = DT2.keyD AND
          DT1.city = 'Dayton' AND
          DT2.date = '1/1/2008'
GROUP BY DT1.city, DT2.date
```

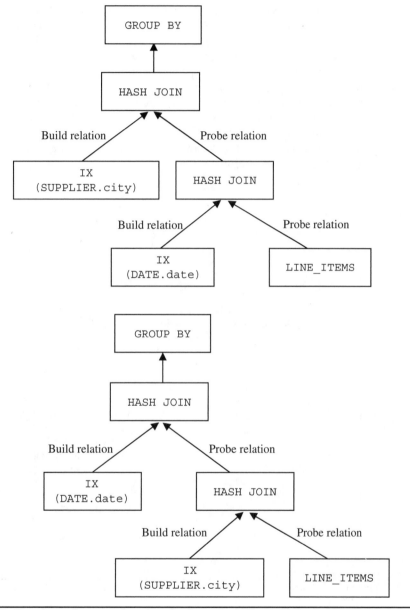

FIGURE 12-7   Two alternative execution plans for the query in Figure 12-6

The strength of rule-based optimizers is that the optimization speed for complex queries can offset poor performance solutions. Moreover, rule-based optimizers do not need statistics to be recalculated and stored to disk regularly, which may use significant space and time. Their weakness is that their failure to take statistical profiles into account may lead to unexpected results. For example, even if one of the attribute conditions is relatively unselective, an index on that attribute may still be used and lead to significantly higher costs than the costs of simple sequential scanning.

Figures 12-8 and 12-9 show part of the optimization algorithm used by the IBM Red Brick Decision Server 6.0 DBMS. The flowchart is the result of a black-box analysis of that system. For this reason, it should be considered only as a reference example, because this type of analysis may well produce incomplete and imprecise results, as we mentioned previously. In particular, the algorithm of Figure 12-9 does not take into account the existence of an appropriate star index.[1] On the contrary, a star index can be very useful to decrease query execution costs. Figure 12-10 shows the execution plan for the query of Figure 12-3 when you apply this algorithm.

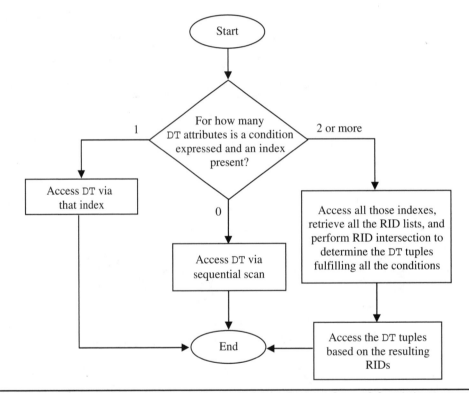

Figure 12-8   Schema for the algorithm used by the Red Brick Decision Server 6.0 optimizer to access the DT dimension table

---

[1]Remember that star indexes are designed to support joins if the attributes involved in joins are in the first index positions. See section 11.4.1 for more details.

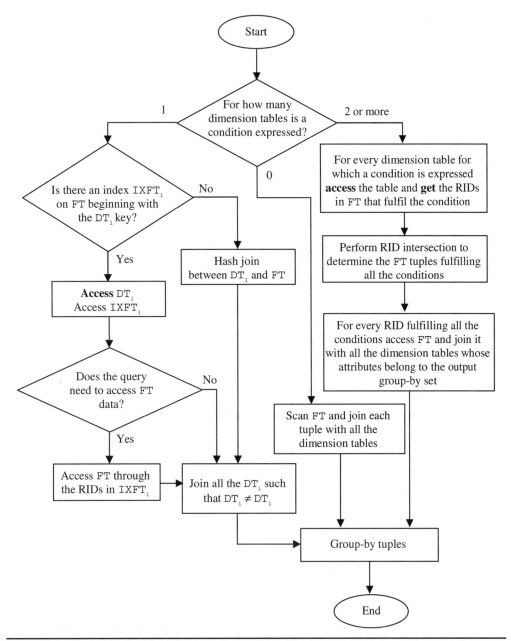

FIGURE 12-9 Part of the Red Brick Decision Server 6.0 optimizing algorithm: the words in boldface indicate operations that require further optimizer choices.

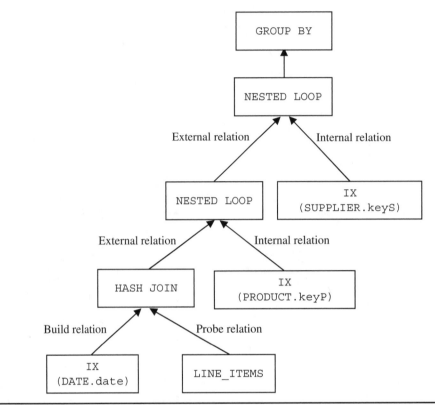

Figure 12-10   An execution plan for the query of Figure 12-3

As soon as designers gain insight into an optimization process, such as the one expressed in Figures 12-8 and 12-9, they will have helpful information at hand to define their physical schemata—for example:

- If a DBMS can use multiple indexes simultaneously, designers can create a wide range of indexes on the dimensional attributes.

- If a DBMS broadly uses indexes on foreign keys of fact tables, designers can create not only indexes on primary keys, but also indexes on individual attributes that make up primary keys.

- If a DBMS always uses indexes built on attributes for which selection conditions are expressed, and if a recurrent condition on an attribute is relatively unselective, it is better not to create any index on that attribute because it will probably be more costly than simply scanning tables.

Note *Rule-based optimization processes do not depend on specific database instance features. This point makes it easier to define a physical schema for a DBMS that uses a rule-based optimizer.*

12.1.2   Cost-based Optimizers

> **Cost-based Optimizers**
> Functions that take into account instance-specific features of databases being queried are necessary to evaluate execution plans in *cost-based* optimizers. The statistical information used is stored to appropriate *catalogues*. For example, this information is about cardinality of tables, cardinality of attribute domains, and distribution of attribute values.

It is theoretically likely that this type of optimizer delivers more accurate solutions than rule-based optimizers. However, we would like to emphasize that the plans chosen by a cost-based optimizer may also result in inefficient solutions if the statistical data stored or the cost functions used are not sufficiently detailed and up-to-date.

The ability of a DBMS to calculate accurate statistics on the basis of data distribution is increasing all the time. The amount of research that has gone into this has already produced much more highly evolved cost-based optimizers, together with significant improvements in the cost functions they use. The basic information stored is minimum value (*minval*), maximum value (*maxval*), and the number of distinct values (*nval*) assigned to each attribute in each relation (Selinger et al., 1979). This information forms the basis of selectivity estimates for the following type of predicates: *<attribute><oprel><value>* (where *<oprel>*∈ {=, >, <, ≥, ≤}). Selectivity estimates can be calculated like this:

$$Sel(= x) = \frac{1}{nval}$$

$$Sel(< x) = Sel(\leq x) = \frac{x - minval}{maxval - minval}$$

$$Sel(> x) = Sel(\geq x) = \frac{maxval - x}{maxval - minval}$$

These formulae are obtained by assuming that the attribute values are uniformly distributed in the [*minval, maxval*] interval. When this distribution is not uniform, as is often the case, those formulae can be highly approximate. The introduction of *histograms* has been one of the major leaps forward in estimating the costs of executing queries. Histograms provide a simple representation of actual value distribution for relation attributes of a specific database instance. See section 12.1.3 for more details on this technique; now we will simply show how statistical profiles can affect execution plans.

Consider again the query shown in Figure 12-3. The execution plan of Figure 12-11 is generated by the cost-based optimizer in the Oracle 8*i* DBMS.[2] It assumes that a B⁺-Tree index is available for the date attribute in addition to the primary indexes for tables.

---

[2] We opted for the 8*i* version because the cost functions used by the optimizer are increasingly sophisticated in later versions. In this way, the execution plans are increasingly complex and make it difficult to show any behavioral examples. In real-world applications, the higher the sophistication level of optimizer logic patterns, the closer the dependency of execution plans on specific database instance features.

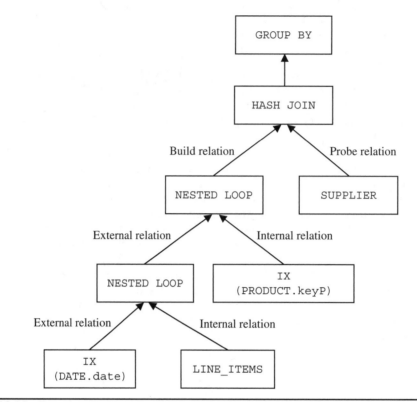

Figure 12-11 Execution plan generated by the Oracle 8*i* cost-based optimizer for the query shown in Figure 12-3

As you can see, this plan is very similar to the one generated by the Red Brick Decision Server 6.0 optimizer (Figure 12-10). However, Oracle prefers a nested loop algorithm for the join to begin with. This is probably because it has estimated that the high selectivity of the date attribute condition makes the hybrid hash join algorithm less efficient.

In contrast to the results achieved by a rule-based optimizer, execution plans change along with query selectivity. Figure 12-12 proves this point and shows how the execution plan generated by Oracle changes if the date condition is rewritten as DT3.date>'1/1/2008'. The join algorithms used are different because the predicate selectivity is also different.

Cost-based optimizers explicitly take into account the cost of executing queries in order to add flexibility. This makes it extremely difficult to predict which execution plan the optimizer will choose. For this reason, the indexes to be created should be selected on the basis of the general rules dictated by the structure of the star schema, as we mentioned at the beginning of section 12.1. They are then valid regardless of any specific data feature. Section 12.2 will discuss those general rules and highlight critical decision-making factors.

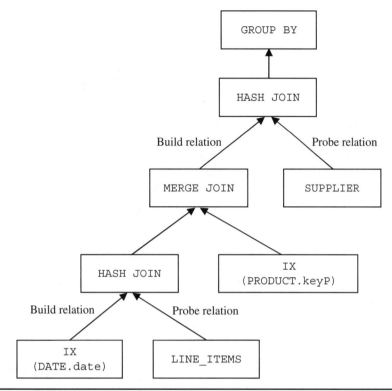

FIGURE 12-12 Execution plan created by the Oracle 8*i* cost-based optimizer for the query with the DT3 . date>'1/1/2008' condition

12.1.3 Histograms

> **Histogram**
>
> A *histogram* provides an approximated representation of the distribution of attribute values within a specific database instance. To obtain this representation, we need to split the range of possible attribute values into several intervals (sometimes called *buckets*) and evaluate for each of them how often internal values appear in relations.

Although the literature proposes many different types of histogram (Kooi, 1980; Piatetsky-Shapiro and Connell, 1984; Ioannidis and Christodulakis, 1993), those used in commercial systems are generally *equi-width* histograms or *equi-height* histograms. Equi-width histograms divide a value space into intervals of equal width. Equi-height histograms select their intervals in such a way that the sum of the frequencies of the attribute values associated with each one of them is the same regardless of the number of values in an interval. In both cases, the information associated with each interval is the average frequency at which interval values appear in a specific database. Equi-height histograms provide more accurate information, but they are more difficult to calculate and keep updated.

> **NOTE** *The statistics related only to the cardinality of individual attributes may be viewed as a degenerate histogram consisting of just one group. Obviously, the smaller the amount of information a histogram contains, the greater the error margin in estimating costs.*

Let us consider the example shown in Figure 12-13 from Piatetsky-Shapiro and Connell. It shows a hypothetical distribution of the age attribute values in the EMPLOYEES relation for a small IT company with 100 employees. The age value varies from 11 (a child prodigy!) to 60 (the company chairman). Figure 12-14 shows a possible equi-width histogram consisting of 10 intervals. Although that histogram is easy to work out—because data has to be analyzed only once in order to create it—the information it provides is not very rich in details. Because of the lack of uniformity, most values range from 20 to 30. If we want to know the percentage of people aged under 27, the estimate returned is

$$0.46 \leq Sel(\text{age}{\leq}27) \leq 0.86$$

This is obtained by calculating the sum of the frequencies up to the immediately adjacent interval to the left and right of the reference value. As you can see, the value estimate given is not very significant and could lead to major evaluation errors. If only the information relating to the minimum and maximum values of the age domain is used, this will result in an even worse estimate:

$$Sel(\text{age}{\leq}27) = \frac{27 - 11}{60 - 11} \approx 0.33$$

If we used an equi-height histogram (Figure 12-15), this would result in a more precise estimate:

$$0.54 \leq Sel(\text{age}{\leq}27) \leq 0.63$$

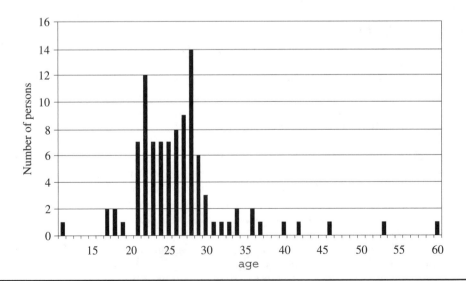

FIGURE 12-13   Possible distribution of the age attribute values

FIGURE 12-14
Equi-width
histogram for the
distribution in
Figure 12-13

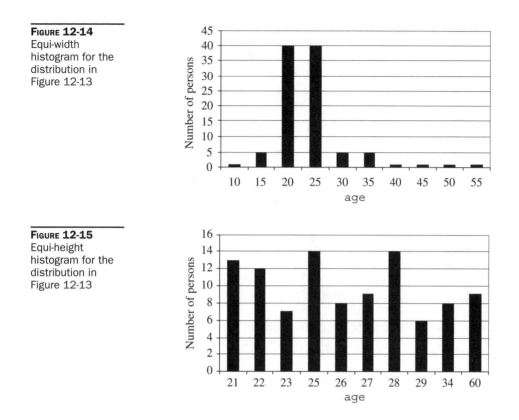

FIGURE 12-15
Equi-height
histogram for the
distribution in
Figure 12-13

This is because of the more detailed information maintained for the intervals where data is more concentrated.

The effectiveness of the estimates produced by histograms depends on histograms' ability to approximate the real-world data distribution, which in turn depends partly on the number of intervals used and partly on the technique adopted to associate elements with intervals. In case of queries involving selection predicates or equi-join predicates, the research conducted has shown that, after setting the β number of intervals to be used, the best estimate is produced by a histogram that minimizes the following sum:

$$\sum_{i=1}^{\beta} p_i V_i$$

where p_i and V_i are, respectively, the number and the variance of the frequencies placed in the interval i. It is possible to prove that this histogram belongs to the class known as *serial* histograms (Ioannidis and Poosala, 1995).

Serial Histogram

In a *serial histogram* the frequencies of the attribute values associated with each interval are either all greater or all smaller than the frequencies associated with every other interval.

In other words, the technique used to create a serial histogram must make it possible to order attribute values on the basis of the frequency at which they appear in a database. This leads to minimizing the frequency variance for each interval and, consequently, the value of the sum shown previously.

Given a specific database instance, you could define a large number of different histograms for an individual attribute, few of which would actually return accurate estimates. Most of the research in this area is concerned with attempts to develop strategies for choosing the most accurate type of histogram. When choosing a technique for creating a histogram, an effective compromise must be reached between the accuracy of the estimate produced and the updating speed and space required to store the information.

12.2 Index Selection

> **Index Selection**
> *Index selection* refers to the process of selecting a set of indexes of different kinds to be created on data mart tables to improve performance. The set of indexes created must comply with the space constraints imposed by users.

This definition poses the problem of the choice of indexes in a way that is very similar to the problem of view materialization. This can be tackled in two phases:

- *Identify the set of useful indexes.* An index's usefulness depends on specific DBMS features, and it can be evaluated only if the features of DBMS optimizers are known. There is no point in creating an index for an execution plan if optimizers cannot take it into account.

- *Select the best subset.* If there is a space constraint, you can only create a subset of useful indexes. Chapter 11 shows the formulae used to calculate the size of indexes. The space factor should not be undervalued, because indexes use on average at least the same amount of space as data.

Each DBMS provides a set of tools to evaluate the size of tables and indexes. These tools can provide good approximations. Table 12-1 shows some examples of size estimates for some indexes that can be created on the line item schema we used earlier in the chapter. Note that the bitmap index size grows as the number of distinct attribute values increases.

Attribute	Distinct Values	Tuples	Index Type	Size (MB)
customerCountry	25	1,500,000	B⁺-Tree	8.6
customerCountry	25	1,500,000	Bitmap	4.5
employee	1000	1,500,000	B⁺-Tree	8.6
employee	1000	1,500,000	Bitmap	179.8
FT primary key	6,001,215	6,001,215	Star index	126.7

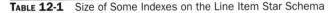 **TABLE 12-1**   Size of Some Indexes on the Line Item Star Schema

For this reason, a bitmap index cannot be used for the `employee` attribute. The size of the star index is also considerable, but this is justified by the number of tuples and the number of attributes involved.

The next sections will present general rules for indexing data mart tables. We do not consider it worthwhile to provide any more specific rules because they vary according to index implementation in every DBMS. For this reason, refer to the manufacturer's manuals.

12.2.1 Indexing Dimension Tables

Dimension table attributes are mainly used to filter the tuples to be retrieved in a fact table. For this reason, either RID-list indexes[3] or bitmap indexes of the types described in sections 11.1, 11.2, and 11.3 can be used to index them. The type of index to use is chosen according to the features of the attribute to be indexed. The greater the attribute cardinality gets, the more suitable it is for RID listing. When efficient bitmap compression techniques or advanced bitmap indexes, such as bitmap-encoded, are available, problems with increased size of bitmap indexes are lessened.

When you choose the attributes to index, you should use a reference workload. This can be put together from user interviews in the design phase and from the DBMS log in the operating phase. Obviously, the greater the number of queries that express conditions for an attribute, the higher the probability that the attribute needs to be indexed. Table 12-2 shows a simple schema that makes it possible to choose the best type of indexes on the basis of attribute features and attribute selections.

Note that projection indexes can be competitive only when the percentage of values to be retrieved and the number of distinct values for the indexed attribute are both high. When both cases apply simultaneously, a bitmap index will be very large because of the high number of distinct values. B+-Tree access can also be difficult because of the large number of internal nodes read for each value to be retrieved as you go down the tree. Under those conditions, advanced bitmap indexes (bit-sliced and bitmap-encoded indexes) can also be highly advantageous because of their small size.

		Distinct values	
		MANY	FEW
Query selectivity	HIGH	B+-Tree	B+-Tree Bitmap
	LOW	Projection index, Advanced bitmap, B+-Tree	Bitmap

TABLE 12-2 Selection Criteria for the Type of Index to Use for a Dimension Table Attribute

---

[3]The term *RID-list index* means all the indexes that explicitly store the Row IDentifier lists associated with every attribute value (for example B-Trees, B+-Trees). These are different from bitmap indexes that associate a bit vector with each attribute value.

We assume that a B+-Tree index on primary keys of dimension tables is always created. This index will often be used to streamline joins with the fact table, as in the execution plan of Figure 12-4. This will also be useful for periodic data updates to check primary and referential integrity. If a snowflake schema is used, it is necessary to index not only primary keys of secondary dimension tables, but also corresponding foreign keys. This makes queries more efficient if their execution plans require access to secondary dimension tables (those for which a condition is expressed) as well as to primary dimension tables (to retrieve the corresponding tuples).

12.2.2   Indexing Fact Tables

Tuples from fact tables are normally retrieved based on their foreign key values, which are selected after accessing one or more dimension tables. For this reason, indexing requirements mainly involve joins and those foreign keys that make up fact table primary keys.

You should assume that primary indexes on fact tables are always available. Unfortunately, fact table primary keys consist of many attributes, so primary indexes cannot always be used in join operations. A join operation from a dimension table (DT) to a fact table (FT) may use only the FT index if the foreign key referencing DT is the first index component, as we already mentioned in Chapter 11. For example, the execution plan shown in Figure 12-5 does not use the LINE_ITEMS primary index precisely because the composite fact table primary key has the foreign key referencing ORDER in the first position. This means that it is essential that you take great care when you decide on the order of the foreign keys in your primary index.

The most frequently used attribute must always be in the first position of composite indexes. This is normally a "date" attribute. However, the resulting index cannot result in an appreciable increase in performance because it makes only one of the possible joins easier. For this reason, we suggest that you create additional indexes. Experience has shown us that you should create a number of join indexes between pairs of tables rather than a single multi-table join index, or *star index*, because join indexes are more flexible in use. When bitmapped-join indexes are available, they are also cost-effective to use. However, remember that there is no point in creating join indexes between fact tables and dimension tables when dimension tables can be completely stored to the central memory during join operations.

TIP   *If your DBMS does not provide any specific index type for join operations, you can create various B+-Tree indexes to index individual components of fact table keys.*

In addition to primary indexes, you may need to create a fact table index to select a subset of tuples on the basis of a measure value. If this is the case, a bit-sliced index will perform best because the attribute to be indexed is numerical and because bit-sliced indexes combine relatively small size with great flexibility in carrying out selections.

CAUTION   *Any index created on a fact table with a very large number of tuples will always be very large. For this reason, you should evaluate very carefully how cost-effective indexes created on measures are.*

12.3 Additional Physical Design Elements

The physical design of a data mart does not end with defining its indexes. You should also define the set of parameters that determine the physical schemata of data marts. Regardless of much of the terminology used for the different DBMSs, the disk space used up by a database is normally divided into *tablespaces*, *data files*, and *data blocks*. Their organization, size, and allocation may have a significant effect on both performance and fault tolerance.

> **Tablespaces**
> *Tablespace* is a logical subdivision of the disk space used by a database. A tablespace must store uniform data sets.

> **Data Files**
> A *data file*, also called a *segment*, is a file storing part of the information on a tablespace. A data file belongs to a single tablespace, and a number of data files may be associated with one tablespace.

> **Disk Blocks**
> A *disk block* is the information unit read or written by DBMSs.

Figure 12-16 shows the hierarchical relationship between these elements. Each tablespace is associated with various data files that consist of a variable number of disk blocks. Each individual database item, such as an index or a table, is associated with a specific tablespace.

12.3.1 Splitting a Database Into Tablespaces

Although all the database data can be theoretically stored to one single tablespace, we suggest that you use this abstraction to split information sensibly into smaller bits. This is a good starting point to improve performance and fault tolerance. To get to this starting point, data files should be properly allocated.

The disk space used up by a database is not the same as the space required to store data, because a DBMS also requires additional space for the following:

- Data dictionaries
- Indexes
- Information for transaction cancellation (*roll-back*)
- Temporary tables
- Procedures and *triggers* that make up the applications

Starting from this functional classification, you can split space into tablespaces to ensure homogeneous tablespace information, types of access, and amounts of data. Table 12-3 shows a generic tablespace division of the information required by a database. It does not take into account the specific data warehouse operation modes that consist of two main statuses:

Tablespace	Description
SYSTEM	Tablespace for data dictionary
DATA1..., n	Tablespace for data
INDEX1..., m	Tablespace for indexes
RBS	Tablespace for standard roll-back
TEMP	Tablespace for temporary data
TOOLS1..., h	Tablespace for stored procedures and triggers

online (analysis performed by users) and offline (loading). Table 12-4 shows a data warehouse-specific division into tablespaces.

The data loading phase features time-demanding batch procedures that read data from operational sources or import data from flat files. Data is copied into temporary tables, where it is cleansed and transformed before properly loading into data marts. The TEMP_ LOAD tablespace should perform this task, and the amounts of data it stores may constantly vary. The primary events loaded into the data mart are stored to one or more tablespaces (DATA1..., n) on the basis of the amount of data, and the related indexes are hosted separately (INDEX1..., n). Secondary events can also be stored separately (AGG1..., m e INDEX_AGG1..., m).

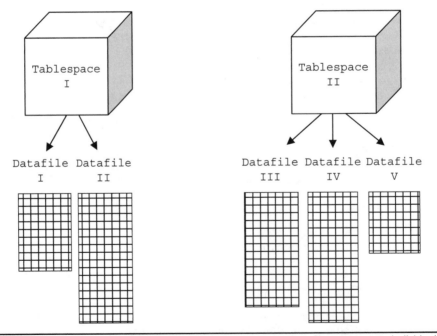

FIGURE 12-16   Physical data allocation to disk. The grid inside the data files represents individual disk blocks.

	Tablespace	Description
TABLE 12-4 A Data Warehouse Split into Tablespaces	SYSTEM	Tablespace for data dictionary
	DATA1..., *n*	Tablespace for data
	AGG1..., *n*	Tablespace for grouped data
	INDEX1..., *m*	Tablespace for indexes
	INDEX_AGG1..., *m*	Tablespace for indexes for grouped data
	RBS	Tablespace for standard roll-back
	RBS_LOAD	Tablespace for roll-back used during loading
	TEMP	Tablespace for temporary data
	TEMP_LOAD	Tablespace for temporary data required during loading
	TOOLS1..., *h*	Tablespace for stored procedures and triggers

TIP *When you create a tablespace, you should specify both its minimum and maximum sizes. It is very important that first the designer and then the DBMS administrator check for the space actually used up by various tablespaces regularly to avoid space waste or errors due to lack of space.*

12.3.2 Allocating Data Files

We can assume that many hard disks are available if the amount of data to be stored is particularly large. As described next, allocating data files to your hard disks gives the opportunity to do the following:

- Improve performance thanks to parallel disk access while your queries are running
- Increase fault tolerance because any disk fault involves only a part of your data

12.3.2.1 Executing Parallel Queries

An in-depth discussion of the problems associated with executing parallel queries would take up a whole book and is beyond the scope of this text. In this section, we limit our discussion to setting out basic instructions, and we concentrate on parallel data reading from disks. Refer to specialist texts (Özsu and Valduriez, 1991; Abdelguerfi and Wong, 1998) and to DBMS manuals for further information.

I/O operations are responsible for most of the cost of queries because disk access time is far greater than the time for CPUs to carry out those I/O operations. However, I/O time can be greatly reduced if you use multiple disks that can be accessed in parallel.

NOTE *Parallel access is possible when each of the various hard disks is linked to its own controller. The observations proposed in the following sections do not apply to partitioned disks and only partly apply to disks sharing an individual controller.*

If you model the logical-physical schema of your database properly, you can exploit parallel access advantages of multiple disks. Database schema optimization can be oriented toward two types of approach to parallel access:

- **Inter-query parallel access**   Schemata are optimized to minimize conflicts arising from multiple queries running simultaneously. To achieve this, you should use different disks to store the information required for separate queries.

- **Intra-query parallel access**   Schemata are optimized to maximize query execution speed. To achieve this, you should use separate disks to store different data portions required for each individual query (*declustering*). This means that you can have a parallel access to data and use multiple processors to execute your queries.

Generally, you should prefer intra-query parallelism to inter-query parallelism in data warehouse systems, because the number of simultaneous accesses to your system is not critical, but the complexity of individual queries is high. You can also apply both types of parallelism at the same time, but the number of disks required to do this is so high that it is hardly feasible.

Intra-query parallelism can be applied to tables. Fact tables and their dimension tables should be stored to separate disks to speed up parallel data reading during join operations. Alternatively, intra-query parallelism can be applied to fragments. Fact tables should be partitioned into fragments allocated to different disks that can be consequently read in parallel. In the second case, you should take into account parallelism in the logical design phase when you can apply appropriate horizontal and vertical fragmentation strategies. On the one hand, the goal of parallelism-oriented fragmentation criteria is to query as many separate fragments as possible. On the other hand, the goal of the criteria oriented to a reduction in the amount of data to read is to query a single fragment that should be as small as possible. For this reason, we suggest that you use fragmentation to reduce the quantity of data to be read, and that you apply declustering to tables only.

12.3.2.2   Fault Tolerance

The term *fault tolerance* describes the system's ability to continue operating when a fault appears in one of its components. Hard disks run major risks of fault due to their wear and tear, many mechanical moving parts, and the tremendous precision required for data reading and writing.[4]

The need to ensure a high degree of fault tolerance in data warehouses is the result of two factors. First, to keep corporate operations under control, relevant information must always be available. Second, it is very difficult to reconstruct data warehouse information. In particular, data warehouses contain history information that may not be stored to operational databases because operational databases normally cover a very short time frame or store only current data.

TIP   *Keep an offline copy of your data warehouse information. To do this, you can use magnetic tapes or optical disks. This suggestion should at least be applied to primary events, because computing secondary views and creating indexes is mainly a matter of time.*

---

[4]Hard disk performance has been improved much more slowly than memory and CPU performance, and this confirms the complexity of hard disks.

The use of multiple disks enables parallel I/O of data, and it also reduces the amount of data lost if one disk fails. But if you increase the number of disks, you will also reduce the period of time between faults, or *mean time to failure*. Intuitively, if hard disk manufacturers specify that the average life of their hard disks is five years and if you use 10 hard disks to store your data, a fault should statistically take place every six months.

These observations show two requirements: on the one hand, the use of multiple disks enables parallel access to data; on the other hand, the risk of losing data can be reduced if you add redundant data.

Data Striping

Data striping refers to the techniques used to allocate a set of data to several disks to read and write at the same time. To stripe data, you can split either single bits or entire data blocks.

Data Redundancy

Data redundancy refers to the techniques used to store redundant data that reduce the probability of data loss. Those storage techniques vary according to the additional control data used. For example, control data can be a single bit for each data unit, *bit parity*, or even the duplication of entire disk devices, *mirroring*. The larger the amount of control data is, the greater the ability to achieve error-free storage results.

These concepts underlie *RAID (Redundant Array of Inexpensive Disks)* technology. A RAID configuration (Chen et al., 1994; Patterson et al., 1988) consists of a number of disks on which data is allocated in different ways. The number of disks used and the redundancy or parity management techniques applied can distinguish every RAID configuration. Figure 12-17 shows three possible configurations that we consider particularly suitable for data warehouses:

- In the RAID 1 configuration, *mirrored disk*, two copies of data are stored to two separate disks. Data will be lost only if both disks fail at the same time.

- In the RAID 0+1 configuration, a *stripe of mirrors*, data is allocated to an array of replicated disks. In this way, both data mirroring and data striping are achieved.

- In the RAID 5 configuration, *block-interleaved distributed parity*, data is allocated to more than one disk, and so is parity. In this configuration, there is no mirroring, because a real data copy is not stored, but instead error-correction techniques are used, such as *Hamming* and *Reed-Solomon* codes, to limit the set of possible errors.

RAID 1 and RAID 0+1 configurations provide great reliability, but they are the most expensive among RAID configurations. The RAID 5 configuration delivers excellent performance when reading and writing large amounts of data.

CAUTION *For each RAID configuration, the capability of running parallel I/O applications greatly depends on the way the disks are configured and the number of disk controllers used. Total parallel access can be achieved only when each disk unit has its own controller.*

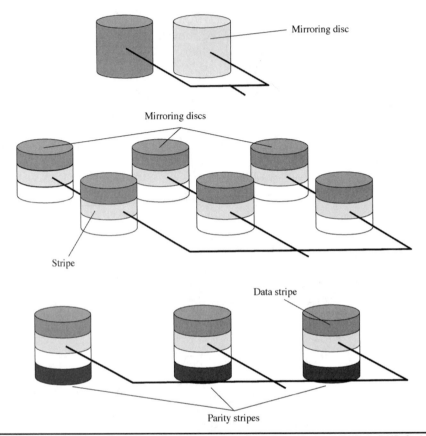

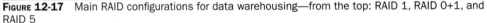

FIGURE 12-17   Main RAID configurations for data warehousing—from the top: RAID 1, RAID 0+1, and RAID 5

Remember that data allocation becomes a physical level issue when RAID techniques are applied. This means that you need not be concerned with data file allocation, because the DBMS automatically allocates data to disks.

12.3.3   Disk Block Size

Each DBMS can specify the size of disk blocks—that is, the number of bytes to be read/written atomically at each disk access. Disk block size normally ranges from 0.5 KB to 256 KB. It can affect or improve system performance, depending on the type of queries to be executed and the features of the tables stored.

Figure 12-18 shows the time necessary to read 1 MB from a hard disk as a function of the disk block size, in case of sequential and random access. You can clearly see that the random access time dramatically reduces as the disk block size increases, as a result of a lower number of hard disk head movements required. However, if the amount of information required is lower than an individual block, the usage of large size blocks leads to reading/writing unnecessary information and this results in an increase of I/O time. For example, to read 1-KB large information stored in 512-byte blocks causes no unnecessary information to be read, while 255 KB of unnecessary information will be read if you use 256-KB blocks.

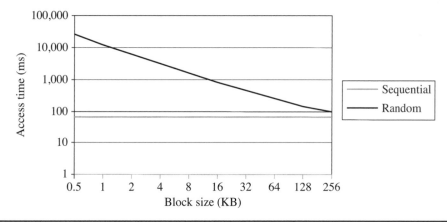

FIGURE 12-18   Disk access time as a function of the disk block size

These observations show that small size blocks are more suitable for storing tables with smaller size tuples and for access involving fewer tuples. On the contrary, large disk blocks are more suitable for storing tables with larger size tuples and for access involving a greater number of tuples. While the former situation is more common in operational databases, the latter is typical for data warehouses. While OLTP queries usually process a small amount of information, OLAP queries need to access large amounts of data, as we have already mentioned several times. As a result, we suggest that you use disk blocks of 32–64 KB for data warehouse systems, while operational systems normally use 2–8 KB disk blocks.

NOTE   *The disk block size that DBMSs should read/write can be different from the disk block size used by operating system file systems. However, experimental evidence shows that the best performance is delivered when both values coincide.*

Data Warehouse Project Documentation

In the preceding chapters, we examined the complex sequence of techniques and actions that lead designers through the various design phases until a detailed design for a data mart and a data warehouse is complete. Along the way, we have looked at some of the formalisms that partially illustrate the design either in graphical or textual form. This chapter looks at how to organize these illustrations into a consistent, well-ordered collection and considers what must be added to produce complete and useful documentation.

The use of wide-ranging documentation is essential for IT projects of all kinds, but above all for those of medium to large size. As far as data warehousing is concerned, projects are so complex that documentation is absolutely essential. By the way, the job of data warehouse design would be much simpler if even operational sources were better documented than most currently are.

In general, a good set of project documents should show the following features. It must

- cover all the phases of the project exhaustively and provide an extensive picture of the process leading from the original specifications to a data warehouse;

- be able to be used at many levels of abstraction. On the one hand, it must be able to provide a concise global overview of all the salient phases of data warehouse projects and architectures. On the other hand, it must include all the relevant details and the crucial decisions defining final conceptual, logical, and physical structures;

- act as an effective support tool for data warehouse maintenance and upgrade;

- allow everyone—including new design teams taking over from previous ones—to understand design solutions in sufficient depth so as to continue data warehouse projects as planned;

- include purely technical illustrations as well as abstract, conceptual illustrations for end users and application domain experts to enable them to discuss, check, and, if necessary, fine-tune design specifications;

- include one or more glossaries to make the terminology relating to the application domain transparent to everyone, including non-experts.

TIP   The documentation does not only become useful when the project is completed, it is essential to ensure quality and accuracy in every design phase. Preparing a structured, standardized set of documents offers designers the opportunity to think of the choices they have made. For this reason, we suggest that you create your documentation as you go, either during or at the end of each individual design phase.

In this chapter we will deal only with design-related documents. Other documentation sections, such as project management documents, user manuals, and administration manuals, will not be considered.

The structured approach to documentation we propose in this chapter suggests illustrations at three different levels of abstraction that will give an exhaustive description of various design features. The following sections will show that each level includes one or more schemata based on graphical and textual representations and integrated with appropriate glossaries.

1. **Data warehouse level**   This describes the overall architecture of a data warehouse and in particular user profiles and types of sources populating a data warehouse.

2. **Data mart level**   This provides an overview of the structure of each data mart. This level documents logical and physical schemata, constraints on data marts, the workload encountered by the data marts, and data mart population.

3. **Fact level**   This conceptually documents each fact designed and issues appropriate glossaries to define attributes, measures, and data volumes.

The introduction of the data mart level is particularly useful when designers adopt a bottom-up approach, as mentioned in Chapter 2.

13.1 Data Warehouse Level

At this level, you must document the global architecture of a data warehouse, its data sources, and the specific data marts of which it is composed. The following sections discuss the aspects of this level that should be documented.

13.1.1   Data Warehouse Schemata

Data warehouse schemata are the "load-bearing" structures of this entire level. They are iconic diagrams that provide a qualitative global view of data warehouses in terms of functionality and data flows. A data warehouse schema shows various data marts that make up a data warehouse; it describes the sources that populate data marts, the users that access data marts, and the types of access granted. It does not show how software applications are deployed to the available hardware; see section 13.1.2 for more details on this point. Figure 13-1 shows the key to the icons.

Figure 13-2 shows an example of a data warehouse schema for a context involving the production and sale of items in a retail chain. Four data marts deal with human resource

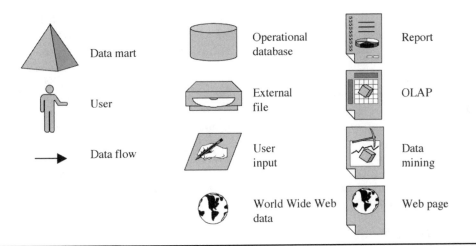

Figure 13-1 Icons showing objects (left), inputs (center), and outputs (right) of a data warehouse schema.

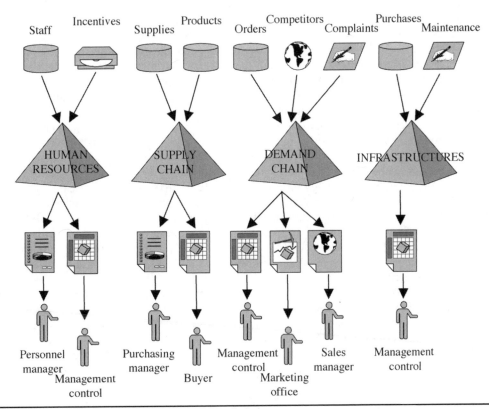

Figure 13-2 Data warehouse schema for a retail chain

management, supply chain, demand chain, and infrastructure, respectively. The human resource data mart may include data on recruitment, resignations, dismissals, transfers, promotions, and incentives. The facts modeled in the supply chain data mart include the production of components, their inventories and delivery, product manufacture starting with components, packaging and dispatch to warehouses, warehouse inventories, and shipment to stores. The demand chain data mart may include sales, orders, invoices, dispatch to customers, and complaints. Lastly, the infrastructure data mart will include data on the acquisition of premises and shelving and on any rebuilding work done in the stores.

The pyramid icons mark the data marts, meant as logical rather than physical units. The person icons show the categories of users who access this data warehouse. Different icons can be used to provide a schematic representation of the sources populating data marts and the main data access methods set for every user group.

13.1.2   Deployment Schema

This schema is strictly linked to and completes data warehouse schemata. While data warehouse schemata show *functional* features, deployment schemata show *static* features. In particular, a deployment schema shows the software applications involved in a data warehouse process, as well as the hardware and network architecture to which these software applications are deployed. For example, a deployment schema can be used to show whether there exists a primary data warehouse where data mart data is redundantly stored; to represent the number of clients and servers, and Intranet or Internet usage; or to show whether data marts are geographically separated (if administrative offices were in different premises from the sales and marketing departments, their respective data marts would probably be in different towns).

As far as representation formalisms are concerned, we suggest you use *deployment diagrams* provided by Unified Modeling Language (UML) (Arlow and Neustadt, 2005). They show hardware devices that can make up any architecture, hardware device connections, and software applications running on each hardware device.

A UML deployment diagram gives you the opportunity to show the physical architecture of systems at different levels of detail. It is a graph showing *processing nodes* (cubes) linked by *communication associations* (lines). A node is a physical object involved in systems operation. It represents a processing resource equipped with at least some memory. Furthermore, it usually can process information. A node may contain software *component* instances, each marked with a rectangle with two smaller boxes inside. This shows that software component instances exist and run in the current node.

Figure 13-3 shows an example of a deployment schema using the UML formalism. The terms in chevron brackets (« and ») define the classes of elements (UML *stereotypes*) that users can add. In our example, we have used the «server», the «client», and the «legacy» stereotypes (their names are easy to understand) for our nodes, and we have used the «DBMS», the «ETL», the «OLAPTool», the «miningTool», the «browser», the «operationalDB», and the «dataMart» stereotypes for our software components.

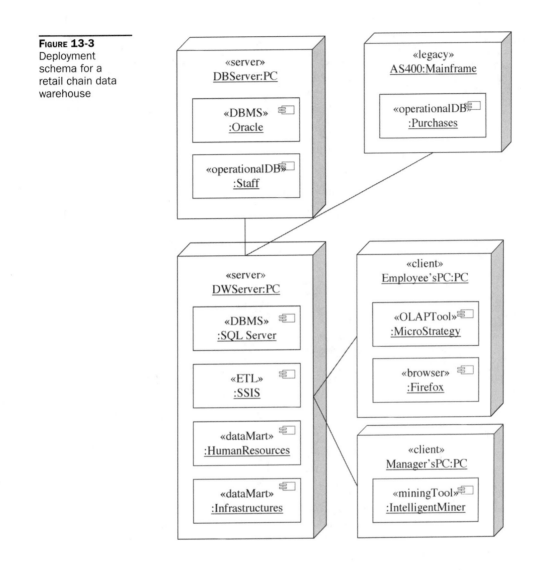

FIGURE 13-3
Deployment
schema for a
retail chain data
warehouse

Each node or component is labeled with an optional object name followed by a colon and the name of the class to which those objects belong. For example, DBServer is a PC class object.

You can also use alternative representations for nodes and components, marking their stereotypes with specific icons. Figures 13-4 and 13-5 show some examples with different levels of detail.

FIGURE 13-4
Deployment
schema for a retail
chain data
warehouse using
icons for
components

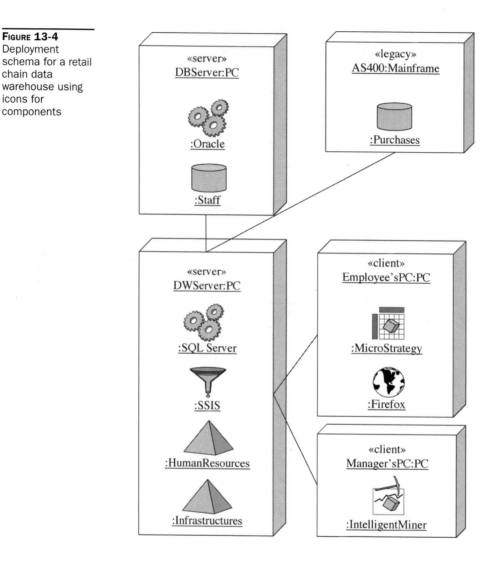

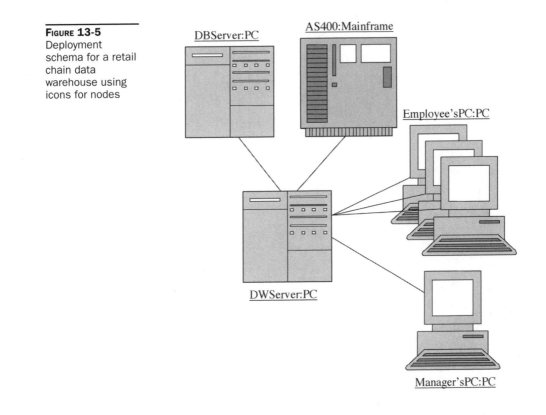

FIGURE 13-5
Deployment
schema for a retail
chain data
warehouse using
icons for nodes

DBServer:PC

AS400:Mainframe

Employee'sPC:PC

DWServer:PC

Manager'sPC:PC

13.2 Data Mart Level

This level is designed for documenting every data mart, specifying details on data mart operational sources and population procedures, showing data mart composition in terms of facts, expressing data mart workload for data mart design, and measuring data mart data volume. This level should also include the documentation relating to logical and physical schemata for data marts, together with logical and physical schema design constraints. The following sections describe the recommended illustrations.

13.2.1   Bus and Overlapping Matrices

The goal of *bus and overlapping matrices* is to summarize the facts that make up data marts and to show overlapping links. See section 5.5 for more details on overlapping fact schemata. This information may be represented by a pair of tables showing complementary information. One of those tables shows which analysis hierarchies appear in each fact. It is called a *bus matrix* because it expresses information similar to the data warehouse bus architecture matrix proposed by Kimball (1998) for logical schemata. The other table, called an *overlap matrix,* specifies which hierarchies can be overlapped.

Tables 13-1 and 13-2 provide examples based on the supply chain data mart. The first table shows which analysis dimensions can be used for the various facts and which ones are degenerate. Obviously, a dimension that is shared between two or more facts can be the key to an overlapped fact schema. However, this is not the only situation that makes it possible

TABLE 13-1 Bus Matrix for a Supply Chain Data Mart; Dimension Roles in Italics.

Dimensions \ Facts	Degenerate	MANUFACTURE	PACKAGING	DISPATCH	INVENTORY	....
date (*production*)		✓				
product		✓	✓	✓	✓	
factory		✓	✓	✓		
quality	✓	✓				
phase	✓	✓				
packageType			✓			
date (*packaging*)			✓			
warehouse				✓	✓	
date (*dispatch*)				✓		
mode	✓			✓		
month (*inventory*)					✓	
......						

to overlap two hierarchies, or part of them. To obtain more information on this subject, you should analyze the other matrix. It shows fully overlapping dimensions with different roles and partially overlapping dimensions where only one subset of attributes is shared.

If overlapping matrices become too complex because of the number of facts and dimensions, they can be replaced by multiple tables associated with individual facts. The columns in each of those tables must contain only the dimensions for a single fact, and the lines must contain only the dimensions of other facts showing at least one overlapping dimension.

TIP *Bus matrices can be used at design time to assess the quality of fact schemata. As a rule of thumb, if your matrix is very sparse, you probably failed to recognize the semantic and structural similarities between apparently different hierarchies. Conversely, if your matrix is very dense, you probably failed to recognize the semantic and structural similarities between apparently different facts.*

This level should also include a table for dynamic features (Table 5-37) that specifies which attribute data from various hierarchies should be logged. See section 5.4.3 for more details.

13.2.2   Operational Schema

Operational schemata are the starting point for data mart design. The data in operational schemata is the main source to populate data marts. For this reason, data mart documentation must absolutely include schemata for the various operational sources involved, in addition to the reconciled schema resulting from normalization and integration, as mentioned in Chapter 3. The minimum requirement for each operational source is a complete logical

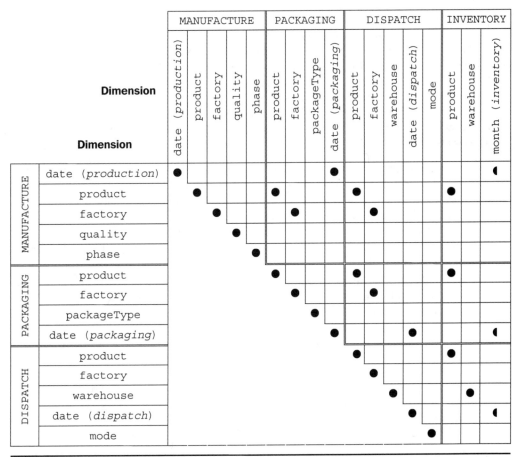

TABLE 13-2   Overlapping Matrix for a Supply Chain Data Mart. The Symbol ● Indicates a Correspondence Between all the Attributes in Both Hierarchies. The Symbol ◀ Indicates that Only Some Attributes Are Overlapping.

schema and any relevant glossaries. We also find it very helpful for future maintenance to make available any corresponding conceptual Entity-Relationship schema obtained from recognition and normalization. As far as nonrelational sources are concerned, record tracks should be included together with any other information considered useful for their descriptions.

The documentation of the reconciled database must certainly relate to the logical level, and presumably the conceptual level if a conceptual formalism was used to complete the integration phase. It is an excellent idea to show the data logging level of the reconciled database, in particular whether this level is different from that of the operational sources.

To complete an operational schema, it is essential that you document *mappings* between your reconciled schema and source schemata. If you adopted a Global-As-View (GAV) approach, you can express your mappings by associating every global schema concept with a view that defines that concept in terms of local schema concepts. See section 3.4 for more details.

13.2.3   Data-Staging Schema

Data-staging schemata include a whole set of illustrations of various kinds. They all aim at accurately documenting procedures for populating data marts. In data warehouse schemata, we have already briefly specified which sources populate each data mart. In the deployment schemata, we have shown how sources are physically allocated, and in operational schemata, we have provided a representation of source structures. Now it is time to model in detail the Extraction, Transformation, and Loading (ETL) process that extracts data from sources, transforms it as required, and loads it into data marts.

The essential points of this operation to be documented can be summed up as follows:

- **Global schema**   This is an overview of the population process that feeds the reconciled database starting from the data sources, and feeds the data mart starting from the reconciled database. It shows the individual processing steps, the archives involved, any use of a staging area, and any manual intervention by an operator. We suggest you use the *Data-Flow Diagram (DFD)* formalism by Stevens and others (1974), because this type of schema is created for functional purposes. Figure 13-6 shows an example of this.

- **Populating the reconciled database**   The processes to be modeled consist of (static or incremental, immediate or delayed, log or timestamp-based) extraction, transformation (conversion, enriching and split/concatenation procedures), cleansing (any approximate merging rules, dictionaries, application domain-specific business rules), and (static or incremental) loading. Because this level mainly involves the documentation of algorithmic aspects, we suggest that you use pseudo-code, flowcharts, or UML *activity diagrams* (Arlow and Neustadt, 2005). Figure 13-7 shows an activity diagram documenting the process of extraction and incremental loading into a data mart. This starts from a source database (SDB in the figure), where every table has an attribute recording when each tuple was last modified, and then it passes through the reconciled database (RDB in the figure), where an

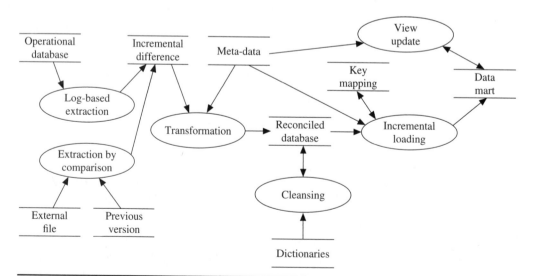

Figure 13-6   An example of a DFD used to document the population process

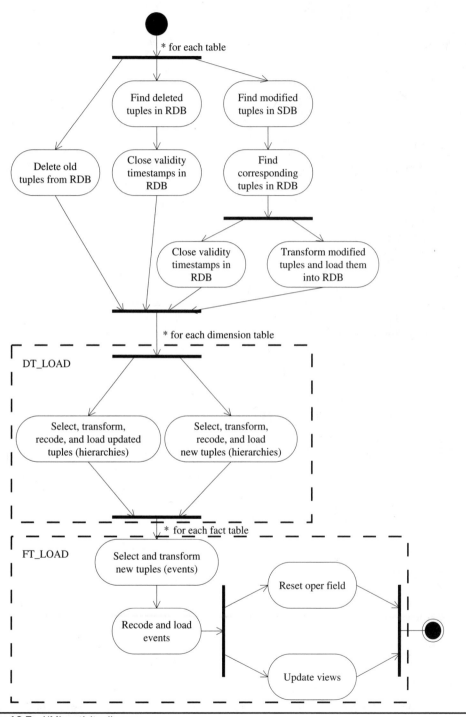

Figure 13-7 UML activity diagram

Process name	FT_LOAD		
Goal	Incremental data loading into the FT starting from reconciled database		
Preconditions	–		
Constraints	Complete updating of the dimension tables involved		
Data Sources	RIC_VERDICTS RIC_MAGISTRATE RIC_SECTION....	Source Type	Reconciled database relations
Data Destinations	FT_VERDICTS		
Activity	Activity Type	Description	Entities Involved
Tuple selection and transformation	Source selection	Extracts new tuples identified by the flag oper= 'I' from the table	RIC_VERDICTS
....	....	....	....

TABLE 13-3   Textual Description of an ETL Process

oper attribute identifies the type of operation that caused each tuple to be extracted. As far as complex ETL processes are concerned, a diagram-based description is of little use unless it is accompanied by an appropriate textual description. Table 13-3 shows an example of this.

- **Populating the data mart**   This requires that you produce the documentation on loading procedures for primary fact tables and dimension tables and show how dynamic hierarchies are handled. Figure 13-8 shows a simple example of an SQL query that loads a new tuple into the stores dimension table.

FIGURE 13-8   Loading query for the STORE dimension table

```
INSERT INTO STORE (store, storeCity, state,
                   country, salesManager, salesDistrict)
    SELECT S.store, C.city, T.state,
           T.country, S.salesManager, S.districtNum
    FROM   STORES S, CITIES C, STATES T
    WHERE  S.inCity = C.city AND
           C.state = T.state
```

- **Updating views and indexes**   Views require documentation of any incremental updating techniques used (section 10.5).

In recent years, scientific literature has suggested some specific approaches to conceptual documentation on ETL. From among these, we will confine ourselves to those proposed by Vassiliadis et al. (2002) and by Trujillo and Luján-Mora (2003).

The Vassiliadis approach introduces a conceptual ETL model with a strong emphasis on the interrelationships between attributes and concepts, and on the transformations that data must undergo during data warehouse population. Interrelationships between attributes and concepts can be captured after mapping data-supplying attributes in sources onto data

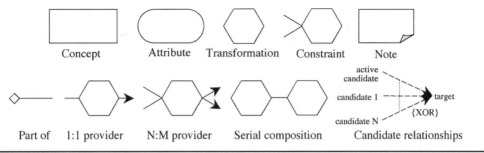

FIGURE 13-9   Generic constructs of the conceptual ETL model proposed by Vassiliadis

warehouse data-consumer attributes. *Transformations* are taken to mean schema restructuring and value formatting. Moreover, this model can show constraints of various kinds and the composition of the transformations. Figure 13-9 shows the generic constructs this model provides. Each designer can specialize this model and define a table containing the ETL operations he or she uses most frequently.

The Trujillo and Luján-Mora approach also aims at a conceptual ETL representation, but it is based on standard UML. Table 13-4 defines a set of basic mechanisms to process data in the form of records consisting of attributes. Each mechanism corresponds to a UML class stereotype. Client-server type dependencies link all the mechanisms to one another in a class diagram.

Stereotype	Description	Icon
Grouping	Data grouped on the basis of a particular criterion	
Conversion	Data item type and format changed or new data derived from existing data	A → B
Filter	Data filtered and checked	
Error	Erroneous data redirected	!!!
Join	Join between two data sources calculated	
Loader	Data loaded	
Log	Operations carried out recorded in the log	LOG
Merge	Two or more data sources with compatible attributes integrated	
Surrogate	Unique surrogate keys generated	123 →
Wrapper	Native data sources transformed into relational form	

TABLE 13-4   ETL Mechanisms and the Corresponding Icons Proposed by Trujillo

Remember, however, that ETL tools typically provide designers with a graphical user interface to "draw" procedures. To do this, ETL tools have proprietary graphical languages for modeling both data and control flows. Illustrations produced by ETL tools are generally an integral part of the ETL documentation. Some examples of these types of tools are IBM DataStage, Microsoft SQL Server 2005 Integration Services (SSIS), and Oracle Data Integration Suite (ODI). Figures 13-10 and 13-11 show a few examples of the graphical representations of ETL flows created by SSIS and ODI.

FIGURE 13-10
ETL Modeling
in SSIS

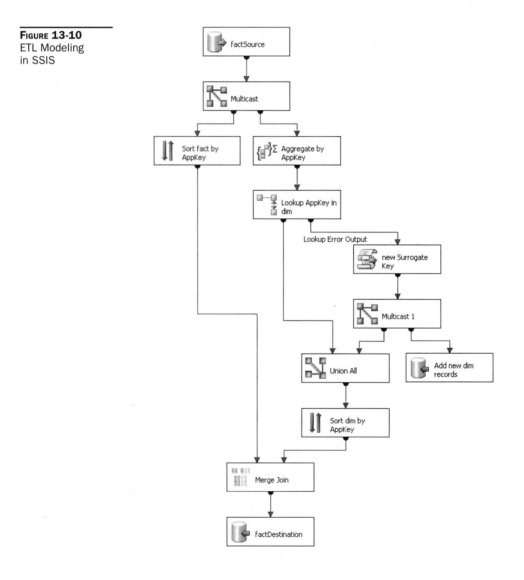

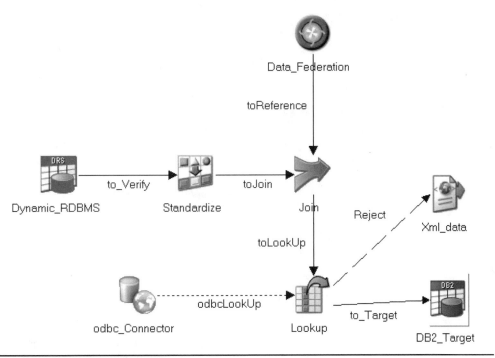

Figure 13-11 ETL Modeling in ODI

Finally, we would like to emphasize the importance of providing suitable documentation for the certification procedures adopted to preserve data quality and to manage the source records rejected by ETL tools in the cleansing phase. This requires the following:

- Describe the quality criteria records must fulfill.

- Carefully document the format of the log files storing rejected records so that data warehouse administrators can quickly realize which quality criteria those records do not meet.

- Properly define the organizational workflow that makes it possible to correct/insert the wrong/missing data. For example, this could entail contacting the owner of each rejected record.

13.2.4 Domain Glossary

It may be useful to prepare a glossary for the various attribute domains. Table 13-5 shows how it should be structured. It should set out the domain properties for all the attributes in data mart fact schemata; in particular, the following properties should be listed for every domain: (primitive or enumerated) type, expected cardinality, a description, and some examples of values that help users understand the precise meaning of a domain. Note that the glossary provides a semantic definition of the data in the fact schemata, even if this is in an informal way.

Name	Description	Values	Type	Cardinality
Products	Product names in catalogue	Pringles, Mars	CHAR(40)	5000
Brands	Manufacturer's brand	Procter & Gamble, Nestlé, Mars	CHAR(20)	800
Cities	Full name of cities	Paris, London	CHAR(40)	100
Countries	Country	France, UK	CHAR(20)	300
Product Types	Level 1 product classification	chocolate bar, potato chips	CHAR(20)	200
Product Categories	Level 2 product classification	snack, appetizer	CHAR(20)	10
Stores	Full name of stores or the chains to which they belong	Happy Candy, BonFruit, Alison Nelson's	CHAR(40)	100
......	......	......	......	......

TABLE 13-5   Domain Glossary for the Supply Chain Data Mart

The goal to share terminology completely at all corporate levels is an ambitious one. It undoubtedly deserves to be fixed and documented definitively on paper. The greater the percentage of attributes shared between the various facts included in the data mart, the more useful such a glossary will be. In particular, a domain glossary makes it possible to emphasize those attributes that are shared, and to represent the information about each domain unambiguously. It also makes it easier to overlap fact schemata. On the contrary, if most attributes in various fact schemata show different semantics, those glossaries become less important and you can directly enter glossary information into your attribute glossaries (see section 13.3.2).

13.2.5   Workload and Users

This section gathers together all the documentation relating to user profiles and most frequently issued and/or most important queries of which the core of data mart operations consists.

As far as user profiles are concerned, a UML *use case diagram* is recommended. Figure 7-5 shows how that diagram should look. Furthermore, you should create a graphical representation (Figure 7-6) or a table (Table 7-4) of the constraints on data access for every user profile.

When documenting the workload, we will consider only user (read-only) queries, because ETL (write-only) queries are documented by data-staging schemata. You should create two tables. The first table lists the main necessary reports classified into themed areas. Each report is coupled with a query formulated through a dimensional expression based on an elementary fact or overlapped fact. The queries are also linked to any particular parameters required and to their expected frequency within a given unit of time. The second table shows how each user profile can use reports (static, semi-static, or OLAP). Table 13-6 shows an example related to a data mart for court of law activities.

Themed Area	Report Code	Report Description	Query	Parameters	Freq.

Economic Analysis	EA_001	Payment made per quarter, office, procedure, and subject matter	`REGISTRATION`
			`[quarter,`
			`  procedure,`
			`  subjectMatter;`
			`  magistrate=<param>`
			`  AND year=<param>]`
			`  .payment`
				year, magistrate	10

	EA_002	Payment made per quarter, section, and type of magistrate	`REGISTRATION`
			`[quarter,`
			`  section,`
			`  magistrateType;`
			`  quarter=<param>`
			`  AND section=<param>]`
			`  .payment`
				quarter, section	5

Report Code	Magistrate	Section Head	Office Head
AE_001	static	semi-static	OLAP
AE_002	—	—	OLAP

TABLE 13-6 Workload Specification for a Data Mart for Activities in a Court of Law

Alternatively, you can use the fact schema formalism to represent your queries in graphical form, as mentioned at the end of section 7.1.1. Figure 13-12 shows an example. This representation contains only those attributes and measures you can navigate for analysis purposes. The attributes marked with a black dot show the starting point group-by set. Here you can also specify the input parameters. If reports should be used semi-statically, we suggest that you use this graphical representation because it shows navigation constraints very clearly. However, remember that this representation is suitable only for simple, non-nested queries.

Figure 13-12
An example of semi-static report documentation. The black dots mark the starting point group-by set. The white dots mark hierarchy aggregation levels that can be reached by OLAP navigation.

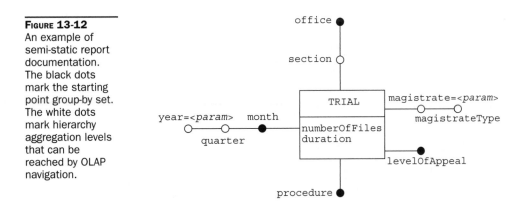

13.2.6 Logical Schema and Physical Schema

Last, but certainly not least, comes this documentation level, which must include logical and physical schemata for data marts.

For Relational OLAP (ROLAP) implementations, logical schemata essentially consist of the relational schemata used to define data mart fact and dimension tables. Those schemata may be star, constellation, or snowflake schemata. To document each table, you can draw a representation of its relational schema or use the SQL *Data Definition Language (DDL)*. Graphical and tabular representations are easier to read, but DDL representations can be transferred immediately to the DBMS in use. Table 13-7 and Figure 13-13, respectively, show a tabular representation of part of the relational schema and the DDL for the star schema of Figure 8-3. Note the non-standard AS IDENTITY clause in the DDL star schema; this clause is used in the DB2 DBMS to set the surrogate keys as sequential numbers managed by the system.

FIGURE 13-13   DDL for the sales star schema

```
CREATE TABLE DATE
(  keyD        INT NOT NULL
   GENERATED ALWAYS AS IDENTITY (START WITH 1, INCREMENT BY 1),
   date        DATE NOT NULL,
   month       CHAR(6),
   quarter     CHAR(5),
   year        CHAR(4),
   day         CHAR(10),
   week        INT,
   holiday     CHAR,
   PRIMARY KEY (keyD) )
CREATE TABLE STORE
(  keyS          INT NOT NULL
   GENERATED ALWAYS AS IDENTITY (START WITH 1, INCREMENT BY 1),
   store         CHAR(40) NOT NULL,
   storeCity     CHAR(40),
   state         CHAR(40),
   country       CHAR(20),
   salesManager  CHAR(10),
   salesDistrict CHAR(10),
   PRIMARY KEY (keyS) )
CREATE TABLE PRODUCT
(  keyP          INT NOT NULL
   GENERATED ALWAYS AS IDENTITY (START WITH 1, INCREMENT BY 1),
   product       CHAR(40) NOT NULL,
   type          CHAR(20),
   category      CHAR(20),
   department    CHAR(20),
   marketingGroup CHAR(20),
   brand         CHAR(20),
   brandCity     CHAR(40),
   PRIMARY KEY (keyP) )
```

```
CREATE TABLE SALES
(  keyD                INT NOT NULL,
   keyS                INT NOT NULL,
   keyP                INT NOT NULL,
   quantity            INT,
   receipts            DEC(10,2),
   unitPrice           DEC(10,2),
   numberOfCustomers SMALLINT,
   PRIMARY KEY (keyD , keyS, keyP),
   FOREIGN KEY (keyD) REFERENCES DATE,
   FOREIGN KEY (keyS) REFERENCES STORE,
   FOREIGN KEY (keyP) REFERENCES PRODUCT )
```

The logical schema should also include relational schemata or DDL statements for each secondary materialized view, although the set of materialized views may change over time because of fine-tuning activities. It may also be helpful to add a diagram showing a graphical representation of the lattice of the materialized views containing roll-up relationships between various group-by sets.

Note that logical schemata are included at the data mart documentation level, rather than the fact level, because one logical schema can relate to more than one fact schema. This applies when there are conformed hierarchies, normally modeled by a single dimension table. This also applies when logical designs include a vertical fragmentation step to create views including measures from two or more separate fact schemata.

The documentation requirements for physical schemata depend partly on individual features of the DBMS used to support a data warehouse. The basic information to be represented relates to the indexes created and index features, although further relevant data can be related to any clustering schemata used or any table partitioning at the DBMS level.

Relation name	PRODUCT			
Conceptual name	product			
Description	Contains all the attributes describing products			
Column	Description	Conceptual name	Type	Source attribute
keyP	Surrogate key	—	INT	—
product	Product names in catalogue	product	CHAR(40)	PRODUCTS.
product type	Level 1 product classification	type	CHAR(20)	TYPES.
type category	Level 2 product classification	category	CHAR(20)	TYPES.category
....	....	....	....	....
Primary key	keyP			
Foreign key	—			

TABLE 13-7   Relational Schema Representation for the PRODUCT Dimension Table

Finally, we suggest that you take note of all the constraints guiding you through the logical and physical design phases (Theodoratos and Bouzeghoub, 2000)—consider the following, for example:

- Space for materializing secondary views
- Space for creating indexes
- Data freshness level
- Maximum user response time
- Maximum loading time

13.2.7   Testing Documents

The documentary records relating to testing must be kept beginning from the initial project phases, because they enable designers and programmers to know the functional and efficiency levels required of the system. Establishing these levels in advance is essential to avoid any disputes arising if design and development are outsourced.

Table 13-8 shows a general schema for the documentation required for each test. You should provide some of the information required in the early design phase; however, other information becomes available only in the development phase or during or as a result of testing. The "Compiled" column specifies the point in the project development cycle at which that document field must be filled in. The values that can be set are: 'D' (design), 'I' (implementation), and 'T' (testing).

Field	Content	Compiled
Test code	Shows the test sequence number	D
Test type	Unit, usability, and so on	D
Test objective	Name of the test module/function	D
Goal	Specifies the aim of the test	D
Pass criteria	Specifies the criteria for passing the test	D
User type	Specifies user skills needed to perform the test	D/I
Prerequisites	Sets out the operations to be carried out before starting the test	I/T
Start-up	Defines the activities to perform to start up the test	I/T
Input data	Shows (possibly generically) the data to be used to perform the test	D/I
Expected output	Specifies the results required in quantitative terms	D/I
System behavior	Describes the behavior of the system during the test	T
Comments	Reports any other observations	T

TABLE 13-8   Test Documentation Schema

13.3 Fact Level

The fact level requires documentation for the information relating to the individual facts making up each data mart. This includes not only fact schemata, but also glossaries for attributes and measures.

13.3.1 Fact Schemata

Naturally, this level focuses on fact schemata, the core of the entire methodology, as we have already discussed at length in Chapter 5. Each elementary fact must be documented in terms of feed interval, history interval, and estimated primary cube sparsity (typically a percentage). Remember that estimated sparsity is defined as $card(G_0)/card_{max}(G_0)$, where G_0 is the primary group-by set, as mentioned in section 7.2. For example, the following text

```
Feed interval: one week
History: 5 years
Sparsity percentage: 10⁻³
```

at the foot of a fact schema shows that data-staging will be carried out every seven days, that the time period covered by that fact is five years, and that only one thousandth of the primary coordinates will actually generate an event $(card(G_0) = card_{max}(G_0)/1000)$.

It is not strictly necessary to document a schema for overlapped facts, although this may be helpful if the workload includes a large number of drill-across queries.

Figure 13-14 shows a simplified summary of the nine fact schemata making up the supply chain data mart.

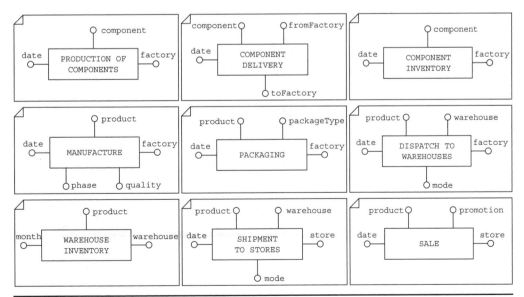

Figure 13-14 Nine supply chain fact schemata

13.3.2   Attribute and Measure Glossaries

Each elementary fact schema must be associated with an attribute glossary and a measure glossary.

The *attribute glossary* (Table 13-9) includes a domain, a cardinality, and a textual description specific for each dimensional attribute. Domains are expressed as they are in domain glossaries, if those have been compiled. If this is not the case, they are expressed in terms of primitive types. It is clear that cardinality values cannot be greater than the domain glossary cardinality values.

The *measure glossary* (Table 13-10) includes a (generally numerical) type and a descriptive field for each measure. To define derived measures, you should refer to the definitions of other measures. Non-derived measures are associated with their defining expressions, starting from the reconciled schema, as we mentioned in section 6.1.7 (Entity-Relationship sources) and section 6.2.3 (relational sources). We want to emphasize that the expression used to define a measure may not be used directly as a population query for a fact table. To issue a query of this kind, you should link to a dimension table to identify the surrogate key values completing the fact table tuples.

This level also requires the compilation of the *additivity matrix* described in Table 5-3. That matrix specifies which aggregation operators can be used for each measure-dimension pair.

Name	Description	Domain	Cardinality
<u>product</u>		Products	5000
brand		Brands	800
brandCity	Where branded products are made	Cities	50
type	(pasta, soft drink...)	Product Types	200
category	(food, clothing...)	Product Categories	10
department	Sales department for the product category	Departments	5
marketingGroup	Product type manager	Marketing Groups	20
<u>store</u>		Stores	100
storeCity		Cities	80
country		Countries	5
. . . .	. . . .	. . . .	. . . .

TABLE 13-9   Attribute Glossary for the Sales Fact Schema; Dimensions Are Underlined

Name	Description	Type	Query

quantity	Quantity of product sold	INT	SELECT SUM(S.quantity)
			FROM SALES S
			    INNER JOIN SALE_RECEIPTS R
			ON R.saleReceiptNum =
			    S.saleReceiptNum
			GROUP BY S.product, R.date,
			         R.store

receipts	Derived measure	DEC(10,2)	unitPrice * quantity

numberOfCustomers	Estimated as the number of receipts issued	SMALLINT	SELECT COUNT(*)
			FROM SALES S
			    INNER JOIN SALE_RECEIPTS R
			ON R.saleReceiptNum =
			    S.saleReceiptNum
			GROUP BY S.product, R.date,
			         R.store

unitPrice	For one product unit	DEC(10,2)	SELECT AVG(S.unitPrice)
			FROM SALES S
			    INNER JOIN SALE_RECEIPTS R
			ON R.saleReceiptNum =
			    S.saleReceiptNum
			GROUP BY S.product, R.date,
			         R.store

TABLE 13-10   Measure Glossary for the Sales Fact Schema

13.4 Methodological Guidelines

This section provides a brief description of some guidelines for integrating your documentation process with your design schedule with reference to the data-driven approach.

You will remember that Chapter 2 states that the bottom-up approach is most commonly used in data warehouse design. This means gradually building new data marts around an initial data mart. For this reason, it is clear that no accurate data warehouse schema can be produced in the initial design phases. And a final version may never be produced, because of the natural evolution process. Despite this, we suggest that you forecast and outline the overall architecture of your data warehouse in terms of data marts in the data warehouse planning phase. Naturally, you should consider this schema entirely open to review and fine-tuning during the actual design process.

The deployment schema will only be partially produced at the time you implement your first data mart so that you can extend it each time you add a new data mart. This also applies for data-staging schemata.

The evolution of operational schemata depends on specific conditions. It may happen that the reconciled schema defined in the source integration phase is valid for multiple data marts. But it may also happen that every data mart implies a separate integration operation and consequently generates its own reconciled schema, which is separate from other reconciled schemata and is, of course, compatible with them.

On the basis of these observations, we can briefly sum up the documentation process in the design phase as follows:

```
0. draw the initial data warehouse schema, and
   insert all the relevant data marts;
1. choose the next data mart for prototyping;
2. for that data mart:
   2.1 identify its sources and its user categories,
       show them in the data warehouse schema;
   2.2 integrate the sources and create (or extend)
       the operational schema;
   2.3 identify its relevant facts and create
       a bus matrix, an overlapping matrix
       and a temporal scenario table that sum up
       all fact properties;
   2.4 identify the level of quality and efficiency required
       and set a testing document;
   2.5 for each fact:
       2.5.1 use the operational schema to define a fact schema;
       2.5.2 compile the attribute and measure glossaries;
   2.6 identify relevant overlapping facts
       and show them in the overlapping matrix;
   2.7 compile the domain glossary;
   2.8 define the workload;
   2.9 define the logical and physical schemata;
3. define (or extend) the data-staging schema;
4. define (or extend) the deployment schema;
5. repeat from point 1.
```

A Case Study

This chapter offers a complete case study to help you put what you have learned in the preceding chapters to the test. The case in point is a large Italian company selling wholesale sportswear. Gruppo Sistema s.r.l., Cesena, Italy, kindly provided us access to this case study and we would like to thank them for all the help they gave us.

14.1 Application Domain

Our company, which we will call *TransSport*, is mainly engaged in wholesale sales. Its sales operation is run by a network of agencies located across Italy. Each agency has a certain number of sales agents who are assigned their own operating territory. Most of the customers are large retail chains with a number of branches in different locations.

A sale is represented by a sales document consisting of one or more lines detailing the units of goods sold. The items offered for sale by TranSport are highly seasonal. This results in extremely variable trends in sales of the different products over the course of the year, with a consequent marked fluctuation in turnover. The calendar year is divided into two main marketing campaigns: fall/winter and spring/summer. Order collection and invoicing for these campaigns take place in separate months of the year.

Shortly before the start of each season's campaign, a price list is compiled that includes the items to be shown to customers for their orders and the subsequent invoices. The products sold are divided into two categories, new and classic. New products are added to the collection to refresh the range and keep this up to date with the latest fashion trends. Classic products sell regularly over several seasons.

The operating budget is drawn up yearly in summer to plan the items to be sold and the amounts to be invoiced in each season. This budget may of course undergo some modifications over the course of the trading year. The budget is then passed on to the sales and marketing department managers, who sort the predicted figures by customer and by product.

14.2 Planning the TranSport Data Warehouse

The planning phase involved two distinct departments: the sales department, which deals mainly with the sales agencies, and the marketing department, which focuses on the items sold. Two data marts will be created: one for each department. Figure 14-1 shows the data

FIGURE 14-1
Data warehouse
schema for
TranSport

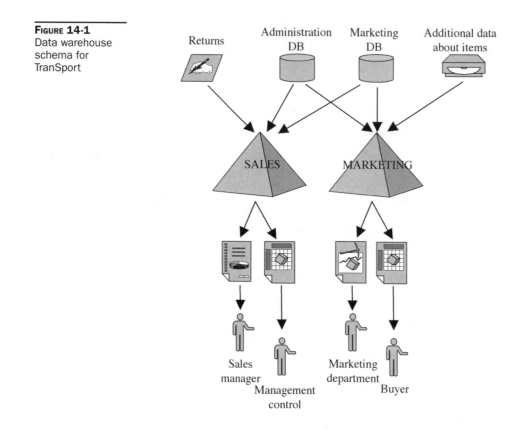

warehouse schema. The sales department was chosen for the first prototype data mart, whose design will be examined in greater detail in this chapter. We decided to adopt a data-driven approach for two reasons. First, the need to integrate two databases to obtain a reconciled schema enabled us to gain sufficient in-depth knowledge of the operational schemata and made it unnecessary to resort to an exclusively requirement-driven approach. Second, the operational data was not complex enough to adopt a mixed approach.

14.3 The Sales Data Mart

Figure 14-2 shows a preview of the bus matrix and overlapping matrix for the sales department. The following sections will give the details of the various design phases, with particular reference to the ORDER fact.

14.3.1 Data Source Analysis and Reconciliation

Data source analysis for the sales data mart was based on that part of the company information system related to the sales and marketing departments. To complete it, we involved the IT staff directly. Our goal was to generate the conceptual and logical schemata for the business area being studied.

	Facts	Degenerate	ORDER	INVOICE	BUDGET
Dimensions					
orderDate			✓		
customer			✓	✓	
deliveryDate		✓	✓		
subCategory			✓	✓	
paymentDueDate		✓	✓		
agent			✓	✓	✓
date (invoiced)				✓	
year		✓			✓
category		✓			✓
season		✓			✓

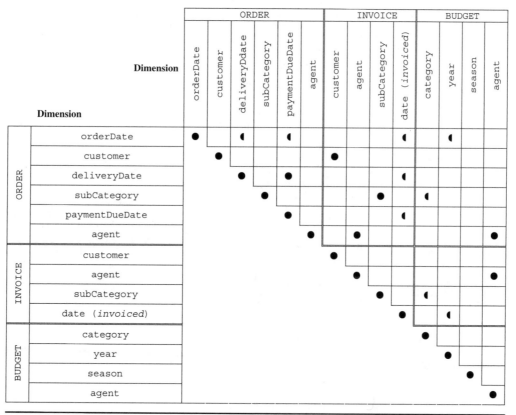

FIGURE 14-2 Bus matrix and overlapping matrix for the sales data mart

14.3.1.1 Recognition

The TranSport information system is managed by an IBM AS/400 system containing two distinct relational databases: the first, the Administration DB, manages orders and invoices; the second, the Marketing DB, is used by the general management and the marketing department to plan and manage marketing campaigns and their predicted results for sales agents and items. Both databases were created at different times. The Administration DB has been in use for more than 15 years to manage those administrative procedures that are most directly linked to sales activities. The Marketing DB has been recently introduced to rationalize sales policy and to provide the company management with a tool for monitoring the progress of the marketing campaigns and the work of agents. Although both databases were created on the same platform, the systems are barely integrated and many overlaps and conflicts have been revealed.

Tables 14-1 and 14-2 show the relations in both databases. A set of lookup tables must be added to those tables to ensure that a correspondence exists between the codes provided for many of the relation attributes and the associated description.

The register and sales relations include a somewhat large number of attributes, many of which will not be used, since they provide little in the way of interesting information.

Relation Name	Description
CUSTOMER	Basic customer details
CUSTOMER_DETAILS	Additional information on customers
BRANCH	Information on each customer's branch offices
ITEM	Basic information on the items to be sold by TranSport
ITEM_DETAILS	Additional information on the items
VENDOR	Sales agents and their agencies
MOVEMENT	Invoice headers
MOVEMENT_LINE	Individual lines in the invoices
ORDER	Sales document headers
ORDER_LINE	Individual lines in the orders (a tuple for each item)

TABLE 14-1 Administration DB Relations

Relationship Name	Description
ITEM	Basic information on the items to be sold by TranSport
ITEM_DETAILS	Additional information on the items
PRICE_LIST	Sale prices of the items
SUB-SEGMENT	Item sub-segments (racing costumes, beach costumes, etc.)
SUB-CATEGORY	Item sub-categories (water textile, gym footwear, etc.)
AGENT	Agents and their agencies
SALES_BUDGET	Data of interest for the sales budget
MARKETING_BUDGET	Data of interest for the marketing budget

TABLE 14-2 Marketing DB Relations

TABLE 14-3
Documentation for
Some Attributes
of the CUSTOMER
Relation

From	To	Name	Type	Length	Description
1	1	CLITRK	A	1	Record type
2	6	CLIDIT	A	5	Company code
7	12	CLICOD	A	6	Customer code
13	41	CLIRG1	A	29	Company name
42	71	CLIIND	A	30	Address

The relations are often denormalized and contain redundant attributes, in some cases entered to increase the response speed.

The initial documentation provided by the IT staff for database inspection is a print-out—created by the DBMS export program—of the description of the attributes in the archives stored in the AS/400 system. Table 14-3 shows a small part of that print-out. The meaning of the columns is as follows:

- *From* indicates the start position of the attribute.
- *To* indicates the end position of the attribute.
- *Name* is the name of the attribute.
- *Type* can be assigned one of two values: 'A' means that the attribute is stored normally, 'P' means that the information is stored in compact form.
- *Length* indicates the number of bytes the attribute occupies.
- *Description* briefly describes what the attribute means.

Following this is the logical schemata for some of the tables, starting with the schema for the Administration DB. The name of the attributes, their domain, a brief description, and any foreign keys are indicated in each table. Attributes that make up primary keys are underlined. If an attribute refers to a lookup table, the generic term *Lookup* is shown.

ORDER

Name	Description	Domain	References
AAORCT	Year of order	Integer	
NRORCT	Order number	Integer	
CLORCT	Order class	String	
CDDICT	Company code	String	BRANCH
CDCLCT	Customer code	String	BRANCH
CDFICT	Branch code	String	BRANCH
CDA1CT	Vendor	String	VENDOR
CDPACT	Payment	String	*Lookup*
DTCOCT	Delivery date	Date	
SCPACT	Discount on payment	Float	
SCINT	Unconditional discount	Float	
CDANCT	Reason for cancellation	String	*Lookup*
DTPACT	Payment-due date	Date	
DTIMCT	Date order entered	Date	
QTTOCT	Total order quantity	Float	
RU07CT	Payment type	String	*Lookup*
RGRCCT	Season	String	

ORDER_LINE

Name	Description	Domain	References
AAORCD	Year of order	Integer	ORDER
NRORCD	Order number	Integer	ORDER
RIORCD	Order line	Integer	
CLORCD	Order class	String	
CDARCD	Item code	String	ITEM
QTTOCD	Quantity ordered	Integer	
DTCOCD	Goods delivery date	Date	
CDANCD	Reason for cancellation	String	*Lookup*
CDA1CD	Vendor	String	VENDOR

ITEM

Name	Description	Domain	References
CDARAR	Item code	String	
DEARAR	Item description	String	
DECOAR	Color description	String	
CDMOAR	Model	String	
CDIVAR	VAT number	String	
UBARAR	Location in warehouse	String	
CDFOAR	Manufacturer	String	*Lookup*
LINEAR	Range	String	*Lookup*

After using the available documentation to conduct a thorough analysis, processing a set of database queries, and taking advantage of IT staff assistance, some inconsistencies were found, including the following:

- In the ORDER relation, the reference to the vendor is redundant because each customer may be serviced by only a single vendor. For this reason, the vendor of a customer is uniquely identified. A clear redundancy also exists in the ORDER_LINE relation.

- The key used in ORDER is in fact a superkey because the numbering of the orders in different years does not depend on the order class. This inconsistency was identified because ORDER_LINE includes only the first two attributes of the ORDER key. To check this, the data was queried. This confirmed that the tuples in ORDER are unequivocally identified by the attributes AAORCT and NRORCT.

- *Order class* indicates how an order is placed (for example, by telephone, from samples), during the season—fall/winter, restock. A possible value for the attribute CLORCT is 'FW2008 sample set', which corresponds to the 'FW' value in the RGRCCT attribute. For this reason, the ORDER relation is denormalized by the functional dependency CLORCT→RGRCCT.

- The CLORCD attribute in ORDER_LINE is redundant because the order class is determined by the order of which the line is a part.

The following tables are from the Marketing DB:

ITEM

Name	Description	Domain	References
CDARAR	Item code	String	
DEARAR	Item description	String	
DECOAR	Color description	String	
CDMOAR	Model	String	
CDTEAR	Subject	String	*Lookup*
AAPRAR	Production year	Date	
STPRAR	Production season	String	
AAATAR	Current price list year	Integer	
STPRAR	Current price list season	String	
LISTAR	Order class	String	
RG10AR	Designer	String	*Lookup*
PREMAR	Average price	Float	
CDFOAR	Manufacturer	String	*Lookup*
SESSAR	Target	String	*Lookup*
LINEAR	Range	String	*Lookup*

PRICE_LIST

Name	Description	Domain	References
AAATLT	Price list year	Integer	
ATATAL	Price list season	String	
CDARLT	Item code	String	ITEM
CL01LT	Order class	String	
PREILT	Unit price	Float	
CL02LT	Order class 2	String	
CL03LT	Order class 3	String	

SUB-SEGMENT

Name	Description	Domain	References
CODSOS	Sub-segment code	String	
DESSOS	Sub-segment description	String	

SUB-CATEGORY

Name	Description	Domain	References
CODSOC	Sub-category code	String	
DESSOC	Sub-category description	String	

SALES_BUDGET

Name	Description	Domain	References
BUDCAN	Sales year	Integer	
RGCLOC	Season	String	
AGCOM	Agent	String	AGENT
CODSOC	Sub-category	String	
BUDCPRR	Predicted returns	Integer	
BUDCQT	Predicted total quantity	Integer	
BUDCPRA	Predicted cancellations	Integer	
BUDCPRS	Predicted discounts	Integer	
BUDCVL	Predicted gross value	Integer	

MARKETING_BUDGET

Name	Description	Domain	References
BUDMAN	Sales year	Integer	
RGCLOC	Season	String	
ARTBUDM	Item code	String	ITEM
CODSOS	Sub-segment	String	
SESSAR	Target	String	
BUDMPRR	Predicted returns	Integer	
BUDMPRA	Predicted cancellations	Integer	
BUDMPRS	Predicted year-end discounts	Integer	
BUDMVL	Predicted gross value	Integer	
BUDMQT	Predicted total quantity	Integer	
BUDMFT	Predicted invoice discount	Integer	

Here are some of the anomalies found in the Marketing DB:

- In ITEM, the information on the price list is completely useless because PRICE_LIST already has the history of all the price lists where an item is located.

- Attributes CL02LT and CL03LT of PRICE_LIST model in a denormalized way an item included in three lists in the same campaign. Of course, the number of price lists will vary from campaign to campaign in a real-world situation. And for this reason even more than three can exist.

- Although ITEM does not have any foreign keys referring to SUB-SEGMENT and SUB-SEGMENT does not have any foreign key referring to SUB-CATEGORY, having spoken to the users, it would seem that the items belong to sub-segments (for example racing costumes, beach costumes), which are in turn grouped into sub-categories (for example water textiles, gym footwear).

- The MARKETING_BUDGET relation is denormalized because of the functional dependency between item and target and between item and sub-segment.

14.3.1.2 Normalization

We used a *reverse engineering* process to derive Entity-Relationship schemata from the logical schemata for both databases. Figures 14-3 and 14-4 show the Entity-Relationship schemata that we obtained. For greater clarity, only those attributes that are part of the identifiers are included. To make the schemata easier to understand, we will use the attribute descriptions to identify them instead of the name from this point on.

Note that the term INVOICE has been introduced into the Administration DB, replacing the term MOVEMENT, which was considered less appropriate. In addition, the problems mentioned in section 14.3.1 have been solved. The CAMPAIGN entity in the Marketing DB indicates a specific campaign identified by a year and a season. It is also necessary to pay attention to the PRICE LIST *entity*, which should not be confused with the PRICE_LIST *relation* of the Marketing DB. The PRICE LIST entity models the heading of a price list identified by class, year, and season. The PRICE_LIST relation implements the many-to-many relationship between the PRICE LIST and ITEM entities.

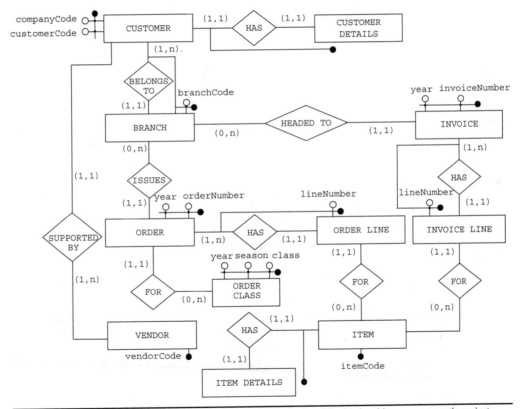

FIGURE 14-3 Entity-Relationship schema for the Administration DB obtained by reverse engineering

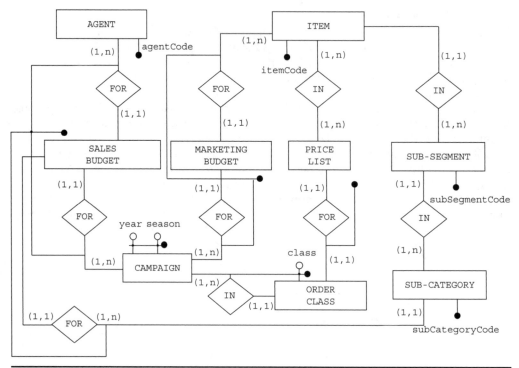

FIGURE 14-4   Entity-Relationship schema for the Marketing DB obtained by reverse engineering

14.3.1.3   Integration

Starting from the local schemata shown in Figures 14-3 and 14-4, we proceeded with the integration phase. We followed the steps indicated in the methodology proposed in Chapter 3. Since there were only two schemata, we were not faced with the problem of choosing an integration technique, and the binary type inevitably had to be used. However, on the advice of the IT staff, we favored the Marketing DB solution when any conflict arose, because it was most recently created. Comparison of the two schemata revealed the following conflicts:

- Clearly the terms AGENT and VENDOR are synonymous. AGENT is the preferred name. Although many of the attributes common to the two schemata had different names, we could easily identify correspondences after we analyzed their descriptions. We had to resolve all attribute name conflicts before we could integrate both schemata.

- After checking the data, the CDFOAR attributes in the ITEM entities in both databases were found to be homonymous. The Administration DB stores the name of the product suppliers and the Marketing DB stores the name of the actual manufacturer.

- The campaign concept is expressed in the Administration DB by the `season` and `year` attributes of the `ORDER CLASS` entity. This is done by an entity in the Marketing DB.

- The `AGENT` and `ITEM` entities are common to both schemata and describe the same concept from different points of view, so they contain different sets of attributes.

At this point, the integration methodology required that both schemata be aligned. This meant that their conflicts had to be resolved. In addition to eliminating synonymy, it was necessary to add the `CAMPAIGN` entity to the Administration DB schema. To resolve the homonymy revealed in the `ITEM` entity, we renamed the `CDFOAR` attribute in the Administration DB to `supplier`. In order for the schemata to be merged, the `AGENT` and `ITEM` entities had to contain the same set of attributes—that is, the union of both sets of attributes.

Then both aligned schemata could be merged. To do this, we overlapped their common concepts. Figure 14-5 shows the reconciled schema obtained in this way. Note that this includes both the `CATEGORY` and `SEGMENT` entities not included in the local schemata because they were added only after creating the Marketing DB. Examples of categories and segments are, respectively, 'swimming' and 'costumes'. The IT staff suggested their inclusion because they represented a useful level of aggregation for decision-making processes. Obviously, when the reconciled schema has been initialized, the data of `CATEGORY` and the `SEGMENT` has been entered manually.

As the users stated, the sales budget was currently drawn up on the basis of categories, while it was drawn up on the basis of sub-categories when the Marketing DB was being designed. This meant that one category was being incorrectly stored in the `CODSOC` attribute for some 10 years! Adding `CATEGORY` gave us the opportunity to solve this problem.

14.3.1.4 Designing the Reconciled Database

While the reconciled database was being defined, we also needed to set a level of data logging. Because the source databases were transient, we opted to retain this situation in the reconciled database. It is nonetheless essential to asses the needs of the data staging process. Data staging should be done incrementally, so we added an `oper` attribute to every relation. This attribute should show whether a tuple has been modified since the last data population procedure was carried out. If this is the case, the attribute should specify the type of operation that generated the modification. See Chapter 10 for more details on this point. Figures 14-6 and 14-7 show the logical schema for the reconciled database shown in Figure 14-5. The notation used is the *Crow's Foot Entity-Relationship Diagram*. In that diagram, the referential integrity constraints are represented by lines terminating in what looks like the claws of a crow's foot, at the end of which the foreign keys can be found.

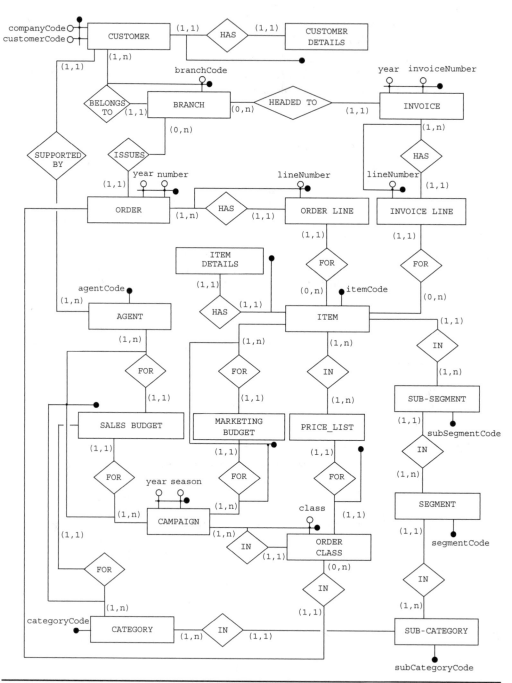

FIGURE 14-5   Conceptual schema of the reconciled database

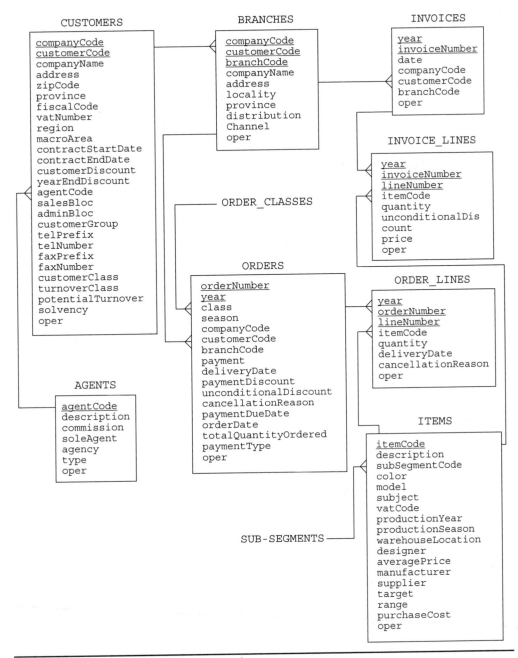

CUSTOMERS

companyCode
customerCode
companyName
address
zipCode
province
fiscalCode
vatNumber
region
macroArea
contractStartDate
contractEndDate
customerDiscount
yearEndDiscount
agentCode
salesBloc
adminBloc
customerGroup
telPrefix
telNumber
faxPrefix
faxNumber
customerClass
turnoverClass
potentialTurnover
solvency
oper

BRANCHES

companyCode
customerCode
branchCode
companyName
address
locality
province
distribution
Channel
oper

INVOICES

year
invoiceNumber
date
companyCode
customerCode
branchCode
oper

INVOICE_LINES

year
invoiceNumber
lineNumber
itemCode
quantity
unconditionalDis
count
price
oper

ORDER_CLASSES

ORDERS

orderNumber
year
class
season
companyCode
customerCode
branchCode
payment
deliveryDate
paymentDiscount
unconditionalDiscount
cancellationReason
paymentDueDate
orderDate
totalQuantityOrdered
paymentType
oper

ORDER_LINES

year
orderNumber
lineNumber
itemCode
quantity
deliveryDate
cancellationReason
oper

AGENTS

agentCode
description
commission
soleAgent
agency
type
oper

ITEMS

itemCode
description
subSegmentCode
color
model
subject
vatCode
productionYear
productionSeason
warehouseLocation
designer
averagePrice
manufacturer
supplier
target
range
purchaseCost
oper

SUB-SEGMENTS

FIGURE 14-6 Reconciled logical schema, part 1

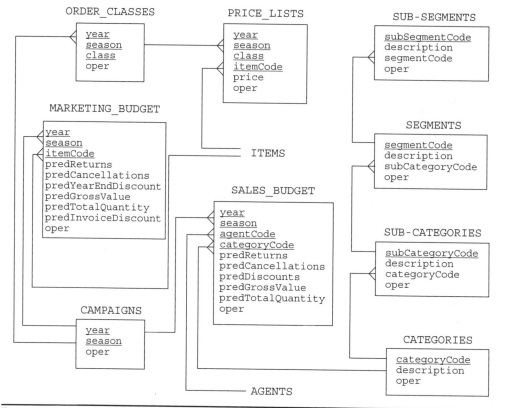

FIGURE 14-7   Reconciled logical schema, part 2

Once the logical schema was available, we defined the second result of the integration phase: the mapping between the relations in the source schemata and those in the reconciled schema. This result was useful in defining the population process. Since the Global-As-View (GAV) approach was used, the mapping consists of a set of SQL instructions that define concepts of the reconciled schema as views of source schemata. Figure 14-8 shows some examples of this.

FIGURE 14-8   SQL queries that define the mapping between the local schemata and the reconciled schema on the basis of the GAV approach

```
// Customer mapping from the Administration DB
CREATE VIEW CUSTOMERS (companyCode, customerCode, companyName, ...) AS
    SELECT C.CLIDIT, C.CLICOD, C.CLIRG1, ...,
            CD.PTELSC, CD.TELSC, ...
    FROM   CUSTOMER AS C, CUSTOMER_DETAILS AS CD
    WHERE  C.CLIDIT= CD.CLIDIT AND
            C.CLICOD = CD.CLICOD
// Campaign Mapping from the Marketing DB
CREATE VIEW CAMPAIGNS (year, season) AS
    SELECT BUDCAN, RGCLOC
```

```
FROM    SALES_BUDGET
UNION
SELECT BUDMAN, RGCLOC
FROM    MARKETING_BUDGET
```

14.3.2 User Requirement Analysis

After talking to the users, we learned that they need three facts from the sales data mart: *invoices, orders,* and *budget*. Table 14-4 shows a glossary of requirements for the granularity required, the main measures identified, and the historical interval. Table 14-5 shows some sample queries extracted from the preliminary workload.

Comparing the requirements expressed by the end users with the reconciled schema made it necessary to define a new attribute to be added to the existing ones: returns, indicating the number of items returned for each order line. The users and the database administrators agreed that the data staging frequency should be one week for orders and invoices and yearly for the budget.

TABLE 14-4
Example of User
Requirement
Glossary

Fact	Possible Dimensions	Possible Measures	History
ORDER	agent, customer, item subCategory, orderDate, paymentDueDate, deliveryDate	quantity, price, discounts, returns, netOrders	5 years
INVOICE	agent, customer, subCategory, invoiceDate	quantity, price, discounts	5 years
BUDGET	year, season, agent, item category	provisional data	5 years

TABLE 14-5
A Sample of
the Preliminary
Workload.

Fact	Query
ORDER	Total annual quantity ordered for a certain item category.
	Average gap between goods delivery date and payment date, by customer.
	Net total orders by agent, customer, and item sub-category.
INVOICE	Total quantity invoiced in each item sub-category for the previous year.
	For a given customer, the receipts from the various item categories in a certain month.
	Annual receipt summary by customer region.
BUDGET	Summary of the predicted total quantity sold, by year and by item category.
	Predicted annual cancellations and returns for the current year, by agent and by season.

In considering the dynamic features of the hierarchies, the users asked to be able to formulate queries based on the today-for-yesterday and today-or-yesterday temporal scenarios with reference to agents assigned to the agencies. Only the today-for-yesterday scenario was required in all the other cases.

14.3.3 Conceptual Design

We started the conceptual design for the sales data mart by selecting the INVOICE, ORDER, and BUDGET facts, corresponding respectively to the INVOICE_LINES, the ORDER_LINES, and the SALES_BUDGET relations.

Let's look in detail at the design for the ORDER fact. Figure 14-9 shows the attribute tree rooted in the ORDER_LINES relation. We will make the first sequence of adjustment operations on this one:

1. For greater clarity, composite keys are replaced by the relation name. For example, year+orderNumber becomes order.

2. The oper attributes are eliminated.

3. The codes and corresponding description attributes are inverted to eliminate the codes and keep the description as the node.

4. The returns attribute is added, as requested by users.

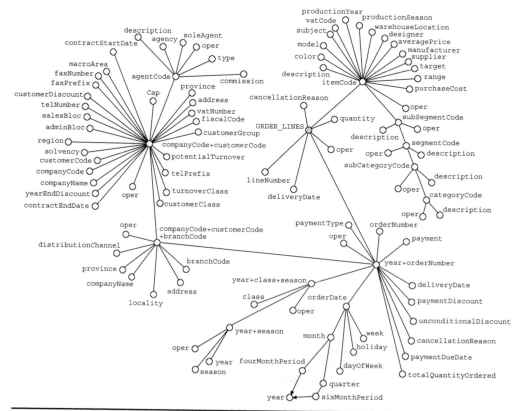

Figure 14-9 Attribute tree

5. The unit price of an order line is unequivocally set, because an order line determines an item and an order class, which in turn determines a price list. An item and a price list determine a price. However, the algorithm navigating the functional dependencies in the reconciled schema is not capable of extracting the dependency between order lines and prices. For this reason, we added the `price` attribute as a root child. The `price` value can then be retrieved if we execute a simple SQL query during the data population process.

6. Functional dependencies not included in the reconciled schema are added (between customer region and macro-area, between customer group and turnover class).

In this way, we obtained the tree shown in Figure 14-10. Then we proceeded with the specific pruning and grafting operations for the sales area data mart.

1. We pruned the nodes of no interest, such as `orderNumber`.

2. We eliminated some functional dependencies to make some attributes become dimensions, such as `customer`, or measures, such as `unconditionalDiscount`.

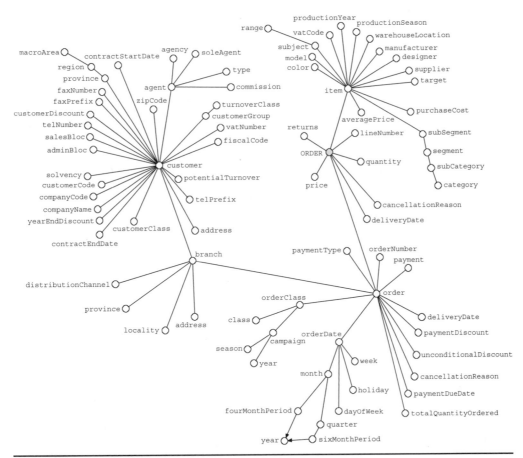

FIGURE 14-10 Modified attribute tree

3. The arc between `customer` and `contractEndDate` was marked as optional.

4. We grafted the node `item` and we retained only its sub-category.

Then we selected the dimensions and measures. Figure 14-11 shows the resulting tree, and Figure 14-12 shows the resulting lossy-grained fact schema. We added some derived measures to the fact schema, summarized in the measure glossary shown in Table 14-6. All the measures are additive along all dimensions because all the discounts are shown as amounts and not as percentages, except for `price` averaged along all dimensions. The attribute `paymentType` may be modeled as a description attribute of the fact since it depends exclusively on the customer. Note the high sparsity value due, on the one hand, to the fact that most customers prefer to place a few large orders during each season and, on the other, to the presence of functional dependencies between dimensions:

$$customer \rightarrow agent$$
$$orderDate \rightarrow paymentDueDate$$

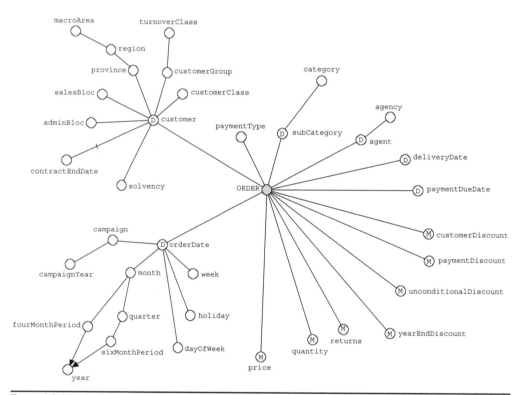

FIGURE 14-11   Attribute tree after pruning and grafting, showing dimensions and measures

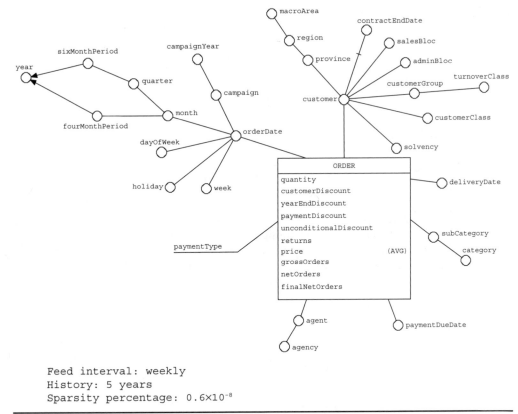

Feed interval: weekly
History: 5 years
Sparsity percentage: 0.6×10^{-8}

FIGURE 14-12   Orders fact schema

Name	Type	Query

quantity	Float	SELECT SUM(L.quantity)
		FROM ORDER_LINES AS L, ORDERS AS O,
		    CUSTOMERS AS C, ITEMS AS I,
		    SUB-SEGMENTS AS SS, SEGMENTS AS S,
		    SUB-CATEGORIES AS SC, AGENTS AS A
		WHERE <L join O> AND <O join C> AND
		    <L join I> AND ...
		GROUP BY O.orderDate, C.companyName,
		    C.customerCode, L.deliveryDate,
		    SC.description, O.paymentDueDate,
		    A.description

grossOrders	Float	quantity * price
netOrders	Float	grossOrders - unconditionalDiscount - customerDiscount - paymentDiscount
finalNetOrders	Float	netOrders - returns

TABLE 14-6   Part of the Measure Glossary for Orders

TABLE 14-7
Part of the
Data Volume

Attribute	Cardinality
item	30,000
subSegment	20
customer	12,000
agent	63
agency	13
deliveryDate	1500
orderDate	1500
paymentDueDate	1500

An extract of the data volume is shown in Table 14-7.

Figures 14-13 and 14-14 show the resulting fact schemata for invoices and budget, respectively. Overlapping the invoices and budget schemata is particularly important for end users because it allows them to check the budget (Figure 4-15).

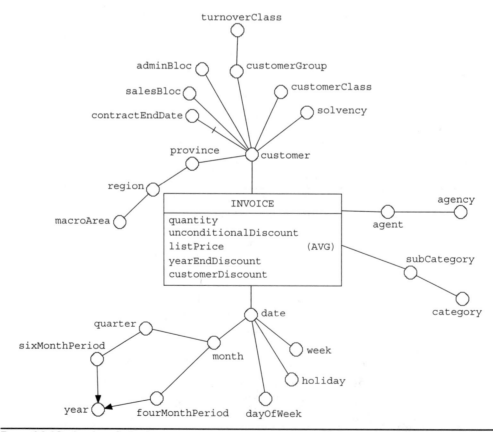

Figure 14-13   Invoices fact schema

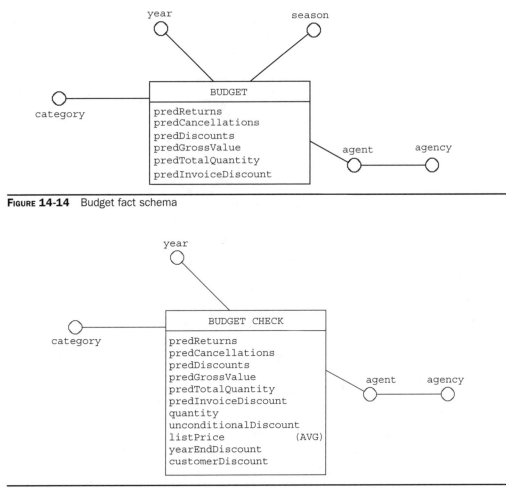

Figure 14-14   Budget fact schema

Figure 14-15   Invoice and budget fact schemata overlapped

14.3.4 Logical Design

At the logical level, we opted for the use of star schemata for all the data marts. Figure 14-16 shows the schemata for orders and invoices. The budget schema is so simple that it has been omitted. Note that the two facts present a number of conformed hierarchies (`agent`, `subCategory`, `customer`, `date`). For this reason, they will not be duplicated. In particular, the `orderDate` hierarchy for the `ORDER` fact contains two more attributes than the hierarchy for `INVOICE`. To obviate this problem, we applied a snowflake solution and added a new `DT_CAMPAIGN` table. This table will be used to query orders only.

The agents hierarchy is managed in dynamic mode because user requirements showed the need to model the transfer of agents between the various agencies. We chose to use a fully-logged dynamic hierarchy because different temporal scenarios should be supported. This requires the timestamps to be entered (`validityStart` and `validityEnd`) to manage valid tuples in addition to a `master` attribute to determine reference tuples.

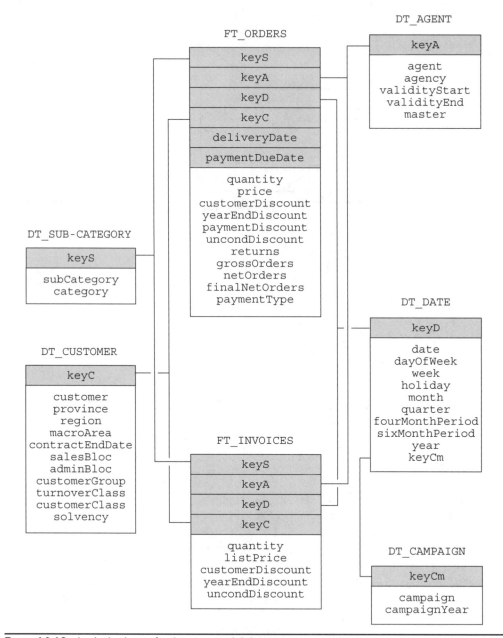

FIGURE 14-16 Logical schema for the commercial data mart

The ORDER fact schema includes two degenerate dimensions, namely paymentDueDate and deliveryDate. We decided to add them as attributes to the primary key of the order fact table, rather than create two more foreign keys referencing DT_DATE to avoid additional joins. The paymentType descriptive attribute is linked to the fact. For this reason, we added paymentType to the fact table.

The main obstacle to creating materialized views was determined by the workload. Figure 14-17 shows some examples of queries, that were derived from interviews with the future data mart users and from the analysis of standard reports previously created by the IT staff. We used dimensional expressions to codify those queries, as explained in section 7.1. On the basis of the volume of data previously collected (150 GB for primary events) and the space limitations imposed by the database administrator (500 GB for the entire data mart), we decided to set aside 100 GB for the materialized views. The price and the listPrice measures in both facts are not additive. This means that the grouped views must contain the count support measure in order to use the AVG operator for aggregations to be carried out starting from other, partially aggregated views. See section 9.1.9 for more details.

FIGURE 14-17   Some workload queries used for view materialization

```
ORDER[year; category='swimming'].quantity
ORDER[deliveryDate, paymentDueDate, customer].(deliveryDate-paymentDueDate)
ORDER[agent, customer, subCategory].netOrders
INVOICE[subCategory; year='2008'].quantity
INVOICE[customer, category; month='12/2008'].
    (quantity*price-unconditionalDiscount-customerDiscount)
INVOICE[region, year].
    (quantity*price-unconditionalDiscount-customerDiscount)
```

View materialization was carried out heuristically without the support of automated tools because of the reduced reliability of the workload collected. In the initial weeks during which the data mart was in use, we had to use the tools made available by the DBMS to compile a detailed list of the queries made by users and carry out the necessary tuning operations. When we defined our views, our goal was to reduce the cost of executing the workload in relation to the space limitation; other optimization principles, such as the update time limitation, were not considered.

Figure 14-18 shows some of the group-by sets defining the views created for the workload. Note that you can use the G_3 group-by set view to solve the first query in Figure 14-17: Even if this view does not have the same group-by set as the query, its level of aggregation is sufficient to produce a notable reduction in the number of tuples accessed. The query can be processed efficiently even because of the stringent selection criterion. Figure 14-17 shows that no view was planned for the second query because its very fine group-by set does not lead to any sharp reduction in the number of tuples accessed. Finally, you can use the G_2 group-by set view to resolve the third query directly.

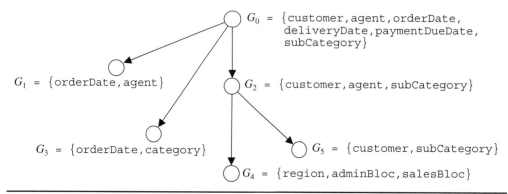

$G_0 = \{\texttt{customer,agent,orderDate,}$
$\qquad\texttt{deliveryDate,paymentDueDate,}$
$\qquad\texttt{subCategory}\}$

$G_1 = \{\texttt{orderDate,agent}\}$

$G_2 = \{\texttt{customer,agent,subCategory}\}$

$G_3 = \{\texttt{orderDate,category}\}$

$G_5 = \{\texttt{customer,subCategory}\}$

$G_4 = \{\texttt{region,adminBloc,salesBloc}\}$

FIGURE 14-18 A part of the multidimensional lattice defining the views to be materialized in the orders schema

14.3.5 Data-Staging Design

Data staging can be divided into two subsequent phases because of the presence of the reconciled layer: from the operational data sources to the reconciled database and from the reconciled database to the star schemata. We decided to export the data to flat files and subsequently importing them into the reconciled database, because the source and destination databases were in different platforms. This approach made it possible to use the DBMS *bulk loader* program that delivers much better performance than SQL commands.

The log-based technique was used for incremental data extraction because the operational DBMS provides a built-in interpretation tool. The transformation operations were not particularly complex, with the exception of merging information on items and agents. Indeed, these two concepts existed in both databases, but they had different attribute sets. There was also a data-cleaning problem with the ITEMS and the AGENTS relations because both sets of information were completely unaligned. The similarity between the tuples in the ITEMS relation was determined by a set of rules based on common attributes: description, color, and model. There was no point in using the item codes as they were represented in different ways in both data sources. Note that after merging data, we had to copy a single code wherever a reference was made to each individual item.

As far as star schemata population from the reconciled database was concerned, we decided to keep a lookup table named LU_*NameDT* in the staging area for each dimension table. This would speed up searches for surrogate key values. Then we created three loading procedures, one for each possible value of the oper attribute. For example, if some tuples in the AGENTS relation change, the loading procedure processes the three queries shown in Figure 14-19. The first query extracts only the modified tuples from the reconciled database. The second query updates the validity-end timestamp to terminate the validity of the tuples modified in the DT_AGENT dimension table. The third query enters the new tuples: the validityStart attribute contains the current date, the validityEnd attribute is set to NULL showing that the tuple is still valid, and the master attribute points at the reference tuple. In the interests of brevity, we do not provide the query updating the LU_AGENT lookup table.

FIGURE 14-19   The three main queries necessary to update the dimension table DT_AGENT

```
// Extraction from the reconciled database
INSERT INTO TEMP1
    SELECT agentCode, description, agency
    FROM    AGENTS
    WHERE   oper='U'
// Update timestamps in the dimension table
UPDATE DT_AGENT
SET     validityEnd = CURRENT_DATE
WHERE keyA IN
  ( SELECT LU.keyA
    FROM    TEMP1 AS T, LU_AGENT AS LU
    WHERE   T.agentCode = LU.agentCode)
// Load modified tuples into the dimension table
INSERT INTO DT_AGENT (agent, agency, validityStart, master)
    SELECT T.description, T.agency, CURRENT_DATE, LU.masterKey
    FROM    TEMP1 AS T, LU_AGENT AS LU
    WHERE   T.agentCode = LU.agentCode
```

The fact table loading process features reconciled-database access to retrieve all the measures and key values relating to the various dimensions. Figure 14-20 shows the queries that extract the reconciled-database data to populate the FT_ORDERS fact table.

FIGURE 14-20   The query for extracting the data to update the FT_ORDERS fact table

```
// Extraction from the reconciled database
INSERT INTO TEMP2
    SELECT C.agentCode, C.customerCode, C.companyCode, S.subCategoryCode,
           O.orderDate, L.deliveryDate,
           O.paymentDueDate, O.paymentType,
           SUM(L.quantityOrdered), AVG(P.price),
           SUM(C.customerDiscount), SUM(C.yearEndDiscount),
           ...... // omitted for brevity
    FROM   ORDER_LINES AS L, ORDERS AS O, CUSTOMERS AS C,
           ITEMS AS I, SUB-SEGMENTS AS SS, SEGMENTS AS S,
           PRICE_LISTS AS P
    WHERE  L.orderNumber = O.orderNumber AND
           L.year = O.year AND
           O.customerCode = C.customerCode AND
           O.companyCode = C.companyCode AND
           L.itemCode = I.itemCode AND
           I.subSegmentCode = SS.subSegmentCode AND
           SS.segmentCode = S.segmentCode AND
           O.year = P.year AND
           O.season = P.season AND
           O.class = P.class AND
           L.itemCode = P.itemCode
    GROUP BY C.agentCode, C.customerCode, C.companyCode, S.subCategoryCode,
             O.orderDate, L.deliveryDate,
             O.paymentDueDate, O.paymentType
```

14.3.6   Physical Design

The main point to be addressed in this phase is the choice of the indexes for fact and dimension tables to be created. After consulting the manuals of the DBMS used for data mart implementation, we could ascertain the following features:

- The DBMS is equipped with a cost-based optimizer.
- It can use B+-Tree, bitmap, and join indexes.
- It implements three join algorithms: nested-loop, sort-merge, and hybrid hash.

We were aware that we would be able to create indexes quite safely because we knew that the DBMS used a cost-based optimizer. If you express a poorly selective predicate for an indexed attribute, the optimizer automatically excludes the index from the execution plan. The only limitation on index creation is the amount of available disk space—we fixed it at 100 GB for the sales data mart. The following list shows the main indexes created:

- B+-Tree index for the primary keys of the primary and secondary dimension tables.
- B+-Tree index for the composite key of the primary and secondary fact tables.
- B+-Tree index for the keyCm attribute of the DT_DATE primary dimension table to manage the join with the DT_CAMPAIGN secondary dimension table.
- B+-Tree index for individual foreign keys of the fact tables to facilitate the join operations.

Additionally, some indexes were created for dimensional attributes in the DT_CUSTOMER and the DT_ITEM tables. No index was created for the dimensional attributes in the other dimension tables because the reduced dimension table size did not cause any particular problems. The choice between B+-Tree and bitmap indexes was made according to the number of distinct attribute values.

14.4 The Marketing Data Mart

The three facts identified for the sales data mart were also used for the marketing data mart. However, the requirement analysis showed that the item descriptions were of greater interest. This had a profound effect on the choice of dimensions and on the way hierarchies were structured in the conceptual design phase. In particular, after comparing the end user requirements with the reconciled schema, it was clear that new attributes would have to be defined and added to the existing ones:

- designerGroup   Group to which the designer of each item belongs
- support   Describes the main material an item is made of (such as nylon, cotton, wool)

Figures 14-21, 14-22, and 14-23, respectively, show the fact schemata for marketing-oriented orders, invoices, and budget. The bus and the overlapping matrices are not shown because they are essentially similar to those of the sales data mart.

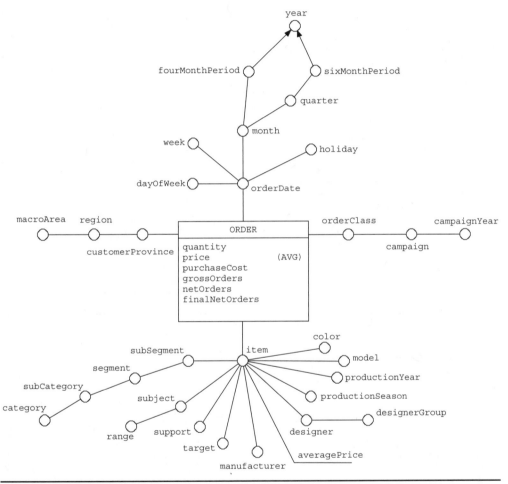

Figure 14-21 Orders fact schema for the marketing data mart

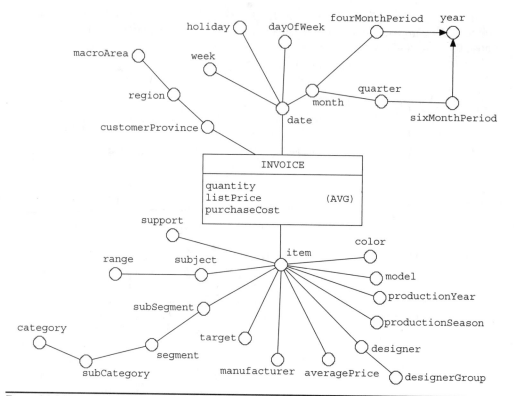

FIGURE 14-22   Invoices fact schema for the marketing data mart

FIGURE 14-23
Budget fact
schema for
the marketing
data mart

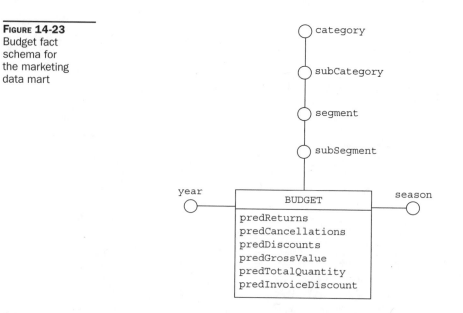

Business Intelligence: Beyond the Data Warehouse

Data warehouse systems are undoubtedly the most widely used electronic decision-making support tools. However, beyond these tools is a set of broader and more varied solutions that are collectively known as *business intelligence (BI)* systems. The techniques on which these systems rely have been available for some time. But it is only now that they are beginning to attract the attention of users whose experience with data warehouses has encouraged them to seek out more sophisticated approaches.

In this chapter, we will examine those BI applications that appear the most promising in terms of their greater capacity to satisfy the information needs of business managers.

15.1 Introduction to Business Intelligence

The set of electronic tools used during the decision-making process is known as the *management portfolio*. This term emphasizes its value as an effective information analysis tool. An alternative term for the same concept is *business intelligence platform*, because appropriate support hardware and software infrastructure is necessary to provide business managers with a powerful and flexible analysis capacity.

> **Business Intelligence**
> *Business intelligence* provides corporate decision-makers with software solutions that help them identify and understand the key business factors to make the best decisions for the situation at the time.

In more detail, business intelligence is a set of tools and procedures that make it possible for companies to extract and process their own business *data* and then transform that data into *information* useful for the decision-making process. The information obtained in this way is then contextualized and enhanced by the decision-makers' own skills and experience, generating *knowledge*. This knowledge is used to define and support business strategies to make conscious and well-informed decisions, and its goal is to gain competitive advantage, improve operating performance and profitability, and in a more general sense to create added value for companies. Finally, the performance achieved by the actions undertaken can be measured to assess the effectiveness of the strategies adopted and correct any, if necessary.

This definition highlights two complementary factors: the technology and the scientific components. Technology helps overcome the problems associated with the sheer size of databases and complex processing involved. The scientific component plays a primary role in ensuring that critical business factors are properly identified and that the most appropriate techniques are used to obtain the information required. The essential contribution to this process comes from joint work between designers and decision-makers. To this end, designers must not only be IT experts, but they must also have knowledge and skills in economics, corporate organization, and project management.

NOTE *The truly professional BI expert is still a rare breed in the corporate world because it is not easy to find a single person who embodies the necessary technical and management profiles. However, it is very likely that this type of individual will be increasingly in demand in the future.*

Our definition of BI is intended to be general, because any attempts to mark out the territory too precisely would create undesirable limitations in this context. On the one hand, the software on offer is in a constant state of evolution; on the other hand, it is difficult to assess when a particular type of analysis falls within the BI context. For example, in a customer relationship–management system, the statistics on the performance of marketing personnel are useful to calculate productivity bonuses in purely administrative terms, and to assess employee skills and capacities in more general management terms. The distinguishing feature of such solutions must be their ability to support the decision-making process effectively. At the same time, they should also be able to deliver sufficient flexibility and efficiency by means of adequate hardware and software infrastructure.

To date, data warehouses have been the main BI tool; and a rapid uptake of these systems has occurred in both large and medium-sized companies. Data warehouses are acknowledged to deliver the following benefits:

- They provide the ability to manage sets of historical data.
- They provide the ability to perform multidimensional analyses accurately and rapidly.
- They are based on a simple model that can be easily learned by its users.
- They are the basis for indicator-calculating systems.

These features have led to the widespread, enthusiastic uptake of data warehouse systems. Once users learn to exploit the full potential of such systems, they become aware of their limitations. As a result, they begin to demand new solutions capable of meeting their ever-growing need for information. Following are some of the most frequent criticisms expressed by data warehouse users:

- Updates are rarely possible at intervals of less than a week/day.
- Data warehouse systems are not very efficient in dealing with complex queries that do not comply with the multidimensional model.
- Current solutions can only record the past and cannot provide predictive scenarios.

These drawbacks are further emphasized in a changed corporate setup. On the one hand, business managers are ever keener to use information technology to support their decision-making. On the other hand, market conditions increasingly force decision-makers to reduce waste and optimize decisions. This has become not only a critical, but vital, factor for companies. Lastly, the use of information technology in the departments of a company that are closest to its practical operations—for example, when there is a need to collect real-time data from production line machinery—makes it necessary to bring new solutions onboard to respond to the need for more information, as summed up here:

- More powerful analysis techniques not based on the multidimensional model
- The ability to analyze data from many heterogeneous sources with faster updates
- The ability to predict the future rather than just analyze the past

These needs have given rise to the *BI pyramid* shown in Figure 15-1. It gives a clearer picture of the distinctions between data, information, and knowledge, and also the roles played by the different technologies in the decision-making process. Indeed, this demonstrates that reports and online analytical processing (OLAP) are no more than the starting point for the application of more advanced techniques that aim at building a bridge to the real decision-making process. In particular, *data mining* consists of a set of advanced analysis techniques that make possible the "automatic" identification of features hidden within data. *What-if* analysis makes it possible to create predictive scenarios based on business models and corporate trends. In sections 15.2 and 15.3 we will offer a brief comparison of the main topics associated with data mining and what-if analysis. Section 15.4 will introduce *business performance management (BPM)*, a framework for corporate performance control to share corporate strategies at all levels.

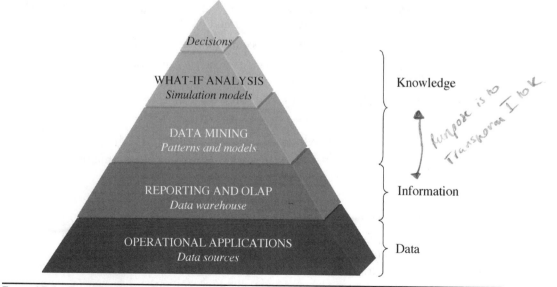

FIGURE 15-1   The business intelligence pyramid

The choice of the topics to examine in greater depth was made on the basis of the amount of interest the different solutions are generating among software producers and their clients (Golfarelli, 2005). Note that BPM is an innovative, predominately technological solution. On the contrary, what-if analysis and data mining are techniques that are well covered in the literature. Because they are considerably more complex than data warehousing, they have to date been largely ignored in the corporate world. However, we believe that today's companies have become sufficiently IT literate to take the leap toward the second generation of BI systems.

15.2 Data Mining

Data mining can be explained in brief as a *technique aimed at finding information hidden in data*. Or more precisely, data mining is *a process that applies algorithms to extract knowledge from large-scale databases. The algorithms identify hidden associations between items of information and make them visible to the user*.

Data mining techniques have been used for years, even before data warehousing, in specialized, non-commercial applications such as geological, medical, military, astronomical, demographic, and meteorological research (Kelly, 1997). Data warehousing has made it possible to transfer data mining from the scientific to the business analysis community. This has opened the doors to a plethora of very useful applications supporting decision-making processes, such as these:

- Market research, such as studies of customer buying patterns, lifestyle analysis, assessing customer satisfaction, and predicting election results
- Marketing effectiveness studies, such as *click-stream analysis* for monitoring web site users
- Market segmentation to identify significant customer profiles to provide them with a better service or for targeted product promotion
- Buying habits analysis for product placement on supermarket shelves
- Corporate planning for workload management, cost and budget control, revenue prediction, and stock control
- Investment modeling to predict share trends on stock exchanges
- Uncovering fraud, such as in the insurance field
- Risk category assessment in the insurance and credit sectors
- Recognizing the similarities between sequences of events (telecommunications network breakdowns, signal analysis)
- Assessment of clinical cases and study of epidemiological models

When very large amounts of data are involved, even such sophisticated analysis tools as OLAP do not always make it possible for system users to identify all the significant *patterns* that exist within the data, such as repeated sequences, relationships and associations between the data, and relevant groupings. Data mining puts together a set of techniques and methodologies from artificial intelligence and pattern recognition, such as genetic algorithms, fuzzy logic, expert systems, and neural networks, to help users in their search for patterns. It is no longer necessary to analyze such data manually. All that is needed is to indicate fairly approximately *what* and *where* you want to research and let an automated tool take the strain out of the computing. However, data mining does in fact only conduct automated analyses of large quantities of data despite the broadly held opinion that data mining is the universal panacea for curing all the ills of advanced data analysis. The ultimate success of any research depends mainly on the correct execution of the process steps and on the skills of researchers.

The process of *knowledge discovery* features two essential elements that are at the heart of data mining: data and patterns. The word *data* here refers to a set of descriptions of events from a database, a data warehouse, or a data stream. A *pattern* is defined as follows, (Rizzi et al., 2003b):

> **Pattern**
> A *pattern* is a synthetic, semantically rich representation of a set of data.

In other words, a pattern is an expression. It is encoded in an appropriate language, and it defines any relevant piece of information extracted from data at an appropriate abstraction level. In general, a pattern expresses a *recurring* schema within data. However, if patterns are *atypical*, this makes them relevant under specific conditions. Furthermore, it is important that

- you are quite confident that patterns are *valid* for your data;
- patterns are *previously unknown* in order to contribute significantly to the decision-making process;
- patterns are *potentially useful* for company business; and
- patterns are syntactically and semantically *comprehensible*.

Data mining may be used for data warehouse data for *descriptive* purposes. This means that data mining can be used to extract a schematic representation of data warehouse data that can be easily interpreted by users. But data mining can also be used to make *predictions*—that is, to determine the future values of some known or previously unknown variables. Here are two simple examples of patterns expressed in everyday language. They can be said to have a predictive function: *Male customers between the ages of 8 and 15 buy video games* (in a marketing context), and *Clients with a monthly salary of less than $1000 do not pay installments on time* (in a financial context).

The knowledge discovery process is intrinsically iterative. This means that it involves progressive refinement of data. Figure 15-2 schematically shows the four phases for knowledge discovery:

1. **Selection and sampling**   Relevant data are selected from sources, such as operational databases or data warehouses, or sampled from a data stream, such as production line machineries.

2. **Transformation and cleansing**   If necessary, data is cleaned and its format transformed as required for the algorithms to be used in the next step.

3. **Data mining**   The selected mining algorithm is launched and its parameters are set to generate patterns.

4. **Evaluation**   Specific visualization front-ends can be generally used to examine and validate patterns. If results are not entirely satisfactory, a retro-action is triggered. Typically, this goes back to the data mining phase to adjust the algorithm settings.

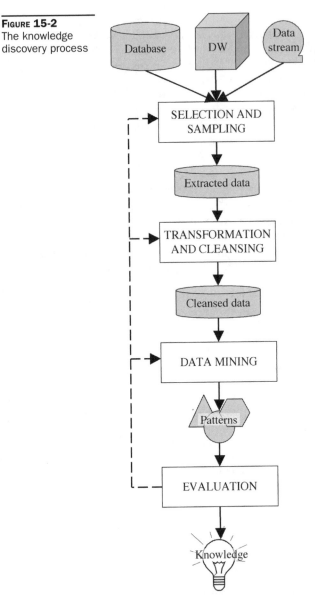

FIGURE 15-2
The knowledge
discovery process

We will now proceed with a brief introduction to the most common types of patterns that can be extracted from data by using data mining techniques. A vast amount of literature on data mining has been published. A detailed review of all the pattern types and the algorithms used to extract them is beyond the scope of our book. See Witten and Frank (2000), Han and Kamber (2001), and Berry and Linoff (1997) for more details.

15.2.1   Association Rules

Association rules make it possible to determine the logical implication rules that exist in databases. In this way, you can identify affinity groups. To help you understand affinity groups, consider the most common example of their use: *market-basket analysis*. This is an analysis of the products bought *together* by customers, and it aims at identifying the most frequent relationships between products. If we had a database of customers recording a set of purchasing transactions, each of which is described by the particular set of products purchased (Agrawal et al., 1993; Srikant and Agrawal, 1995), an association rule would look like this:

$$X \Rightarrow Y$$

where X and Y are sets of products. The intuitive meaning of this rule is that transactions containing the products in X tend to contain those in Y, too.

Of course, only the most widely checked rules can express the most common purchasing habits. For this reason, two measures are commonly added to evaluate how useful this rule is: *support* and *confidence*. The support measure stands for the percentage of transactions containing both X and Y. The confidence measure stands for the percentage of transactions that also contain Y among the ones that contain X:

$$support\ (X \Rightarrow Y) = \frac{\#\text{transactions containing } X \cup Y}{\#\text{total transactions}}$$

$$confidence\ (X \Rightarrow Y) = \frac{\#\text{transactions containing } X \cup Y}{\#\text{transactions containing } X}$$

For example, the rule

{beer} $\Rightarrow$ {potato chips}, support=70%, confidence=85%

shows that 85 percent of the customers buying beer also buy potato chips. But it also shows that this association accounts for 70 percent of the recorded transactions. See Figure 15-3 for an example.

Extracting association rules normally involves determining all the rules whose support and confidence figures are above a certain threshold. The literature on this subject provides a number of different algorithms for extracting association rules. The most well-known is undoubtedly the *APriori* algorithm (Agrawal and Srikant, 1994) based on the identification of the most frequent item sets.

Studies on buying habits for targeted advertising, product placement on supermarket shelves, and variations in sales in case of lacking products belong to the many applications of association rules.

15.2.2   Clustering

Given a population of objects as points in a multidimensional space, in which each dimension corresponds to a particular *feature*, and given a function expressing how close or similar two points are, *clustering* refers to grouping these objects together in a reduced number of sets (*clusters*) better characterizing the population (Jain and Dubes, 1988). Usually each cluster contains items that are very similar or close to one another, while items in other clusters are not similar or are far apart. Figure 15-4 shows this point intuitively. In some cases, clusters can be overlapped rather than disjointed, or you can arrange clusters hierarchically to create a *dendrogram*.

In general, we can state that clustering identifies and highlights the similarities between items. Since the item categories have not been identified beforehand, the literature on pattern recognition also refers to *unsupervised learning*. The applications of clustering include segmenting customers into categories to provide better services for each one or to achieve a targeted promotion of new products, the evaluation of clinical cases on the basis of symptoms, epidemiological analysis, and identification of geologically dangerous areas.

FIGURE 15-3
Source data and
association rules

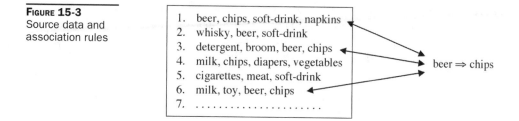

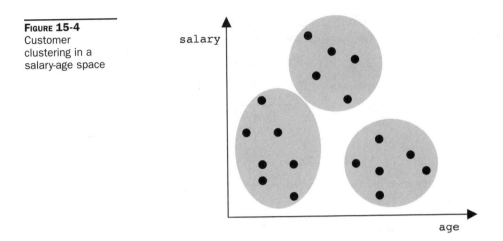

FIGURE 15-4
Customer clustering in a salary-age space

15.2.3   Classifiers and Decision Trees

If we have a set of categories known beforehand and a set of items already labeled with the category to which they belong (*training set*), a *classifier* is an algorithm that can create a descriptive profile for each category, based on the features of the data in the training set. The model generated by the classifier can then be used to assign other items not belonging to the training set to the appropriate category. This makes it particularly suitable for predictions. The following criteria determine how effective a classifier is:

- *Predictive accuracy*, the ability to predict a correct category for new or previously unexamined data
- *Speed*, computational costs of generating and using this model
- *Robustness*, the ability of this model to make correct predictions even when data is noisy or incomplete
- *Scalability*, the ability to create this model efficiently for large quantities of data
- *Interpretability*, the level of comprehensibility provided to users

Decision trees are a particular type of classifiers. They are used to understand a specific phenomenon because they can prioritize the causes leading to a specific event. In a decision tree, each intermediate node models a choice. To do this, it normally takes a condition that compares a constant to an attribute. Each arc from a node is a possible outcome of the condition it contains and each leaf is a final decision. This type of pattern is easy to understand for users and this is its main advantage.

Decision trees are typically used for the assessment of customer risk categories for companies granting mortgages and loans. Figure 15-5 shows a simple example of a decision tree based on a set of data for the risk categories of customers for an insurance policy: the initial data are on the left and the decision tree is on the right, and age groups are the main discriminating property.

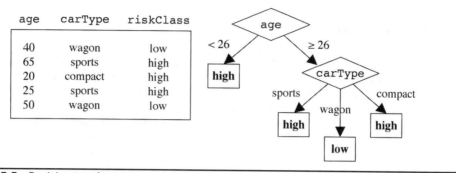

FIGURE 15-5   Decision tree for customer risk assessment

15.2.4 Time Series

The goal here is to identify recurring or atypical patterns in complex data sequences (Keogh and Pazzani, 1998). The fields of application range from economics to meteorology and astrophysics. Some significant examples include identifying associated growth schemata in shares on stock exchanges, revealing anomalies in monitoring systems, studying the relationships between different time series, identifying companies with similar developmental models, and analyzing navigation routes on web sites. Figure 15-6 shows an example of a time series study.

Time series analysis involves two main types of query: *complete match* and *partial match*. In complete match queries, the sequence searched for is as long as the database sequences. In partial match queries, the sequence searched for may be a sub-sequence of the sequences retrieved from the database. In any case, you should take into account the opportunity to shift, normalize, and stretch both sequences to evaluate the match degree of both sequences.

FIGURE 15-6
A recurrent time
series study

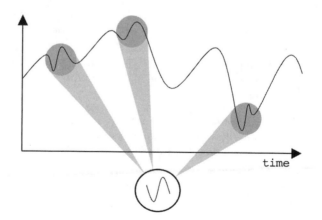

15.3 What-If Analysis

What-if analysis can be described as a data-intensive simulation whose goal is to inspect the behavior of a complex system (that is, the enterprise business or a part of it) under some given hypotheses (called *scenarios*). More pragmatically, what-if analysis measures how changes in a set of independent variables affect a set of dependent variables on the basis of a *simulation model*. A simulation model generates a simplified representation of company business. It is designed to display significant features of business and should be adjusted according to historical enterprise data (Kellner et al., 1999). For this reason, what-if analysis is capable of performing previsional analyses with the aim of responding to the following types of questions:

- If the unit price of the Spinach rolls product were discounted by 5 percent for a period of two months, what effect would this have on sales of the Broccoli product?
- What would happen if we divided the overall budget differently between various corporate departments?
- How will personnel costs vary over the next five years on the basis of the current recruitment plan?

This type of analysis overcomes one of the basic limitations of reporting and OLAP—that is, the fact that they are capable of recording only the past, but they are unable to analyze future scenarios. To achieve this goal, analysts should be able to design a model that reproduces a good approximation of the behavior of the system under investigation. Obviously, the closer the model is to reality, the more accurate will be the estimates obtained. The model is normally created in an iterative way. This means that comparison with a set of historical data (*training set*) is necessary to define the accuracy of the first version of this model and validate it. Any irregular behavior of this model can be identified after a comparison with an additional dataset (*test set*). The irregular behavior is then used to apply changes until the model behavior is as close as possible to a real-world behavior. Data warehouses are typically used for the validation phase because they are the main storage medium to record historical data on corporate events. For example, if on December 31, 2008, we want to create a scenario to predict the sales of a certain product in 2009, the 2006–2007 sales data can be used to identify the factors influencing sales over 2008–2009. In this way, we can check for the 2008 estimates to match the data actually recorded in the data warehouse for 2008.

We can classify what-if analysis techniques on the basis of the approach used to create the simulation model:

- **Inductive techniques**   These attempt to model a system on the basis of the behavior that the system has over a specific period of time. They are also known as *extensional* techniques because they are based on a set of past events.
- **Deductive techniques**   Their goal is to identify and characterize cause and effect relationships between the components of a system. These relationships may also generate retroactive cycles when interacting parts of a system mutually affect their behavior.

Both types of model are examined in greater detail in the next two sections. Section 15.3.3 also provides some notes on methodological aspects (Golfarelli et al., 2006b).

15.3.1   Inductive Techniques

Solutions of this type are simpler to create because they do not have to take into account the causes of a system behavior, but only the effects. However, they are less effective to show the behavior of particularly complex systems. To model the behavior of a system, split it into sub-parts. To model each sub-part, use statistics and interpolating functions calculated from the available history series. To obtain the overall system behavior, merge the sub-models.

Let us consider the example in Figure 15-7 that models the problem of working out the optimal quantity of goods to keep in stock. On the one hand, keeping surplus goods in stock incurs costs. On the other hand, being unable to meet customer demand because the goods are out of stock implies loss of revenue. What is the best compromise if you think that some data is sometimes unreliable? The system works out the optimal stock quantity in every period of the year on the basis of demand, reorder time, and warehousing costs. Minimizing the quantity in stock decreases warehousing costs, but it may easily lead to stock-out if you consider the uncertainty of the reorder time. Although stock-out results in loss of revenue, having no goods available for sale may still be economically viable if the loss is offset by the saving in warehousing costs. If we use this model as a starting point to adjust the basic parameters, such as fall-off in demand and reorder times, we can simulate various scenarios.

Figure 15-7 shows a model in which predictions are based on events that occurred in the past. For example, we can make price estimates by using a linear regression based on the price trends in previous periods. Figure 15-8 shows that the long-term trend can be approximated as constant growth, even if the product price does not vary uniformly over time.

An inductive model can function only as a "black box." And this is the limitation of this model, because it assumes that a system behavior is consolidated and fully described by history observations, without taking into account the real relationships that exist between variables. In practice, the use of this technique is tantamount to saying *if this was the trend before, it will be the same afterward*. As a result, this system becomes less effective whenever a variation in trend cannot be predicted from the historical data. For example, what happens if price increases undermine consumers' purchasing power and reduce demand drastically?

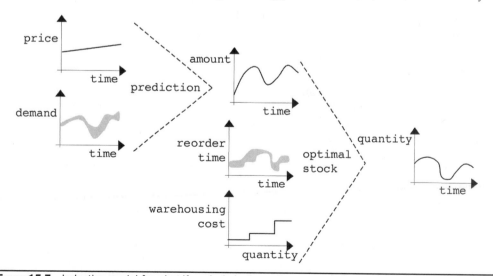

FIGURE 15-7   Inductive model for what-if analysis in the optimum goods in stock problem. The gray areas indicate uncertainty in the value of variables.

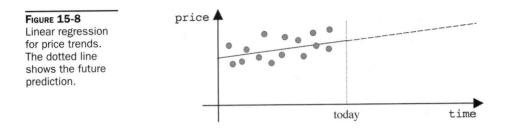

Figure 15-8
Linear regression for price trends. The dotted line shows the future prediction.

15.3.2 Deductive Techniques

Deductive techniques can potentially overcome the problems with inductive techniques, because they imply in-depth knowledge of the rules governing system dynamics to generate a model that takes in the *cause-effect* relationships underlying the behavior of the system itself. The effectiveness of deductive approaches hinges on the expressive power of the constructs used to create models, and on the ability of models to evolve from their original statuses. An easy-to-use spreadsheet recording a set of relationships between variables can also be viewed as a deductive model. However, a solution of this type will display its limitations as soon as the modeling requires nonlinear relationships and retroactive cycles. These cycles are necessary whenever the interacting parts of a system mutually affect their behaviors. In this way, they generate the so-called *complex systems*. The behavior of complex systems cannot be analyzed by decomposition techniques because the interaction between various sub-systems is not equal merely to the sum of individual behaviors.

System dynamics is one of the disciplines that best addresses the problems of studying complex systems. System dynamics was developed in the 1960s by Jay Forrester of MIT, and although it is virtually unknown in BI, it is widely used in such other contexts as corporate organization and project management. In more than 40 years, it has generated a vast amount of scientific literature.

What makes system dynamics different from other approaches is its ability to model retroactive cycles. Stocks and flows are the building blocks of these models. They describe which retroactive cycles are available in a system and when retroactive cycles result in nonlinear situations. For example, they show when even a small stimulus can have a wide-ranging effect. Computer simulations are used to determine how the status of these systems will evolve.

These days, many tools are available to create system dynamics simulations, such as Powersim and Vensim. These tools make the complexity of the models and the techniques used for their evolution clear to designers, who use appropriate graphic formalisms to define them. Moreover, these tools can make probability-based assumptions, such as *The delay in delivering a particular product follows a normal distribution characterized by a mean of 5 days and a standard deviation of 2 days*. The outcome of the simulation can return not only the trends in the variables taken into account, but also the statistical evaluations associated with the occurrence of particular events, such as *on the basis of the model created, what is the confidence interval relative to the probability of achieving a turnover of $40,000?*.

The simulations based on system dynamics models support what-if analysis. This means that they are able to track the evolution over time of a complex system from an initial scenario. Figure 15-9 shows a possible model for the stock control example. In purely qualitative terms, you can see that revenues increase according to the quantity of customer requests satisfied, and that this is in turn influenced positively by the quantity of stock

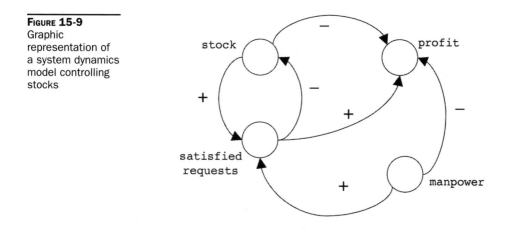

FIGURE 15-9
Graphic
representation of
a system dynamics
model controlling
stocks

available and the available manpower. Both last elements are a cost, and they have a negative influence on profit. The model shows a retroactive cycle between `stock` and `satisfied requests`, which have a mutual influence on one another.

15.3.3   Methodological Notes

As we mentioned, what-if application hinges on a *simulation model*. The simulation model establishes a set of complex relationships between *business variables* corresponding to significant business entities, such as products, branches, customers, costs, revenues, and so on. To make simulation model specifications easier and help users understand them, simulations can be split into a set of *scenarios*. Each scenario provides one or more alternative ways to make a *prediction* in which users may be interested. Predictions are typically represented as multidimensional cubes, so users can use OLAP front-end applications to explore interactively the dimensions and measures of predictions.

To design a what-if analysis application, you should refer to a methodological framework. The methodological framework we introduce here is discussed by Golfarelli and others (2006b). Figure 15-10 shows its seven phases.

1. **Goal analysis**   Aims at determining which business events should be simulated and how business events should be characterized. To express goals, the set of business variables users want to monitor and business variable granularity have to be specified, and relevant scenarios should be outlined on the basis of the variables users want to control to manage their simulations.

2. **Business modeling**   Creates a simplified model of an application domain to help designers understand business events, allow them to refine scenarios, and give them some early hints on what should be neglected or simplified for future simulations.

3. **Data source analysis**   Aims at understanding which information is available to manage a simulation, how information is structured, and how it has been physically deployed, with particular regard to the cube(s) that store historical data.

4. **Multidimensional modeling**   Considers the static part of the business model created in phase 2 and fulfils the requirements expressed in phase 1 to provide a structural description of predictions. Prediction structures are very often coarse-grained views of cube(s) that store historical data.

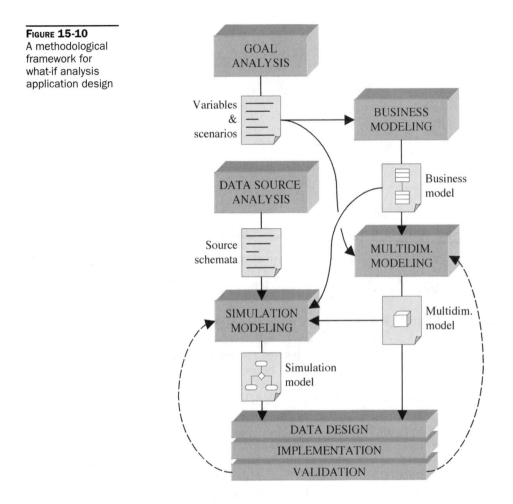

Figure 15-10
A methodological
framework for
what-if analysis
application design

5. **Simulation modeling**   Creates the simulation model that allows predictions to be derived from source data for every scenario.

6. **Data design and implementation**   At this stage, multidimensional schemata for predictions and simulation models are implemented on a platform to create a prototype for testing purposes.

7. **Validation**   Assesses how faithful a simulation model is in comparison with a real-world business model and how reliable predictions are. If the approximation introduced by the simulation model is considered as unacceptable, phases 4 through 7 are iterated to create a new prototype.

The five analysis/modeling phases (1 to 5) require a supporting formalism. Standard UML can be used for phases 1 (use case diagrams), 2 (a class diagram coupled with activity and state diagrams), and 3 (class and deployment diagrams). The Dimensional Fact Model (DFM) can be effectively adopted for phase 4. Finding in literature a suitable formalism to provide a broad conceptual support to phase 5 is a very difficult task. Golfarelli et al. (2006b) suggested that an extended form of a UML activity diagram should be used.

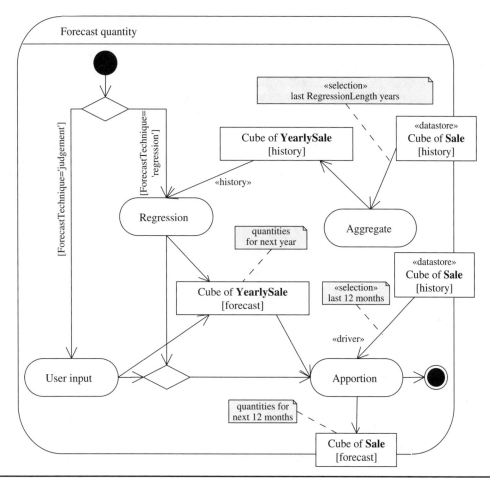

FIGURE 15-11 UML activity diagram for monthly quantity prediction of next year's sales

Figure 15-11 shows an example that documents how to make monthly quantity prediction of next year's sales. This prediction can be made by judgment (users directly specify next year's monthly quantities) or by regression (based on the total quantities sold during the last RegressionLength years and on the monthly quantities sold during the last 12 months), depending on the value given to the ForecastTechnique parameter.

15.4 Business Performance Management

The approach to business management has changed radically over the last ten years. To reduce running costs and to keep in step with the market, today's buzz words are *performance optimization*. Many businesses rely on a process-based model to achieve this goal. This model may also involve customers and suppliers to enable them to synchronize all corporate activities. It requires two complementary elements: organizational structure and processes.

Organizational structure consists of a hierarchy of departments defining duties and responsibilities. This structure normally shows three levels: The *strategic level* is concerned with corporate strategy, and in practice it coincides with higher management. The *tactical level* consists of a set of departments, each controlling a specific set of functions. The decisions made at this level are closely connected to these specific functions and they must also be compatible with the global strategy. Lastly, the *operating level* is the level at which the company's core business is carried out. Here, decision-making power is limited to optimizing specific production activities, also in a way that is compatible with the global strategy.

In addition to the organizational structure, *processes* are a set of logically related activities that attempt to achieve a global corporate goal. Processes do not depend on the organizational structure because the activities included within them may be undertaken by different departments and they may require decisions to be made at different levels.

NOTE   *As you optimize the process efficiency and effectiveness, even to the detriment of individual divisional functions, the strength of this kind of corporate management intuitively lies in the attention paid to general corporate goals, which is greater than attention paid to individual department goals.*

If employees are to be able to bring their own work into line with an overview that is broader than their own specific role, they must share in the corporate strategy goals at all levels. To achieve this, you should translate what has been decided at a strategic level into a set of goals that are more specific to the lower levels, whereby each will be associated with a specific results indicator, or *key performance indicator (KPI),* and its objective value. Employees and decision-makers at all levels within a company will aim to engage in their own activities and make the decisions associated with these to bring the current indicator values into line with the strategic corporate goals. This method of imposing and sharing corporate strategy is known as *metric-driven management* and is shown in Figure 15-12.

NOTE   *A corporate strategy is undoubtedly a highly complex entity, and representing this by means of a set of indicators, however broad they may be, provides an extremely simplistic picture. To date, attempts made to deploy company policies defined at the strategic level to lower levels of the operation have failed, because each employee tends to have only a partial and subjective vision of his company. However, the strength of the KPI method is that it allows management to establish rules that are unambiguous and not open to personal interpretation. This is not the case when company codes of conduct and directives are used for the same purpose.*

To implement metric-driven management, it is necessary to measure company performance constantly, and the phrase coined to describe this in BI is *business performance management (BPM).*

> ### Business Performance Management (BPM)
> *Business performance management* is the set of activities designed to measure individual performance and put a premium on effective corporate processes and the efficient use of human, material, and economic resources.

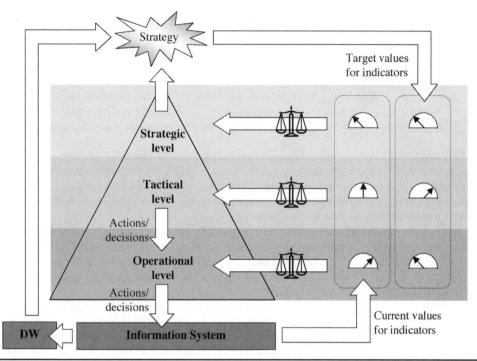

Figure 15-12   The information decision-making flow typical of metric-driven management

Other versions of this term, which are often abused in IT magazines and software producers' brochures, include *corporate performance management* (CPM) and *enterprise performance management* (EPM). Note that the same BPM acronym is often used for *business process management*, which refers to the aforesaid process-oriented approach to enterprise management.

BPM requires that indicator values be constantly updated and made available to a specific level at just the right time in an appropriate form to support decision-makers' activities in the most suitable way. The following features distinguish this from classic data warehouse solutions:

- **Users**   Users are always decision-makers, but at tactical and operating levels rather than strategic levels. This means that they have a more limited vision of corporate strategy and tend to concentrate only on the set of indicators relevant to their own particular tasks.

- **System response time**   Decisions at the tactical and operating levels must be made much faster than those at the strategic level. For this reason, information updates should occur more frequently. BPM systems are considered to be *right-time* systems—that is, they must be able to update information frequently enough to enable timely decisions to be made, even if they are not real-time systems (Dresner and Buytendjik, 2003).

- **Information lifetime and detail degree** The information requested from BPM systems is normally more detailed than that extracted from data warehouse systems, because it covers specific events related to detailed activities. Moreover, the lifetime of this information is limited since users are interested in the current performance levels for their own activities.

- **User interfaces** Most BPM users do not have the time or the ability to carry out OLAP sessions. For this reason, information must normally be delivered by reports and dashboards, or by alerts automatically triggered by business rule control systems.

By now, it must be clear that major distinctions exist between data warehouse and BPM systems and that they can be seen as complementary. While data warehouse systems are used by management to define corporate strategies, BPM systems help employees understand these strategies. From a less cooperative point of view, BPM systems help the company management to impose their strategies.

The technology designed for data warehouses can only partially cope with the requirements of BPM. These days, software manufacturers try to meet users' demands by combining customized OLAP solutions with specialized Extraction, Transformation, and Loading (ETL) tools. The leading BI vendors are currently working on the technology gap expected to be filled within the next three to five years.

Figure 15-13 shows an example of the sort of architecture that we believe will eventually appear on the market (Golfarelli et al., 2004). The left side of the figure shows the typical data warehouse architecture: the data extracted from the information system using an ETL tool is loaded first into a reconciled database (*operational data store*, or *ODS*) and then into the data warehouse to enable OLAP and reporting tools to be used. The right side of the figure shows the architectural components that support the reactive flow necessary for the BPM system, generally referred to by the term *business activity monitoring (BAM)*.

To provide full support for the functions described, the system should include the following:

- A *right-time integrator (RTI)* able to promptly integrate data from operational databases, data warehouses, *enterprise application integration (EAI)* systems, and real-time data sources

- A *dynamic data store (DDS)*, a data manager able to store data for short periods of time and provide quick access to them to carry out data mining and to calculate rules

- A *KPI manager* able to calculate the necessary indicators for all BPM levels

- A set of *mining tools* that can identify relevant patterns, even from real-time sources

- A *rule engine* that can monitor constantly the events filtered by RTI systems or identified by data-mining modules to send out alerts promptly

Despite the claims that dedicated software manufacturers would have us believe, the architecture described here does not yet exist, and many problems remain to be solved.

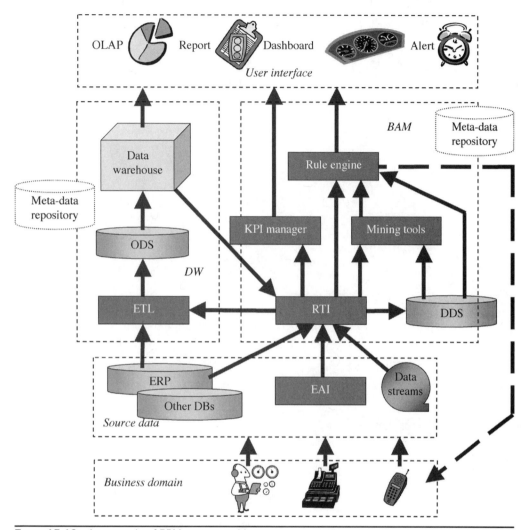

FIGURE 15-13   An example of BPM system architecture

For example, as far as the problems associated with complex integration, such as approximate merge of tables (Baxter et al., 2003) are concerned, today's solutions imply a materialized reconciled layer. For this reason, they are not able to operate in real-time. Furthermore, data stream manipulation poses yet more challenges. At present, complex operations are performed offline, while queries made in real-time actually use just simple filters (Koudas and Srivastava, 2003).

Glossary

Additivity A measure property related to a hierarchy. It specifies whether you can or cannot use the SUM operator when you aggregate measures along that hierarchy.

Aggregate navigator A software module designed for rewriting an OLAP query on the materialized view yielding the minimum execution cost.

Aggregation A way to sum up data in the multidimensional model. It can group events into a single event that sums them all up.

Attribute A name given to a relation column in the relational model. A (generally alphanumeric) finite domain field that describes a dimension in the multidimensional model and in the Dimensional Fact Model (DFM).

Business activity monitoring (BAM) Generic name for a technology supporting business performance management development.

Business intelligence BI allows corporate decision-makers to use software applications for understanding business key factors, so that they can then make the best decisions.

Business performance management (BPM) An approach to corporate management based on business strategy sharing through a set of key performance indicators that specify business goals. BPM helps companies optimize business performance by encouraging process effectiveness and the efficient usage of human, material, and economic resources.

Business process management (BPM) The development and automation of new and integrated business processes to assist in real-time business visibility and decision-making. BPM includes workflow design and modeling and automated process integration and management.

Cleansing A phase of the data warehousing process that improves data quality.

Conceptual design A design phase that aims at providing an abstract description of a data mart. It needs to define relevant facts and create fact schemata.

Convergence   This DFM construct is used when two or more arcs end in an individual attribute.

Corporate data warehouse   See *Primary data warehouse*.

Cross-dimensional attribute   A DFM attribute whose value is defined by the combination of two or more attributes belonging to different hierarchies.

Cube   A metaphor used to represent data in the multidimensional model. Every event that occurs is considered a *cube cell*, whose edges are analysis dimensions.

Data mart   A data warehouse data subset or aggregation that includes information relevant to a specific business area, a specific business department, or a specific category of users.

Data mining   Tasks aimed at extracting information in the form of patterns or models, such as association rules, clusters, and time series, concealed by data.

Data staging   A procedure used to extract data from operational sources, integrate them, make them consistent, and then load them into a data warehouse.

Data warehouse   A subject-oriented, integrated, consistent, nonvolatile data repository showing data evolution over time and supporting decision-making processes.

Data warehousing   Methods, techniques, and tools that help knowledge workers conduct data analyses aimed at decision-making and improving corporate information assets.

Decision support systems   A set of information techniques and tools designed for information extraction from a set of data stored to electronic media.

Descriptive attribute   A DFM attribute providing additional information on a dimensional attribute in a hierarchy. It cannot be used for aggregation.

Dimension   A (generally alphanumeric) finite-domain attribute defining minimum fact granularity.

Dimension table   In a star schema, a dimension table is a denormalized relational table that includes a surrogate key and a set of attributes belonging to a hierarchy.

Dimensional Fact Model (DFM)   A conceptual model for data warehouse design.

Drill-across   An OLAP operator that establishes a link between two or more cubes interrelated to compare their data. For example, a drill-across can calculate expressions involving measures from both cubes.

Drill-down   An OLAP operator reducing cube data aggregation and adding a detail level.

Drill-through   An OLAP operator linking multidimensional cube data to operational data in sources or in reconciled databases.

Entity-Relationship model   A common conceptual model for operational database design.

Event   The basic information cell in a multidimensional cube. An *n*-ple of values given to cube dimensions single it out.

Extension   Relation extension stands for its data set or its set of tuples.

Extraction   A phase of the data warehousing process extracting any relevant data from sources.

Extraction, Transformation, and Loading (ETL)   Tools integrating heterogeneous schemata, extracting, transforming, cleansing, validating, filtering, and loading data form sources into a data warehouse.

Fact   A concept relevant to decision-making processes. A fact models a set of business events occurring in an enterprise.

Fact schema   Basic DFM element. This schema represents a fact and fact measures, dimensions, and hierarchies.

Fact table   A relational table including all the fact measures in a star schema. The primary key of a fact table is the composition of a set of foreign keys referencing dimension tables.

Foreign key   A set of relation attributes whose values are constrained to be a subset of the values of a unique key in another (or in the same) relation.

Fragmentation   Used in the logical design phase for relational databases to partition table tuples or attributes to reduce table size.

Functional dependency   A functional dependency exists between two attributes in a relation schema when an individual value of the second attribute corresponds to each value of the first attribute in every tuple of every legal schema instance.

Group-by set   A set of DFM hierarchy attributes defining a query aggregation level.

Hierarchies   A set of attributes, linked by many-to-one associations, that describe a dimension.

History interval   Specifies the width of the time frame for data storage for every fact schema.

Incomplete hierarchy   A hierarchy missing a few instance values at one or more aggregation levels.

Index   A data structure that can be associated with a table to speed up data access.

Integration   A process that merges more operational schemata into one consistent schema.

Intension   The intension of a relation is the relation schema, that consists of a relation name and a set of attributes.

Join   Given two relations and a Boolean predicate involving both relation attributes, the join operator connects all the tuple pairs from both relations that meet that predicate.

Key performance indicator (KPI)   An indicator used alone or in combination with other indicators to measure the quantifiable goals a company has reached.

Legacy systems   Corporate applications generally stored to mainframes or minicomputers. Even if they are currently used for operational system management, legacy systems do not meet state-of-the-art standards and modern architecture requirements. For this reason, systems recently implemented can only barely access and integrate them.

Loading   A phase of the data warehousing process that loads data into a data warehouse after cleansing and transforming it.

Logical design   A data mart development phase defining relational schemata to model facts. This phase involves optimization techniques such as view materialization and fragmentation.

Lossless grain   A property of a fact schema in which each primary event corresponds to a single transaction recorded in the source operational database.

Lossy grain   A property of a fact schema in which each primary event sums up a set of many transactions recorded in the source operational database.

Measure   A field defined by (generally numeric) continuous value-based domains. It provides a quantitative description of facts.

Meta-data   Data defining other data. In data warehousing, meta-data specifies sources, values, usage, and functions of data warehouse data and defines how data is altered and transformed at every architecture level.

MOLAP (Multidimensional OLAP)   A multidimensional model implementation based on an ad hoc logical model in which position-based access arrays are used to represent multidimensional data.

Multidimensional model   A basic data warehouse model considering data as points in space with as many dimensions as possible analysis dimensions. Each point represents an event that has occurred in a company and is described by a set of measures relevant to decision-making.

OLAP (online analytical processing)   An interactive data processing system for dynamic multidimensional analyses.

OLTP (online transactional processing)   An interactive data processing system based on transactions.

Operational data store (ODS)   A repository for reconciled data.

Operational database   An operational database stores data from business operations performed in management processes.

Overlapping   A way to combine two or more fact schemata with shared attributes to create a new fact schema to be used for drill-across queries.

Pattern   A compact and significant representation of a large data set, extracted by data mining techniques. It typically captures a recurring scheme in data.

Physical design   A data mart development phase that defines a physical schema, including indexes and instructions for data allocation.

Pivot   An OLAP operator that causes a change in cube representation. The pivot aims at analyzing an individual set of information from a different viewpoint.

Population   See *Data staging*.

Primary data warehouse   A global centralized repository for all the summarized data. Data marts extract (and further sum up, if necessary) a fraction of data relevant to a specific application domain from the primary data warehouse.

Primary key   An attribute set whose values single out a specific tuple in a relation.

Reconciled data   The operational data available after integrating and cleansing source data. Reconciled data is integrated, consistent, correct, volatile, current, and detailed.

Reconciled schema   Operational schema obtained from the integration of operational source schemata. It stores reconciled data.

Recursive hierarchy   A hierarchy with instances that can be different in their length.

Relation   A relation (or table) is the basic element of the relational model, and is formally defined as a subset of the Cartesian product of a set of domains. A relation consists of a schema and an instance. The schema (or intension) includes the relation name, a set of attributes, and a set of integrity constraints. The instance (or extension) includes a set of tuples that conform to the schema.

Relational model   A logical model for data storage in the form of relations.

Report   A static summary of information, designed for users in need of periodic access to information with unchanging structure.

ROLAP (Relational OLAP)   A multidimensional model implementation based on the relational model and generally based on star schemata.

Roll-up   An OLAP operator that aggregates a set of cube events to reduce event detail level.

Row IDentifier (RID)   The physical reference to a single relation tuple.

Slice-and-dice   An OLAP operator that reduces the number of cube cells being analyzed by applying a selection criterion.

Slowly changing dimension   A hierarchy whose instances dynamically evolve over time.

Snowflake schema   A star schema variant with dimension tables partially normalized.

Star schema   A basic schema used for representing multidimensional data with the relational model. It consists of a fact table and set of dimension tables.

Surrogate key   A relational database attribute whose unique values are automatically generated by a DBMS.

System dynamics   An area of study on complex systems able to model real-world domains and simulate domain evolution over time in comparison with an initial scenario.

Transactional database   See *Operational database*.

Transformation   A phase of the data warehousing process that converts data from its operational source format into the format used in the reconciled database or in the data warehouse.

Tuple   A single table row in the relational model.

View   An aggregate fact table that stores the result of a group-by query. It can reduce query execution costs.

View materialization   Used in the logical design phase for a data mart to improve data mart performance by storing redundant data.

What-if analysis   A data-intensive simulation whose goal is to inspect the behavior of a complex system under some given hypotheses called scenarios.

Bibliography

Abdelguerfi, M., and K. Wong (1998). *Parallel Database Techniques*. Wiley-IEEE Computer Society.

Abelló, A., J. Samos, and F. Saltor (2006). YAM²: A multidimensional conceptual model extending UML. *Information Systems*, 31(6):541–567.

Abiteboul, S., R. Hull, and V. Vianu (1995). *Foundations of Databases: The Logical Level*. Addison-Wesley.

Abiteboul, S., P. Buneman, and D. Suciu (2000). *Data on the Web: From Relations to Semistructured Data and XML*. Morgan Kaufman Publishers.

Agrawal, R., A. Gupta, and S. Sarawagi (1995). Modeling multidimensional databases. *IBM Research Report*, IBM Almaden Research Center.

Agrawal, R., T. Imieliski, and A. Swami (1993). Mining association rules between sets of items in large databases. In *Proceedings ACM SIGMOD Conference on Management of Data*, Washington, D.C., pp. 207–216.

Agrawal, R., V. Narasayya, and B. Yang (2004). Integrating vertical and horizontal partitioning into automated physical database design. In *Proceedings ACM SIGMOD Conference on Management of Data*, Paris, pp. 359–370.

Agrawal, R., and R. Srikant (1994). Fast algorithms for mining association rules in large databases. In *Proceedings 20th International Conference on Very Large Data Bases*, Santiago, pp. 487–499.

Arlow, J., and I. Neustadt (2005). *UML 2 and the Unified Process: Practical Object-Oriented Analysis and Design*. Addison-Wesley Object Technology Series.

Atzeni, P., S. Ceri, S. Paraboschi, and R. Torlone (1999). *Database Systems: Concepts, Languages and Architectures*. McGraw-Hill.

Baralis, E., S. Paraboschi, and E. Teniente (1997). Materialized view selection in multidimensional database. In *Proceedings 23rd International Conference on Very Large Data Bases*, Athens, pp. 156–165.

Barquin, R., and S. Edelstein (1996). *Planning and Designing the Data Warehouse*. Prentice Hall.

Batini, C., M. Lenzerini, and S.B. Navathe (1986). A comparative analysis of methodologies for database schema integration. *ACM Computing Surveys*, 18(4):323–364.

Baxter, R., P. Christen, and T.A. Churches (2003). A comparison of fast blocking methods for record linkage. In *Proceedings Workshop on Data Cleaning, Record Linkage and Object Consolidation*, Washington D.C.

Bayer, R., and E.M. McCreight (1972). Organization and maintenance of large ordered indices. *Acta Informatica*, 1:173–189.

Bebel, B., J. Eder, C. Koncilia, T. Morzy, and R. Wrembel (2004). Creation and management of versions in multiversion data warehouse. In *Proceedings ACM Symposium on Applied Computing*, Nicosia, Cyprus, pp. 717–723.

Beckmann, N., H. Kriegel, R. Schneider, and B. Seeger (1990). The R*-tree: An efficient and robust access method for points and rectangles. In *Proceedings ACM SIGMOD International Conference on Management of Data*, Atlantic City, New Jersey, pp. 322–331.

Beizer, B. (1990). *Software Testing Techniques 2nd Edition*. International Thomson Computer Press.

Beneventano, D., S. Bergamaschi, S. Castano, A. Corni, R. Guidetti, G. Malvezzi, M. Melchiori, and M. Vincini (2000). Information integration: The MOMIS project demonstration. In *Proceedings 26th International Conference on Very Large Data Bases*, Cairo.

Berge, C. (1985). *Graphs*. North-Holland Mathematical Library.

Berry, M., and G. Linoff (1997). *Data Mining Techniques for Marketing, Sales, and Customer Support*. John Wiley & Sons.

Blanco, J.L., A. Illarramendi, and A. Goni (1994). Building a federated relational database system: An approach using a knowledge-based system. *Journal of Intelligent and Cooperative Information Systems*, 3(4):415–455.

Blaschka, M. (2000). FIESTA: A framework for schema evolution in multidimensional databases. PhD Thesis, Technische Universitat Munchen, Germany.

Bliujute, R., S. Saltenis, G. Slivinskas, and C.S. Jensen (1998). Systematic change management in dimensional data warehousing. In *Proceedings International Baltic Workshop on Databases and Information Systems*, Riga, Latvia, pp. 27–41.

Bonifati, A., F. Cattaneo, S. Ceri, A. Fuggetta, and S. Paraboschi (2001). Designing data marts for data warehouses. *ACM Transactions on Software Engineering and Methodology*, 10(4):452–483.

Bouzeghoub, M., and Z. Kedad (2000). A quality-based framework for physical data warehouse design. In *Proceedings 2nd International Workshop on Design and Management of Data Warehouses*, Stockholm.

Bresciani, P., P. Giorgini, F. Giunchiglia, J. Mylopoulos, and A. Perini (2004). Tropos: An agent-oriented software development methodology. *Journal of Autonomous Agents and Multi-Agent Systems*, 8(3):203–236.

Bruckner, R., B. List, and J. Schiefer (2001). Developing requirements for data warehouse systems with use cases. In *Proceedings 7th Americas Conference on Information Systems*, pp. 329–335.

Bunke H. (1993). Structural and syntactic pattern recognition. In C. Chen, L. Pau, and P. Wang (Eds), *Handbook of Pattern Recognition & Computer Vision*. World Scientific.

Cabibbo, L., and R. Torlone (1998). A logical approach to multidimensional databases. In *Proceedings 6th International Conference on Extending Data Base Technology*, Valencia, Spain, pp. 183–197.

Calvanese, D., G. De Giacomo, M. Lenzerini, D. Nardi, and R. Rosati (1998). Description logic framework for information integration. In *Proceedings 6th International Conference on Principles of Knowledge Representation and Reasoning*, Trento, Italy, pp. 2–13.

——— (1999). A principled approach to data integration and reconciliation in data warehousing. In *Proceedings 1st International Workshop on Design and Management of Data Warehouses*, Heidelberg, Germany.

Cardenas, A.F. (1975). Analysis and performance of inverted database structures. *Communications of the ACM*, 18(5):253–263.

Carey, M.J., L.M. Haas, P.M. Schwarz, M. Arya, W.F. Cody, R. Fagin, M. Flickner, A. Luniewski, W. Niblack, D. Petkovic, J. Thomas, J.H. Williams, and E.L. Wimmers (1995). Towards heterogeneous multimedia information systems: The Garlic approach. In *Proceedings RIDE-DOM*, pp. 124–131.

Chan, C., and Y. Ioannidis (1998). Bitmap index design and evaluation. In *Proceedings ACM SIGMOD Conference*, Seattle, pp. 355–366.

——— (1999). An efficient bitmap encoding scheme for selection queries. In *Proceedings ACM SIGMOD Conference*, Philadephia, pp. 215–226.

Chaudhuri, S., and K. Shim (1994). Including group-by in query optimization. In *Proceedings 20th International Conference on Very Large Data Bases*, Santiago, pp. 354–366.

Chaudhuri, S., and U. Dayal (1997). An overview of data warehousing and OLAP technology. *SIGMOD Record*, 26(1):65–74.

Chawathe, S., H. Garcia-Molina, J. Hammer, K. Ireland, Y. Papakonstantinou, J. Ullman, and J. Widom (1994). The TSIMMIS project: Integration of heterogeneous information sources. In *Proceedings IPSI Conference*, Tokyo.

Chen, P.M., E.K. Lee, G.A. Gibson, R.H. Katz, and D.A. Patterson (1994). RAID: High-performance, reliable secondary storage. *ACM Computing Surveys*, 26(2):145–185.

Chu, W., and I. Oieong (1993). A transaction-based approach to vertical partitioning for relational database system. *IEEE Transactions on Software Engineering*, 19(8).

Ciaccia, P., M. Golfarelli, and S. Rizzi (2003). Bounding the cardinality of aggregate views through domain-derived constraints. *Data and Knowledge Engineering*, 45(2):131–153.

Colliat G. (1996). OLAP, relational and multidimensional database systems. *SIGMOD Record*, 25(3):64–69.

Cui, Y., and J. Widom (2000). Lineage tracing in a data warehousing system. In *Proceedings 16th International Conference on Data Engineering*, San Diego, California.

Datta, A., and H. Thomas (1997). A conceptual model and algebra for on-line analytical processing in data warehouses. In *Proceedings 7th Workshop for Information Technology and Systems*, pp. 91–100.

Deutsch, A., M. Fernandez, D. Florescu, A. Levy, and D. Suciu (1999). A query language for XML. *WWW8 / Computer Networks*, 31(11–16):1155–1169.

Devlin, B. (1997). *Data Warehouse: From Architecture to Implementation*. Addison Wesley Longman.

Dresner, H., and F. Buytendjik (2003). Business intelligence and data warehousing scenario: Key trends and evolving markets. *Gartner Symposium ITXPO*, Cannes, France.

Eder , J., C. Koncilia, and T. Morzy (2002). The COMET metamodel for temporal data warehouses. In *Proceedings International Conference on Advanced Information Systems Engineering*, pp. 83–99.

Elmasri, R., and S. Navate (2006). *Fundamentals of Database Systems*. Addison-Wesley.

English, L.P. (1999). *Improving Data Warehouse and Business Information Quality*. John Wiley.

Ezeife, E.I. (2001). Selecting and materializing horizontally partitioned warehouse views. *Data & Knowledge Engineering*, 36(2):185–210.

Fahrner, C., and G. Vossen (1995). A survey of database transformations based on the Entity-Relationship model. *Data & Knowledge Engineering*, 15(3):213–250.

Fayyad, U.M., G. Piatetsky-Shapiro, and P. Smyth (1996). The KDD process for extracting useful knowledge from volumes of data. *Communications of the ACM*, 39(11):27–34.

Ferrandez-Medina, E., J. Trujillo, R. Villaroel, and M. Piattini (2004). Extending UML for designing secure data warehouses. In *Proceedings International Conference on Conceptual Modeling*, pp. 224–237.

Few, S. (2006). *Information Dashboard Design*. O'Relly.

Finkel, R.A., and J.L. Bentley (1974). Quad-Trees: A data structure for retrieval on composite keys. *ACTA Informatica*, 4(1):1–9.

Forrester, J. W. (1958). Industrial dynamics: A major breakthrough for decision makers. *Harvard Business Review*, 36(4):37–66.

Franconi, E., and U. Sattler (1999). A data warehouse conceptual model for multidimensional aggregation. In *Proceedings 1st International Workshop on Design and Management of Data Warehouses*, Heidelberg, Germany.

Gaede, V., and O. Günther (1998). Multidimensional access methods, *ACM Computing Surveys*, 30(2).

Galhardas, H., D. Florescu, D. Shasha, E. Simon, and C. Saita (2001). Declarative data cleaning: Language, model, and algorithms. In *Proceedings 27th International Conference on Very Large Data Bases*, Rome, pp. 371–380.

Garcia-Solaco, M., F. Saltor, and M. Castellanos (1995). A semantic-discriminated approach to integration in federated databases. In *Proceedings 3rd International Conference on Cooperative Information System*, Vienna.

Giorgini, P., E. Nicchiarelli, J. Mylopoulos, and R. Sebastiani (2003). Formal reasoning techniques for goal models. *Journal of Data Semantics*, 1.

Giorgini, P., S. Rizzi, M. Garzetti (2008). GRAnD: A Goal-Oriented Approach to Requirement Analysis in Data Warehouses. *Decision Support Systems*, 45(1):4–21.

Golfarelli, M. (2005). New trends in business intelligence. In *Proceedings 1st International Conference on Business Intelligence Systems*, Opatija, Croatia.

———. (2009). From user requirements to conceptual design in data warehouse design: A survey. In *Data Warehousing Design and Advanced Engineering Applications: Methods for Complex Construction*, L. Bellatreche (Ed). IGI Global.

Golfarelli, M., J. Lechtenbörger, S. Rizzi, and G. Vossen (2006a). Schema versioning in data warehouses: Enabling cross-version querying via schema augmentation. *Data and Knowledge Engineering*, 59(2):435–459.

Golfarelli, M., D. Maio, and S. Rizzi (1998). The Dimensional Fact Model: A conceptual model for data warehouses. *International Journal of Cooperative Information Systems*, 7(2–3):215–247.

——— (2000a). Applying vertical fragmentation techniques in logical design of multidimensional databases. In *Proceedings 2nd International Conference on Data Warehousing and Knowledge Discovery*, Greenwich, pp. 11–23.

Golfarelli, M., and S. Rizzi (1999). Designing the data warehouse: Key steps and crucial issues. *Journal of Computer Science and Information Management*, 2(1):1–14.

——— (2000b). View materialization for nested GPSJ queries. In *Proceedings 2nd International Workshop on Design and Management of Data Warehouses*, Stockholm.

——— (2000c). Comparing nested GPSJ queries in multidimensional databases. In *Proceedings ACM International Workshop on Data Warehousing and OLAP*, Washington, D.C., pp. 65–71.

——— (2007). Managing late measurements in data warehouses. *International Journal of Data Warehousing and Mining*, 3(4):51–67.

Golfarelli, M., S. Rizzi, and I. Cella (2004). Beyond data warehousing: What's next in business intelligence? In *Proceedings ACM International Workshop on Data Warehousing and OLAP*, Washington D.C.

Golfarelli, M., S. Rizzi, and A. Proli (2006b). Designing What-if analysis: Towards a methodology. *Proceedings ACM International Workshop on Data Warehousing and OLAP*, Arlington, Virginia, pp. 51–58.

Golfarelli, M., S. Rizzi, and B. Vrdoljak (2001). Data warehouse design from XML sources. In *Proceedings ACM International Workshop on Data Warehousing and OLAP*, Atlanta.

Gopalkrishnan, V., Q. Li, and K. Karlapalem (2000). Efficient query processing with associated horizontal class partitioning in an object relational data warehousing environment. In *Proceedings 2nd International Workshop on Design and Management of Data Warehouses*, Stockholm.

Graefe, G., A. Linville, and L. Shapiro (1994). Sort versus hash revisited. *IEEE Transactions on Knowledge and Data Engineering*, 6(6).

Gray, J., A. Bosworth, A. Layman, and H. Pirahesh (1997). Data cube: A relational aggregation operator generalizing group-by, cross-tab, and sub-totals. *Data Mining and Knowledge Discovery*, 1(1):29–53.

Griffin, T., and L. Libkin (1995). Incremental maintenance of views with duplicates. In *Proceedings ACM SIGMOD International Conference on Management of Data*, San Jose, California, pp. 328–339.

Gupta, A., V. Harinarayan, and D. Quass (1995). Aggregate-query processing in data-warehousing environments. In *Proceedings 21st International Conference on Very Large Data Bases*, Zurich.

Gupta, A., H. Jagadish, and I.S. Mumick (1996). Data integration using self-maintainable views. In *Proceedings 5th International Conference on Extending Database Technology*, Avignon, France, pp. 140–144.

Gupta, A., and I.S. Mumick (1998). *Materialized views*. MIT Press.

Gupta, H. (1997a). Selection of views to materialize in a data warehouse. In *Proceedings 6th International Conference On Database Theory*, Delphi, Greece, pp. 98–112.

Gupta, H., V. Harinarayan, A. Rajaraman, and J. Ullman (1997b). Index selection for OLAP. In *Proceedings 13th International Conference on Data Engineering*, Birmingham, UK, pp. 208–219.

Gupta, H., and I.S. Mumick (1999). Selection of views to materialize under a maintenance cost constraint. In *Proceedings 7th International Conference on Database Theory*, Jerusalem.

Guttman, A. (1984). R-trees: A dynamic index structure for spatial searching. In *Proceedings ACM SIGMOD Conference*, Boston, pp. 47–57.

Gyssens, M., and L.V.S. Lakshmanan (1997). A foundation for multi-dimensional databases. In *Proceedings 23rd International Conference on Very Large Data Bases*, Athens, pp. 106–115.

Haas, P.J., J.F. Naughton, S. Seshadri, and A.N. Swami (1995). Sampling-based estimation of the number of distinct values of an attribute. In *Proceedings 21st International Conference on Very Large Data Bases*, Zurich.

Halevy, A.Y. (2000). Theory of answering queries using views. *SIGMOD Record*, 29(4):40–47.

Han, J., and M. Kamber (2001). *Data Mining: Concepts and Techniques*. Morgan Kaufmann Publishers.

Harinarayan, V., A. Rajaraman, and J. Ullman (1996). Implementing data cubes efficiently. In *Proceedings ACM SIGMOD Conference*, Montreal, pp. 205–216.

Hernandez, M.A., and S.J. Stolfo (1995). The purge/merge problem for large databases. In *Proceedings ACM SIGMOD Conference*, San Jose, California, pp. 127–138.

—— (1998). Real-world data is dirty: Data cleansing and the purge/merge problem. *Journal of Data Mining and Knowledge Discovery*, 2(1):9–37.

Hoffer, J., F. McFadden, and M. Prescott (2005). *Modern Database Management*. Pearson Prentice Hall.

Hou, W., and G. Özsoyoglu (1991). Statistical estimators for aggregate relational algebra queries. *ACM Transactions On Database Systems*, 16(4):600–654.

Hull, R., and G. Zhou (1996). A framework for supporting data integration using the materialized and virtual approaches. *SIGMOD Record*, 25(2):481–92.

Hüsemann, B., J. Lechtenbörger, and G. Vossen (2000). Conceptual data warehouse design. In *Proceedings 2nd International Workshop on Design and Management of Data Warehouses*, Stockholm.

Inmon, W.H. (2005). *Building the Data Warehouse*. John Wiley & Sons.

Ioannidis, Y., and S. Christodulakis (1993). Optimal histograms for limiting worst-case error propagation in the size of join results. *ACM Transactions On Database Systems*, 18(4):268–277.

Ioannidis, Y., and V. Poosala (1995). Balancing histogram optimality and practicality for query result size estimation. In *Proceedings ACM SIGMOD Conference*, San Jose, California, pp. 233–244.

Jain, A.K., and R.C. Dubes (1988). *Algorithms for Clustering Data*. Prentice Hall.

Jarke, M., M. Lenzerini, Y. Vassiliou, and P. Vassiliadis (2000). *Fundamentals of Data Warehouse*. Springer.

Jennings, M. (2004). *Universal Meta Data Models*. John Wiley & Sons.

Jensen, M., T. Moller, and T.B. Pedersen (2001). Specifying OLAP cubes on XML data. *Journal of Intelligent Information Systems*, 17(2–3):255–280.

Jones, M.E., and I.-Y. Song (2005). Dimensional modeling: Identifying, classifying and applying patterns. In *Proceedings ACM International Workshop on Data Warehousing and OLAP*, Bremen, Germany, pp. 29–38.

JPivot (2009). JPivot Project. http://jpivot.sourceforge.net/.

Kaser, O., and D. Lemire (2003). Attribute value reordering for efficient hybrid OLAP. In *Proceedings ACM International Workshop on Data Warehousing and OLAP*, New Orleans, pp. 1–8.

Katic, N., G. Quirchmayr, J. Schiefer, M. Stolba, and A.M. Tjoa (1998). A prototype model for data warehouse security based on metadata. In *Proceedings International Conference on Database and Expert Systems Applications*, Vienna, pp. 300–308.

Kellner, M., R. Madachy, and D. Raffo (1999). Software process simulation modeling: Why? What? How? *Journal of Systems and Software*, 46(2–3):91–105.

Kelly, S. (1997). *Data Warehousing In Action*. John Wiley & Sons.

Kendall, K., and J. Kendall (2002). *System Analysis and Design*. Prentice-Hall International.

Keogh, E., and M. Pazzani (1998). An enhanced representation of time series which allows fast and accurate classification clustering and relevance feedback. In *Proceedings 4th International Conference on Knowledge Discovery and Data Mining*, New York, pp. 239–243.

Kimball, R. (1996). *The Data Warehouse Toolkit*. John Wiley & Sons.

Kimball, R., L. Reeves, M. Ross, and W. Thornthwaite (1998). *The Data Warehouse Lifecycle Toolkit*. John Wiley & Sons.

Kimball, R., and J. Caserta (2004). *The Data Warehouse ETL Toolkit*. John Wiley & Sons.

Kirkgöze, R., N. Katic, M. Stolda, and A.M. Tjoa (1997). A security concept for OLAP. In *Proceedings International Conference on Database and Expert Systems Applications*, Tolouse, France, pp. 619–626.

Kooi, R.P. (1980). *The optimization of queries in relational databases*. Ph.D. thesis, Case Western Reserve University, Cleveland, Ohio.

Koudas, N., and D. Srivastava (2003). Data stream query processing: A tutorial. In *Proceedings International Conference on Very Large Data Bases*, Berlin.

Labio, W.J., D. Quass, and B. Adelberg (1997). Physical database design for data warehouses. In *Proceedings 13th International Conference on Data Engineering*, Birmingham, UK.

Lakshmanan, L., J. Pei, and Y. Zhao (2003). QC-Trees: An efficient summary structure for semantic OLAP. In *Proceedings ACM SIGMOD Conference on Management of Data*, San Diego, California, pp. 64–75.

Lechtenbörger, J. (2001). *Data warehouse schema design*. DISDBIS 79, Akademische Verlagsgesellschaft Aka GmbH.

Lee, D., and W.W. Chu (2000). Constraints-preserving transformation from XML Document Type Definition to relational schema. In *Proceedings 19th International Conference on Conceptual Modeling*, Salt Lake City. Utah.

Lenz, H.J., and A. Shoshani (1997). Summarizability in OLAP and statistical databases. In *Proceedings 9th International Conference on Statistical and Scientific Database Management*, Washington, D.C., pp. 132–143.

Levy, A.Y. (2000). Logic-based techniques in data integration. In J. Minker (Ed), *Logic Based Artificial Intelligence*. Kluwer Publishers.

Li, C., and X.S. Wang (1996). A data model for supporting on-line analytical processing. In *Proceedings International Conference on Information and Knowledge Management*, pp. 81–88.

Li, Z., and K.A. Ross (1999). Fast joins using join indices. *VLDB Journal*, 8(1):1–24.

Lim, Y., and M. Kim (2004). A bitmap index for multidimensional data cubes. In *Proceedings International Conference on Database and Expert Systems Applications*, Zaragoza, Spain, pp. 349–358.

List, B., R. Bruckner, K. Machaczek, and J. Schiefer (2002). A comparison of data warehouse development methodologies: Case study of the Process Warehouse. In *Proceedings International Conference on Database and Expert Systems Applications*, Zaragoza, Spain, pp. 203–215.

Lomet, D., and B. Salzberg (1990). The H *Data & Knowledge Engineering* b-Tree: a multidimensional indexing method with good guaranteed performance. *ACM Transactions on Database Systems*, 15(44):625–658.

Luján-Mora, S., and J. Trujillo (2003). A Comprehensive method for data warehouse design. In *Proceedings International Workshop on Design and Management of Data Warehouses*, Berlin.

Luján-Mora, S., J. Trujillo, and I. Song (2002). Multidimensional modeling with UML package diagrams. In *Proceedings 21st International Conference on Conceptual Modeling*, Tampere, Finland, pp. 199–213.

——— (2006). A UML profile for multidimensional modeling in data warehouses. *Data & Knowledge Engineering*, 59(3):725–769.

Maniezzo, V., A. Carbonaro, M. Golfarelli, and S. Rizzi (2001). ANTS for data warehouse logical design. In *Proceedings 4th Metaheuristics International Conference*, Porto, Portugal, pp. 249–254.

Mannila, H., and K.J. Räihä (1994). Algorithms for inferring functional dependencies. *Data & Knowledge Engineering*, 12(1).

Markl, V., F. Ramsak, and R. Pieringer (2001). The TransBase HyperCube RDBMS: Multidimensional indexing of relational tables. In *Proceedings 17th International Conference on Data Engineering*, Heidelberg, Germany.

Markl, V., M. Zirkel, and R. Bayer (1999). Processing operations with restrictions in relational database management systems without external sorting. In *Proceedings 15th International Conference on Data Engineering*, Sydney.

Marotta, A., F. Piedrabuena, and A. Abello (2006). Managing quality properties in a ROLAP environment. In *Proceedings 18th International Conference on Advanced Information Systems Engineering*, Luxembourg, Belgium, pp. 127–141.

Mattison, R. (2006). *The Data Warehousing Handbook*. Lulu.com.

Mayers, G. (2004). *The Art of Software Testing 2nd Edition*. John Wiley & Sons.

Mazón, J. N., J. Pardillo, and J. Trujillo (2007a). A model-driven goal-oriented requirement engineering approach for data warehouses. In *Proceedings ER Workshops*, Auckland, New Zealand, pp. 255–264.

Mazón, J. N., J. Trujillo, and J. Lechtenbörger (2007b). Reconciling requirement-driven data warehouses with data sources via multidimensional normal forms. *Data & Knowledge Engineering*, 63(3):725–751.

Miller, R., M. Hernández, L. Haas, L. Yan, H. Ho, R. Fagin, and L. Popa (2001). The Clio Project: Managing heterogeneity. *SIGMOD Record*, 30(1):78–83.

Mondrian (2009). Mondrian Project. http://mondrian.pentaho.org/.

Monge, A., and C. Elkan (1996). The field matching problem: Algorithms and applications. In *Proceedings 2nd International Conference on Knowledge Discovery and Data Mining*, Portland, Oregon.

——— (1997). An efficient domain-independent algorithm for detecting approximately duplicate database records. In *Proceedings Workshop on Research Issues on Data Mining and Knowledge Discovery*, Tucson, Arizona.

Moody, D., and M. Kortink (2000). From enterprise models to dimensional models: A methodology for data warehouse and data mart design. In *Proceedings 2nd International Workshop on Design and Management of Data Warehouses*, Stockholm.

Muralikrishna, M., and D.J. DeWitt (1988). Equi-depth histograms for estimating selectivity factors for multi-dimensional queries. In *Proceedings ACM SIGMOD Conference*, Chicago, pp. 28–36.

Navathe, S.B., and L. Kerschberg (1986). Role of data dictionaries in information resource management. *Information and Management*, 10(1).

Nguyen, T.B., A.M. Tjoa, and R. Wagner (2000). An object-oriented multidimensional data model for OLAP. In *Proceedings 1st International Conference on Web-Age Information Management*, Shanghai, pp. 69–82.

Niemi, T., J. Nummenmaa, and P. Thanisch (2001). Logical multidimensional database design for ragged and unbalanced aggregation hierarchies. In *Proceedings 3rd International Workshop on Design and Management of Data Warehouses*, Interlaken, Switzerland.

Nievergelt, J., H. Hinterberger, and K.C. Sevcik (1984). The Grid File: An adaptable, symmetric multikey file structure. *ACM Transactions on Database Systems*, 9(1):38–71.

Object Management Group (2000). Catalog of OMG Modeling and Metadata Specifications. www.omg.org/cwm/.

O'Neil, P. (1987). Model 204 architecture and performance. In *Proceedings 2nd International Workshop on High Performance Transactions System*, Asilomar, California.

O'Neil, P., and G. Graefe (1995). Multi-table joins through bitmapped join indices. *SIGMOD Record*, 24(3):8–11.

O'Neil, P., and D. Quass (1997). Improved query performance with variant indexes. In *Proceedings ACM SIGMOD International Conference on Management of Data*, Tucson, Arizona.

Orenstein, J.A., and T.H. Merret (1984). A class of data structures for associate searching. In *Proceedings SIGMOD-PODS Conference*, Portland, Oregon.

Otoo, E., D. Rotem, and S. Seshadri (2007). Optimal chunking of large multidimensional arrays for data warehousing. In *Proceedings ACM International Workshop on Data Warehousing and OLAP*, Lisbon, pp. 25–32.

Özsu, M.T., and P. Valduriez (1991). *Principles of Distributed Database Systems*. Prentice Hall.

Paim, F., and J. Castro (2003). DWARF: An approach for requirements definition and management of data warehouse systems. In *Proceedings International Conference on Requirements Engineering*, Monterey, California.

Papadimitriou, C.H., and K. Steiglitz (1982). *Combinatorial Optimization*. Prentice Hall.

Patel, J.M., M.J. Carey, and M.K. Vernon (1994). Accurate modeling of the hybrid hash join algorithm. In *Proceedings ACM SIGMETRICS*, Santa Clara, California.

Patterson, D., G. Gibson, and R. Katz (1988). A case for redundant arrays of inexpensive disks. In *Proceedings ACM SIGMOD Conference*, Chicago, pp. 109–116.

Pedersen, T.B., and C. Jensen (1999). Multidimensional data modeling for complex data. In *Proceedings 15th International Conference on Data Engineering*, Sydney, pp. 336–345.

Piatetsky-Shapiro, G., and C. Connell (1984). Accurate estimation of the number of tuples satisfying a condition. In *Proceedings ACM SIGMOD Conference*, Boston, pp. 256–276.

Poess, M., and C. Floyd (2000). New TPC benchmarks for decision support and web commerce. *ACM SIGMOD Record*, 29(4).

Power, D.J. (2002). *Decision Support Systems: Concepts and Resources for Managers*. Quorum Books.

Prakash, N., and A. Gosain (2003). Requirements driven data warehouse development. In *Proceedings CAiSE Short Papers*, Klagenfurt/Velden, Austria.

Priebe, T., and G. Pernul (2000). Towards OLAP security design: Survey and research issues. In *Proceedings ACM International Workshop on Data Warehousing and OLAP*, McLean, Virginia, pp. 33–40.

Quass, D. (1996). Maintenance Expressions for views with aggregation. In *Proceedings SIGMOD Workshop on Materialized Views*, pp. 110–118.

Quix, C. (1999). Repository support for data warehouse evolution. In *Proceedings 1st International Workshop on Design and Management of Data Warehouses*, Heidelberg, Germany.

Qian, X. (1996). Query folding. In *Proceedings 12th International Conference on Data Engineering*, New Orleans.

Reddy, M.P., B.E. Prasad, P.G. Reddy, and A. Gupta (1994). A methodology for integration of heterogeneous databases. *IEEE Transactions on Knowledge and Data Engineering*, 6(6):920–933.

Rissanen, J. (1977). Independent components of relations. *ACM Transactions on Database Systems*, 2(4):317–325.

Rizzi, S. (2006). Conceptual modeling solutions for the data warehouse. In *Data Warehouses and OLAP: Concepts, Architectures and Solutions*, R. Wrembel and C. Koncilia (Eds). IRM Press.

——— (2008). Data warehouse. In *Encyclopedia of Computer Science and Engineering*, B. W. Wah (Ed). John Wiley & Sons.

Rizzi, S., and E. Saltarelli (2003a). View materialization vs. indexing: Balancing space constraints in data warehouse design. In *Proceedings 15th Conference on Advanced Information Systems Engineering*, Velden, Austria, pp. 502–519.

Rizzi, S., E. Bertino, B. Catania, M. Golfarelli, M. Halkidi, M. Terrovitis, P. Vassiliadis, M. Vazirgiannis, and E. Vrachnos (2003b). Towards a logical model for patterns. In *Proceedings 22nd International Conference on Conceptual Modeling*, Chicago, pp. 77–90.

Romero, O., and A. Abelló (2007). Automating multidimensional design from ontologies. In *Proceedings International Workshop on Data Warehousing and OLAP*, Lisbon, pp. 1–8.

Rosenthal, A., and E. Sciore (2000). View security as the basic for data warehouse security. In *Proceedings 2nd International Workshop on Design and Management of Data Warehouses*, Stockholm, pp. 1–8.

Ross, K., and D. Srivastava (1997). Fast computation of sparse datacubes. In *Proceedings 23rd International Conference on Very Large Data Bases*, Athens, pp. 116–125.

Sapia, C., M. Blaschka, G. Hofling, and B. Dinter (1998). Extending the E/R model for the multidimensional paradigm. In *Proceedings International Conference on Conceptual Modeling*, Singapore.

Savnik, I., and P. Flach (1993). Bottom-up induction of functional dependencies from relations. In Piatesky-Shapiro (Ed), *Knowledge Discovery in Databases*. AAAI.

Selinger, P.G., M.M. Astrahan, D.D. Chamberlin, R.A. Lorie, and T.G. Price (1979). Access path selection in a relational database management system. In *Proceedings ACM SIGMOD Conference*, Boston, pp. 82–93.

Serrano, M., C. Calero, J. Trujillo, S. Luján-Mora, and M. Piattini (2004). Empirical validation of metrics for conceptual models of data warehouses. In *Proceedings 16th International Conference on Advanced Information Systems Engineering*, Riga, Latvia, pp. 506–520.

Serrano, M., R. Romero, J. N. Mazón, J. Trujillo, and M. Piattini (2007). A proposal for a conceptual data warehouse quality model. In *Proceedings 19th International Conference on Software Engineering & Knowledge Engineering*, Boston, pp. 477–482.

Shanmugasundaram, J., H. Gang, K. Tufte, C. Zhang, D. DeWitt, and J.F. Naughton (1999). Relational databases for querying XML documents: Limitations and opportunities. In *Proceedings 25th International Conference on Very Large Data Bases*, Edinburgh.

Shukla, A., P. Deshpande, J.F. Naughton, and K. Ramasamy (1996). Storage estimation for multidimensional aggregates in the presence of hierarchies. In *Proceedings 22nd International Conference on Very Large Data Bases*, Mumbai.

Simitsis, A., P. Vassiliadis, and T. Sellis (2005). Optimizing ETL processes in data warehouses. In *Proceedings 21st International Conference on Data Engineering*, Tokyo, pp. 564–575.

Sismanis, Y., A. Deligiannakis, Y. Kotidis, and N. Roussopoulos (2003). Hierarchical dwarfs for the rollup cube. In *Proceedings ACM International Workshop on Data Warehousing and OLAP*, New Orleans, pp. 17–24.

Soler, E., V. Stefanov, J.N. Mazón, J. Trujillo, E. Fernández-Medina, and M. Piattini (2008). Towards comprehensive requirement analysis for data warehouses: Considering security requirements. In *Proceedings 3rd International Conference on Availability, Reliability and Security*, Barcelona, pp. 104–111.

Song, I.-Y., W. Rowen, C. Medsker, and E. Ewen (2001). An analysis of many-to-many relationships between fact and dimension tables in dimensional modeling. *Proceedings 3rd International Workshop on Design and Management of Data Warehouses*, Interlaken, Switzerland, pp. 6.1–6.13.

Song, I.-Y., R. Khare, and B. Dai (2007). SAMSTAR: A semi-automated lexical method for generating star schemas from an entity-relationship diagram. In *Proceedings ACM International Workshop on Data Warehousing and OLAP*, Lisbon, pp. 9–16.

Sprague, R.H., and E.D. Carlson (1982). *Building Effective Decision Support Systems*. Prentice Hall.

Sprague, R.H., and H.J. Watson (1993). *Decision Support Systems: Putting Theory into Practice*. Prentice Hall.

Srikant, R., and R. Agrawal (1995). Mining generalized association rules. In *Proceedings 21st International Conference on Very Large Data Bases*, Zurich.

Stevens, W., G. Myers, and L. Constantine (1974). Structured Design. *IBM Systems Journal*, 13(2), pp. 115–139.

Tansel, A., J. Clifford, V. Gadia, A. Segev, and R.T. Snodgrass (Eds) (1993). *Temporal Databases: Theory, Design and Implementation*. The Benjamin/Cummings Publishing Company.

Theodoratos, D., and M. Bouzeghoub (2000). A general framework for the view selection problem for data warehouse design and evolution. In *Proceedings ACM International Workshop on Data Warehousing and OLAP*, McLean, Virginia.

——— (2001). Data currency quality satisfaction in the design of a data warehouse. *International Journal of Cooperative Information Systems*, 10(3):299–326.

Thomsen, C., and T.B. Pedersen (2005). A survey of open source tools for business intelligence. In *Proceedings 7th International Conference on Data Warehousing and Knowledge Discovery*, Copenhagen, pp. 74–84.

Tozer, G. (1999). *Metadata Management for Information Control and Business Success.* Artech House Publishers.

Trujillo, J., and S. Luján-Mora (2003). A UML based approach for modelling ETL processes in data warehouses. In *Proceedings International Conference on Conceptual Modeling*, Chicago, pp. 307–320.

Tryfona, N., F. Busborg, and J.G. Borch Christiansen (1999). starER: A conceptual model for data warehouse design. In *Proceedings ACM International Workshop on Data Warehousing and OLAP*, pp. 3–8.

Tsois, A., N. Karayannidis, and T. Sellis (2001). MAC: Conceptual data modeling for OLAP. In *Proceedings 3rd International Workshop on Design and Management of Data Warehouses*, Interlaken, Switzerland, p. 5.

Tziovara, V., P. Vassiliadis, and A. Simitsis (2007). Deciding the physical implementation of ETL workflows. In *Proceedings ACM International Workshop on Data Warehousing and OLAP*, Lisbon, pp. 49–56.

Ullman, J.D. (1997). Information integration using logical views. In *Proceedings International Conference on Database Theory*, Delphi, Greece, pp. 19–40.

Vaisman, A., A. Mendelzon, W. Ruaro, and S. Cymerman (2002). Supporting dimension updates in an OLAP server. In *Proceedings International Conference on Advanced Information Systems Engineering*, pp. 67–82.

Valduriez, P. (1987). Join indices. *ACM Transactions on Database Systems*, 12(2):218–246.

Vassiliadis, P. (1998). Modeling multidimensional databases, cubes and cube operations. In *Proceedings 10th International Conference on Statistical and Scientific Database Management*, Capri, Italy.

———— (2000). Gulliver in the land of data warehousing: Practical experiences and observations of a researcher. In *Proceedings 2nd International Workshop on Design and Management of Data Warehouses*, Stockholm.

Vassiliadis, P., A. Simitsis, and S. Skiadopoulos (2002). Conceptual modeling for ETL processes. In *Proceedings ACM International Workshop on Data Warehousing and OLAP*, McLean, Virginia, pp. 14–21.

Vrdoljak, B., M. Banek, and S. Rizzi (2003). Designing web warehouses from XML schemas. In *Proceedings 5th International Conference on Data Warehousing and Knowledge Discovery*, Prague, pp. 89–98.

Wache, H., T. Vögele, U. Visser, H. Stuckenschmidt, G. Schuster, H. Neumann, and S. Hübner (2001). Ontology-based integration of information: A survey of existing approaches. In *Proceedings IJCAI Workshop on Ontologies and Information Sharing*, pp. 108–117.

Whang, K., and R. Krishnamurthy (1991). The Multilevel Grid File: A dynamic hierarchical multidimensional file structure. In *Proceedings International Symposium on Database Systems for Advanced Applications*, Tokyo, pp. 449–459.

Winter, R., and B. Strauch (2003). A method for demand-driven information requirements analysis in data warehousing projects. In *Proceedings Hawaii International Conference on System Sciences*, pp. 1359–1365.

Witten, I., and E. Frank (2000). *Data Mining*. Morgan Kaufmann Publishers.

Wong, H.K.T., H-F. Liu, F. Olken, D. Rotem, and L. Wong (1985). Bit transposed files. In *Proceedings 11th International Conference on Very Large Data Bases*, Stockholm.

W3C, World Wide Web Consortium (2000). XML 1.0 Specification. www.w3.org/TR/2000/REC-xml-20001006.

——— (2002a). XML Schema. www.w3.org/XML/ Schema.

——— (2002b). XQuery 1.0: An XML query language (Working Draft). www.w3.org/TR/xquery/.

Wrembel, R., and C. Koncilia (2007). *Data Warehouses and OLAP*. IRM Press.

Wu, M.C., and A. Buchmann (1998). Encoded bitmap indexing for data warehouses. In *Proceedings 14th International Conference on Data Engineering*, Orlando, Florida.

Wu, K., E. Otoo, and A Shoshani (2006). Optimizing bitmap indices with efficient compression. *ACM Transactions on Database Systems*, 31(1):1–38.

Yan, W.P., and P. Larson (1995). Eager aggregation and lazy aggregation. In *Proceedings 21st International Conference on Very Large Data Bases*, Zurich.

Yang, J., K. Karlapalem, and Q. Li (1997). Algorithms for materialized view design in data warehousing environment. In *Proceedings 23rd International Conference on Very Large Data Bases*, Athens, pp. 136–145.

Yu, E. (1995). *Modelling Strategic Relationships for Process Reengineering*. PhD Thesis, University of Toronto, Department of Computer Science.

Zhao, Y., P.M. Deshpande, and J.F. Naughton (1997). An array-based algorithm for simultaneous multidimensional aggregates. In *Proceedings ACM SIGMOD International Conference on Management of Data*, Tucson, Arizona.

Zhuge, Y., H. Garcia-Molina, and J.L. Wiener (1996). The Strobe algorithms for multi-source warehouse consistency. In *Proceedings Conference on Parallel and Distributed Information Systems*, Miami.

Index